THE ECONOMICS OF JOAN ROBINSON

Joan Robinson is widely regarded as the greatest female economist and a major figure in the post-Keynesian tradition. In this volume a distinguished international team of scholars analyses her extraordinarily wide-ranging contribution to economics.

Various contributions address her work on:

- the economics of imperfect competition
- the development of the Keynesian tradition at Cambridge
- her response to Marx and Sraffa
- growth, development and dynamics
- technical innovation and capital theory
- her preference for 'history' rather than equilibrium as a basis for methodology

Her published work spanned six decades, and the volume includes a bibliography of her work that lists some 450 items, which will be a major resource for students of the development of modern economic analysis.

Maria Cristina Marcuzzo is Associate Professor of Economics at the Università di Roma 'La Sapienza'. Her previous publications include *Ricardo and the Gold Standard* (co-author, 1991) and numerous journal articles. **Luigi L. Pasinetti** is Professor of Economics at Università Cattolica del S. Cuore, Milan. As well as publishing articles on capital theory, economic growth, income distribution and structural dynamics, he is the author of *Growth and Income Distribution* (1974), *Lectures on the Theory of Production* (1977), *Structural Changes and Economic Growth* (1981) and *Structural Economic Dynamics* (1993). **Alessandro Roncaglia** is Professor of Economics at the Università di Roma 'La Sapienza'. His publications include *Sraffa and the Theory of Prices* (1978), *Petty: The Origins of Political Economy* (1985) and *The International Oil Market* (1985).

ROUTLEDGE STUDIES IN THE HISTORY OF ECONOMICS

The history of economics offers a rich store of ideas about the economic dimension of human activity. This series makes new, original material of a high quality accessible to an international readership. The series does not limit itself to any single approach or historical period and includes volumes based on critical themes or issues, major figures, and important schools of thought.

1 ECONOMICS AS LITERATURE
Willie Henderson

2 SOCIALISM AND MARGINALISM IN ECONOMICS
Ian Steedman

3 HAYEK'S POLITICAL ECONOMY
Steve Fleetwood

4 ON THE ORIGINS OF CLASSICAL ECONOMICS
Tony Aspromourgos

5 THE ECONOMICS OF JOAN ROBINSON
Edited by Maria Cristina Marcuzzo, Luigi L. Pasinetti and Alessandro Roncaglia

THE ECONOMICS OF JOAN ROBINSON

Edited by

Maria Cristina Marcuzzo,
Luigi L. Pasinetti
and Alessandro Roncaglia

Routledge
Taylor & Francis Group
LONDON AND NEW YORK

First published 1996
by Routledge
2 Park Square, Milton Park, Abingdon, Oxfordshire OX14 4RN

Simultaneously published in the USA and Canada
by Routledge
711 Third Avenue, New York, NY 10017

First issued in paperback 2014

Routledge is an imprint of the Taylor & Francis Group, an informa business

Typeset in Times by
Solidus (Bristol) Ltd, Bristol

British Library Cataloguing in Publication Data
A catalogue record for this book is available from the British Library

Library of Congress Cataloging in Publication Data
The Economics of Joan Robinson / edited by Maria Cristina Marcuzzo, Luigi L. Pasinetti, and Alessandro Roncaglia.
p. cm.
Includes bibliographical references and index.
ISBN 0-415-13616-4 (cloth: alk. paper)
1. Robinson, Joan, 1903–1983. 2. Robinson, Joan, 1903–1983 —Bibliography. 3. Economics—History—20th century. 4. Economists—Great Britain. 5. Keynesian economics. I. Robinson, Joan, 1903–1983. II. Marcuzzo, Maria Cristina, 1948–. III. Pasinetti, Luigi L. 1930– IV. Roncaglia, Alessandro, 1947–.
HB103.R63E273 1996
330.1′092–dc20 95–19891
CIP

ISBN 13: 978-0-415-13616-7 (hbk)
ISBN 13: 978-0-415-75681-5 (pbk)

CONTENTS

CONTRIBUTORS

Amit Bhaduri, Professor of Economics, Institute for Advanced Studies, Berlin
Salvatore Biasco, Professor of International Economics, Università di Roma 'La Sapienza'
Jack Birner, Professor of Economics, Rijksuniversiteit Limburg, Maastricht
Pierluigi Ciocca, Banca d'Italia
Marco Dardi, Professor of Economics, Università di Firenze
Nicolò De Vecchi, Professor of Economics, Università di Pavia
Pierangelo Garegnani, Professor of Economics, Terza Università di Roma
Giorgio Gilibert, Professor of Economics, Università di Modena
Geoffrey Harcourt, Reader in the History of Economic Theory, University of Cambridge, UK
Bruno Jossa, Professor of Economics, Università di Napoli 'Federico II'
Jan Kregel, Professor of Economics, Università di Bologna
Marco Lippi, Professor of Economics, Università di Roma 'La Sapienza'
Siro Lombardini, Professor of Economics, Università di Torino
Maria Cristina Marcuzzo, Professor of Economics, Università di Roma 'La Sapienza'
Ferdinando Meacci, Professor of Economics, Università di Padova
Giangiacomo Nardozzi, Professor of Economics, Politecnico di Milano
Luigi Pasinetti, Professor of Economics, Università Cattolica del S. Cuore, Milan
Massimo Pivetti, Professor of Economics, Università di Roma 'La Sapienza'
Alessandro Roncaglia, Professor of Economics, Università di Roma 'La Sapienza'
Andrea Salanti, Professor of Economics, Università di Bergamo
Neri Salvadori, Professor of Economics, Università di Pisa
Roberto Scazzieri, Professor of Economics, Università di Bologna
Bertram Schefold, Professor of Economics, J. W. Goethe Universität, Frankfurt a.M.

CONTRIBUTORS

Annamaria Simonazzi, Professor of Economics, Università di Roma 'La Sapienza'

Paolo Varri, Professor of Economics, Università Cattolica del S. Cuore, Milan

Fernando Vianello, Professor of Economics, Università di Roma 'La Sapienza'

Stefano Zamagni, Professor of Economics, Università di Bologna

INTRODUCTION

The papers collected in this book have been selected from those presented at a conference in memory of Joan Robinson, held in the tenth year after her death (5 August 1983). The conference took place in Turin in December 1993 and was jointly organized by Società Italiana degli Economisti (SIE), Fondazione Einaudi, and a Research Group on 'Distribuzione del reddito, progresso tecnico e sviluppo economico' of the Consiglio Nazionale delle Ricerche (CNR). We are grateful to Giacomo Becattini, President of SIE, the late Mario Einaudi and Terenzio Cozzi of the Einaudi Foundation, and Carlo D'Adda, Chairman of the CNR Research Group, for their help and Silvia Brandolin for her skilful editorial assistance.

Our thanks, of course, extend to the authors of the papers, most of whom, like the three editors, had the privilege of attending Joan's lectures and seminars in Cambridge, UK, as students and colleagues. The common effort for this volume testifies to our gratitude and admiration for her teachings and for her intellectual freedom.

When in 1922 – not yet nineteen years old (she was born on 31 October 1903) – Joan Robinson went to Cambridge to study economics, women had just been admitted to degree courses. In 1923 they were admitted to the University Library and to University lectures, and became eligible for all University teaching offices. However, women had to wait until 1948 to be admitted to full membership of the University of Cambridge. This background left its mark on Joan Robinson, who had to fight uphill for most of her academic career. In Cambridge her passionate participation in intellectual debates in the various fields of economics immediately revealed the fierce character that allowed her to establish herself as a dominant figure in academic and non-academic circles.

Joan Robinson took her Tripos in 1925 at a time when economics in Cambridge was identified with just one person: Alfred Marshall. But she learned economics in the version taught by Pigou, who had 'worked the hard core of Marshall's analysis into a logical system of static theory' (Robinson 1951: viii).

After graduation, she went to India with her husband, Austin Robinson.

When she came back to Cambridge in 1928, she made acquaintance with two persons who were to become crucial, intellectually and emotionally, throughout her life: Richard Kahn, who was at that time preparing his fellowship dissertation on *The Economics of the Short Period*, and Piero Sraffa, whose lectures on 'advanced theory of value' were 'calmly committing the sacrilege of pointing out inconsistencies in Marshall' (Robinson 1951: vii). These were the years leading to the Keynesian Revolution, whose analytical foundations – the economics of the short period, and the critiques of Pigou's version of the Marshallian theory of value and the firm – were laid in Cambridge. Joan Robinson's own contribution to these themes was her first classic book, *The Economics of Imperfect Competition*, published in 1933.

The essays in Part I of the present volume refer to this first stage of development in Joan Robinson's thought. The paper by Maria Cristina Marcuzzo (Chapter 1) addresses the issue of the relationship between Kahn and Robinson by looking at their common work on imperfect competition and short-period analysis. Marco Dardi's paper (Chapter 2) provides a bridge from these aspects to the following period, focusing on the implications of short-period analysis for the development of Keynesian economics. Nicolò De Vecchi's paper (Chapter 3) illustrates the immediate impact of Joan Robinson's theory of imperfect competition on the outside world from a specific though important angle, discussing the reception of her book by Schumpeter.

When Keynes' *Treatise on Money* was published in October 1930, a lively debate on his ideas had already started within a close circle of immediate disciples. The publication of the *Treatise* gave it impetus. Together with Richard Kahn, Piero Sraffa, James Meade and Austin Robinson, Joan Robinson played an important role in this small group of selected disciples who coupled enthusiasm for the new ideas with critical – occasionally, hypercritical – vigilance. In the crucial years of Keynes' transition from the *Treatise* to the *General Theory* his theory was dissected. Detailed critical remarks and hints for improvements were provided. Joan, more than the other members of the group, was interested in translating Keynes's complex theoretical construction into simplified expositions with the aim of attracting a wider audience and extending the Keynesian approach in different directions. These contributions materialized in a number of papers – most of which were collected in a book, *Essays in the Theory of Employment*, published in 1937 – and in her *Introduction to the Theory of Employment*, also published in 1937, 'a told to the children version of the *General Theory*', as she put it to Keynes in a letter dated November 8, 1936 (Keynes 1979: 185).

Although Joan Robinson's ideas on imperfect competition underwent substantial changes after their original presentation, her adhesion to the Keynesian revolution, though not acritical, remained with her for the whole of her life, and constituted a stronghold from which to fire against the unfaithful and, especially, against the attempts to absorb the Keynesian revolution into the main body of neoclassical orthodoxy.

The second group of essays in this volume explore different aspects – including some policy implications – of Joan Robinson's role in the development of a truly Keynesian tradition centred in Cambridge. Jan Kregel (Chapter 4) discusses Joan Robinson's critical attitude towards both 'prodigal sons' and 'bastard progeny', namely towards the development of both post-Keynesian and post-neoclassical modern economics. Kregel uses as an interpretative key the contrast between 'history' and 'equilibrium', a crucial element that comes up for further consideration in other papers. Pierangelo Garegnani (Chapter 5) takes issue with Robinson's first attempt – in a paper published in 1936, more or less simultaneously with Keynes' *General Theory* – to develop a long-period theory of output and employment within a Keynesian framework. According to Garegnani, this attempt is vitiated by a persistent adherence to marginalist premises. In a similar critical vein, Massimo Pivetti (Chapter 6) discusses Robinson's views on the rate of interest. A contrasting stand is taken in Giangiacomo Nardozzi's paper (Chapter 7), where Keynes' theory of interest as a conventional phenomenon is considered through the interpretation of the working of financial markets given by Joan Robinson and is then used for a critique of present-day economic policies. Similarly oriented to present-day policy issues is Annamaria Simonazzi's paper (Chapter 8). This provides a comparison of policy choices in the 1930s and the 1980s as the background for an assessment of Joan Robinson's contributions to international economics.

On the fringes of the Keynesian 'circle' and partly overlapping with it, strong intellectual influences other than Keynes' were present in the Cambridge of the 1930s. The emergence of the Fascist regime in Italy and the Nazi regime in Germany and, later, the outbreak of the Spanish civil war generated a counteraction in the form of a certain popularity for communism, and an intellectual interest in Marxism. Joan Robinson read Marx with some sympathy, but also with a critical attitude, endeavouring to separate what she considered interesting (mainly accumulation and economic growth) from what she saw as muddled or plainly wrong (mainly the labour theory of value). As early as in 1942 she published *An Essay on Marxian Economics* where, while re-evaluating many points of Marxian analysis, she rejected Marx's value theory. She felt later that she 'has been treated as an enemy by the professed Marxists ever since' (Robinson 1979: 276). Her interest in Marx was also stimulated by her friendship with the Polish economist Michal Kalecki, who had independently developed a theory of output and employment based on aggregate demand similar to that presented in Keynes' *General Theory*. Kalecki's blend of Keynesian-like doctrines with elements of Marxism was an important stimulus in Joan Robinson's search for a relationship between the theory of functional income distribution, the theory of output and employment and the theory of accumulation. Equally important

– although highly controversial – was the connection between Marxism and the classical (Ricardian) approach to the theory of value, and here Joan Robinson responded to the impact of Piero Sraffa's strong personality. Her attitude to Sraffa's attempt to reinstate the classic approach was marked by alternate phases of adhesion and strong critical reaction.

Joan Robinson's attitude to Marxism and to Sraffa's analysis is the main subject of the third group of papers of this volume, while the relationship between Joan Robinson's and Kalecki's economics is considered from various viewpoints in many of the papers concerning dynamics. Marco Lippi (Chapter 9) offers a revaluation of Joan Robinson's criticisms of the labour theory of value, in which Sraffa's analytical results on the determination of prices of production play a crucial role, with some notes on the debate on 'Marx after Sraffa'. Fernando Vianello (Chapter 10) contrasts Joan Robinson's notions of 'normal prices' and 'normal rate of profits' with an analysis of 'fully adjusted situations' in which flexibility in the degree of utilization of productive capacity is admitted. Giorgio Gilibert (Chapter 11) discusses a specific aspect of her intellectual relationship with Piero Sraffa, the 'corn model' and the 'standard commodity', stressing her perplexities with regard to Sraffian analysis.

The idea of building a long-run theory of output and accumulation as a complement to Keynes' short-run analysis is apparent in Joan Robinson's writings from the 1930s on, but it came to occupy the central role in her research in the 1950s. A kind of springboard was provided by the publication in 1948 of Harrod's *Towards a Dynamic Economics*. The results of Joan Robinson's research on this subject is presented in *The Accumulation of Capital* (1956), *Exercises in Economic Analysis* (1960), *Essays in the Theory of Economic Growth* (1962). In this field we have what may be considered Robinson's main analytical contributions. She tried to bridge the analysis of 'golden ages' – connected with the 'equilibrium method' – and the 'historical method' that she discovered in the classical economists and in Marx. Her central model incorporates Keynesian, Kaleckian, Marxian and classical ideas. Saving behaviour is class determined and income distribution is determined by the savings ratios, which affect determination of the level and rate of profits through the impact of the rate of capital accumulation. Planned accumulation depends on expected profitability (itself related to current profitability). When accumulation generates an income distribution implying that this profitability has been achieved, equilibrium is attained, but full employment may not be obtained.

The themes underlying her dynamic analysis – the relations between accumulation, income distribution, economic development and economic policy – are the topic of the fourth group of papers in the present volume. Siro Lombardini (Chapter 12) sympathetically illustrates Joan Robinson's views on economic development in their difficult relationship between theoretical analysis and historical intuitions. Salvatore Biasco (Chapter 13) offers a specific example in the pure spirit of Robinsonian dynamic analysis. Roberto Scazzieri (Chapter 14) assesses Joan Robinson's theory of accumulation from the standpoint of contemporary dynamic structural analysis (as presented in Pasinetti's *Structural Change and Economic Growth*, 1981). Paolo Varri (Chapter 15) compares Roy Harrod's and Joan Robinson's versions of dynamic analysis, stressing the differences behind the apparent similarities and the common elements behind their reciprocally critical attitudes. Pierluigi Ciocca (Chapter 16) contrasts the idea of a continuous unimpeded process of development implicit in the notion of the 'golden age' with Joan Robinson's critical attitude towards capitalism and with her views on practical development issues. Finally, Amit Bhaduri (Chapter 17) relates Robinson's contribution to growth theory to Kaldorian and Kaleckian themes. He takes capital theory elements into consideration, and thus provides a bridge to the following section of the book.

A new phase in Cambridge economics was opened by Sraffa's 'Introduction' to his edition of Ricardo's *Principles* (1951) and then by his classic book on *Production of Commodities by Means of Commodities* (1960). While Sraffa was carefully – and slowly – building up his devastating 'prelude to a critique' of the traditional marginalist theory of value and distribution, focusing precisely on the notion of capital as a factor of production, Joan Robinson opened fire against the aggregate production function in a famous article published in 1954. There she also hinted at the phenomenon of reswitching, which was going to play a crucial role in the debates on capital theory of the 1960s.

The relationship between Sraffa's criticism of the marginalist theory of value and distribution and Joan Robinson's own attack on it is discussed in three papers. Luigi Pasinetti (Chapter 18) clarifies the nature of Joan Robinson's multifaceted criticisms of the prevailing orthodoxy, stressing that, paradoxically, she did not use reswitching as an argument in her own contributions. The same issue is again considered in the paper by Stefano Zamagni (Chapter 19), who argues that the target of Joan Robinson's criticism is more methodological than theoretical. Jack Birner (Chapter 20) reconstructs the story of the 'Cambridge controversies', showing that reswitching did not play a crucial role in the first stages of the debate, which were dominated by Robinson's attack on the production function. The crucial role of reswitching in Sraffa's critique was recognized – and came to occupy a central role – only later, after Pasinetti's disproof of Levhari's non-switching theorem.

Joan Robinson's criticism of neoclassical capital theory was quite independent of the reswitching phenomenon. It had, as its background, her own analysis of accumulation, in which capital theory and the theory of technical progress are connected. Neri Salvadori (Chapter 21) offers a critical examination of the analytical tool developed in this context by Joan Robinson in her *Accumulation of Capital* (1956), i.e. the so-called productivity curves.

Ferdinando Meacci (Chapter 22) discusses, in an Austrian vein, Joan Robinson's treatment of the transition to a higher degree of mechanization in the light of the distinction between choice and change of techniques. Bruno Jossa (Chapter 23) surveys Joan Robinson's analysis of technical progress.

The conviction that in economics it is possible to keep the scientific and ideological levels of analysis separate was at the core of Joan Robinson's stand in her 1962 methodological book, *Economic Philosophy*. She sought to apply the criteria of this methodology in two ways. First, in her study of the history of economic theories she endeavoured to discriminate, after the manner of Schumpeter, the elements of fact and logic from the elements that she saw as 'metaphysical'. Secondly, and more fundamentally, she denounced the strategy employed in orthodox economics of seeking consensus rather than establishing scientific propositions.

In her work of reconstructing an alternative and truly 'post-Keynesian' economics Joan Robinson at times also found herself in disagreement with some of her allies in the battle against the prevailing neoclassical orthodoxy. Her stress on 'history' versus 'equilibrium' came to be at odds with the Sraffian analytical structure of prices of production and uniform profit rate. She felt uneasy about a method based on long-run equilibrium, favouring short-period and historical analysis. Here, her passion for strong positions may have led her to see counterpositions where others were looking for integration or for the necessary compromises.

The last group of papers in the present volume addresses these issues. Andrea Salanti (Chapter 24) illustrates her views on method and their evolution in time. Bertram Schefold (Chapter 25) concentrates on a specific theme, namely the historical specificity of economic theories, tackling it through reference to different forms of economic life and finding some evidence of Joan Robinson's adhesion to an historicist view. Finally, Geoff Harcourt (Chapter 26) surveys Joan Robinson's intellectual career and assesses the relationship between her contribution and present-day post-Keynesians and neo-Ricardians.

Joan Robinson's multifarious interests branched out in many directions. Between 1930 and 1983, when active as a writer, she published books, articles in scholarly journals, short papers in newspapers and magazines, and many reviews. The bibliography of Joan Robinson's writings by Maria Cristina Marcuzzo, consisting of 443 items, is presented as a conclusion to this volume, attesting to Joan Robinson's extraordinary range of interests and productivity.

It is still too early to try to figure out what place, among the economists of the twentieth century, the history of economic ideas will assign to such a remarkable woman as Joan Robinson.

Her fierce independence of spirit, which never deserted her throughout her life, led her to espouse causes without regard to prevailing fashions and prejudices. Her academic career was never easy. She aroused great enthusiasm among crowds of students, but received little symphathy from colleagues and no honour from the establishment, even when her scientific merits became clear.

At the end of her life, like all the members of that extraordinary group of Keynesians who happened to be concentrated in Cambridge in the post-war period, Joan Robinson became increasingly dissatisfied with the way economics was developing. She became more and more disillusioned with the prevailing economics as a body of knowledge that could be used to solve problems in the real world. Her extensive travels in India, China and other less developed countries convinced her that economic theory was unfit for the task of dealing with the problem of underdevelopment. At the same time, she became concerned with wider issues that, as she felt, could even be obscured, rather than clarified, by contemporary economic theory.

In the spirit of a scholarly tribute to the uncompromising personality of Joan Robinson, this collection of essays aims at a critical evaluation of her contributions to different areas of economics. We should like to think that, along with all their different viewpoints, these papers share her critical attitude towards the dominant wisdom, though offering different evaluations of many aspects of her thinking. We also hope that this will appear an appropriate homage to Joan Robinson's social concern and passionate quest for rationality.

M.C.M., L.L.P., A.R.

REFERENCES

Harrod, R. F. (1948) *Towards a Dynamic Economics. Some Recent Developments of Economic Theory and Their Applications to Policy.* London: Macmillan.

Keynes, J. M. (1971) *A Treatise on Money.* In D. Moggridge, ed., *The Collected Writings of John Maynard Keynes*, vols V–VI. London: Macmillan.

——— (1973) *The General Theory of Employment, Interest and Money.* In D. Moggridge, ed., *The Collected Writings of John Maynard Keynes*, vol. VII. London: Macmillan.

——— (1979) *The General Theory and After. A Supplement.* In D. Moggridge, ed., *The Collected Writings of John Maynard Keynes*, vol. XXIX. London: Macmillan.

Pasinetti, L. L. (1981) *Structural Change and Economic Growth. A Theoretical Essay on the Dynamics of the Wealth of Nations.* Cambridge: Cambridge University Press.

Robinson, J. (1951) *Collected Economic Papers*, vol. I. Oxford: Blackwell.

——— (1979) *Collected Economic Papers*, vol. V. Oxford: Blackwell.

Sraffa, P. (1951) Introduction to D. Ricardo, *Principles of Political Economy and Taxation*, in P. Sraffa, ed., *The Works and Correspondence of David Ricardo*, vol. 1. Cambridge: Cambridge University Press.

——— (1960) *Production of Commodities by Means of Commodities. Prelude to a Critique of Economic Theory.* Cambridge: Cambridge University Press.

Part I

THE HERITAGE OF MARSHALL

1

JOAN ROBINSON AND RICHARD KAHN

The origin of short-period analysis[1]

Maria Cristina Marcuzzo

The most easily identifiable heritage of Marshall, in the 'new' Cambridge School of Economics, is the short period. The short period of Keynes, Kahn and Joan Robinson has a peculiar meaning, whose origin can be traced back to the late 1920s and early 1930s. Those years saw the transition from the *Treatise on Money* to *The General Theory* and the transformation of the Marshallian–Pigouvian apparatus that culminated in *The Economics of Imperfect Competition*.

This paper is concerned with three points in particular. The first is the importance of Kahn's work in providing the link between the short-period determination of price and quantity of a single commodity and the short-period theory of the level of prices and output in aggregate. The second is comparison between Kahn's fellowship dissertation, *The Economics of the Short Period*, and Robinson's *The Economics of Imperfect Competition*, with a view to pointing out their common ground. The third point is the peculiarity of Joan Robinson's position as regards the importance of short period in economic analysis.

THE TRANSITION FROM THE *TREATISE* TO THE *GENERAL THEORY*

In his 1924 essay on Marshall, although showing his appreciation of the distinction between long and short periods, Keynes wrote: 'this is a quarter in which, in my opinion, the Marshall analysis is least complete and satisfactory, and where there remains most to do' (Keynes 1972: 206–7).

The task was undertaken by Kahn, who actually chose it as the topic for his dissertation, 'The Economics of the Short Period'. This work, which Kahn started in October 1928 (Marcuzzo 1994a: 26n) and completed in December 1929, earned him a fellowship at King's College, Cambridge, in March 1930. The dissertation turned out to be an important step in the development of Keynesian ideas, although, as Kahn remarked sixty years later at the time of its publication, 'neither he [Keynes] nor I had the slightest idea that my work on the short period was later on going to influence the development of Keynes's own thought' (Kahn 1989: xi).

Kahn began his collaboration with Keynes in the final drafting of the *Treatise*, which was completed in September 1930;[2] the same month saw the beginnings of his intellectual partnership with Joan Robinson.[3] In fact, in the transition to the *General Theory* a major role is assigned by Moggridge to the 'core pair' of Joan Robinson and Richard Kahn (Moggridge 1977: 66).

We know that in the *Treatise* Keynes declared his unwillingness to be led 'too far into the intricate theory of the economics of the short period' (Keynes 1971: 145),[4] but soon after the publication of the book, in a letter to Hawtrey of 28 November 1930, he wrote:

> I repeat that I am not dealing with the complete set of causes which determine volume of output. For this would have led me an endlessly long journey into the theory of short period supply and a long way from monetary theory; – though I agree that it will probably be difficult in the future to prevent monetary theory and the theory of short-period supply from running together.
>
> (Keynes 1973b: 145–6)

It was while following this line of research that Keynes came to write his most famous book. The intention of writing the *General Theory* became apparent in the summer of 1932 after a period of long discussions with the participants in the Circus, who urged him to tackle the question of the causes of variation of output in aggregate. This at least is Kahn's opinion, who wrote: 'It is my strong belief – based on our several and joint memories – that the Circus encouraged the development indicated by Keynes to Hawtrey' (Kahn 1985: 48–9).

One crucial element in the transition from the *Treatise* to the *General Theory*, – the adoption of the theory of demand and supply, i.e. 'in a given state of technique, resources and costs' (Keynes 1973a: 23), to determine the short-period level of prices – was attributed by Keynes himself to Kahn.[5]

As is well known, Kahn brushed aside any implicit or explicit suggestion that his role in the writing of the *General Theory* was that of a co-author rather than of a remorseless critic and discussant.[6] However, in a letter to Patinkin of 11 October 1978 he wrote: 'I claim that I brought the theory of value into the *General Theory* in the form of a concept of the supply curve as a whole and that this was a major contribution' (Patinkin 1993: 659).

In order to clarify this question we have first to single out the relevant works produced by Kahn in this area. The obvious starting point is the so-called 'multiplier article', to which Keynes refers, but this was written after the dissertation, which, as we have seen, was the first step in the development of short-period analysis. Two further works must be added to the list: the unfinished and unpublished book that has the same title as the dissertation, 'The Economics of the Short Period', where the nature of the short period is further explored, and the lectures on the 'Economics of the Short Period', which Kahn gave from 1931 onwards. These lectures came to us in the form of a summary of their main content, written by Tarshis on the basis of the notes he took when attending Kahn's lectures in the Michaelmas term of 1932.

In the following section we shall take together the multiplier article, published in 1931, with Kahn's lectures, in both of which we find the construction of an aggregate supply curve of consumption goods and output in aggregate. We shall then go on to examine its bearing on the concept of the short period.

KAHN'S AGGREGATE SUPPLY FUNCTION

In his 'multiplier' article, Kahn maintains that the determination of the level of price and output of consumption goods cannot but be derived from the theory of demand and supply.[7] The aggregate supply curve of consumption goods, just like the supply curve of a single commodity, indicates the price necessary for each level of demand for consumption goods for that quantity to be produced, the demand for consumption goods being a function of total employment. Thus, the aggregate supply curve of the consumption goods sector represents 'all the situations in which the price level is such as to confirm production and employment plans made by the firms in this sector' (Dardi 1990: 8).

Following a change in employment (brought about by the building of roads financed by the government) we can study its effects on the prices and output of consumption goods, in other words the increase in production beyond the increase in investment, by looking at the shape of the supply curve of consumption goods. The latter must be derived according to 'the point of view of the particular period of time that is under consideration – long, short or otherwise' (Kahn 1972: 6).

As we know, Kahn claims here that:

> At normal times, when productive resources are fully employed, the supply of consumption-goods in the short period is highly inelastic ... But at times of intense depression, when nearly all industries have at their disposal a large surplus of unused plant and labour, the supply curve is likely to be very elastic.
>
> (Kahn 1972: 10)

Thus, in the former case, the increase in secondary employment is small and the increase in price high, while in the latter the change in secondary employment is large and the increase in price negligible.

The effects of a change in demand and in employment in the short period are made dependent on the state of demand and the pattern of costs. Thus, in the short period, we can have an increase in output and employment, or only an increase in prices. If demand is sustained, the increase in costs (and therefore in prices) is accounted for by capacity being fully utilized. If demand is low, plants and machinery are not fully utilized and production can be increased without any increase in costs. If marginal costs are assumed to be fairly constant (because there is spare capacity since demand is low) there need not be a large increase in price to call forth an increase in output (the aggregate supply curve is elastic); in contrast, if marginal costs are increasing, because we are closer to full capacity, then prices also will increase or, rather, only if they increase will it be profitable to increase production.

Kahn's construction of the aggregate supply curve is meant to solve two problems: (a) what the price must be in order that a given quantity of consumption goods be produced; (b) how much employment is generated by the increase in the quantity of consumption goods that it is profitable to produce. However, the answers to these two questions are kept separate in his argument. The answer to (a) depends on the assumed pattern of costs, on the value and pattern of the elasticity of demand, and on the rule of behaviour assumed to be followed by firms (profit maximization); whereas the answer to (b) depends on the hypotheses about labour productivity and money wages.

Once hypotheses are made relatively to (a) and (b), we can calculate the increase in price and production for any given increase in the primary employment, which is of course the multiplier.

The multiplier article can be seen then as the first step towards a theory based on aggregate supply and demand curves, although its application is limited here to the consumption goods sector. Extension of this analysis to output as a whole is accomplished in the discussion of the aggregate supply function as we find it in the lectures given by Kahn in 1932. Unfortunately, the only published evidence we have here is contained in an article by Tarshis (1979), where he states that it conveys the substance of the argument put forward by Kahn in his lectures.[8]

The starting point for the construction of the aggregate supply curve is the same as in the multiplier article. The difference is that now on the vertical axis we have the expected proceeds necessary to induce entrepreneurs to produce a given output, while on the horizontal axis we can have the level of output (ASF-O)[9] so that the question – what the price must be – is substituted by what the proceeds must be in order that a given quantity be produced.

To derive the aggregate supply curve, we start from the determination of the supply curve of each level of output for a single firm. The supply price answers the question: given marginal and average costs, associated with a given level of output, O_i, what must the price be in order that the firm that maximizes its profits be willing to produce precisely that level of output?

The level of output, O_i, will be produced only if profits are at a maximum; that is to say, only if in O_i marginal revenue equals marginal cost.[10] Thus, for the well-known relationship between price and marginal revenue, for a given elasticity of demand measured at O_i, the supply price, p_i, is:

$$p_i = \left(\frac{k}{k-1}\right) MC_i,$$

where k = elasticity of demand and MC_i = marginal costs at O_i.

The supply curve is then given by:

$$Z(O_i) = p_i O_i = \left(\frac{k}{k-1}\right) MC_i O_i.$$

It is worth noticing that the above is a *general* formulation, which does not require special assumptions about market form or the shape of the marginal cost curve. Specific assumptions are reflected in the shape of the supply curve and in the value of its elasticity. According to Tarshis, the different possibilities were discussed in Kahn's lectures (Tarshis 1979: 369n).

The aggregation problem is 'solved' by assuming that, for any given level of output, the distribution among firms of their individual share is known. The aggregate level of output, O, is then:

$$\sum_{k=1}^{m} O^k$$

m = number of firms; O^k = output produced by the k'th firm.

The total output of the economy is measured by a production index; to avoid double counting, intermediate products are of course subtracted from the total production, so that a measure in terms of value added is obtained.

The importance of the aggregate supply curve, drawn in the expected proceeds–aggregate output space, is that the derivation from it of the 'level of prices' is straightforward: for each level of output, it is given by the ratio of expected proceeds to output. This means that the level of price can be determined by the same forces as the level of output and not by the Quantity of Money. This was an important step in the development of Keynesian ideas, as Joan Robinson reminded us years later: 'A short period supply curve relating the level of money prices to the level of activity (at given money-wages rates) led straight from Marshall to the General Theory' (Robinson 1969b: 582).

The short-period aspect relevant in the construction of the aggregate supply curve is that profit maximization is the sole stopping rule for changes in production. For long-run equilibrium, the additional condition is required that firms earn the normal rate of profit, which is established through changes in the number of firms within a given industry.

However, profit maximization requires knowledge of the costs and revenue functions relevant to it, on both an 'objective' and a 'subjective' point of view. On the 'objective' side, short period is defined as the time interval that is required before changes take place in the size of plants and in the number of firms. On the 'subjective' side it is defined as the time interval when a change in the condition of demand is not expected to last. There is a 'normal' level of demand, relative to which changes in demand are perceived as either temporary or permanent. If a change in demand is not expected to last, capacity will not be altered.

Profit maximization can be given as the *general* behavioural stopping rule, which defines short-period equilibrium, only if it can be extended to cases when competition is not perfect; this means knowing, in the revenue function, how price is related to quantity, i.e. the value of the elasticity of demand, when the assumption of perfect competition is abandoned.

These two issues – how equilibrium is established when market imperfection is introduced and what sets the limits to the short period – were tackled jointly by Richard Kahn and Joan Robinson in the early 1930s. In the discussion of their work, in the next three sections, we follow the chronological rather than the logical order – first the dissertation, which – as we saw – Kahn wrote between October 1928 and December 1929; then the *Economics of Imperfect Competition*, which Joan Robinson started writing between the end of 1930 and the beginning of 1931; and finally the unfinished book 'The Economics of the Short Period', which Kahn wrote probably between the second half of 1930 and the last months of 1932.

The reason for doing so is to give an account of the beginnings of the collaboration between Kahn and Joan Robinson and to point out their common ground.

THE DISSERTATION

In the dissertation,[11] Kahn starts from Marshall's definition of short period as the situation in which machinery and the organization of production are assumed to be constant. Apparently – he noted – it would seem illogical to yoke together with the same criterion, i.e. how fast they can be altered, two so very different entities. In fact 'fixed plant increases rapidly but decreases slowly' (Kahn 1989: 3), whereas 'organization can be easily and rapidly cut down but can only slowly and with difficulty be enlarged' (Kahn 1989: 3). Thus, the possibility of considering them alike, i.e. as constant from the point of view of the short period, is given by the fact that the decision to alter them is the same and depends on whether or not demand conditions are considered permanent relatively to a level considered to be 'normal'. If changes in demand are assumed to be transitory, the decision to modify the plant or the organization will not be taken.

In the short period, 'firms carry on at a loss in the hope of an improvement, but in the longer period such firms have to close down, either in despair or through necessity' (Kahn 1989: 4). Thus, in a depression: 'It is the hope of the return to prosperity that sustains a firm through a period in which existence is possible only at the expenses of a loss' (Kahn 1989: 3).

The point of the dissertation is to prove that, when the aim is to minimize losses, as in a depression, the relevant average and marginal cost curves have the shape of an inverted L. Because the average unit cost curve is horizontal for the relevant range, only the imperfection of competition can account for an equilibrium level of production below full capacity.

The apparatus used by Kahn to produce this result is built upon very special assumptions. Besides the assumption that the average unit cost curve is linear, it is the assumption that the demand curve is also linear that allows Kahn to determine the equilibrium level of output, by using only the concept of 'maximum monopoly net revenue' introduced by Marshall (1961: 397) to obtain the equilibrium output of a monopolist producer (Marcuzzo 1994a). The generality of the result obtained was therefore limited by the peculiarity of the assumptions made and by the analytical tool adopted.

The assumption that short-period average unit costs are constant up to capacity output was later abandoned by Kahn, who did not propose it again in his multiplier article.[12] The reasons that led him towards a more orthodox line are possibly to be found in the criticism by Pigou of the restrictive nature of the assumption of linearity (Marcuzzo 1995), but more probably – as we shall see – in the construction built upon the concept of marginal revenue, which is presented in its most complete and refined form only in *The Economics of Imperfect Competition*. It is in fact this construction that eliminates the need for any restriction to the shape of the cost and demand curves.

A generalized application of marginal analysis was also provided by Kahn in his lectures. This allowed for a representation, in the aggregate supply function, of different hypotheses about the shape of marginal cost and demand curves, bypassing the need for restrictive assumptions. Unfortunately, generalization of the results was gained at the expense of the 'realism' of the dissertation, where the actual behaviour of cotton firms during the depression was accounted for precisely by L-shaped cost curves.

JOAN ROBINSON AND RICHARD KAHN: *THE ECONOMICS OF IMPERFECT COMPETITION*

The first letter we have to document the beginnings of the collaboration between Joan Robinson and Kahn is dated 15 March 1930. In this letter Joan Robinson expresses, in her typical style, her pleasure that Kahn got the fellowship: 'I am so glad – tho' not surprised. I congratulate King's on showing sense.'[13]

For more than fifty years the correspondence between them continued almost uninterruptedly, witnessing a lasting emotional and intellectual partnership. Elsewhere I have dealt with the origin of that encounter in the climate of Cambridge in those years (Marcuzzo 1991). The focus here is rather the importance for short-period analysis of the results achieved in *The Economics of Imperfect Competition*.

Joan Robinson began writing *The Economics of Imperfect Competition* between the end of 1930 and the beginning of 1931.[14] The occasion that started everything off was related by Austin Robinson. One day, when Richard Kahn was lunching at 3, Trumpington Street, where Joan and Austin lived in those days, he reported that a pupil of his – C. Gifford – had just invented an interesting concept, which was later christened by Austin Robinson 'marginal revenue'; according to his reconstruction, the book started 'as a joint game between Joan and Richard Kahn' (Leith and Patinkin 1977: 80; A. Robinson 1994: 7–8).

The drafting of the book, which Joan Robinson nicknamed 'my nightmare', was tormented. The exchanges with Kahn were pressing and demanding, because Kahn checked every single passage, as he did with Keynes. Physical distance did not seem to matter, since the revision of proof was done by mail, back and forth between Cambridge (UK) and Cambridge (USA), where Kahn had been visiting since the end of December 1932. Eventually, by early February 1933, he was able to write to her:

> I have finished your book and feel that I might be allowed to write to you . . . It is an amazing piece of work. I find that I usually take it for granted, but whenever I stop to think about it I just can't believe it is true. Do you by any chance realize what you have done? In the course of two years of your young life?
>
> (Letter by RFK to JVR of 7/2/1933; RFK Papers 13/90, King's College Library, Cambridge)

Early in November 1932, the typescript of the book was taken to Macmillan, who asked Keynes' opinion. After only two weeks, Keynes recommended publication, but hesitated to stress the originality of the book (Keynes 1973c: 866–7).

Perhaps Keynes was right in warning that the book was 'predominantly a discussion of the development of ideas which have been started by others, and which are now widely current, not only for learned articles, but in oral discussion at Cambridge and Oxford'. However, this does not invalidate the conclusion that it is only with Joan Robinson's book that the generalization of the development of a method of analysis based on the equality of marginal cost to marginal revenue was really accomplished.

The starting point[15] of *The Economics of Imperfect Competition* is Sraffa's proposal – later dismissed by him – 'to re-write the theory of value, starting from the conception of the firm as a monopolist' (Robinson 1969a: 6), but with the aim of extending the marginal technique to market forms other than perfect competition. By doing so it is possible to unify the analysis of monopoly and perfect competition according to a single principle. Joan Robinson considered this an advance on Marshall's approach, because:

> It is clear that the marginal method of analysis will produce exactly the same results as the method, used by Marshall, of finding the price at which the area representing 'monopoly net revenue' is at a maximum, since net revenue is at a maximum when marginal revenue and marginal cost are equal. Both methods can be applied to problems of competition and monopoly.
>
> (Robinson 1969a: 54n)

It was rightly argued that Robinson provided for the first time 'a full and unified treatment of profit-maximizing equilibrium for a firm facing a fixed market environment' (Whitaker 1989: 187). Without addressing the question of priority as regards the discovery of the main relevant analytical points,[16] it was undoubtedly through that book that perfect competition was shown to be a special case in a general theory of competition.

The Economics of Imperfect Competition is built upon a general relation between average value, marginal value and elasticity of the average value. If e is the elasticity of the average value, A the average value, M the marginal value, then:

$$e = \frac{A}{A - M}; \quad M = A\frac{(e - 1)}{e}; \quad A = M\frac{e}{(e - 1)}$$

The above set of relationships (Robinson 1969a: 36)[17] can be applied both to the average and marginal revenue curve and to the average and marginal cost curve. For the revenue curve, there are two points to note. First, it is only with a downward-sloping demand curve that the marginal revenue becomes a distinct curve.[18] Secondly, with a downward-sloping demand curve, *any* assumption about the shape of the marginal cost curve provides for the determinacy of equilibrium. The generality of the statement that, both in competition and in monopoly, production will be carried up to the point where marginal cost is equal to marginal revenue lies in the fact that it can equally accommodate constant, decreasing and increasing costs.

The Economics of Imperfect Competition is concerned mainly with long-period analysis, and the study of short-period conditions is confined to the discussion of the shape of cost curves. As in Kahn's dissertation, we find the proposition that in the short period the marginal cost curve is constant for a wide range of output (Robinson 1969a: 49), but, unlike the dissertation, this book makes no mention of expectations relative to the level of demand, which are, as we have seen, an important factor in the definition of short period.

Joan Robinson later became a severe critic of the book that brought her fame and distinction. A few years later it was dismissed as a 'blind alley' (Robinson 1979: x), and already in the second edition she listed a number of blemishes (Robinson 1969a: vi–vii). However, although *The Economics of Imperfect Competition* may appear as a *detour*, or, to borrow Loasby's expression, 'a wrong turning' (Loasby 1991), if compared with the positions favoured by Joan Robinson later on, the book provided the key to the possibility of extending the theory of supply and demand to the *general* case (Marcuzzo 1994b). The other key was provided by a book that was not published and that did not get any public recognition, but that was equally important for the issue we are examining here.

THE ECONOMICS OF THE SHORT PERIOD

While he was helping Joan Robinson with her *Economics of Imperfect Competition*[19] and assisting Keynes in getting his ideas into focus, Kahn was trying to write his own book, where the main findings of the dissertation could be presented in an improved form. The book, which bears the same title as the dissertation, remained unfinished. The extant copy, which was found among Kahn's papers in King's College Archives, contains a few comments pencilled by Joan Robinson, who read it at the beginning of 1933.[20] Of the planned eleven chapters, according to the index, chapters I, III and IV remained unwritten, while chapter VII was left unfinished.[21] Since Joan Robinson's book is quoted as *The Theory of Monopoly* and we know that its title was changed in January 1933;[22] and since we know that Kahn left for America in December 1932 and the latest reference in the book is an article published in February 1932, it is safe to date the extant version to the last quarter of 1932.

The most striking feature of the book is the attempt to define the short period with the utmost precision; the result is that, compared with the dissertation, the issue of the imperfection of competition is overshadowed.[23] The nature of the short period is described as a matter of fact, rather than a conceptual experiment, where certain variables are kept constant:

> The whole usefulness of the device of the Short Period is based on the fact that the life of fixed capital is considerably greater than the period of production, greater that is to say than the life of working capital. It cannot be too strongly emphasized that this is a *fact*, which could not be deducted by *a priori* reasoning. In a different kind of world in which, for example, the plough wore out after a single season's use (or, better still, in which crops took as long to reach fruition as ploughs to reach decrepitude), quite a different kind of analysis would be appropriate.
>
> (Kahn 1932, Chap. II: 2; 1989: xiii)

If there were a complete range of continuous variation in the lives of the different means of production, the notion of short period could not be employed. But, in reality, as far as the range of variation is concerned:

> Between raw materials, on the one hand, and productive plant, on the other hand, there is a desolate and sparsely populated area. As a general rule, the life of physical capital is illustrated either by the mayfly or by the elephant.
>
> (Kahn 1989: xiii)

The reality of the 'economics of the short period' is, then, rooted in the nature of the production process, which gives meaning to a time interval where productive capacity is given and only its utilization varies. When we study the effects of a change in demand on the equilibrium of an industry, we have to keep in mind that 'there are changes that occur rapidly and completely (such as the alteration in the amount of employment) and there are changes that occur only slowly (such as the alteration, quantitative and qualitative, in fixed plant)' (Kahn 1932, Chap. II: 6).[24]

The other element entering the definition of the short period is the expectations of the level of demand relative to the level perceived as the normal level. In fact, 'the situation in which businessmen are expecting a fairly rapid return to more normal conditions ... provides par excellence the atmosphere that the short period thrives on' (Kahn 1932, Chap. II: 22).[25]

In a depression, the short period is a longer time interval, because expectations are that demand will return to its normal level, whereas suspending production or reducing the productive capacity to zero would require the belief that demand will continue to remain low. According to Kahn's taxonomy, in the 'ideal short period', when the number of firms is fixed, 'any change that occurs is not expected to be permanent' (Kahn 1932, Chap. II: 10).[26] On the contrary, when profits are high and the depression is over, firms react very rapidly by increasing production and capacity, and the short period is consequently 'shorter'. Moreover, to measure the length of the short period not only are demand expectations relevant, but also market form, since 'The monopolist is far quicker in adapting himself to new conditions than is a competitive industry' (Kahn 1932, Chap. X: 7).[27]

As we have seen, the book by Kahn remained unfinished but the way to short-period analysis was paved.

JOAN ROBINSON'S SHORT PERIOD

Joan Robinson, as we saw, became increasingly dissatisfied with her *Economics of Imperfect Competition*, especially as far as the distinction between short and long period was concerned. In the following years she endeavoured to make this distinction more clear cut,[28] and she returned to this very issue in her last paper (Robinson 1985). Thus, in reviewing Joan Robinson's later work on this issue, the question arises whether short and long period should be interpreted as two aspects of the same theory or whether this distinction is thought to be feasible only on the basis of two distinct theories.

In her *Accumulation of Capital*, the distinction between short period and long period is derived on the basis of four criteria (Robinson 1969c: 179–82):

1 *Short- and long-period variables*. Changes in production, employment and prices belong to short-period analysis, whereas changes in capital stock, labour force and techniques belong to long-period analysis.
2 *Short- and long-period expectations*. Short-term expectations guide entrepreneurs in their decisions on the level of output, whereas long-term expectations guide entrepreneurs in their decisions on the stock of productive capacity.
3 *Short- and long-period aspects of the same variable*. From the point of view of the short period, investment is a determinant only of the level of aggregate demand, whereas from the point of view of the long period it enters as a determinant of the rate of accumulation and in the choice of techniques.
4 *Short- and long-period market forms*. Competition and monopoly (oligopoly) have both a short-period and a long-period aspect. Competition in its short-period aspect is described as a situation where there are many independent producers and each of them takes the price as given by the market. Each producer tries to keep his costs as low as possible and obtain the maximum profit that is feasible at that price. In oligopoly, price is not given by the market, but each producer must take into account how rivals react to his price policy. This represents the short-period aspect of oligopoly. The long-period aspect of competition is reflected in the relative ease in entering the market and in the pressure to adopt innovations in order to remain in the market. The long-period aspect of oligopoly is also reflected in how easily potential rivals can enter the market, so that a monopolist can be strong in controlling his market in the short period, but may not be able to prevent others taking control of the market.

In her 1956 book, Joan Robinson thus appears unwilling to give up the idea of having a theory that can deal with both short- and long-run issues. Later on she appears to be wavering between the idea that they can be approached within the same theory (by applying to the long period the same forces that are at work in the short period) and the resigned acceptance that the only option is to have separate theories.

Thus, the question is whether or not the distinction between short and long period can be made independent from the particular theory underlying it. We saw that in order to define a short-period equilibrium a stopping rule is needed for the system, resulting in the absence of any further incentives to change decisions. As far as the theory of effective demand is concerned, the rule that defines short-period equilibrium is given by the equality between saving and investment brought about by changes in income. This proposition, within the framework of analysis employed by Keynes and Kahn, was established through the adoption of aggregate demand and supply curves. However, extension to the long period of the same proposition, established within that *particular* theory, faces the well-known difficulties related to the need to measure the quantity of capital (Garegnani 1979).

Within the framework of analysis provided by the theory of demand and supply, the short-period equilibrium level of output is determined when we are given the rule of behaviour of profit maximization, which in its most general form can be expressed by the equality of marginal cost to marginal revenue.[29] However, extension to the long period of the theory of demand and supply, needed in order for the rate of profit to be determined, is impaired by the difficulty of giving meaning to the concept of a quantity of capital.

After acknowledging the difficulty of extending to the long period the particular theory adopted for short-period problems, i.e. the theory of output and competition on the basis of supply and demand functions, Joan Robinson drew two conclusions. On the one hand she opted for a long-period theory of value and distribution, which does not encounter the same difficulties as the theory of supply and demand of 'factors of production'. On the other, she held firmly to the idea that the short period could not be introduced in a framework of analysis where expectations of demand and various degrees of capital utilization do not have any role to play.[30]

CONCLUSIONS

In this paper I looked into the meaning of the short period, examining its development at the origin of Keynesian macroeconomics. In the work of Richard Kahn and Joan Robinson the short period emerges as a framework where some decisions are taken and their effects are revealed (level of output) while others are not (plants and productive capacity). Two justifications for short-period analysis are given. The first is rooted in the nature of the productive process itself: the time horizon of decisions about the level of utilization of the labour force is shorter than that of decisions about the degree of utilization of productive capacity. The second is grounded in the nature of decisions in the pricing and production process: expectations about demand are made with respect to a level perceived as 'normal' and only changes that are perceived as permanent involve variations in plants, machinery and the choice of techniques.

This is a meaning of short period as a situation describing decisions taken on the basis of expectations. However, what matters is the divergence between the expected and the 'normal' values of selected variables, not the divergence between fulfilled and unfulfilled expectations. It follows that the short period is *not* a 'short' time interval, a temporary state when the so-called permanent forces of the system have not yet worked out their effects. The 'Cambridge' idea of short period is, rather, a position that is maintained as long as the set of decisions depending upon the expected values of those variables does not change (Dardi, Chapter 2 in this volume).

Whereas Richard Kahn always remained faithful to the original formulation of short-period analysis, Joan Robinson's position evolved during the years, branching out in more than one direction. On this issue there was disagreement with Kahn, to whom she once wrote bluntly: 'Cannot we agree on Piero's prices for the long run and on Keynes' prices for the short run and leave it at that?'[31]

Thus, it would appear that her legacy is to solve what she saw as a dilemma between a Keynesian (short-period) and a Sraffian (long-period) approach.

NOTES

1 I wish to thank, without implicating them, Marco Dardi, Andrea Ginzburg, Luigi Pasinetti, Alessandro Roncaglia, Anna Simonazzi, Maurizio Zenezini and especially Annalisa Rosselli for their comments on earlier versions of this paper. I also wish to express my gratitude to the former Vice-Provost, Ian Fenlon, the Librarian, Peter Jones, and especially the Modern Archivist, Jackie Cox, for the privilege I was granted to consult Kahn's papers before they were catalogued. Finally, I am very grateful to David Papineau for permission to quote from the unpublished writings of R. F. Kahn.

2 'Keynes did not want to divert me from my writing my dissertation, and it was only after December 1929 that he started giving me for comments the proofs of the *Treatise*' (letter from R. F. Kahn to D. Patinkin of 9/3/1974, published in Patinkin and Leith 1977: 148; see also Kahn 1985: 44). After he had submitted the dissertation, on 7 December 1929, Kahn was free to give his time to Keynes to help him in the final revision of the *Treatise*. In a letter to Keynes of 17/12/1929, he was already raising the issue: 'Do you think that any attention ought to be devoted to the effects of short period influences in the Trade cycle: i.e. the effects of limited capacity and of surplus capacity on prices and profits?' (Keynes 1973b: 121).

3 In the same letter to Patinkin, Kahn added: 'Before I had finished the index [of the *Treatise*], I went away for a holiday in the Alps and left Joan Robinson to finish it' (Patinkin and Leith 1977: 148). It was during the same holiday in the Austrian Tyrol that Kahn began his multiplier article (Kahn 1984: 91).

4 In fact, according to Kahn: 'The *General Theory* is . . . short period theory, whereas . . . the *Treatise* is essentially long-period' (Kahn 1984: 68).

5 'It was Mr. Kahn who first attacked the relation of the general level of prices to wages in the same way as that in which that of particular prices has always been handled, namely as a problem of demand and supply in the short period rather than as a result to be derived from monetary factors' (Keynes 1973a, Appendix: 400n). Keynes is referring here to the 'multiplier' article.

6 However, whatever Kahn's real contribution to the development of ideas presented in the *General Theory* may have been, there is not agreement in the literature. At one extreme there is Patinkin (1993), who belittles Kahn's influence in establishing what he sees as the main proposition of the *General Theory*, i.e. the theory of effective demand. At the other extreme there is Samuelson (in Patinkin and Leith 1977 and Samuelson 1994), who, on the contrary, believes that the theory of effective demand is 'logically equivalent' to the multiplier. Closer to the interpretation given here is the work done by Harcourt and O'Shaughnessy

(1985), Harcourt (1994) and Dardi (1983), who stress the importance of Kahn in the development of short-period analysis, and by Dardi (1990), who worked out the macroeconomic model underlying the formula of the multiplier. See also Pasinetti (1992).

7 There is agreement in the literature that this was an original contribution by Kahn. See, for instance, Shackle (1951) and Cain (1979).

8 Tarshis was a student of Keynes and Kahn between 1932 and 1935.

9 Keynes chose to measure the level of economic activity in terms not of aggregate output but of employment, because the latter was believed to be less exposed to aggregation problems. This is the reason why, according to Tarshis, we do not find the ASF-O in the *General Theory*.

10 In addition the price must be at least as high as the variable unit cost, otherwise the entrepreneur would earn more (or, in this instance, lose less) by suspending production.

11 Kahn's interest in the short period is witnessed for the first time in a paper, 'Short period equilibrium', that he read at the Political Economy Club on 12 November 1928 and that later earned him the Adam Smith Prize. In the paper we find the following, striking comment: 'While long period economics deals with things as they should be, and never are, short period economics is concerned with things as they are – and one fears, usually never should be' (R. F. Kahn Papers [henceforth RFK] 3/8/1, King's College Library, Cambridge).

12 Defending himself from criticism for his acceptance of the inverse relationship between real wages and employment, Keynes attributed the responsibility to Kahn, who had allowed him to retain the hypothesis of rising marginal costs in the *General Theory* (Marcuzzo 1993).

13 RFK 13/90. Copyright The Provost and Scholars of King's College, Cambridge, 1994. Permission from King's to publish this quote is gratefully acknowledged.

14 See letter of April 1931, from RFK to Joan Robinson (henceforth JVR): 'I feel I must write at once and congratulate you on making such a fine beginning and also to thank you. For it is tremendously pleasant to see it all rolling off – or at least beginning to roll off (it is going to be quite a big work) – so beautifully. I am so very pleased it has begun' (RFK 13/90). In October of 1931, the drafting of the book must have gone far enough to worry Shove, who asked for 'some acknowledgment' for his part in developing imperfect competition (see letter of 24/10/1931 to JVR; Turner 1989: 27).

15 This part is mainly derived from Marcuzzo (1994a).

16 Comparison with Shove is difficult, because most of his papers were destroyed; comparison with Harrod is easier and supports the interpretation that Harrod had a similar project of providing a general theory of competition. On this point, see Besomi (1993).

17 The algebraic demonstration of the relation between the curves of average and marginal values is given by Harrod (1931).

18 As has been noted, 'nobody had previously wanted the *general* concept of marginal revenue since they conceived of marginal revenue in the special form of *price*' (Shackle 1967: 42).

19 As in the case of Keynes, Kahn reacted strongly to the suggestion that he co-authored the ideas presented in *The Economics of Imperfect Competition*. In a letter of 28/3/1933 he wrote to her: 'you are attributing to me much more than I am responsible for. What I did was to read what you had written. Most of my attempts to do constructive work (e.g. in regard to Discrimination and Exploitation) ended in failure and it was almost invariably you who found the clue . . . My place in the scheme of things is apparently to correct arithmetic' (RFK 13/90).

20 See letter of 24/1/1933 from JVR to RFK: 'I have read your book . . . It is certainly a very impressive work. I hope you are going to let me help you with polishing it up' (RFK 13/90. Copyright The Provost and Scholars of King's College, Cambridge, 1994. Permission from King's to publish this quote is gratefully acknowledged).

21 Part of this chapter merged into an article, 'The Marginal Principle', which Kahn took with him to America and submitted to Taussig for publication in *The Quarterly Journal of Economics*. The article was rejected and remained unpublished.

22 See letter from JVR to RFK of 23/1/1933: 'I enclose the blurb of my book – Austin wrote it for me. The latest idea is to call it "The Economics of Imperfect Competition", what do you think? The text does not bear much relation to it, but I do not think that matters. I would have preferred to stick to the original title, but Maynard won't let me' (RFK 13/90. Copyright The Provost and Scholars of King's College, Cambridge, 1994. Permission from King's to publish this quote is gratefully acknowledged).

23 In his Introductions to the Italian (1983) and English (1989) editions of the dissertation, which include the only reference to the unfinished book, Kahn wrote: 'In the course of the following three or four years I did rewrite seven chapters, intending them for publication. On looking at them I am amazed to find that they are almost entirely confined to conditions of perfect competition; whereas the importance of my dissertation largely rested on its treatment of imperfect competition (Kahn 1989: xii).

24 RFK 2/7.

25 Ibid.

26 Ibid.

27 Ibid.

28 There are many quotations to support this; perhaps the following is worth noting: 'I am working on my book on Marx. Its chief purpose is to show that economics is no good – either Marxists' or ours – except for short period analysis. This ought to please Maynard' (letter of JVR to RFK of 22/5/1941; RFK 13/90. Copyright The Provost and Scholars of King's College, Cambridge, 1994. Permission from King's to publish this quote is gratefully acknowledged).

29 It is the most general form because, given the hypothesis of optimizing behaviour, it allows for different assumptions about the shape of cost functions and the value of elasticity of demand. Only when these functions exhibit some kind of discontinuity – as in the case of L-shaped average unit cost curves – is the condition required weaker (see Marcuzzo 1995).

30 The following quote is fairly representative of her view: 'Sraffa offers long-period analysis in the sense that the stock of means of production for a particular technique is supposed to be always used at its designed capacity' (Robinson 1980: 131).

31 Letter from JVR to RFK of 2/5/1961; RFK 13/90. Copyright The Provost and Scholars of King's College, Cambridge, 1994. Permission from King's to publish this quote is gratefully acknowledged.

REFERENCES

Besomi, D. (1993) Roy Harrod, la concorrenza imperfetta e la possibilità di una teoria dinamica, *Studi Economici*, 50: 41–70.

Cain, N. (1979) Cambridge and Its Revolution: A Perspective on the Multiplier and Effective Demand, *Economic Record*: 108–17.

Dardi, M. (1983) Introduzione. In R. F. Kahn, *L'Economia del breve periodo*. Turin: Boringhieri.

——— (1990) Richard Kahn, *Studi Economici*, 41: 3–85.

Garegnani, P. (1979) Notes on Consumption, Investment and Effective Demand II, *Cambridge Journal of Economics*, 3: 63–82.

Harcourt, G. C. (1994) Kahn and Keynes and the making of *The General Theory*, *Cambridge Journal of Economics*, 18: 11–23.

Harcourt, G. C. and O'Shaughnessy, T. J. (1985) Keynes's Unemployment Equilibrium: Some Insights from Joan Robinson, Piero Sraffa and Richard Kahn. In G. C. Harcourt, ed., *Keynes and His Contemporaries*. London: Macmillan.

Harrod, R. (1931) The Law of Decreasing Costs, *Economic Journal*, 41: 566–76.

Kahn, R. F. (1932) The Economics of the Short Period. Unpublished manuscript. King's College Library, Cambridge.

——— (1972) *Selected Essays on Employment and Growth*. Cambridge: Cambridge University Press.

——— (1984) *The Making of Keynes's General Theory*. Cambridge: Cambridge University Press.

——— (1985) The Cambridge 'Circus'. In G. C. Harcourt, ed., *Keynes and His Contemporaries*. London: Macmillan.

——— (1989) *The Economics of the Short Period*. London: Macmillan.

Keynes, J. M. (1971) *A Treatise on Money*. In D. Moggridge, ed., *The Collected Writings of John Maynard Keynes*, vols V–VI. London: Macmillan.

——— (1972) *Essays in Biography*. In D. Moggridge, ed., *The Collected Writings of John Maynard Keynes*, vol. XI. London: Macmillan.

——— (1973a) *The General Theory of Employment, Interest, and Money*. In D. Moggridge, ed., *The Collected Writings of John Maynard Keynes*, vol. VII. London: Macmillan.

——— (1973b) *The General Theory of Employment, Interest, and Money: Preparation*. In D. Moggridge, ed., *The Collected Writings of John Maynard Keynes*, vol. XIII. London: Macmillan.

——— (1973c) *Economic Articles and Correspondence: Investment and Editorial*. In D. Moggridge, ed., *The Collected Writings of John Maynard Keynes*, vol. XII. London: Macmillan.

Loasby, B. J. (1991) Joan Robinson's 'Wrong Turning'. In I. Rima, ed., *The Joan Robinson Legacy*. Armonk, NY: M. E. Sharpe.

Marcuzzo, M. C. (1991) Joan Robinson e la formazione della Scuola di Cambridge. In J. Robinson, *Occupazione, distribuzione e crescita*, ed. M. C. Marcuzzo. Bologna: Il Mulino.

——— (1993) La relazione salari-occupazione tra rigidità reali e rigidità nominali, *Economia Politica*, 10: 439–63.

——— (1994a) R. F. Kahn and Imperfect Competition, *Cambridge Journal of Economics*, 18: 25–39.

——— (1994b) At the Origin of the Theory of Imperfect Competition: Different Views? In K. I. Vaughn, ed., *Perspectives in the History of Economic Thought*. Aldershot: Elgar.

——— (1995) Alternative Microeconomic Foundations for Macroeconomics: The Controversy over the L-shaped Cost Curve Revisited. *Review of Political Economy*, 7: 447–65.

Marshall, A. (1961) *Principles of Economics*, ed. C. W. Guillebaud. London: Macmillan.

Moggridge, D. (1977) Cambridge Discussion and Criticism Surrounding the Writing of the General Theory: A Chronicler's View. In D. Patinkin and J. C. Leith, eds, *Keynes, Cambridge and the General Theory*. London: Macmillan.

Pasinetti, L. L. (1992) Richard Ferdinand Kahn 1905–1989, *Proceedings of the British Academy*, 76: 423–43.
Patinkin, D. (1993) On the Chronology of the *General Theory*, *Economic Journal*, 103: 647–63.
Patinkin, D. and Leith, J. C., eds (1977) *Keynes, Cambridge and the General Theory*. London: Macmillan.
Robinson, A. (1994) Richard Kahn in the 1930s, *Cambridge Journal of Economics*, 18: 7–10.
Robinson, J. V. (1969a) *The Economics of Imperfect Competition*, 2nd edn. London: Macmillan.
——— (1969b) Review of A. Leijonhufvud, *On Keynesian Economics and the Economics of Keynes*, *Economic Journal*, 79: 581–3.
——— (1969c) *The Accumulation of Capital*, 3rd edn. London: Macmillan.
——— (1979) *Contributions to Modern Economics*. Oxford: Blackwell.
——— (1980) *Further Contributions to Modern Economics*. Oxford: Blackwell.
——— (1985) The Theory of Normal Prices and Reconstruction of Economic Theory. In G. R. Feiwel, ed., *Issues in Contemporary Macroeconomics and Distribution*. London: Macmillan.
Samuelson, P. A. (1994) Richard Kahn: His Welfare Economics and Lifetime Achievement, *Cambridge Journal of Economics*, 18: 55–72.
Shackle, G. L. S. (1951) Twenty Years on: A Survey of the Theory of the Multiplier, *Economic Journal*, 61: 241–60.
——— (1967) *The Years of High Theory. Invention and Tradition in Economic Thought 1926–1939*. Cambridge: Cambridge University Press.
Tarshis, L. (1979) The Aggregate Supply Function in Keynes's General Theory. In M. J. Boskin, ed., *Essays in Honor of Tibor Scitovsky*. New York: Academic Press.
Turner, M. S. (1989) *Joan Robinson and the Americans*. Armonk, NY: Sharpe.
Whitaker, John K. (1989) The Cambridge Background to Imperfect Competition. In G. F. Feiwel, ed., *The Economics of Imperfect Competition and Employment. Joan Robinson and Beyond*. London: Macmillan.

2

IMPERFECT COMPETITION AND SHORT-PERIOD ECONOMICS

Marco Dardi

The Economics of Imperfect Competition (Robinson 1933) is commonly regarded as a milestone in Joan Robinson's intellectual career and in the development of Cambridge economics. However, doubts have been expressed, *in primis* by the author herself, as to the effective relevance of this work. The contention of the present paper is that these doubts are better understood, and a more critical evaluation of Joan Robinson's work on imperfect competition is gained, if what she set out to do in the early 1930s is considered in the light of the contemporaneous efforts that Keynes was making to turn short-period economics into a full-fledged explanation of recession and unemployment.

Robinson's later qualms at having poured time and energies into a project that she herself now considered a 'wrong turning' (Robinson 1951: vii–viii; see also Robinson 1953) are comprehensible. With the 1933 book she accomplished a task that helped her to establish a reputation for herself as a standard economist, but it was a task that ran counter to her deep-seated intellectual sympathies and political inclinations. These were all on the side of Keynes' quest for a radical breakthrough in the way in which economists look at the actual workings of economic systems. But whereas Keynes pursued this aim by trying to realign analysis along the short-period perspective – in a sense that I shall shortly explain – Joan Robinson's work led to an official divorce between that particular line of research and the theory of imperfect markets and industrial structure. In the late 1920s, in the wake of Sraffa's article in the 1926 *Economic Journal*, it had seemed likely that imperfect competition might represent a second line of theoretical renovation, parallel to Keynes' investigations of short-period economics. Sraffa did not do much with it, but Richard Kahn's 1928 fellowship dissertation (Kahn 1989) made some strides in that direction.[1] After Robinson had severed the links tying imperfect competition to short-period economics, however, the former lay exposed for what it was: a mere extension of the orthodox theory of value, filling the gap between the cases of pure competition and pure monopoly in a scholastic and predictable way.

What all this reveals, as I shall argue, is that the innovative drive existing in Cambridge during the period under examination lay elsewhere than in the field of imperfect competition; rather, it mostly lay in the field of short-period economics. From here it was extended to the field of imperfect competition, but only in as much as the two had certain things in common. To substantiate these claims I shall first try to clarify in what sense Keynes' attack on orthodox theory may be said to have taken its cue from short-period economics; and then I shall try to explain why it was that imperfect competition *by itself* could not provide the way out that the young generations of Cambridge economists were looking for.

Saying that Keynes intended to develop short-period analysis into a new theory that would be radically critical of the extant economic orthodoxy seems to imply some sort of paradox. In Cambridge, orthodox theory could mean only Marshall and Pigou, but it was also Marshall who, of all previous economists, had brought the notion of the short period into greatest theoretical prominence. In fact, Keynes' objections had nothing to do with the content and relevance of the notion, and only concerned the way in which Marshall utilized it in theoretical reasoning.

To Marshall and Keynes alike, 'short period' meant a situation of partial equilibrium, i.e. a state of things in which certain agents do what they believe to be their best in the given circumstances, but where the circumstances themselves involve differences in rates of return (positive or negative quasi-rents) that point to profitable ways of redirecting invested resources. Interest in this notion of equilibrium is justified by the assumption that the economy is hardly ever in a state of *complete* equilibrium or disequilibrium, but is usually in a mixed state, with some economic activities being settled in regular routines while others undergo processes of revision and change. The short period is, therefore, a situation of *partial* regularity or normality, characterized by the local equalization of rates of return in certain sectors of the economy, but immersed, so to speak, in the flow of movement induced by agents competing for the remaining differential profits. As the pressure of competition gradually squeezes these differential profits out, and provided that no unpredictable sources of new differential profits crop up for a while, the area of regularity or normality in the economy will expand monotonically until, in a 'theoretically perfect long period' (Marshall 1961, I: 379n), it ends up covering the whole system, and a state of general equilibrium or, in Marshall's own words, a 'stationary state' eventually emerges.

It does not matter that Marshall viewed the stationary state as only a virtual state, the actual attainment of which is indefinitely postponed in historical time by the continual occurrence of technological and organizational innovations that bring the process of construction of equilibrium back to a state of partial disarray, from where it starts again. The essential point is that

Marshall assumed that the tendency to construct and expand the areas in which regularity or normality prevails, however disturbed, is always at work in the economy. This faith in the ordering power of competition implies the belief that there are always enough knowledgeable agents around who can discern where profitable opportunities lie and how to exploit them, so that, sooner or later, resources will be directed towards the most beneficial utilizations.

It is at this very point that Keynes parted company with Marshall. As illustrated in the *General Theory*, Keynes' main argument was that, in most cases, agents simply do not know what to do or how to move in order to put right an unsettled situation. In his *General Theory*, Keynes laid special emphasis on the case of financial operators and wealth-owners in general, who in the last instance shape the asset composition of the whole economy, and whose decisions are conditioned to the highest degree by ignorance and doubt. Earlier in the 1920s, however, as a recent paper by Roberto Marchionatti (1995) reminds us, Keynes' concern was also with industrialists who lacked the entrepreneurial skill and foresight required to come through awkward circumstances.[2] The theory he was to work out was not one of errors in allocative decisions, but one of self-fulfilling expectations or 'bootstraps'. When uncertainty as to the profitability of different lines of investment is particularly high, agents fall back on the well-established tenet 'when in doubt, do nothing', which means avoiding commitment to new projects or changing current patterns of behaviour. The consequence is that existing resources lie unused and potential ones are not produced. The ensuing state of depression corroborates the belief that doing nothing is the right thing, so that the current state of affairs tends to reproduce itself through time, at least until something breaks down somewhere.

The novelty of Keynes' intuition is in showing that, in their own way, bootstraps are an expression of economic rationality. They therefore provide theoretical ground for the thesis that short-period equilibria may last a long time or, put in another way, that the Marshallian assumption that short-period equilibria evolve into long-period ones lacks general foundations. Competition as a normalizing device requires a greater amount of knowledge and confidence than may be taken for granted. The path from short- to long-period equilibria gets bogged down whenever agents have no clear ideas about the right direction to take and prefer the relative safety of staying put. In brief, the gist of Keynes' theoretical reorientation may be said to lie in his stripping the Marshallian short period of its essential quality, i.e. temporariness.

If this is a fair account of what Keynes was about at the turn of the 1930s, it is easy to understand why the contemporaneous attacks on perfect competition had a minor role to play. First of all, the target of criticism was not the same as Keynes's. If by perfect competition is meant price-taking behaviour (Robinson 1933: 18), then there is no possible relationship with Marshall's theory of competitive markets, as Keynes himself and others in

Cambridge (for example Shove) knew all too well.[3] A competitive market was, in Marshall's view (1919: 397–8), a system of 'conditional' or 'provisional monopolies', admittance to which costs time and resources because firms have to fight to conquer and defend their own market niches. In the *Principles*, explicit references can be found to the notions (although not with their proper denominations) of 'marginal revenue', as distinct from market price, and of marginal productivity in value, as distinct from the value of marginal (physical) productivity (Marshall 1961, I: 849–50). They both imply that each producer faces a downward-sloping particular demand curve. Price-taking is at times assumed as a convenient simplification, but nowhere does it play an essential part in the Marshallian analysis of competitive markets. This is not to say once more that 'it was all in Marshall'. What catches the modern reader's attention in the passages I have just mentioned is the total insouciance with which Marshall dropped his marginal formulas as a matter of course that was hardly worth notice. This may be seen as evidence that he was not aware of their importance, or that from his point of view they actually *were* of little importance. I would opt for the second interpretation on the basis of the discussion that follows.

The mere existence of a gap between price and marginal revenue, and in equilibrium between price and marginal cost, is not such as to disturb Marshall's view of the normal operations of an economy. The gap may well be associated with extra-normal profits, but if we consider profits over the whole life-cycle of a representative firm, as should be done in a Marshallian perspective, then these extra-profits are counterbalanced by the less-than-normal profits the firm earns while trying to make a name for itself and, later on, when it enters the inevitable phase of decadence. If we take all the stages that a firm typically passes through into consideration, therefore, deviations from the competitive norm may or may not cancel themselves out – and the presence of a monopoly rent may or may not turn out to be a delusion – according to whether the firm's life-cycle is representative of a long- or short-period equilibrium situation. There is thus no necessary relationship between short-period phenomena and the extra-profits allowed by the Marshallian notion of competition. Marshall's conditional monopoly, like Joan Robinson's imperfect competition a few decades later, was perfectly compatible with long-period normality or equilibrium.

This is so much so that it was only by means of a completely different route that Kahn came across the relationship between imperfect competition and the short period, which was the object of his 1928 dissertation. His starting point was an industry in a state of depressed demand and generalized excess capacity, modelled after the pattern of the British coal and cotton industries in the 1920s. The situation was clearly a short-period one, because the extent and duration of excess capacity went beyond the limits of normal fluctuations around a long-period equilibrium. Imperfect competition stepped in by making the partial utilization of plants compatible with the assumption (which

Kahn considered the most likely) of constant marginal costs below capacity output. The two may coexist in short-run equilibrium only if the total revenue function is concave, i.e. if each firm has a separate market of its own with demand price decreasing in the firm's own output. Once admitted onto the scene, however, imperfection took up an additional role. Each firm's particular demand is an asset whose value depends on the firm's expectations: negative quasi-rents are not by themselves a good enough reason for leaving the market. In Kahn's picture, expectations are such as to justify the decision to hold out, at least as long as there are residual financial resources, and also to abstain from any kind of innovative investment. Consequently, the industry neither collapses nor revives, and stagnation corroborates extant expectations, so that 'the short period may run into decades' (Kahn 1989: 2).

One may well conclude that in Kahn's case it was historical experience that, by confronting him with a peculiar combination of depression and imperfection, suggested the idea of short-period equilibria turning into bootstraps. I have argued elsewhere (in section 5 of Dardi 1982) that there is a close analogy between Kahn's entrepreneurs refusing to abandon their particular markets in times of distress, and Keynes' financial operators seeking safety in the most liquid abodes of wealth in periods of high uncertainty. Both phenomena provide convergent explanations of why new investments may remain blocked for a long time, and point to external (political) intervention as the only means for unlocking the situation before it turns sour.

I believe that this is where imperfect competition and Keynesian economics might have joined forces.[4] Events, however, took a different turn. For reasons of his own, Keynes preferred to concentrate on the monetary side of the short-period problem, leaving the theory of markets entirely to Joan Robinson, who chose to develop it in the way we know. It thus happened that Keynes took the short period out of the Marshallian world of 'normalizing' economies, whereas Robinson found herself trapped in a particular region of that world, while working on the analytical and geometric implications of Marshall's marginal formulas. The schism resulted in Kahn's being pushed in opposing directions, his devotion for both his friends compelling him to render assistance to two completely independent projects. We may only conjecture that his unfinished book on the short period might have met a different and better fate had he felt free to follow his own inclinations.

One final question that one might ask in connection with the chasm that Keynes introduced between short- and long-period economics is the following. Is it still possible to consider these as two different perspectives encompassed by a single theory, as they were in the original Marshallian formulation, or is it inevitable that, after Keynes, each one become the object of a separate theory? In Chapter 1, Cristina Marcuzzo depicts Joan Robinson as wavering between the alternatives, with perhaps a certain bias (at least in her maturity) for theoretical separation. This bent is borne out by a passage from an unpublished letter to Kahn of 1961, quoted by Marcuzzo at the end of her paper (this volume, p. 24). Separation also seems to be the key of Marcuzzo's interpretation of short-period analysis 'in the heritage of the school of Keynes, Kahn and Joan Robinson'.

I am unable to decide if this really was Robinson's final option, but were it so I would not agree that it belongs to the same heritage as Keynes. The very fact of taking seriously the hypothesis of a split between short- and long-period theory seems to imply complete surrender to the static interpretation of the short/long distinction that prevails in textbooks. This is out of line with both the original (classical and Marshallian) view and the Keynesian view of the short period. Seeing the latter as a phase – not necessarily a transitory one, as we saw above – in the process of construction of more complex equilibria implies the project of a dynamic theory aiming at showing how the forces that make for economic change combine and eventually exhaust their strength. The object is the path of the economy; short and long periods are simply conventional ways of looking at its opposite ends. In spite of Keynes' favourite maxim 'we may dispense with the long period', the object of the *General Theory* was well within the scope of the project. In that work, in fact, the main question was why it is that the economy may get trapped in a position that does not have the characteristics of a long-period equilibrium, or, in other words, what other attractors compete against long-period equilibria in actual dynamical processes. The fact that a truly dynamic theory of the short/long relationship was beyond his reach does not mean that Keynes would have been prepared to give up the project and accept the idea of a theory split into two parts. (Neither, I think, would he have accepted the parallel split between microeconomics and macroeconomics to which mainstream theory acquiesced for some decades after Keynes.) Robinson's resignation, in her 1961 letter, at having 'Keynes for the short run, Sraffa for the long' looks rather like an indication that her confidence in the possible development of economic dynamics was at its lowest ebb; a temporary mood, perhaps, which I would not take as representative of her 'true' theoretical position.

NOTES

1 Later on, a somewhat different attempt at entwining the two strands was made by Harrod (1934), especially in part III.

2 It may be worth recalling that Keynes' interest in the crisis of the Lancashire cotton industry prepared the way for Kahn's later work on the economics of the short period: see Kahn (1989: xi), and further on in this paper.

3 Keynes' doubts as to the originality of Robinson's book (voiced in a letter to Harold Macmillan of 25 November 1932, reproduced in Keynes 1983: 866–8) are, in the light of what follows, rather telling. The case of Shove is noteworthy because he always asserted that the theory of imperfect competition, which he had taught in Cambridge during the late 1920s, did not imply any breakaway

from Marshall's theory of the firm and industry, but rather amounted only to developing 'a simplified version' of the latter (Shove 1933: 657). Schumpeter's observations on Robinson *vis-à-vis* Marshall, contained in his 1934 *Journal of Political Economy* review of Robinson's book, are also pertinent – see Chapter 3 in this volume.

4 This refers only to the period we are considering, the early 1930s. I do not exclude that imperfect competition may turn out to have other important implications for Keynesian macroeconomics, as some recent 'New Keynesian' literature maintains. Assessing these claims is, however, beyond the scope of the present paper.

REFERENCES

Dardi, M. (1982) Introduzione. In R. F.Kahn, *L'economia del breve periodo*. Turin: Boringhieri.

Harrod, R. (1934) Doctrines of Imperfect Competition, *Quarterly Journal of Economics*, 48: 442–70.

Kahn, R. F. (1989) *The Economics of the Short Period*. London: Macmillan.

Keynes, J. M. (1983) *Economic Articles and Correspondence. Investment and Editorial*. In D. Moggridge, ed., *Collected Writings of John Maynard Keynes*, vol. XII. London: Macmillan.

Marchionatti, R. (1995) Keynes and the Collapse of the British Cotton Industry in the 1920s. A Microeconomic Case against Laissez-faire, *Journal of Post Keynesian Economics*, 17: 427–45.

Marshall, A. (1919) *Industry and Trade*. London: Macmillan.

——— (1961) *Principles of Economics*, 9th (Variorum) edition. London: Macmillan.

Robinson, J. (1933) *The Economics of Imperfect Competition*. London: Macmillan.

——— (1951) *Collected Economic Papers*, vol. I. Oxford: Blackwell.

——— (1953) Imperfect Competition Revisited, *Economic Journal*, 63: 579–93.

Shove, G. F. (1933) Review of *The Economics of Imperfect Competition* by J. Robinson, *Economic Journal*, 43: 657–61.

Sraffa, P. (1926) The Laws of Returns Under Competitive Conditions, *Economic Journal*, 36: 535–50.

3

SCHUMPETER'S REVIEW OF *THE ECONOMICS OF IMPERFECT COMPETITION*

Another look at Joan Robinson[1]

Nicolò De Vecchi

Of those works that Joan Robinson wrote and in part published during the period 1931–3, there are four that significantly express her theoretical orientation: 'Teaching Economics', *Economics is a Serious Subject*, *The Economics of Imperfect Competition*, and *The Theory of Money and the Analysis of Output.*[2] Outside the Cambridge circle, Schumpeter was among the first to comment on them. He interprets them as constituent parts of a coherent programme of research, separable from each other only because they deal with matters that fall into different sectors of economics.

The strongest cohesive element in the four works is a proposal of method. Joan Robinson presents and discusses it in two of them. In her opinion, controversies over the assumptions which sustain any theory whatsoever will never cease. But economists need to proceed with research by common accord, and to this end they must concentrate their attention on analytical tools (Robinson 1932 and 'Teaching Economics'). This proposal is actually implemented in the other two works. Joan Robinson demonstrates that a 'box of tools' is already available with which, on the one hand, to formulate an axiomatic theory of the firm that takes account of the different degrees of competition, and, on the other, to begin an 'analysis of output' of the economic system as a whole.

Her book *The Economics of Imperfect Competition* is a step in the first direction. Although working on a declared, very simplified level, she looks forward to a continuous refinement of the analytical tools so as to approximate ever more closely to the firm's 'real' behaviour.

The second line of research, proposed contemporaneously with the first, is based on an interpretation of Keynes' *A Treatise on Money.* Joan Robinson maintains, on the basis of this work, that the relationships between consumption, saving, investment, the volume of employment, etc. can be studied using analytical tools similar to those used in the partial equilibrium approach (Robinson 1932: 5; 1951a).

Schumpeter was greatly interested in all these matters. The fact that these were proposed and discussed by an economist member of the Cambridge circle increased his curiosity, because he wanted to understand how the new lines of research tied in with Alfred Marshall's teachings. After having expressed himself privately on the manuscript of 'Teaching Economics',[3] he decided to review the more ponderous work, *The Economics of Imperfect Competition*. However he took advantage of the review to survey the other works too,[4] thereby demonstrating that he considered them the fruit of a single coherent thought process.

His review was one of the most detailed (eight pages) and most favourable that the book received. However here and there and in the final summing up he expresses some perplexities with regard to various points in Joan Robinson's overall programme. As we shall see, Schumpeter appreciates the expositive style of the book and the idea of developing research for analytical tools, but at the same time he dares to disregard Joan Robinson's rules of procedure because he objects to her 'fundamental assumption' for constructing her theory of the firm taking various degrees of competition into account. He also notes the static character of her theory and makes veiled hints about the doubt – which later he was to reinforce – about compatibility between the analytical procedure adopted by Joan Robinson and that of Marshall. Finally, while approving of the need to construct a theory for the system as a whole, he warns against the temptation of taking it as a mirror of the partial equilibrium approach, in the sense that it could be conducted with instruments similar to those that Joan Robinson proposes for analysing the firm.

We shall consider the different aspects separately.

ANALYTICAL TOOLS AND ASSUMPTIONS

The Economics of Imperfect Competition seems to Schumpeter 'one of the best textbooks ever written'. Joan Robinson is an inspired teacher and reveals 'a mind eminently gifted for, and almost passionately fond of, teaching'. Her contribution is of paramount importance where she demonstrates the complete analytical symmetry of supply and demand schedules with reference to the individual firm manufacturing a single commodity, and where she identifies a single formula for determining the price for all forms of competition and clearing out the existing 'patchwork' on the subject (Schumpeter 1934: 252–3).

In short, Schumpeter read *The Economics of Imperfect Competition* while under the influence of 'Teaching Economics' and *Economics is a Serious Subject*. It is undeniable that, in writing her book, Joan Robinson considered increasing everyone's awareness of economics to be a duty and that she made an effort to combine simple language with analytical severity, but it is equally certain that her ambitions were directed elsewhere (Robinson 1969: 1–12).

Schumpeter adds that Joan Robinson achieved such sober and essential results and such a clear and elementary graphical treatment because she was successful in her intention to propose simplifying assumptions, and it is irrelevant that many who work in the same field and are used to dealing with much more complicated situations may find her tools clumsy (Schumpeter 1934: 253). In any case, she has taught 'certain fundamental truths' in the most efficient way possible and has provided a demonstration of what she herself meant by the serious work of the economist: avoiding disagreement and controversies on assumptions and setting oneself to seek or refine specific tools for defined analytical fields. According to Schumpeter, within her assumptions, she has achieved an absolutely illuminating classification and analytical arrangement of degrees of competition. Therefore she provides 'an excellent example of what serious theory should be and well lives up to the standard of rigour set . . . in a pamphlet entitled *Economics is a Serious Subject*' (Schumpeter 1934: 251; Robinson 1932: 3–4).

Schumpeter also approved of the idea that economic theory is essentially the same thing as the economist's box of analytical tools. Joan Robinson did not invent it. She inherited it from illustrious members of the Cambridge school, but it was she who made it the flagship of future research. She starts from the observation that economists never stop squabbling over assumptions, simply because they are of different temperaments. It follows that any difference on assumptions cannot be decided and that, if one wishes to widen one's knowledge, one can only move to another level, independent of the previous one: that of analytical tools. In short, the subjects that economists deal with must be 'neither more nor less' than their own techniques. It is enough to add here that the tools are never definitive, but they are perfectible, in order to sustain that any controversy on this level can be resolved. In fact each instrument or set of instruments will be continually superseded by another and, by successive approximations, more and more faithful representations of the 'real world' will be attained (Robinson 1932: 3–8; 1969: 1, 12, 327).

Joan Robinson (1932: 5) argues so incontrovertibly and confidently as to disallow any shades of opinion: 'the time has come when the economists must stake their faith on their technique. And when they do so a thousand tiresome controversies will be cleared up.'

In *History of Economic Analysis* (1954) Schumpeter adopts her thesis as a guiding principle for reconstructing the history of the analytical tools of economics, but adds to this such a lot of premises, restrictions, possible exceptions and qualifications that he ends up by highlighting its intrinsic weaknesses. He states that the set of tools is so constructed as to be ready for use on any problem whatsoever, but he adds cautiously 'within wide limits' and does not bother to clarify what he means by this phrase. He does not deny that the history of economic analysis shows that many boxes of tools, although accurately worked out, have turned out to be useless if not downright harmful. In spite of this statement, he insists on the progress achieved by economists in this field of research but he does not clearly define the scale of reference for measuring this progress. Finally he adds that tools and assumptions are linked, and thus contradicts, as he did earlier in the 1934 review, the crucial principle in Joan Robinson's theory, that the analytical tools proposed for formulating a theory are independent of the assumptions that support the theory itself. So, implicitly he acknowledges that it is difficult to agree on the tools without agreeing on the assumptions (Schumpeter 1954: 14–20, 43–4, 474).[5]

DISCUSSING THE ASSUMPTIONS

After praising Joan Robinson's excellent ability in perceiving and organizing such an analytically innovative field of theory, Schumpeter observes that the 'machine' that she presents 'stops of itself' after a certain point. This happens not so much, as she believes, because its parts are as yet imperfect but nevertheless perfectible by means of successive approximations, but because it is built according to a fundamental design that has numerous limitations and is exposed to general objections (Schumpeter 1934: 254–5).

To understand what Schumpeter means, the key points in the development of Joan Robinson's thought need to be remembered.

In the first place, in keeping with her concept of the economist's work, she sets herself the objective of formulating an axiomatic theory of the firm, using average and marginal revenue curves and average and marginal cost curves.[6] The next step consists in introducing the assumption of maximizing rationality implicit in the analytical tools proposed. Joan Robinson defines it as the 'fundamental assumption' and puts it as follows: 'each individual acts in a sensible manner in the circumstances in which he finds himself from the point of view of his own economic interests'.[7]

She adds that this type of behaviour is opposed to that resulting from 'neuroses and confused thinking'. After extracting the maximizing component from the complex of motives underlying individual action, she gets rid of the rest without worrying too much about its content. She limits herself to observing that at the moment suitable analytical tools for formulating an axiomatic theory of the firm would be missing, should one want to take neuroses and confused thinking into account.[8]

Now Joan Robinson can face the equilibrium analysis of the firm. She first deals with the monopolistic case and shows that it can 'engulf' the case of perfect competition from the analytical point of view (Robinson 1969: 4–5). Then she moves on to cases that do not enjoy the simple properties of these two extremes, and that she presents as hybrids or mixtures of both. Digressions by no means secondary[9] relate her theory to other fields of economic research or demonstrate the consequences of it on political action. Her theory remains static and does not even consider an analysis of the shifts of average and marginal revenue curves and average and marginal cost curves due to circumstances exogenous or endogenous to the firm.[10]

Faced with this construction, Schumpeter makes two types of comments. In the first place, from the analytical point of view, he identifies the book's greatest limitations in the insularity of Joan Robinson's economic culture, in the excessive caution she displays when forced to introduce a marginal utility schedule, and above all in her silence on the problem of determinateness of equilibrium for hybrid market structures.[11]

But Schumpeter concentrates his attention on another front. More than by direct criticism, he expresses his misgivings in questions, as if he expects to be contradicted by effective future research developments. However the passage of time will reinforce his doubts and in *History of Economic Analysis* he will repeat the self-same objections more fully.

He latches on to the assumption of maximizing rationality. Although he acknowledges that it enables a theory of the firm to be formulated with the marginal technique, Schumpeter considers it too reductionist to account for entrepreneurship. He observes that Joan Robinson, in proposing the stark distinction between 'rational-maximizing' action and 'irrational-confused' action, considers the former 'to be an unique and clear-cut type, of the nature of a statistical norm and invariant as to time, race and place'.

Had she but remembered Marshall's normal businessman she would have realized that the maximizing principle is insufficient to express his motives to act (Schumpeter 1934: 255).

Associating Marshall and Joan Robinson in this way is the first step to comparing them. Schumpeter sees many affinities between these two economists. *The Economics of Imperfect Competition* is 'Marshallian to the core': the manner of reasoning, certain prejudices with regard to economic concepts introduced by continental economists, the pressing reform commitment, even the general social vision (Schumpeter 1934: 253–4). Yet when the two economists express themselves on the businessman's motives to act, there appears 'a subtle difference in attitude [towards the problem of individual firms] that is not easy to convey' (Schumpeter 1954: 975). Returning to the question in *History of Economic Analysis*,[12] Schumpeter asks himself whether this difference is not symptomatic of more fundamental disagreement, concerning the very objective that each of them pursues in their theory and the analysis procedure that each of them adopts.

A TERM OF REFERENCE: ALFRED MARSHALL

To answer the question in *History of Economic Analysis* Schumpeter reconsiders how Marshall views the problems of individual firms. In his opinion, Marshall 'was bent on salvaging every bit of real life he could possibly leave in' and immediately connected businessmen's action with the formation of 'special markets' (Schumpeter 1954: 974–5; Marshall 1969: 1, 4–8, 238–42, 244–9, 262–4, 378–81).

According to Marshall, the businessman, to begin production and keep it going in time, tries to distinguish himself from other manufacturers and pursues this end with all available means. He makes an effort to create his own internal organization of the firm, his own sphere of action, his own particular market. He does not limit himself to repetitive work, nor does he passively accept the conditioning of his surrounding environment. On the contrary, he makes every possible kind of change, not only to defend his own position against other's actions in time, but to make his influence felt on the general market. His action therefore has specifically dynamic characteristics.

Gaining profit is undoubtedly among his motives, both when he decides to start up his activity and while he continues it in time. However the maximization of gains cannot be assumed as 'the' principle of action that completely explains his behaviour. In the first place there is no absolute criterion to define the time referred to, so that the principle in question can, if anything, serve to assess in isolation single operations that he carries out in the course of the firm's life. But, above all, it does not account for the outstanding feature of his action, which consists in continuously planning and carrying out schemes to distinguish himself from his competitors (Schumpeter 1954: 975).

In short, for Marshall, modern man's action is characterized by deliberateness, i.e. independence, free choice and careful deliberation of the line of conduct that seems to him the best suited to attaining his ends, and not by selfishness (Marshall 1969: 4–5).[13] If one takes account of the function that Schumpeter attributes to the entrepreneur in his own theory of the capitalist process, it becomes evident why he emphasizes and appreciates these observations of Marshall's on the modern forms of industrial life.

FROM MASTER TO DISCIPLE: CONTINUITY AND BETRAYAL

As has been seen, for Marshall, competition between businessmen inevitably causes the market to split up into many 'special markets'.

Each businessman performs 'special work' in the sense and for the reasons given, but he cannot be described as an absolute monopolist.[14] If anything he is a 'conditional monopolist' because at any moment others can equip themselves in like manner, and because consumers of his commodity can at any moment behave in such a way as to nullify any advantage he derives from producing (Marshall 1970: 196, 397–8).

On the other hand, it cannot be maintained either that this 'open trade' situation (Marshall 1970: 196) is comparable to perfect competition, if this is defined according to two features: excluded price strategy and no more than one price for each homogeneous commodity at any moment.[15]

So, from Marshall's point of view, when looking at business behaviour,[16] absolute monopoly and (even more so) perfect competition seem limit cases with regard to the normality of 'special markets'. It is also a question of cases, Schumpeter adds, where individual action assumes simpler and more unitary features, so that it is easier for the observer to focus on the underlying motives. In fact, by definition, the businessman's need to distinguish himself from other producers is already completely satisfied in monopoly, whereas it cannot be satisfied in perfect competition. By definition too, the monopolist must no longer try to turn market conditions to his own, instead of his competitors', advantage, while the producer in perfect competition must exclude the purpose of influencing the market. In these cases, in short, 'the content of actual business behaviour has been refined away' to such an extent that they 'lend themselves to treatment by means of relatively simple and (in general) uniquely determined rational schemata' (Schumpeter 1954: 975).

If now we go back to Joan Robinson, it can be established with Schumpeter that, by adapting pre-existing analytical tools to the 'fundamental' and 'genuine' pattern of monopoly, she has not simply identified a valid analytical procedure for studying the other 'genuine' pattern and the 'hybrids' of these two cases. What counts most is that the path she took is contrary to that taken by Marshall,[17] and that the results are very different.

She has attained a general axiomatic analysis of the degrees of competition, but it is static and subordinate to accepting a principle of univocal rationality. Marshall instead, starting from the situation of special markets, treats absolute monopoly and perfect competition as 'degenerate' cases and, above all, emphasizes that the businessman's motives are manifold and his action has a typically dynamic character. Schumpeter (1954: 974–5) concludes on this point: '[Marshall] was however singularly unfortunate in this part of his teaching. Neither theorists nor institutionalist enemies of theory saw the hints that they could have developed'.

And he elsewhere repeats:

> *Unlike the technicians of today* who, so far as the *technique of theory* is concerned, are as superior to him as he was to A. Smith, he understood the working of the capitalist process. In particular he understood business, business problems and businessmen better than did most other scientific economists, not excluding those who were businessmen themselves. He sensed the intimate organic necessities of economic life even more intensively than he formulated them, and he spoke therefore as one who has power and *not like the scribes – or like the theorists who are nothing but theorists.*
>
> (Schumpeter 1954: 836, italics added)[18]

Schumpeter keeps on at this idea, indeed drawing the 'moral of this story', although discreetly placed in a note:

> dissecting a phenomenon into logical components and working on the pure logic of each may cause us to lose the phenomenon in the attempt

> to understand it: the essence of a chemical compound may be in the compound and not in any or all of its elements.
>
> (Schumpeter 1954: 975 n9)

One can apply this comment only to Joan Robinson or to any others who were moving in the same direction as her within the theory of the firm. This then sounds like a criticism of the decision to interpret univocally, and certainly reductively, the signposts provided by Marshall. But one can interpret it more loosely and say that perhaps no generation of economists can or will resist the temptation to perform an academic exercise, can or will resist the lure of scrupulously refining some detail of an existing theory, without worrying about having first grasped its overall significance, or understanding if and what contribution it makes to knowledge and if and how much is sufficient to interpret certain phenomena. Seen in this light, *The Economics of Imperfect Competition* turns out to be emblematic of a recurring tendency.[19]

AN EXAMPLE OF INTELLECTUAL INTEGRITY

Joan Robinson herself was soon convinced that she had achieved little more than a scholastic exercise. She criticized herself with an integrity and frankness that raised her head and shoulders above the majority of her colleagues. She also recognized the static nature of her theory and many other limitations (Robinson 1960a: 222).

She continued however to defend her 'fundamental assumption' and justified this by answering her critics in 'the immortal words of Old Bill: "if you know a better 'ole, go to it"'. Naturally her defence is correct only from her point of view, i.e. seeking to formulate an axiomatic theory of the firm.

But Joan Robinson also came to admit that 'the profit motive may be mixed with many other impulses' and that 'the struggle of a firm to survive and grow cannot be expressed in terms of maximizing any precise quantity at a particular moment of time' (Robinson 1960a: 225–6, 238). The compromise she makes is reasonable, and it is acceptable but only on condition that she is also willing to concede that the classification and ranking of degrees of competition proposed in her book are meaningless outside statics. In fact, those clear and distinct forms merge into one another as soon as one accepts that the outstanding feature of entrepreneurial action is the continual search for diversity, using more and more refined means.

Joan Robinson seems to have realized this limitation to her work also and it is significant that she hints at this in a review of Schumpeter, where she admits that 'the competitive system of the text-book type is simply impracticable in a dynamic world' and states that Schumpeter's argument on entrepreneurial competition in the capitalist process 'blows like a gale through the dreary pedantry of static analysis' (Robinson 1951b: 153; 1960b: 241–2).

FROM PARTIAL EQUILIBRIA TO THE ECONOMIC SYSTEM AS A WHOLE

In his concluding remarks to the review and interspersed with comments on the limitation of the theory of the firm, Schumpeter makes two suggestions for future research that seem to have no direct bearing on the theory of the firm. They are as follows:

> 1) The element of money cannot any longer remain in the background to which long and good tradition has relegated it. We must face the fact that most of our quantities are either monetary expressions or corrected monetary expressions, a fact which puts the index problem to the fore.
> 2) In some lines of advance the time has probably come to get rid of the apparatus of supply and demand, so useful for one range of problems but an intolerable bearing-rein for another. This should, incidentally, prevent us from forcing it on the theory of money, where it can in any case do but little good.
>
> (Schumpeter 1934: 256–7)

It was certainly reading *The Theory of Money and the Analysis of Output* at the same time as the book reviewed that inspired him to make these pronouncements. Apart from anything else, shortly before, he had mentioned this work as the 'complement' to the analysis of partial equilibria proposed in the book itself (Schumpeter 1934: 253, 255).

Schumpeter's two proposals cited above seem to be a signal marking his disassociation from the content of Joan Robinson's article.[20]

This article has three basic sections. It opens with the statement that the traditional theory of money is an attempt to determine the price level in a similar way to the price of one commodity, adapting the supply and demand mechanism to money. Then comes the opinion that economists worry about the price level in particular because its variations can influence income, volume of employment and wealth in the economic system.[21] Finally Joan Robinson launches her proposal: 'if we are interested in the volume of output, why should we not try what progress can be made by thinking in terms of the demand for output as a whole, and its cost of production, just as we have been taught to think of the demand and cost of a single commodity?'

The connection between the two lines of research would take place at the toolbox level in the sense that demand and cost schedules could be directly referred to the volume of output, bypassing the 'devious route' through the quantity theory of money. This would yield the advantage, it seems legitimate to add, of evading the obstacle of measuring purchasing power (Robinson 1951a: 55, 58).

Schumpeter, who for a long time had maintained that there was a need for 'monetary analysis', i.e. a theory of the social output and of the movements of a 'money economy',[22] cannot accept this proposal. It ignores, or takes for granted, questions that he considers of prime importance. In what unit are variables such as social product, effective demand, consumption, saving and investment expressed? Is it reasonable to deal with the circumstances that alter these variables, with reference to the economic system as a whole, using similar procedures to those used to study alterations in the corresponding variables for one commodity or the individual?

The two propositions that appear in the review summarize his doubts on the matter.

Schumpeter and Joan Robinson seem to be in agreement in establishing that price level is a different concept from the price of one commodity, because of a question not 'of degree' but 'of substance'. In fact, it is possible to distinguish, among those circumstances that cause the price of one commodity to vary, those that affect it directly from the indirect ones that first cause variations in the price of other goods, and from those that influence all prices, although at different rates and in different ways. The price level, whether general or sectional, according to the theoretical objective taken, changes as a result of a combination of all these movements undergone by each of its components, so that distinguishing the causes of its variations becomes problematic.[23]

It follows that the supply and demand schedules system used to study the price variations of a commodity becomes inadequate to deal with the price level.[24] On the other hand, one cannot really be satisfied with the approximation given by index numbers constructed as averages of independent elements, because the price level components lack precisely 'the requirement of independence and causality of the deviations from the norm', which instead is assumed for the components of index numbers.[25]

It must have been the very difficulty of the concept of price level that prompted the concluding proposal in Joan Robinson's article (1951a: 58; see also 1932: 9): let us assume, on the one hand, that the theory of money continues to deal with that problem and we shall relieve it 'of its too-heavy task' of acting also as a theory of income; on the other hand it will be possible to frame a theory of income without the encumbrance of the problem of the value of money,[26] and without having to worry about the unit of measurement in which to express the variables to be considered.[27]

This is precisely what Schumpeter disputes in his review.

For Schumpeter, a theory of income is above all a 'money' theory of income. This means, in the first place, that the variables considered are expressed in money and that the presence of money exerts influence over the state and the movements of an economic system. But, once money comes into the analysis, the problem of price level crops up once more, the problem that Joan Robinson thought she could exclude from the theory of income.

According to Schumpeter, even if we are obliged to acknowledge that the concept of price level is indeterminate, we still cannot neglect or defer the problem of identifying a unit of measurement in which to express the economic variables within a theory. This is the significance of the first proposition quoted at the beginning.

In short, with regard to the problem of measuring economic variables, Joan Robinson proves to be 'a workmanlike mind impatient of any loss of time and energy in the midst of questions of burning interest', exactly as she was when dealing with the theory of the firm and she imposed without any discussion her 'fundamental assumption' on the entrepreneur's maximizing rationality. Here, as on that occasion, Schumpeter's warning (1934: 255) is appropriate: 'if in spite of the presence of more urgent tasks we do want to look at our tools before using them, we must do so more thoroughly than is done here, or we shall make existing misunderstanding still worse.'

A BRIEF CONCLUSION

In one of his rare spoken comments on his own theoretical work, Schumpeter declared that he had set himself the task of opening closed doors. Joan Robinson has flung several doors wide open. She never did it gently. This has always served to revive interest in problems that professional economists had set aside. At times she did it impulsively and impatiently: this has not always been a bad thing for the future of political economy.

NOTES

1 This research has been financed by the Italian National Research Council (CNR).

2 The first work remained in manuscript form. For the others see Robinson (1932, 1969 and 1951a).

3 Harcourt (1990: 422–4) noted in Schumpeter's letters to Joan Robinson 'old-world charm, courtesy, and subtle (perhaps!) flattery'. But the consummate professor allows himself a touch of gentle irony when he refrained from the 'impertinence to ask [her] to go to the trouble of lecturing [him] on the teaching of economics' and asks her for a copy of her work, presumably equally amazed and amused at the fact that such a serious academic subject should trouble a young researcher.

4 Schumpeter (1934: 251, 253) quotes respectively Robinson (1932) and (1951a). With regard to 'Teaching Economics', Schumpeter indirectly takes it into account in his review because, as will be seen, he attributes great importance to the didactic style of the book.

5 On these questions see Aufricht (1958) and Jensen (1987: 137–42). With regard to Joan Robinson it must be said that she herself (Robinson 1962: 13–15, 21–5) was to underline the connection between the tools proposed by a researcher and his cultural background. As neatly observed by Becattini (1966: 11): 'Tools here can always be traced back to their sources of inspiration, to the social philosophy upon which the respective toolmakers drew in framing their problems.' Again

Becattini (ibid.: 26) makes a comment that ought to be conclusive evidence that the theory of the neutrality of analysis is sterile: 'Economic categories soon wither, it only needs the ideal vision according to which they were fashioned to fade in man's heart and they are transformed from tools to chains on the intellect.'

6 The story Joan Robinson tells of how her research began is significant in this context (1969: vi): 'I remember the moment when it was an exciting discovery (made by R. F. Kahn) that where two average curves are tangential, the corresponding marginal curves cut at the same abscissa. The apparatus which we worked out took on a kind of fascination for its own sake (though by modern standards it is childishly simple) and I set about to apply it in the analysis of price discrimination'. On the differences between Joan Robinson and R. Kahn in stating the problem of market imperfections, see Marcuzzo (1994). On the procedure adopted by Joan Robinson and on the results produced, see Moss (1984: 307, 311–14).

7 Robinson (1969: 4 et seqq., 15 et seqq., 211 et seqq.; 1932: 10). In (1969: 6) she displays very clearly that 'the assumption [of maximizing rationality] underlies the device of drawing marginal curves'.

8 See the quotation in the previous note. Robinson (1969: 16) states: 'When the technique of economic analysis is sufficiently advanced to analyse the results of neuroses and confused thinking, it will study them only insofar as they produce statistically measurable effects', thereby reproposing the thesis that economic research is mainly a search for analytical tools to apply to variables that can be measured statistically. See Robinson (1932: 11) and note 27 below.

9 Schumpeter (1934: 254) observes that in this lie Joan Robinson's real personal contributions.

10 Schumpeter (1934: 256) criticizes this limit. Shove (1933: 661), too, attributes great importance to the question.

11 On this last point Shove (1933: 659–60).

12 In Schumpeter (1934) the comparison is sketched out in one line, whereas it is considerably developed in Schumpeter (1954) where Marshall is compared not only with Joan Robinson, but also with Chamberlin. Here Schumpeter also deletes a statement contained in Schumpeter (1934: 249) on Marshall's responsibility in encouraging the tendency to handle perfect competition and monopoly with different analytical models without much connection between them.

13 Dardi (1991) notes that Marshall's thought is characterized by the simultaneous presence of a, never totally mechanical, subjectivism and a, not completely precluding, organicism that take account of the forces acting at the level of the individual. When he considers individual action Marshall sets the moral quality of motives alongside their utilitaristic component (ibid.: 90). It follows that individual action can be explained partly on the basis of the maximizing principle and partly on the basis of the evolutionary adaptation of organisms to environment through processes of differentiation and innovation (ibid.: 94). In the case of entrepreneurial activity, there would be a search for the points of maximum profit on any possible line of investment, while the distinguishing element would be limited qualitatively to the types of representative firms in existence and the barriers these set to potential newcomers (ibid.: 102).

14 Meaning a sole seller who can appreciably influence the price by varying the quantity supplied. See Robinson (1969: 5–6) and Schumpeter (1954: 975–82).

15 This is how Schumpeter (1954: 972–4) defines perfect competition. He credits, respectively, Cournot and Jevons with having highlighted the two salient features

mentioned. In his review he reproves Joan Robinson for not having paid 'her respects' to Cournot in addition to having ignored the contributions of Walras and Pareto (ibid.: 253).

16 It must be remembered that Marshall developed an axiomatic theory of price not for the individual firm but for industry, defined as a collection of firms producing for the same common market but at different stages of the normal life-cycle. Industry includes nearly all the conditions of real life, it has more or less constant composition and achieves a more or less constant production level. On this point, Moss (1984: 308–11).

17 Many commentators have dealt with the differences between Marshall's and Joan Robinson's analysis of the firm. Observations similar to those of Schumpeter are to be found both in Hutchison (1953: 309–15) and in Moss (1984: 307–11). Becattini (1962: 88–125, 143–58), starting from the concept of industry, reaches conclusions on the differences between Marshall and Joan Robinson on the concept of entrepreneurial activity that are close to those of Schumpeter.

18 The relationship between Marshall and the Cambridge school is seen in Schumpeter's work under both its components (of continuity and betrayal): see Schumpeter (1954: 833, 836, 840, 987 n17) and Schumpeter (1952: 95, 99–100, 105–6).

19 Shove (1933: 660) maintains that Joan Robinson's book could be described as 'an essay in geometrical political economy'. Loasby (1991: 41) observes: 'Joan Robinson's first book gave a powerful impulse towards the development of formalism which has been so characteristic of the last fifty years, and which she came to regard with such dismay.'

20 Schumpeter cannot even agree on Joan Robinson's interpretation of Keynes's *A Treatise on Money* contained in the same article. She uses some examples to demonstrate that Keynes was formulating not a theory of money but a theory of income. She also suggests that Keynes had no clear perception of the potential of his research in this direction (see Robinson 1951a: 55–8; 1979: 169 et seqq.). Schumpeter had a profound respect for Keynes' writings from the 1920s, which culminated in *A Treatise on Money* (direct and indirect evidence of this is too numerous to list here), but he interpreted his book primarily as a theory of money (functions of money, types of money, problems of purchasing power and its appropriate measurement according to the purpose of the research) and as a 'monetary analysis' of the capitalist process (credit cycle, effects of monetary policy, problems of the international standard).

21 Both propositions are in Robinson (1951a: 52). In the course of the article Joan Robinson once more proposes the quantity theory of money using the Cambridge equation and with great dexterity demonstrates the logical muddle that its supporters got themselves into. Then she mentions *A Treatise on Money* and gives the interpretation mentioned briefly in the previous note.

22 Schumpeter (1954: 276–82). The questions of money as unit of account, of the meaning of the purchasing power of money, of the effects of money and credit policy on the amount and distribution of income are considered particularly in Schumpeter (1917) and (1970).

23 These statements summarize observations in Schumpeter (1917: 652–4, 678–81) and Schumpeter (1970: 252–62). The question is dealt with exhaustively in Keynes (1971): in book two from the conceptual point of view, and in the course of the entire volume II from the empirical point of view. For an acknowledgement of the importance of Keynes' analysis of this matter see Schumpeter (1954: 1095).

24 This conclusion seems implicit in the first part of Robinson (1951a). It is explicit,

however, in Schumpeter's second proposition cited at the beginning of the section. Schumpeter (1936: 793) repeats with reference to the Cambridge theoreticians of the 1930s: 'There is . . . little justification for this [application] of the "Marshallian Cross" . . . to the case of money, which has remained a besetting sin of the Cambridge group to this day.'

25 Schumpeter (1970: 260). See also Keynes (1971, vol. V: 68–84).

26 Robinson (1932: 9) declares that it is absolutely useless to bring a technique of analysis into disrepute, by pretending to talk about the price level, in that it is 'an entity which has no real existence'. She probably meant by this statement that the price level is not an entity liable to measurement in the same way as physical dimensions.

27 In (1932: 11) Joan Robinson appreciates the need some economists have to find units of measurement for economic variables that are similar to those used for the physical world. If this is not possible, some unit, however imprecise, must be used. See on this point Harcourt (1990: 418–19), who also refers to the preface of *The Accumulation of Capital*, where this opinion is confirmed. See also note 8 above. Vice versa Joan Robinson displays unwillingness to accept the problem of measurement in a different sense: when it is a question of finding, within a theory, a unit of measurement that permits all the variables considered in the theory itself to be homogeneous. In (1962: 31–2), after mentioning the problem of measurement dealt with by Ricardo, she concludes 'we know that when you cannot get an answer, there is something wrong with the question . . .', but she does not go on to say how the question ought to be reformulated. The problem of measurement in the sense just mentioned is however crucial for Keynes, starting from his paper on index numbers in 1909 up to *The General Theory*, as demonstrated by Carabelli (1992).

REFERENCES

Aufricht, H. (1958) The Methodology of Schumpeter's 'History of Economic Analysis', *Zeitschrift für Nationalökonomie*, 18(4): 384–441.

Becattini, G. (1962) *Il concetto di industria e la teoria del valore*. Turin: Boringhieri.

——— (1966) *Introduzione a J. Robinson 'Ideologie e scienza economica'*. Florence: Sansoni.

Carabelli, A. (1992) Organic Interdependence and the Choice of Units in the 'General Theory'. In B. Gerrard and J. Hillard, eds, *The Philosophy and Economics of J. M. Keynes*. Aldershot: Elgar.

Dardi, M. (1991) The Concept and Role of the Individual in Marshallian Economics, *Quaderni di storia dell'economia politica*, 9(2,3): 89–114.

Harcourt, G. C. (1990) Joan Robinson's Early Views on Method, *History of Political Economy*, 22(3): 411–27.

Hutchison, T. W. (1953) *A Review of Economic Doctrines 1870–1929*. Oxford: Oxford University Press.

Jensen, H. E. (1987) New Lights on Joseph Alois Schumpeter's Theory of the History of Economics? In W. J. Samuels, ed., *Research in the History of Economic Theory and Methodology*, vol. 5. London: JAI Press.

Keynes, J. M. (1971) *A Treatise on Money*. In D. Moggridge, ed., *The Collected Writings of John Maynard Keynes*, vols V and VI. London: Macmillan.

Loasby, B. J. (1991) Joan Robinson's 'Wrong Turning'. In I. Rima, ed., *The Joan Robinson Legacy*. Armonk, NY: M. E. Sharpe.

Marcuzzo, M. C. (1994) At the Origin of the Theory of Imperfect Competition:

Different Views? In K. I. Vaughn, ed., *Perspectives in the History of Economic Thought*. Aldershot: Elgar.

Marshall, A. (1969) *Principles of Economics*, 8th edn. London: Macmillan.

——— (1970) *Industry and Trade. A Study of Industrial Technique and Business Organization; and of their Influence on the Conditions of Various Classes and Nations*, 4th edn. New York: Kelley.

Moss, S. (1984) The History of the Theory of the Firm from Marshall to Robinson and Chamberlin: The Source of Positivism in Economics, *Economica*, 51: 307–18.

Robinson, J. (1932) *Economics Is a Serious Subject. The Apologia of an Economist to the Mathematician, the Scientist and the Plain Man*. Cambridge: Heffer & Sons.

——— (1951a) *The Theory of Money and the Analysis of Output*. In *Collected Economic Papers*, vol. I. Oxford: Blackwell.

——— (1951b) *Capitalism, Socialism and Democracy* by J. A. Schumpeter. In *Collected Economic Papers*, vol. I. Oxford: Blackwell.

——— (1960a) *Imperfect Competition* Revisited. In *Collected Economic Papers*, vol. II. Oxford: Blackwell.

——— (1960b) *Imperfect Competition* Today. In *Collected Economic Papers*, vol. II. Oxford: Blackwell.

——— (1962) *Economic Philosophy*. London: C. A. Watts & Co.

——— (1969) *The Economics of Imperfect Competition*, 2nd edn. London: Macmillan.

——— (1979) What Has Become of the Keynesian Revolution? In *Collected Economic Papers*, vol. V. Oxford: Blackwell.

Schumpeter, J. A. (1917) Das Sozialprodukt und die Rechenpfennige, Glossen und Beiträge zur Geldtheorie von heute. *Archiv für Sozialwissenschaft und Sozialpolitik*, 44: 627–715.

——— (1934) Robinson's *Economics of Imperfect Competition*, *Journal of Political Economy*, 42: 249–57.

——— (1936) J. M. Keynes, *The General Theory of Employment, Interest and Money*, *American Statistical Association*, 31: 791–5.

——— (1952) *Ten Great Economists. From Marx to Keynes*. London: Allen & Unwin.

——— (1954) *History of Economic Analysis*. New York: Oxford University Press.

——— (1970) *Das Wesen des Geldes*. Göttingen: Vandenhoek & Ruprecht.

Shove, G. F. (1933) Review of *The Economics of Imperfect Competition* by J. Robinson, *Economic Journal*, 43: 657–61.

Part II

IN THE TRADITION OF KEYNES

4

OF PRODIGAL SONS AND BASTARD PROGENY[1]

J. A. Kregel

There is a thread running from the satirical 'Lecture Delivered at Oxford by a Cambridge Economist'[2] to the pamphlet *History versus Equilibrium* (Robinson 1974), written around twenty-five years later, which clearly identifies what Joan Robinson considered to be the essential point of Keynes' (and her own) approach to economics. The lecture is built around the necessity of making a careful distinction between a static equilibrium position and the process of change required to reach that equilibrium: 'In time, there is an exceptionally strict rule of one-way traffic.... the distance between today and tomorrow is twenty-four hours forwards, and the distance between today and yesterday is eternity backwards' (Robinson 1953: 256). As a result you can '[n]ever talk about a system getting into equilibrium, for equilibrium has no meaning unless you are in it already' (ibid.: 262).[3]

The main point of the Oxford lecture was to lay the groundwork for the defence against the counter-argument to Keynes' theory that, although it might have some practical application in the 'short period', in the 'long run' the forces of competition would be fully operative and lead to the full utilization of resources. This is a possible interpretation of Keynes' theory that she had already identified while working through the proofs of the *General Theory* (see Robinson 1937) and that was to become her major post-war preoccupation (see 'The Generalisation of the General Theory' reprinted in Robinson 1952), leading to her magnum opus *The Accumulation of Capital* (Robinson 1956) and which set off the notorious 'Cambridge Controversies' in Capital Theory.

Her point of departure for the linkage of the short and long run was the relation between Keynes' short-period theory of investment and a post-Keynesian theory of capital accumulation. The absence of an explicit theory of capital had been the basis of Hayek's criticism of Keynes' *Treatise on Money*, and Sraffa[4] was called in to provide deadly sniper fire to divert attention from the question. The impetus behind her reconsideration of this relation was Sraffa's 'Introduction' to his Royal Economic Society edition of Ricardo, and she refers the reader to it at the end of the lecture.

The Oxford lecture may thus serve as a concise summary of the issues that Joan Robinson continued to confront for the remainder of her career. In the end, she opted for 'history' over equilibrium, for 'process' over stationary states. This would eventually separate her from those who worked from Sraffa's interpretation of Ricardo and Marx to provide a non-neoclassical theory of capital. Not only was it necessary to have been in equilibrium since 'The Fall of Man' to make sense of the quantity of capital, once you started to reason in this way, you could never get out of equilibrium; better not to start there in the first place. There was no going back to the Garden of Eden, so better to enjoy the original sin of the real world, rather than deny the fruits of the tree in the hopes of creating purity outside its confines.

I do not want to use this leitmotiv of equilibrium and process (or history), or long and short period, to provide a critical survey of Joan Robinson's life work. This is done elsewhere in this book. Rather, I would like to use it as an interpretative key to her criticism of the development of modern economics of both a post-Keynesian and post-neoclassical nature – to what in the title I have called the 'prodigal sons' and the 'bastard progeny'.

THE FIRST GENERATION OF BASTARD PROGENY

The first printed reference that I have been able to find to illegitimate offspring from the ideas of the Keynesian revolution is in an *Economic Journal* review (1962; partially reprinted in Robinson 1965: 100–2) of a book by Harry Johnson containing his *American Economic Review* essay celebrating the twenty-fifth anniversary of the *General Theory*. While Joan Robinson could be extremely disobliging, Harry Johnson had spent enough time in Cambridge to have learned the art to perfection, and this piece was one of the first in a distinguished line of papers he was to produce in that vein. As in the Oxford lecture, the point of discrimination is the handling of the concept of capital. The bastard Keynesian position (which in the review is also identified with Hicks and Meade) argues that at any point in time a given quantity of capital is capable of providing full employment if only real wages are permitted to fall to their equilibrium level, i.e. where the supply and demand for labour are equal.

Her criticism of this position is on two levels. The first is the (traditional) failure to distinguish between real and money wages, and the second is the (more recent) failure to identify the relationship between relative prices and the general price level because the latter 'was treated in a separate volume and another course of lectures, under the heading of Money. This was the setting into which Keynes irrupted with the contention that the price level was mainly connected with the level of money-wage rates, while the monetary system was mainly connected with the rate of interest' (Robinson 1965: 100). But, more important than this was that Keynes 'had . . . a sense of time. The short period is here and now, with concrete stocks of means of production in existence'. This she credits to Marshall's influence, a counter to Johnson's criticism of the excessive influence of Marshall on Keynes.

Thus, even if there were a level of real wages at which a capital stock appropriate to the existing quantity and quality of labour might have been constructed so as to produce full employment, you could not reach that equilibrium state by means of a reduction in money wages. She identified the contrary affirmation as 'bastard' Keynesian, because it relied on 'arguments which are purely Keynesian (though formalistic and silly), showing how the effect upon prices of changes in money-wage rates reacts upon liquidity preference and the propensity to consume' (ibid.: 100).

This is just what every student learns (or at least used to, before the New Classical Macroeconomics textbooks appeared) in the textbook version of IS–LM extended to aggregate supply and demand. Unemployment (output) above (below) some critical level causes money wages to fall and, with fixed mark-ups, prices follow. The increase in the real money supply (or decline in the demand for nominal money balances) is then clothed in Keynesian terminology as a reduction in liquidity preference. The resulting fall in the rate of interest causes an increase in investment and, via the multiplier, higher income. In addition, the lower prices increase households' real wealth, leading to an increase in consumption spending, which may be interpreted as a rise in the consumption function. In this version, fixity of the nominal money supply replaces the malleability of capital to allow flexible wages and prices to restore full employment. This automatic adjustment process was absent in Keynes' theory because he assumed

> that money-wage rates are rigid – more accurately, that the supply of liquidity is very much more flexible upwards than money-wage rates are downwards. Of course he did. The contemporary world, inhabited by bankers and financiers (who do not depend on a fixed physical quantity of gold or cowrie shells to carry out monetary transactions) and managers and trade unionists (or for that matter mistresses and charwomen) is not reflected in the model in which money-wage rates can fall indefinitely, or in which the quantity of money remains constant when they are rising.
>
> (Robinson 1965: 101)

But the fatal flaw in the argument is that, even if it were possible to show that '[a]ny arbitrarily fixed quantity of money... is compatible with full employment, in conditions of short-period equilibrium at some level of money-wage rates, the level being lower the smaller the postulated quantity of money, and the larger the labour force to be employed', this in no way provides logical argument 'to justify the contention that falling wages and prices are good for trade' (ibid.: 101).

There is an equivalence between the automatic adjustment produced by flexible wages and prices in conditions of a fixed quantity of capital and of a fixed quantity of money. While capital must be sufficiently 'malleable' to allow changes in the amount of capital per man to absorb available labour in the former case, in the latter changes in the level of wages must produce a change in the interest rate causing an increase in investment spending and, via the multiplier and the propensity to consume, an increase in consumption spending sufficient to provide full employment. Joan Robinson considered both versions 'bastard' progeny. But this is not so much because of the assumed 'malleability' of the fixed stocks of capital and money as of the failure to distinguish between equilibrium and history, between the impact of a change in the interest rate or in the wage rate on the process of development of the system and of equilibria defined by different values of the rate of interest and wage rates, which have prevailed since the Garden of Eden.

THE SECOND GENERATION – NEOCLASSICAL SYNTHETICS

It is enlightening that the first generation of bastard Keynesian progeny closely resembles the modern textbook aggregate supply and demand fare. Although this was served up as the topping on the fixed wage, price and money supply IS–LM model in response to the monetarist criticisms that there is no discussion of inflation in the model and the supply-side criticism that there is no explanation of supply responses, in 1962 Joan Robinson was still citing Hicks' *Theory of Wages* as the source of 'bastard' Keynesianism. However, as time went by she became increasingly preoccupied with the Hicks(–Hansen–Samuelson) IS–LM model known as the 'neoclassical synthesis' because it openly admitted joining neoclassical micro theory with Keynesian macro theory.

Although Joan Robinson's criticisms of this approach are similar to those levied against Harry Johnson, there is an interesting change in emphasis. Although the fixed quantity of money that provides the explanation of the determination of the slope of the LM curve is noted, she concentrates her criticism on the relation between the theory of investment and the theory of capital as represented in the determination of the slope of the IS curve. As generations of students have learned, the IS curve slopes down because of the inverse relation between the rate of interest and the amount of investment given by the marginal efficiency of capital schedule.

Joan Robinson notes that Keynes' theory had liberated the general level of prices from the (quantity) theory of money, and the rate of interest from the theory of relative prices; the former was determined by money wages and other costs, while the latter was determined by the monetary system. There was thus no necessary, or direct, relation between the rate of interest and investment. Indeed, this is why Keynes introduced the 'efficiency' of capital.

The most that could be said about the relation between the rate of interest and investment was that

> Relatively to given expectations of profit, a fall in interest rates will stimulate investment somewhat, and by putting up the Stock Exchange value of placements, it may encourage expenditure for consumption. These influences will increase effective demand and so increase employment. The main determinant of the rate of interest is the state of expectations. When bond-holders have a clear view of what is the normal yield which they expect to be restored soon after any temporary change, the banking system cannot move interest rates from what they are expected to be. It is the existence of uncertainty or 'two views' that makes it possible for the banks to manipulate the money market. But even when the rate of interest can be moved in the required direction, it may not have much effect. The dominant influence on the swings of effective demand is swings in the expectation of profits.
>
> (Robinson 1971: 79–80)

Thus, a fall in the rate of interest, given the marginal efficiency of capital, would increase investment and consumption and create

> a boom which will not last because after some time the growth in the stock of productive capacity competing in the market will overcome the increase in total expenditure and so bring a fall in the current profits per unit of capacity, with a consequent worsening of the expected rate of profit on further investment.
>
> (ibid.: 83)

Put simply, this means that there can be no such thing as investment and accumulation in a given state of expectations, and we are directly transported from the static analysis of the impact of the rate of interest on investment into the cyclical world of Harrod and Domar.

On the other hand, using Hicks' IS curve, 'a permanently lower level of the rate of interest would cause a permanently higher rate of investment'. This Keynes 'could never have said' for it confused equilibrium with a process of change: 'Keynes' contention was that a fall in the rate of interest relatively to given expectations of profit would, in favourable circumstances, increase the rate of investment' (ibid.). But, this would cause expectations to change and the marginal efficiency of capital curve to shift, and presumably the IS curve with it. An IS schedule could not be built upon the static relation between interest and investment.

It is also clear why this point should have been considered to be of utmost importance, for it was the basis of the long-period argument of the bastard Keynesians that the quantity of capital could adjust to provide full employment if wages were lowered sufficiently. Here, a reduction in the rate of interest, given the wage rate, produces an increase in the rate of investment and a larger quantity of capital and employment. It was the analogue to the argument that unemployment is caused by real wages being too high, given the real rate of interest: if the real rate of interest is too high, relative to the wage rate, to provide full employment, this could be remedied by a reduction in interest rates.

For sceptics who think this is a retrospective defence of Keynes' theory of investment, consider this passage from the closing portion of the Oxford lecture:

> Now let us try the long period. The short period means that capital equipment is fixed . . . In the long period capital equipment changes in quantity and in design. So you come slap up to the question: What is the quantity of capital? . . . Let us apply the notion of equilibrium to capital. What governs the demand for capital goods [i.e. investment]? Their future prospective quasi-rents. What governs the supply price? Their past cost of production. For hard objects like blast furnaces . . . demand is of its very nature ex ante, and cost is of its very nature ex post. . . . There is only one case where the quantity of capital can be measured . . .; that is when the economy as a whole is in equilibrium at our old friend E[quilibrium]. . . . Capital goods are selling today at a price which is both their demand price based on ex ante quasi rents, and their supply price, based on ex post costs.
>
> (Robinson 1953: 16–17)

It follows directly that any change in the rate of interest that causes a change in the level of investment will change *ex ante* expected profits and thus expectations, making it impossible to quantify the resulting change in the capital stock. Not only is it impossible to say that a fall in the rate of interest leads to a permanent increase in the level of income, it is impossible to say that a fall in the rate of interest leads to a permanent increase in the 'quantity' of capital per man employed in equilibrium.

In her more technical article on the issue the same point is made: 'The heavy weight which this method of valuing capital puts upon the assumptions of equilibrium emphasizes the impossibility of valuing capital in an uncertain world' (Robinson 1960: 126). 'In short, the comparison between equilibrium positions with different factor ratios cannot be used to analyse changes in the factor ratio taking place through time, and it is impossible to discuss changes (as opposed to differences) in neoclassical terms' (ibid.: 129).

THE THIRD GENERATION – THE NEO-NEOCLASSICALS

The 'neoclassical synthesis' generation of bastard Keynesians were soon reincarnated as 'neo-neoclassicals', defending simple 'parables' in which the monotonic relation between the rate of interest and the aggregate quantity of capital assures the automatic establishment of full employment. The growth models of Swan, Solow and a host of others built on the aggregate production function were criticized on two grounds: the impossibility of identifying an aggregate quantity of capital independent of the rate of interest, and the inability to distinguish between comparison of equilibria and change. The latter was not only a methodological criticism, it was at the basis of the logical criticism of the relation between the rate of interest and the rate of investment that gave these models their bastard Keynesian nature. The debate over the measurement of the quantity of capital thus joined the theory of growth and capital accumulation in the debate over the possibility of the long-period restoration of the orthodox theory.

THE FOURTH GENERATION – THE NEW ORTHODOXY

It was from this debate that the 'new orthodoxy' emerged, based on a sharp division between micro and macro theory. This was primarily due to the fact that the study of capital in long-period equilibrium conditions seemed to require 'assumptions to make it seem plausible that a private-enterprise economy would continuously accumulate, under long-period equilibrium conditions, with continuous full employment of a constant labour force, without any cyclical disturbances, in face of a continuously falling rate of profit' (Robinson 1960: 132–3). Given the obvious absurdity of the assumptions required, it was easier simply to assume that an enlightened Keynesian government undertook the budgetary policy necessary to achieve this result. In the 'new orthodoxy', Say's Law was replaced by 'work[ing] out what saving would be at full employment in the present short-period situation, with the present distribution of wealth and the present hierarchy of rates of earnings of different occupations, and arrang[ing] to have enough investment to absorb the level of saving that this distribution of income brings about. Then hey presto! we are back in the world of equilibrium where saving governs investment and micro theory can slip into the old grooves again' (Robinson 1973: 96–7). Of course, the 'old grooves' mean the traditional explanation of the operation of flexible wages and prices to assure full utilization of resources. Joan Robinson considers Keynes himself not completely innocent in this respect, for the drafting of the final chapter of the *General Theory* left open such an interpretation of his theory.[5]

But the assumption that the government carries out Keynesian policy in order to assure full employment cannot be a justification for the application of orthodox theory.

> Apart from logical incoherence, the flaw in the new orthodoxy destroys the validity of its message. The deepest layer in neo-classical thought was the conception of society as a harmonious whole, without internal

> conflicts of interest. Society, under the guidance of the hidden hand, allocates its resources . . . between present consumption and accumulation to permit greater consumption in the future. Accumulation is presented by Robinson Crusoe transferring some of his activity from gathering nuts to eat to making a fishing rod . . . saving means a sacrifice of present consumption or leisure to increase productivity for the future; saving and investment are two aspects of the same behaviour. Keynes destroyed this part of the analogy by showing that, in a private enterprise economy, investments are made by profit-seeking firms and it is they who decide for society how much it will save.
>
> (Robinson 1971: xiv)

The 'new orthodoxy' thus eliminated the possibility of unemployment as a natural state of affairs in a free enterprise economy and caused its practitioners to miss the main contribution of Keynesian theory. Once Keynes' contribution has been understood, economics can move on from the question of why there is unemployment to the question 'what form should employment take?' and to confront what Joan Robinson called the 'Second Crisis in Economic Theory', the analysis of the problems 'of the persistence of poverty – even hunger – in the wealthiest nations, the decay of cities, the pollution of environment, the manipulation of demand by salesmanship, the vested interests in war, not to mention the still more shocking problems of the world outside the prosperous industrial economies. The complacency of neo-laisser faire cuts the economists off from discussing the economic problems of today just as Say's Law cut them off from discussing unemployment in the world slump' (ibid.: xiv–xv).

The scandal of the use of Keynes' theory to justify ignoring the most important questions facing the economy became the theme of Joan Robinson's Ely lecture to the American Economic Association in New Orleans in December 1971. There she decried the fact that, '[b]y this one simple device [bringing traditional micro theory back intact by assuming the government automatically provides for full employment], the whole of Keynes' argument is put to sleep' (Robinson 1973: 96). She goes on to repeat her basic contention in the Oxford lecture that 'the main point of the *General Theory* was to break out of the cocoon of equilibrium and consider the nature of life lived in time – the difference between yesterday and tomorrow. Here and now, the past is irrevocable and the future is unknown' (ibid.: 95). The point that is ignored by the bastard Keynesian position now simply disappears from view because of the separation between micro and macro. Since all of these questions deal with problems of money and macro theory, they are swept away by the assumption of full employment, leaving free play to Walrasian general equilibrium theory but, she warns, 'Walras leaves out the very point that Keynes was bringing in – historical time' (ibid.: 96). This opens the way to the discussion of the micro foundations of macroeconomics, which results in the elimination of Keynesian macroeconomics, bastard or not, as well as the discussion of the pressing real-world problems, exposing 'the evident bankruptcy of economic theory which for the second time has nothing to say on the questions that, to everyone except economists, appear to be most in need of an answer' (ibid.: 105).

This speech was warmly applauded, more in respect for advanced age than in admiration for its wisdom, and was widely ignored – in hindsight for good reason, for this mutation of bastard Keynesian was sterile; within a decade there were none who would have dared suggest that a Keynesian government could provide full employment by means of the 'appropriate policy'. Rather government was perceived as the main cause of unemployment. But dropping the assumption and the implicit acceptance of the government as the guarantor of the level of employment turned the question back to the first crisis, which promptly made its appearance at the end of the 1980s in the form of the first global slump since the 1930s. Clearly, the assumption of a Keynesian government was not sufficient to make the traditional analysis legitimate.

THE MODERN GENERATION – THE NEW KEYNESIANS

Before concluding, I cannot resist some reference to the so-called 'New Keynesians'. How would Joan Robinson have responded to this new approach? First, I think she would have applauded their acceptance of the fact that prices are not perfectly flexible, and that things could not be improved if they could be made so. She also would have looked favourably on their attempt to analyse a Marshallian 'world [which] is peopled with types ... who have different roles to play ... each with his own characteristic motives and problems' (Robinson 1973: 101) in the form of the analysis of firms, bankers and workers. Beyond these general statements, it is difficult to pin down the theoretical underpinnings of this approach. There seem to be two main strands. The best known seeks to imagine rational behaviour that might lead utility-maximizing individuals in a general equilibrium framework to keep prices rigid in the face of excess demand. This is a line that started in the fix-price temporary equilibria of Hicks as extended by Clower and then Barro and Grossman and others to fixed-price equilibria.

However, the ad hoc nature of the price rigidities led to attempts to justify them on the basis of general equilibrium theory. There are two basic explanations, one for the role of flexible wages in producing equilibrium in the labour market, and one for the role of the rate of interest in producing a level of investment sufficient to absorb full employment savings. As there are a number of different versions I will give my understanding of the basic ideas.

Start by assuming that employers have imperfect monitoring ability concerning the marginal productivity of new relative to already employed workers. In the absence of better information, assume that workers equate real wages with the marginal disutility of work.[6] In the presence of an excess supply of labour there would then be no incentive for an employer to hire unemployed labour that offers to work for a lower wage because he must assume that its marginal productivity will be lower than that of his existing labour. Further, if he did hire new labour at a lower wage, thereby forcing down the general level of wages, this would lead to an overall fall in average productivity, which would offset the change in wages and leave profitability unchanged. Thus, there is no incentive to do so. A similar argument works for an increase in wages. Thus, it is rational for employers not to reduce wages in the face of excess labour supply even if workers are willing to work at those wages. Workers who are unemployed and (irrationally) are willing to offer greater than average effort for the current wage cannot manage to get themselves hired even by offering to work for real wages below the average productivity of the employed labour force, because employers cannot verify the disutility functions of the individual unemployed (or employed) workers. In Clower's language, there is a mutually beneficial exchange that is blocked because it cannot be arbitraged. This is supposed to offer an improvement over Keynes' observation[7] that workers resisted wage reductions by providing a 'theoretical' explanation.

For 'New Keynesians', 'Keynes' analysis of investment was, however, basically a neoclassical analysis: it was failure of the real interest rate (the long-term bond rate) to fall sufficiently that was the source of the problem' (Greenwald, Stiglitz and Weiss 1984: 194). A more 'Keynesian' approach would instead rely on the existence of credit rationing preventing entrepreneurs from obtaining the finance required for the level of investment that produces full employment saving. Assume that bankers have imperfect information concerning the disutility functions of entrepreneurs, or, more realistically, concerning the production function and the real rate of return of investment projects that entrepreneurs want to borrow to finance. In the absence of better information, assume that the banker believes that there is an inverse relation between investment and the rate of return on projects (alternatively that projects offering higher rates of return have higher risk). In the presence of an excess demand for finance there is no incentive for the bank to raise interest rates because the expected return on the project is thought to be below the current lending rate. An entrepreneur who believes he has a project with a rate of return greater than the bank's lending rate cannot get financing even if he offers to pay a higher rate of interest. Better to leave interest rates unchanged, even in the presence of excess demand for loans.

Thus supply and demand may not operate to produce market-clearing equilibrium: wages do not fall to eliminate an excess supply of labour (the marginal disutility is below the marginal productivity of labour), and interest rates do not rise to eliminate the excess demand for loans (the marginal productivity of capital is above the interest rate). This produces the 'New Keynesian' explanation of equilibrium in conditions of imperfect information in which there is excess supply of labour and excess supply of investment and no market force to match the unemployed labourers with the unfilled jobs in the unfinanced investment projects.

Clearly, this is a very different mutation of bastard Keynesian. What sort of criticism would Joan Robinson have made of this approach? It is very difficult to apply the equilibrium versus change argument, for it is not the difference between changes in prices and wages and different equilibrium configurations that is at issue here, but rather the limitation on information. Obviously perfect information should lead to full utilization of resources. What if employers or bankers seek to improve their information?

A final 'New Keynesian' argument is required to show that, even if agents attempt to obtain perfect information, full utilization is impossible in a competitive market system. Assume that there are a few individuals who decide to become informed, and that this allows them to make better employment or lending decisions, increasing their profits. Drawn by the higher profits, more individuals become informed until all are equally well informed. If the profits of being informed come at the expense of the uninformed, then there is no longer any advantage to seeking better information, and the paradoxical result is that no one seeks information. Because full information is not a stable equilibrium, the system exhibits information imperfection and an increase in information does not lead to a permanent increase in investment or employment.

Joan Robinson would surely have pointed out that the information that is required to make fully informed decisions – the marginal product of labour and the marginal product of capital – cannot be discovered in an economy 'living in time', since it depends on measuring the quantity of capital. We are either in equilibrium, in which case the information required concerning the marginal products can be discovered, or we are not, in which case it cannot.

Finally, Joan Robinson would certainly have pointed out that in the New Keynesian world, if real wages could be lowered, employment would be higher, and if the real rate of interest were higher, more investment would be undertaken.[8] The introduction of imperfect information just conceals the true neoclassical parentage of this class of bastard Keynesian models.

Recently Stiglitz (1992) and Greenwald and Stiglitz (1993) have taken distance from the 'rational' explanation of price rigidities to outline an approach in which 'risk' rather than imperfect knowledge plays a crucial role, and price flexibility may itself be a cause of instability. But Joan Robinson would have argued that in this approach they are only disputing with Keynes' 'bastard progeny'. Ironically, the analysis recalls aspects of Hicks' presentation of portfolio decisions in terms of shifts in portfolio composition leading to changes in investment and producing cycles. It is as if the wheel has come round, in which case this variety of New Keynesian belongs in the category Joan Robinson defined as 'pre-Keynesian theory' after Keynes.

THE PRODIGAL SONS

As noted above, Joan Robinson spent the major portion of her professional career attempting to work out an extension of Keynes' theory to the analysis of the problems of capital accumulation and technical progress. This required the specification of what was being accumulated and the relation between investment, capital accumulation and productivity. Making this problem manageable required simplifying assumptions. She first tried the assumption of zero net savings (cf. Kregel 1983). When this proved unfruitful she moved on to the stationary state in conditions of equilibrium in which '[t]he Keynesian freedom of entrepreneurs to invest as they please has not been sacrificed to the neo-classical conditions, but to the postulate that equilibrium is never ruptured' (Robinson 1960: 134). From this came her well-known insistence on the necessity of making 'dynamic comparisons' of equilibrium growth paths in conditions of tranquillity, rather than statements about the process of change.

However, the longer she worked on these problems, the less satisfying these assumptions became. She fobbed off those who were impatient to get on with the analysis of changes with the comment that we have to work out the simple conditions of steady growth before we can reach the interesting questions of money and dynamics. But in the end she became impatient herself and realized that this was no better than pretending that one was still in the Garden of Eden. Finally, the realization that 'the long-period aspect of investment is the change that it is bringing about in the stock of the means of production often accommodating technical innovations' led her to the conclusion that the simplifications required to make the problem tractable in fact precluded any meaningful analysis. And, just as she had argued in the Oxford lecture that there could be no such thing as accumulation in conditions of a given state of expectations, she concluded that 'there is no such thing in real life as accumulation taking place in a given state of technical knowledge' (Robinson 1975: 39).

Thus, at the end of her life she turned away from 'equilibrium' and embraced 'history'. This led to tension with two groups of economists who, in contrast to the 'bastard Keynesians', might be considered legitimate offspring. They followed two diametrically opposed paths, but by the fact that they struck out on their own, thinking that they had found an easier or better way, we might classify both groups as prodigal sons.

One, with the aid of Sraffa's reconstruction of classical theory, returned to study the explanation of growth and distribution in Smith, Ricardo and Marx. The other went back to recover the monetary elements of Keynes' theory that had been cast to one side in the analysis of long-period growth.

Those who blended the implications of Sraffa's work into the analysis of capital accumulation chose equilibrium in the form of steady states or centres of gravitation, rather than the unpredictable unfolding of actual history. After being initially attracted to this approach – indeed much of her own analysis was from stimulus of Sraffa's work – she found it difficult to discard Keynes' emphasis on the importance of decision-making in the 'here and now' of the short period that the neo-Ricardian approach seemed to require.

At the same time, a second group of predominantly American economists interpreted Joan Robinson's insistence that today is a break between an unchangeable past and an unknowable future as support for the position that the existence of uncertainty makes the analysis of long-period equilibrium an anachronism. Since there is no need for the analysis of money, the visible expression of the fact of uncertainty, in long-period equilibrium, they argued that analysis should be limited to short-period equilibrium states. Although such an approach was more congenial to her later views, it could not deal with the problems of growth and accumulation she still wanted to explain.[9]

Thus, although there is no question that both of these approaches are legitimate extensions of Keynes' work, they were nonetheless considered to have shown insufficient respect for the wisdom of their elders in indicating that analysis should go beyond equilibrium, whether short or long period.

NOTES

1 I am grateful to G. C. Harcourt and L. R. Wray for comments on an initial draft, and to V. Chick for suggestions on a subsequent draft. I am also extremely grateful to M. Tonveronachi, the original discussant of the paper, for anticipating his comments. All declined responsibility for the final version.

2 It was published in a small pamphlet *On Re-Reading Marx* in 1953. It reflects the influence of her reading of Marx, which she undertook as a 'distraction' during the war, as well as study for the Introduction to Rosa Luxemburg's *Accumulation of Capital*. Its direct stimulus, however, was Sraffa's Introduction to his edition of Ricardo (see the introduction to the reprint in Robinson 1973: 247).

3 That this represents a watershed in her work, created by her thinking during the war, can be seen by comparing the following quotation from her *Economics of Imperfect Competition*: 'No reference is made to the passage of time ... no study is made of the process of moving from one position of equilibrium to another, and it is with long-period equilibrium that we shall be mainly concerned' (Robinson 1933: 16).

4 As on a previous occasion to counter Dennis Robertson in the Symposium on 'Increasing Returns and the Competitive Firm' in the *Economic Journal*, 1930.

5 A careful reading of that chapter in its historical context suggests that Keynes is referring not to 'classical theory' per se, but rather to the 'classical system' of free enterprise in contrast to the preference for full-scale economic planning that was favoured at the time by both the far right and far left. Keynes was, after all, a liberal and considered an advantage of his theory the fact that it would leave 'a wide field for the exercise of private initiative and responsibility. Within this field the traditional advantages of individualism will still hold good'. This is far from reinstating classical theory. Cf. Kregel (1986: 37).

6 That is, the 'second classical postulate' applies for the individual employed worker but not for the unemployed. Insider–outsider theories follow directly.

7 For those who have read the *Treatise on Money* it is evident that Keynes placed importance on analysis on differentials, in part created by the diverse response of wages in sheltered and unsheltered industries.

8 Margaret Thatcher to lower wages and Michael Milken to provide high-yield financing could between them get the system to full employment.

9 For those who are not part of the extended family and have difficulty in identifying 'representative' prodigal sons, the first group may be linked to the work of Pasinetti and Garegnani, and the second to Weintraub, Davidson and Minsky.

REFERENCES

Greenwald, B. and Stiglitz, J. E. (1993) New and Old Keynesians, *Journal of Economic Perspectives*, 7: 23–44.

Greenwald, B., Stiglitz, J. E. and Weiss, A. (1984) Informational Imperfections in the Capital Market and Macroeconomic Fluctuations, *American Economic Review*, 74: 194–9.

Kregel, J. A. (1983) The Microfoundations of the 'Generalisation of *The General Theory*' and 'Bastard Keynesianism': Keynes's *Theory of Employment in the Long and the Short Period, Cambridge Journal of Economics*, 7: 343–61.

——— (1986) Laws of the Market and Laws of Motion: An Essay in Comparative Social History. In H.-J. Wagener and J. W. Drukker, eds, *The Economic Law of Motion of Modern Society: A Marx–Keynes–Schumpeter Centennial.* Cambridge: Cambridge University Press.

Robinson, J. (1933) *The Economics of Imperfect Competition.* London: Macmillan.

——— (1937) *Essays in the Theory of Employment.* London: Macmillan.

——— (1951) *Collected Economic Papers*, vol. I. Oxford: Blackwell.

——— (1952) *The Rate of Interest and Other Essays.* London: Macmillan.

——— (1953) *On Re-Reading Marx.* Cambridge: Students' Bookshops.

——— (1956) *The Accumulation of Capital.* London: Macmillan.

——— (1960) [1953] The Production Function and the Theory of Capital. In *Collected Economic Papers*, vol. II. Oxford: Blackwell.

——— (1965) *Collected Economic Papers*, vol. III. Oxford: Blackwell.

——— (1971) *Economic Heresies.* London: Macmillan.

——— (1973) *Collected Economic Papers*, vol. IV. Oxford: Blackwell.

——— (1974) History versus Equilibrium. Thames Papers in Political Economy. London: Thames Polytechnic.

——— (1975) The Unimportance of Reswitching, *Quarterly Journal of Economics*, 89(1): 32–9.

Stiglitz, J. E. (1992) Capital Markets and Economic Fluctuations in Capitalist Economies, *European Economic Review*, 36(2–3): 270–306.

5

THE LONG-PERIOD THEORY OF AGGREGATE DEMAND IN A 1936 ARTICLE BY JOAN ROBINSON[1]

Pierangelo Garegnani

I shall here consider an article that Joan Robinson printed in the *Zeitschrift für Nationalökonomie* in 1936, the same year in which the *General Theory* was published. In that article we find a first attempt at what was to become Joan Robinson's central commitment in the rest of her life: to develop a long-period theory of aggregate activity and labour employment. This first attempt is, however, in a direction radically different from those that were to follow and, in spite of its deficiencies,[2] the article has, in my opinion, elements of considerable interest, to which I shall come in the conclusions to this paper.

THE CENTRAL IDEA

Let us first summarize Robinson's essay. The argument is very simple in its close adherence to marginalist premises. The central idea is the same as we find in Chapter XVI of the *General Theory*, where Keynes writes:

> We have seen that capital has to be kept scarce enough in the long-period to have a marginal efficiency which is at least equal to the rate of interest.... What would this involve for a society which finds itself so well equipped with capital that its marginal efficiency is zero and would be negative with any additional investment ... and in conditions of full employment [is still] disposed to save? ... The stock of capital and level of employment will have to shrink until the community becomes so impoverished that the aggregate of saving has become zero.... Thus for a society such as we have supposed, the position of equilibrium, under conditions of *laissez faire*, will be one in which employment is low enough and the standard of life sufficiently miserable to bring savings to zero.
>
> (Keynes 1936: 217)

The problem that Keynes raises here is a problem altogether internal to orthodox theory, though, as far as I know, it had not been raised before – in the convinction, it seems, of an indefinitely high elasticity of the capital intensity of the economy at low interest rates. Only such an elasticity could have ensured that, even in the absence of population growth (or appropriate technical progress), the economy would have absorbed any amount of investment, without the interest rate ever having to fall to zero or to the minimum below which savers would no longer be willing to lend. The problem was however there: what if the rate of interest were to reach such a minimum, so that it could not fall any further, and net investment fell accordingly to zero, but, at the same time, net saving decisions remained positive at full employment income? Only some rigidity could then prevent money wages from falling to zero. And, with such a rigidity, the answer compatible with the theory could only be that given by Keynes: the scale of activity, i.e. the stock of capital and the employment of labour, would both fall, keeping to each other the proportion dictated by the capital intensity of the economy corresponding to that minimum rate, until the point is reached where people would be poor enough to make the net savings of the community equal to zero.

ROBINSON'S ARGUMENT

If the central idea of Joan Robinson's 1936 article is the same just seen in Keynes, her attempt is to generalize it beyond the case of a zero or minimum rate of interest. For that attempted generalization she relies on a very special notion of long-period equilibrium. She refers, that is, to the equilibrium defined by an interest rate that is assumed to have remained constant for a period of time long enough to let the capital stock adjust fully to it, so that the 'marginal rate of return' on that capital is equal to the given interest rate *and net investment has accordingly fallen to zero* (Robinson 1936: 75). She then points out that there is no reason for which, at that rate of interest, net savings decision should be zero in conditions of the full employment of labour. And, as contemplated in Keynes' above passage, equilibrium would require – with the money wage rigidity implied for the assumed interest rigidity – that the quantities of capital and labour employed should diminish in step with each other[3] until income has fallen sufficiently to annul net saving decisions.

It is only at this point of her argument that Joan Robinson considers the illegitimacy of assuming a rigidity of the rate of interest in the presence of labour unemployment. The effects on the real quantity of money of either a flexibility of money wages and prices or an elastic monetary policy imposed by the unemployment of labour could, she admits, decrease interest. She compares then an initial equilibrium such as that described above with the analogous one reached at a lower rate of interest when, that is, the capital stock will again have adjusted fully to the new lower interest rate and investment will again have become zero.

She can then argue that there is no more reason than there was in the old situation why in the new equilibrium, with a lower interest rate, full employment savings should be zero and allow for full employment of labour. The new level of equilibrium employment will then be higher (lower) than before according to whether a zero propensity to save now corresponds to a higher (lower) amount of labour employment. Since, she notes, the influence of the interest rate on the individual propensity to save out of a given income is uncertain in its sign, the effect of the fall in interest on savings will above all depend on its effect on the relative shares of workers and capitalists with their different propensities to save. That effect will therefore depend, she argues, on the elasticity of substitution betweeen capital and labour. In particular, the propensity to save out of any given social income is likely to decrease only if the elasticity of substitution is less than unity and the share of interest (profits) in income accordingly decreases as the interest rate falls. However, even in that case an increase in labour employment will not follow simply from the increase in the social output at which net decisions to save are zero; it will be necessary for that increase to be more than in proportion to the increase in output per worker owing to the increase in capital intensity consequent upon the lower interest rate. And, above all, there is no reason why the elasticity of substitution should be smaller, rather than larger, than unity.[4]

Thus, Joan Robinson argues, the long-term effect of a decrease in interest may well be a decrease rather than an increase in the employment of labour. And she can conclude that '[i]t is thus impossible to argue that there is any self-righting mechanism in the economic system which makes the existence of unemployment impossible even in the longest of runs' (1936: 83).

A FLAW IN THE ARGUMENT

That conclusion concerning the possibility of long-period unemployment does not, however, seem to be justified on the basis of the theory Joan Robinson is following there. It is in fact unclear why the flexibility of the interest rate that Robinson admits as a consequence of the unemployment of labour should arrive on the scene only *after* net investment has become zero and the capacity has adjusted to the zero savings output, causing the long-term unemployment we have described. That flexibility could have appeared *before* net investment became zero, and have acted gradually, keeping investment equal to full employment saving, at least as an average over booms and slumps.

That kind of *continued* gradual flexibility of the rate of interest is evidently what was claimed within the theory of distribution adopted here by Joan Robinson – the same flexibility that, in the hands of Hicks (1937), Modigliani (1944) and others, led to the 'neoclassical synthesis' and the re-absorption of

Keynes in long-run orthodox theory. In fact that flexibility means that it will be possible to maintain the equality between investment and full employment savings until the interest rate has become zero, or has reached the minimum below which there no longer is any incentive to lend.[5] Only in that case, which, as we saw, is also the only one considered by Keynes in Chapter XVI of the *General Theory*, will it be possible to have the long-term unemployment claimed by Joan Robinson. And this is also the case that orthodox theorists (and Keynes himself in one of his moods; cf. 1936: 207) would argue has never occurred yet, and is unlikely ever to occur, given the high interest elasticity of the capital intensity of the economy.

ROBINSON'S ARTICLE IN THE LIGHT OF CONTEMPORARY DISCUSSION

I will now summarize the elements of interest that this article of Joan Robinson has in my opinion. I will distinguish three such elements.

In the first place, her conclusion regarding the possibility of long-period labour unemployment does not rest on those elements of the erroneousness and uncertainty of expectations that characterize such a large part of her subsequent analysis.[6] The analysis rests instead upon long-period positions characterized by the uniform rate of return on capital to which the economy is supposed to tend, and which are independent of the above elements (except in the limited form in which they may underlie the assumed partial rigidity of the interest rate). It should also be noticed that those positions have nothing in common with the positions of steady growth to which Joan Robinson was to refer in her subsequent work as the only ones for which we may legitimately refer to a uniform rate of return on capital.

The article seems thus to provide an indication from Joan Robinson's own work of how natural it was for her, involved though she was in the ideas of the *General Theory*, to leave aside the elements of expectations and uncertainty when approaching a theory of the behaviour of labour employment and aggregate demand in the process of accumulation – how natural it was for her, that is, to base such a long-period theory on the method characterized by what I have elsewhere called 'long-period positions' of the system.[7]

A second element of interest is that, when the flaw in Joan Robinson's 1936 argument is corrected, the article brings clearly into light the inconsistency between the premises of marginal theory and any conclusions about long-period labour unemployment (at least until the economy has reached the minimum level of the rate of interest). The realization of this basic inconsistency may well have been what induced Joan Robinson to reconsider those premises, on the one hand, in the direction of an alternative theory of distribution, and, on the other, towards a reliance on Keynes' uncertainty and erroneousness of expectations also for a long-period analysis.

Those are in fact the two lines along which she would actually move in her subsequent work, with an increasing and, at the end of her life, almost exclusive stress on the second line, as more and more obstacles were met by her in attempting to explain distribution and relative prices by means of the incentive to invest.[8]

A third element of interest in the 1936 article is that it brings into clear light how at the centre of the above incompatibility between long-period labour unemployment and marginal theory there lies the theory of distribution, and in particular the assumed long-period inverse relation between the interest rate and capital intensity. It is that inverse relation that ensures that a gradual lowering of the interest rate would always suffice to keep investment at the level of full employment savings even in the absence of technical progress or population growth. With this, the 1936 article by Joan Robinson seems to bring out once more the importance that the criticism of the marginal theory of distribution – and, in particular, of the notion of capital on which the theory rests in all its versions[9] – assumes for such a long-period analysis.[10]

That article also brings out the importance for a long-period theory of labour unemployment of another aspect of recent critical work: the revival of the theory of the classical economists. Once Ricardo's erroneous identification between savings and investment has been clarified, the possibility of limits of aggregate demand to aggregate output in the long period, as well as in the short one, follows in an altogether natural way within the classical approach to distribution.

ON A DIFFERENT VIEW OF THE IMPLICATIONS OF ROBINSON'S ARTICLE FOR CONTEMPORARY DISCUSSION

We have thus found in Robinson (1936) reasons confirming the complementarity between the Keynesian analysis of aggregate demand on the one hand and, on the other, the criticism of the marginalist concept of capital and revival of classical theory. It behoves us, therefore, to discuss the argument to the contrary which Jan Kregel derives from the same Robinson essay in the article (1983) he contributed to the Robinson memorial issue of the *C.J.E.*

Two elements may be usefully distinguished in that argument by Kregel: one regards the role of expectations and the marginal efficiency of capital in the *General Theory*; the other concerns the criticism on capital.

With respect to the first element, Kregel finds in Robinson (1936) support for rejecting the thesis that the absorption of Keynes' analysis in orthodox theory was eased by Keynes' concept of 'marginal efficiency of capital' and by his reliance on expectations and the short period. Kregel finds such a support because in 1936 Robinson appears to reach Keynesian conclusions despite an entirely orthodox treatment of investment, long period assumptions, and no resort at all to expectations. This, Kregel comments, makes it clear that 'the ease with which traditional theory was re-introduced into the analysis of Keynes was not due to his emphasis on expectations, . . . and [his] own preservation of certain remnants of marginalist distribution theory such as . . . the marginal efficiency of capital schedule'. And he continues:

> Nor could it be argued that the neoclassical resurgence was due to a failure to treat the problems of the long period, or that the classical theory of value is a prerequisite to the preservation of Keynes's results in the long period. It would seem that the answer must be sought elsewhere, in what Joan Robinson identifies as 'bastard Keynesian' analysis.
>
> (Kregel 1983: 353)

It is, however, evident that this argument of Kregel rests on the consistency of Robinson's analysis: it loses its basis once it is realized that, as we argued above, her Keynesian conclusions do not follow from her orthodox long-period premises.

The second element of Kregel's argument is that the comparison between potential equilibria under given technical conditions, on which the criticism of the marginalist concept of capital is based, constitutes an 'anachronism' with respect to the theory Robinson was trying to develop, 'where . . . the technical conditions of production are linked to investment and accumulation' (Kregel 1983: 359).

What seems to be overlooked here is that that comparison between equilibria is imposed by the purpose of the criticism, which is to demonstrate that the marginalist attempt at a logical deduction of 'demand forces' for productive factors from the facts of alternative techniques and consumer choice, is faulty. Now in order to bring out that logical fault the critics have to move within the premises of the theory criticized and, in particular, have to compare its equilibria. However, the problem of the capital criticism was only that of clearing the field from the marginal theory of distribution and relative prices, so as to open it for an alternative theory. In such an alternative theory the question of whether long period positions should be adopted or not will have to be judged according to its merits. And it was indeed with that meaning and purpose in mind that, I believe, Joan Robinson herself started and participated in that debate – before coming, somewhat surprisingly, to claim the 'unimportance of reswitching' (Robinson 1975).

NOTES

1 I wish to thank Cristina Marcuzzo, Luigi Pasinetti and Alessandro Roncaglia for useful comments. Aid from the Italian Research Council and the Italian Ministry of University and Scientific Research (MURST) is gratefully acknowledged.

2 The paper was reprinted only up to 1953 in the first two editions of Robinson (1937). Kregel, (1983) suggests that Joan Robinson abandoned that line of argument because of the deficiencies of the marginal premises she was using: the

specific flaw of Joan Robinson's argument that I shall indicate below does not seem to be noticed.

3 The long-period assumptions evidently entail that aggregate productive capacity, besides having taken the form appropriate to the techniques and relative outputs corresponding to the given interest rate, will expand or contract in step with labour employment.

4 However, as the interest rate approaches zero and therefore the profit share in the net social income also approaches zero, the elasticity of substitution between capital and labour cannot but lie below unity (Robinson 1936: 86). In her article Joan Robinson does not seem to consider the effect on savings of the level of unemployment, which would presumably act, other things being equal, for a decrease of the proportion saved as income falls (e.g. working-class families would have even fewer possibilities to save, and may have to borrow, when some of their members are unemployed).

5 What Joan Robinson may have had at the back of her mind is a rigidity of the rate of interest that, though not absolute (as we saw she admits a fall in interest in the presence of labour unemployment), is however insufficient to keep a full employment level of investment, even only as an average over booms and slumps. This seems in fact to be the import of passages such as the following.

> At best the process of forcing down the rate of interest, even with highly plastic wages, would be both slow and uncertain in its operation.
> (Robinson 1936: 83)

> Thus the run required to reduce the rate of interest to a given extent, by this route, is likely to be far longer than the period in which equilibrium to a given rate of interest can be established.
> (ibid.: 84)

The second statement is, however, not easy to interpret. The period in which 'equilibrium to a given rate of interest' can be established implies nothing less than the destruction of productive equipment down to where the corresponding social product is low enough to give zero net savings, and it seems therefore unlikely to be shorter than the period required for some fall in the interest rate. Above all, it seems incorrect to say:

> In a community with *perfectly plastic* money wages the level of prices may be always moving towards zero without setting up any tendency permanently to reverse the situation which is causing prices to fall.
> (Robinson 1936: 83; italics added)

With 'perfectly plastic' money wages the fall in prices and interest could always be conceived to be fast enough to keep investment at its full employment average. Moreover, even if we interpreted the above passages in the sense we indicated of a rigidity of the rate of interest just sufficient to prevent it from falling fast enough for that result, it would not be easy to see why that partial rigidity should take the discontinuous form necessary for Robinson's argument. Periods of constancy of the interest rate, lasting long enough for productive capacity to approach whatever level corresponds to a zero-savings social product, are there assumed to be followed by sudden falls to equally lasting lower levels of that rate. In the absence of specific arguments to the contrary, it would seem more natural to envisage that partial rigidity in terms of a lag in the actual fall of the interest rate behind the fall required to keep average investment at its full employment level. Now, this second kind of partial rigidity would still entail a fall in productive capacity below the level required for full employment, but the fall would be to a level still allowing for positive, and not for zero net savings.

6 Cf. e.g. Robinson (1974).

7 Garegnani (1976: 26ff). In the section 6 she adds to a section 5 itself drastically revised in her 1937 reprinting of the 1936 article, Joan Robinson writes:

> Before adjustment is reached to a given set of circumstances, circumstances change ... Even if circumstances remain unchanged, the system would not run smoothly into an equilibrium position ... Our analysis of long period equilibrium cannot therefore be regarded as a prediction of the course of history.
>
> (Robinson 1937: 98–9)

These lines do not however appear to differ from the traditional Marshallian caveats on the use of long-period equilibria; the basic fact remains that the analysis is carried out in terms of just those equilibria.

8 Cf. Garegnani (1992).

9 Reliance on the concept of capital as a single magnitude is not in fact confined to the attempt to treat social production in terms of a single 'aggregate production function', or even to the attempt to determine the traditional long-period general equilibria of Walras, Wicksell or Marshall. As I have argued elsewhere, the same concept underlies the contemporary versions in terms of intertemporal general equilibrium.

10 We may incidentally note how the substantial coincidence, which has been sometimes disputed, is between Keynes' 'marginal efficiency of capital' and the marginalist demand for capital is indirectly confirmed by Robinson's treatment of investment demand in her article.

REFERENCES

Garegnani, P. (1976) On a Change in the Notion of Equilibrium in Recent Work on Value. In M. Brown, K. Sato and P. Zarembka, eds, *Essays in Modern Capital Theory*. Amsterdam: North Holland.

——— (1992) Some Notes for an Analysis of Accumulation. In E. J. Nell, J. Halevi and D. Leibman, eds, *Beyond the Steady State*. London: Macmillan.

Hicks, J. R. (1937) Mr. Keynes and the Classics: A Suggested Interpretation, *Econometrica*.

Keynes, J. M. (1936) *The General Theory of Employment, Interest and Money*. London: Macmillan.

Kregel J. (1983) The Microfoundations of the 'Generalisation of the *General Theory*' and 'Bastard Keynesianism': Keynes's *Theory of Employment in the Long and Short Period, Cambridge Journal of Economics*, 7: 343–61.

Modigliani, F. (1944) Liquidity Preference and the Theory of Interest and Money, *Econometrica*.

Robinson, J. (1936) The Long Period Theory of Employment, *Zeitschrift für Nationalökonomie*, 7: 74–93.

——— (1937) The Long Period Theory of Employment. In *Essays in the Theory of Employment*. London: Macmillan, 75–100.

——— (1974) *History versus Equilibrium*, Thames Papers in Political Economy. London: Thames Polytechnic; reprinted in *Collected Economic Papers*, Oxford: Blackwell, 1979, vol. V, 48–58.

——— (1975) The Unimportance of Reswitching, *Quarterly Journal of Economics*, vol. 89, 53–5.

6

JOAN ROBINSON AND THE RATE OF INTEREST

An important change of view on a topical issue

Massimo Pivetti

I should like to focus on what appears to me as a crucial watershed in Joan Robinson's work; one that seems likely to have contributed not unsubstantially – albeit indirectly – to the theoretical restoration of the present time. I refer to the development of her ideas on the subject of *interest* – the subject at the very centre of Keynes' 'long struggle' to escape from traditional ways of thinking.

In 1930 Keynes still regarded Wicksell's 'natural rate of interest' as a very useful and significant concept; accordingly, the general British-led return to the Gold Standard, round about the mid-1920s, was referred to in the *Treatise* as an event 'which served to maintain the market rate of interest somewhat regardless of the underlying realities of the natural rate' (1930, II: 379).

In fact, an important implication of the concept of an 'equilibrium' or 'natural' rate of interest determined by real forces is scepticism that monetary policies can *persistently* affect real interest rates. Whatever part monetary policy may play in governing the actual course of the market rate of interest, the existence of a 'natural' equilibrium of time preference by consumers–savers and the marginal productivity of capital would ultimately make long-term real interest rates beyond the reach of policy. Given the state of Productivity and Thrift, the impact on the price level, or on real output and accumulation, of any lasting discrepancy between the course of the market rate of interest and that of the natural rate would force the authorities to act so as to make the former move in sympathy with the latter.

By 1936 Keynes' view had finally changed, and he 'no longer' regarded the concept of a 'natural' rate of interest as 'a most promising idea' (1936: 243). The actual experience of the British cheap-money programme, inaugurated in the summer of 1932 by the successful Great War Loan conversion operation, certainly played a decisive role in the development of Keynes' ideas after 1930. Basically that experience and the combination of manoeuvres through which the fall in interest rates was made effective are what Keynes had in mind when, in 1936, he wrote that 'the rate of interest is a highly conventional phenomenon' – a magnitude, that is to say, that is largely governed by the 'prevailing view' as to what its normal level is regarded as being – and that the level of the long-term rate established by convention 'will not be always unduly resistant to a modest measure of *persistence and consistency of purpose* by the monetary authorities' (ibid.: 203 and 204; italics added).

The rate of interest thus ceased to be seen as a variable beyond the reach of policy, and, for several years after the elapse of the twenty-year period of cheap money, constraints on the action of the authorities were very rarely related to the existence of a 'natural' rate of interest.

The relevance to the real world of Keynes' new concept of interest as a conventional monetary phenomenon – 'determined from outside the system of production', as Sraffa was later to put it (1960: 33) – became especially clear after World War II, in connection with the system designed at Bretton Woods under the influence of the British economist. In April 1942, in a letter to Harrod on the forthcoming conversations with the Americans on post-war planning, Keynes wrote:

> In my view the whole management of the domestic economy depends upon being free to have the appropriate rate of interest without reference to the rates prevailing elsewhere in the world. Capital control is a corollary to this ... my own belief is that the Americans will be wise in their own interest to accept this conception.
>
> (Keynes 1942: 147)

And he kept stressing the same conception in 1943 and 1944:

> It is not merely a question of curbing exchange speculations and movements of hot money, or even of avoiding flights of capital due to political motives; though all this is necessary to control. The need, in my judgement, is more fundamental. Unless the aggregate of the new investments which individuals are free to make overseas is kept within the amount which our favourable trade balance is capable of looking after, we lose control over the domestic rate of interest.
>
> (Keynes 1943: 275)

> We intend to retain control of our domestic rate of interest, so that we can keep it as low as suits our own purposes, without interference from the ebb and flow of international capital movements or flights of hot money... whilst we intend to prevent inflation at home, we will not accept deflation at the dictate of influences from outside. In other words, we abjure the instrument of Bank rate and credit restriction operating through the increase of unemployment as a means of forcing our domestic economy into line with external factors.
>
> (Keynes 1944: 16)

The rate of interest emerges clearly from these propositions as a policy-determined variable, and one that, as a crucial component of *general* economic policy, the government of each country should endeavour to keep as much as possible under its control. Hence the primacy given in the Bretton Woods settlement to national macroeconomic autonomy, with the explicit right accorded to every member government to control all capital movements. And in fact, in the twenty-five years before the breakdown of the par-value system in 1973, each country was left free to be its own judge, in the field of capital control, and to act as it deemed best in its own interest.

It is well known how far we have moved from all this over the past twenty years – through theoretical routes that, by leading to the idea of 'rules' that bind national policy actions over time as requirements for a well-designed monetary 'regime', have caused economists to regard any loss of policy autonomy on the part of national governments with undiluted favour, with the EMU project and the Maastricht Treaty as the most significant policy outcome of the entire theoretical course (see on this Pivetti 1993).

Let us now take a look at the position of Joan Robinson and the strand of post-Keynesianism that has been the most influenced by her contribution. What is especially worth stressing here is that Keynes' interpretation of the rate of interest as a monetary phenomenon susceptible to policy determination – provided the authorities act with a sufficient measure of 'persistence and consistency' – was fully endorsed after his death by his chief pupils: Richard Kahn and, indeed, Joan Robinson. Thus the latter wrote in 1951, in the last section of her famous article 'The Rate of Interest',[1] with respect to the possibilities of a cheap money policy:

> If the authorities take it gently and do not try to push the rate down too fast, and if they stick consistently to the policy, once begun, so that the market never has the experience of today's rate being higher than yesterday's, it is hard to discern *any limit* to the possible fall in interest rates.
>
> (Robinson 1952: 30; italics added)

As to Kahn, he thus answered in 1958 when called as a witness by the Committee on the Working of the Monetary System and asked to express a view as to the difficulty of controlling the long-term rate of interest:

> If you are thinking of the difficulty of making money very cheap again in the light of the abandonment of the 2½ regime,[2] without asking me to express a view as to whether either then or now it would be desirable, I would say that, if it was thought desirable, it could be done; once the market realises that the authorities are serious they will dash in and help the authorities ... if they really wanted 2½ per cent not tomorrow, but as something to aim at in the near future, I certainly believe that they could get it, provided that they did not mind how much the quantity of money went up in the process.
>
> (Kahn 1960: 743)

Now the point is that a view such as the one expressed in these passages by Robinson and Kahn can hardly coexist with a concept of the normal rate of return on capital employed in production as a magnitude determined by *real* factors – unless one is prepared to deny any long-run connection between the rate of interest and the rate of profit. Naturally this connection was not denied by Keynes, who, consistently with his monetary explanation of interest, regarded the *latter* 'as setting the pace' in the necessary equalization of 'the advantages of the choice between owing loans and assets': 'instead of the marginal efficiency of capital determining the rate of interest', he wrote in 1937, 'it is truer . . . to say that it is the rate of interest which determines the marginal efficiency of capital' (Keynes 1937: 122–3; on the interest–profit connection in economic theory, see Pivetti 1991: Part II).

As I have already pointed out, those who believe instead in the existence of a 'natural' rate of interest, determined by consumers' preferences and the marginal productivity of capital, will naturally be led to rule out the possibility that the authorities can drive interest rates up or down to a chosen level, and keep them there. But the traditional concept of money interest as a subordinate phenomenon, substantially beyond the reach of policy, can hardly be avoided, not only by all those who share the neoclassical theory of distribution, but also by anyone who maintains that the normal rate of profit is governed by the rate of capital accumulation, given the propensities to save. Indeed, with a normal profitability of capital determined in this way, the monetary authorities would be deprived of any substantial power: no matter how large a 'measure of persistence and consistency of purpose' they applied to their action, neither a situation of high interest rates nor one of cheap money could be maintained for any length of time, irrespective of the 'underlying reality' represented by the course of the rate of accumulation.

The development of Joan Robinson's position on interest as her life's work progressed neatly reflects what has just been pointed out.

In the first reprint of the article 'The Rate of Interest' that followed *The Accumulation of Capital* (1956), its last section on the cheap money policy was omitted. Apparently she thought that it had been rendered 'obsolete' by her main work (cf. Robinson 1960: v), where she had written that '[t]he objection to Keynes's treatment is that it seems to leave no place for the influence upon interest rates of the "fundamental phenomena of Productivity and Thrift"' (1956: 398, where 'productivity' is taken to mean the potential growth rate of an economy). In fact, in *The Accumulation of Capital*, after having maintained that in a golden age the level of interest rates is governed by the rate of profit 'appropriate' to that particular golden age,[3] she had thus proceeded to argue:

> in the far from golden age in which we live . . . there is, at any moment, a low level of interest such that, if obtained, inflation would set in . . .

> and a high level such that if obtained would be regarded as intolerable and some kind of reaction would set in to get it brought down. These two levels . . . are governed, roughly speaking, by the prospect of profit on investment . . . Actual interest rates must be somewhere between these two levels.
>
> (1956: 399–400)

In 1979 'The Rate of Interest' was again reprinted, this time in full, at the end of the volume *The Generalisation of the General Theory and Other Essays*. But in her new Introduction to that volume Joan Robinson referred to the essay on interest as 'quite old fashioned', since '[i]t does not deal either with an open system or with inflation, now the topical monetary problems. It only expanded and consolidated the theory as Keynes had left it' (1979: xxvii). By 1951, however, at the time she had first published the essay on the rate of interest, Keynes' theory *had* already been 'expanded' to deal with the problems of an open system and of inflation, as should have been apparent to Joan Robinson from the great influence that Keynes' view on these matters had exerted on the system of fixed (but adjustable) exchange rates established at Bretton Woods in 1944 (see above).

Much more to the point, therefore, as regards the 'old-fashioned' nature ascribed by Joan Robinson to her 1951 essay on interest, is the fact that in that same Introduction to *The Generalisation of the General Theory* she explicitly criticizes as 'unnatural' the concept of the rate of interest as an independently determined monetary phenomenon that governs the rate of profit: 'Over the long run', she writes, reversing Keynes' point of view, 'the interest that rentiers can exact is dominated by the profits that entrepreneurs can earn, not the other way round' (1979: xxii).

What conclusion follows from the above overview on Joan Robinson and her interpretation of interest? To me it seems that there is perhaps a sense in which it can be said that the so-called Keynesian theory of distribution has facilitated the propagation of current macroeconomic thinking. Not directly, of course, in the same way as can be said of the neoclassical synthesis (Joan Robinson's 'bastard Keynesianism'), but indirectly, on account of its incompatibility with the Keynesian idea that, under capitalism, monetary phenomena are central to the explanation of real ones – that is to say, with the very aspect of Keynes' thought that is more in contrast with all orthodoxy, past and present.

NOTES

1 According to F. Hahn (1985: 909), Joan Robinson's best work, together with her other contributions to monetary economics contained in *The Rate of Interest and Other Essays* (1952).

2 Kahn is referring here to the ultra-cheap money policy attempted by the post-war Labour government of 1945–51: the objective of 2½ per cent for long-term

government debt was achieved but not held, and the policy was abandoned at the end of 1947 with the resignation of the Chancellor of the Exchequer, Hugh Dalton. On Dalton's policy, see Howson (1987: 433–52).

3 'Given the rate of profit appropriate to a particular golden age there is only one level of interest that can be obtained without destroying the golden-age conditions, for if interest were too low excess-investment (financed by external borrowing) would be stimulated so much as to create inflation, and if it were too high investment would be brought to a halt' (Robinson 1956: 397–8).

REFERENCES

Hahn, F. (1985) Robinson–Hahn Love–Hate Relationship: An Interview. In G. R. Feiwell, ed., *Joan Robinson and Modern Economic Theory.* New York: New York University Press.

Howson, S. (1987) The Origin of Cheap Money, 1945–7, *Economic History Review* (2nd ser.), 40(3).

Kahn, R. (1960) Evidence before the Committee on the Working of the Monetary System. In Committee on the Working of the Monetary System, *Minutes of Evidence*. London: HMSO.

Keynes, J. M. (1930) *A Treatise on Money* (2 vols). London: Macmillan, 1965.

——— (1936) *The General Theory of Employment, Interest and Money.* London: Macmillan, 1964.

——— (1937) The General Theory of Employment, *Quarterly Journal of Economics*, February; reprinted in D. Moggridge, ed., *The Collected Writings of John Maynard Keynes*, vol. XIV, ch. 2. London: Macmillan, 1973.

——— (1942) Letter to R. F. Harrod, 19 April 1942. In D. Moggridge, ed., *The Collected Writings of John Maynard Keynes*, vol. XXV, ch. 2. London: Macmillan, 1980.

——— (1943) Speech before the House of Lords, 18 May 1943. In D. Moggridge, ed., *The Collected Writings of John Maynard Keynes*, vol. XXV, ch. 3. London: Macmillan, 1980.

——— (1944) Speech before the House of Lords, 23 May 1944. In D. Moggridge, ed., *The Collected Writings of John Maynard Keynes*, vol. XXVI, ch. 1. London: Macmillan, 1980.

Pivetti, M. (1991) *An Essay on Money and Distribution*. London: Macmillan.

——— (1993) Bretton Woods, through the Lens of State-of-the-Art Macrotheory and the European Monetary System, *Contributions to Political Economy,* 12: 99–110.

Robinson, J. (1951) The rate of interest, *Econometrica*, 19: 92–111.

——— (1952) *The Rate of Interest and Other Essays*. London: Macmillan.

——— (1956) *The Accumulation of Capital*. London: Macmillan.

——— (1960) *Collected Economic Papers*, vol. II. Oxford: Blackwell.

——— (1979) *The Generalisation of the General Theory and Other Essays*. London: Macmillan.

Sraffa, P. (1960) *Production of Commodities by Means of Commodities*. Cambridge: Cambridge University Press.

7

JOAN ROBINSON AND THE RATE OF INTEREST THESE DAYS[1]

Giangiacomo Nardozzi

Keynes' theory of interest as 'a highly conventional, rather than a highly psychological, phenomenon' is not among the topics mostly dealt with by the neo-Keynesian school of Richard Kahn, Nicholas Kaldor and Joan Robinson. In Chapter XV of the *General Theory*, Keynes viewed the rate of interest from the perspective of the active investor that he was and considered it as the outcome of the working of financial markets. His neo-Keynesian followers regarded it mainly from the point of view of its significance for his theory of income and employment. They were more concerned with appraising the significance of the liquidity preference as a building block of Keynesian theory and policy rather than with the insights it provided for understanding the working of financial markets.

As early as 1939, in his 'Speculation and Economic Stability', Kaldor went into Keynes' theory of interest to argue that it contains two separate propositions:

> The first regards interest as the price to be paid for parting with liquidity, and arises on account of the uncertainty of the future prices of non-liquid assets. The second concerns the dependence of the current rate of interest on the interest rates expected in the future. While the first proposition provides an explanation of why long dated bonds should normally command a higher yield than short term paper, it is the second which explains why the traditional theory of the working of the capital market is inappropriate – why, in other words, saving and investment are brought into equality by movements in the level of income far more than by movements in interest rates. And this second effect will be the more powerful the less is the uncertainty concerning the future, or the greater the firmness with which the idea of 'a normal price' is embedded in the minds of professional speculators and dealers.
>
> (Kaldor 1986a: 12)

The second proposition is, according to Kaldor, much more important than the first. And the liquidity preference theory is not essential to it (Kaldor 1986b).

In any case Kaldor maintains that speculation is related not to the choice between holding money and bonds but to that between short-term bills and bonds. He then argues, following Hicks, that the current long-term rate depends on the expected future short-term rates. More precisely, the expected long-term rate depends on the average of the expected short rates along the lifetime of the bonds. Since the short rate can be considered as a datum, determined by the central bank, there is no need to refer to demand and supply of money to determine the long-term rate (Kaldor 1939). From his refusal to look at the determination of the long-term rate through the schedule of the demand and supply of money, which later he saw as responsible for the rise of monetarism, Kaldor several years later went on to develop his argument of endogeneity of money.

According to the Hicksian and Kaldorian interpretations of Keynes' theory, the conventional character of the long-term rate of interest lies in the speculation on the future course of the short rate rather than of the long-term rate itself. The possible conventions adopted by investors to make their speculations are thus restricted to one: guess the next move of the central bank in its fixing of the short rate.

This view was opposed by Kahn in *Some Notes on Liquidity Preference*. Kahn argued that, in choosing between short-term bills and bonds, the speculator

> is . . . concerned with the probable behaviour of bond prices during the lifetime of the bills but not with anything beyond that span. The Hicks school seems to argue as though a decision to hold bills at the moment implied an indissoluble contract to remain in bills in perpetuity and as though a decision to hold bonds at the moment implied an indissoluble contract never to sell the bonds and switch into bills.
>
> (Kahn 1954: 75)

Kahn's point is that

> a decision to go long rather than short, or vice versa, is not indissoluble. When a bill is bought rather than a bond the only relevant expectation determining the decision is what the bond rate will be when the bill matures. That expectation is certainly related to the expectation of what the bill rate will itself be at that same date. Furthermore, the expectation of what the bond rate will be at more distant dates, in their turn are related to expectations of what the bill rates will be at those same dates. All this is, however, a very different thing from saying that the bond rate depends on expectations about the future of the bill rate itself, rather than of banking and monetary policy generally.
>
> (Kahn 1954: 78)

There is no need for the speculator to explore central bank moves over a period covering such a distant future as that referring to the lifetime of the bond. It can be argued that no rational basis for expectations covering such a long span of time exists. It is more rational, given the uncertainty regarding the future, for speculators to try to guess how present monetary policy will be judged by the market via the long-term rate that is expected to prevail.

If, in the choice between bonds and bills, the relevant expectation is that regarding the bond rate, and not the bill rate, it is convenient to accept the assumption in Keynes' liquidity preference schedule, which is to ignore the existence of bills and to refer simply to bonds and money on which no interest is paid. Keynes' liquidity preference theory of the rate of interest is thus reaffirmed by Kahn against the critique of Kaldor. The question of supposed exogeneity of the money supply does not arise because 'the supply and demand for money [are] the obverse of the supply of securities in the hands of the public and the demand for securities by the public' (Kahn 1954: 80).

The occasion for the diffusion of the neo-Keynesian ideas on money and interest arose with the establishment of the Radcliffe Committee to which both Kaldor and Kahn submitted a memorandum. The limits of monetary policy as the main instrument of economic policy, as evidenced especially by Kaldor and nicely summarized by Kahn with the expression 'monetary mystique', were found to lie in its ineffectiveness as a stimulus for the economy. However, no particular attention was given by these memoranda to the long-term rate of interest as a conventional phenomenon or to the reasons why, according to Keynes, it can be 'recalcitrant'.

Economic policies being implemented during present times are not governed by the wisdom of the Radcliffe Report (Committee on the Working of the Monetary System 1959). Rather they mainly rely on monetary manouevres.

Faced with the longest recession since World War II, the economies of the G-7 group have relied mainly on wishful effects of lower interest rates to stimulate recovery. Short-term interest rates were consistently reduced from late 1991 until the second half of 1993 when in the USA they reached a historical low.

Long-term rates are now also much lower, even if their decline has not been as steep as that of short rates. At present (end of 1993) they are already moving upwards both in the USA and in Continental Europe. In the USA the rise is due to fears of a return of inflation, which, however, has not yet appeared in forecasts, while Continental Europe is still in recession. In real terms, when expected inflation is taken into account, long-term rates are still high with respect to the expected rates of growth of GDP.

The Radcliffe wisdom explains rather well the slow reaction of economies to the cheap money policy. But the point now at stake is why, having chosen to act mainly through a cheap money policy, money turns out to be not cheap enough. The problem lies with the working of financial markets; and, to understand it, the Kaldorian interpretation of Keynes' theory of interest does not suffice. For what we have observed is that, despite decreasing inflation and short-term rates having reached their historical low, long-term rates have remained high in the USA. At the same time, the Deutsche Bundesbank now finds it difficult to reduce the real long rate. During a period of general expansionary monetary policy with decreasing rates of inflation, the Kaldorian argument of long-term rates depending on expectations about short ones does not explain the stickiness of long rates. Kahn's argument on the dependence of the long rate on its expected variation in the near future, as determined by the market valuation of the monetary policy, seems to fit better. But it must be developed further. This can be achieved by going back to Keynes' theory of interest as a theory of the working of financial markets through the interpretation given by Joan Robinson.

In her agenda for research, Joan Robinson did not attach much importance to the financial aspects of the economy and to financial markets. She was mostly concerned with the aim of providing a long-period theory, that is a growth theory, to complete Keynes' General Theory. Her essay on the rate of interest was immediately republished in a small book that is presented as an 'analysis of a dynamic economic system' (Robinson 1952: v). Nevertheless, the essay provides us with insights into how the long-term rate is established by the market – a theme that is hardly developed by the two other neo-Keynesian authors I have considered.

Following her concern with long-run equilibria, Joan Robinson first considered the full employment rate of interest. This is, in Joan Robinson's words, 'strongly influenced by the real forces of thrift and, if not by the real force of productivity, at least by the beliefs about the future profitability of capital which is related to it'. In fact,

> If the full employment rate were ever above the actual rate inflation would set in through a rise in money-wage rates and the rate of interest would be driven up. The full employment value of the rate of interest may therefore be regarded as, in a certain sense, a lower limit to the possible value of the rate.
>
> (Robinson 1952: 4)

Thus, according to Joan Robinson, the full employment rate of interest is ruled by the forces called on by the traditional neoclassical theory to explain why there is such a thing as a positive rate of interest.

When the full employment equilibrium assumption is dropped, the level of the interest rate can no longer be ruled by the real forces called on to explain why a rate of interest should exist at all. Once multiple, less-than-full employment equilibria are admitted, for each of them there is a different 'natural' rate of interest, as Keynes argued in the *General Theory* (Ch. XVII) rethinking on his treatment of the rate of interest in the *Treatise on Money*. The question then is that of understanding how financial markets determine the levels of these rates of interest, which Harrod (1973: Ch. 6) more properly called 'market rates' to avoid confusion. The answer to this question is provided by the liquidity preference theory that relates to the behaviour of financial investors who are confronted with day-to-day decisions to be taken outside the certain world assumed by the neoclassical full employment equilibrium. In general, investors are not confronted, as in the neoclassical paradigm, with 'the sole and only reason why there ever had been or could be interest' (ibid.). It is then true that

> We have very little knowledge of the influences shaping expectations. Past experience is no doubt the major element in expectations, but experience, as far as one can judge, is compounded in the market with a variety of theories and superstitions and the whole amalgam is played upon from day to day by the influences (including the last bank chairman's speech) which make up what Keynes called 'the state of the news'. Any theory that is widely believed tends to verify itself, so that there is a large element of 'thinking makes it so' in the determination of interest rates.
>
> (Robinson 1952: 19)

Expectations that enter in this behaviour are shaped by many influences. Economic, not only monetary, policy plays an important part both in shaping the expectations and in determining confidence in them. Joan Robinson was ready to accept that real forces can also exert their influence on expectations even if the economy is far from full employment.

How does this idea fit into Keynes' conception of uncertainty? What room is there for neoclassical real forces of productivity and thrift determining the rate of interest? The room is provided by Keynes himself when he writes:

> Nevertheless, the necessity for action and for decision compels us as practical men to do our best to overlook this awkward fact and to behave exactly as we should if we had behind us a good Benthamite calculation of a series of prospective advantages and disadvantages, each multiplied by its appropriate probability, waiting to be summed.... I accuse the classical economic theory of being itself one of these pretty, polite techniques which tries to deal with the present by abstracting from the fact that we know very little about the future.
>
> (Keynes 1937: 114–15)

The conventional character of the rate of interest does not preclude speculators in financial markets from relying on these 'pretty, polite techniques' if we look at conventions as rules of action adopted by speculators facing uncertainty.

When Joan Robinson writes of 'a variety of theories and superstitions' she seems to refer to conventions in this sense. Apart from instinct and imitation of others – which, as 'animal spirits' and 'beauty contest', are well known in the Keynesian literature – conventions can consist of rationalizations provided by economic theories and models. The neoclassical model of interest is just one of these. It is true that it assumes that speculators do not experience Keynesian uncertainty. However, as far as it provides a rationalization to face uncertainty, it can be adopted by speculators if they are given good reasons to believe in it (Carabelli 1991; Dow 1991).

Coming back to present economic policies, if we were close to full employment, there would be reasons for financial markets to adopt the neoclassical model as a convention, that is to look at the rate of interest as being determined by the real forces leading to natural equilibrium. However, these reasons should, in principle, not hold when far from full employment. Yet it cannot be excluded that they hold if markets are led by economic policy to rely on this neoclassical convention.

When there is full employment, economic policy does not provide many convincing arguments for financial markets to accept a real interest rate lower than the one they think is the natural one. When far from full employment it is the financial markets that are short of arguments for resisting a policy aimed at lowering the interest rate. The present economic policies in Europe do not seem to be conscious of the strength they are given by the recession in their confrontation with financial markets. Instead of taking advantage of recession and high rates of unemployment that deprive financial markets of arguments to resist a reduction in real interest rates, economic policy makers behave as if economies were already at full employment. They try to persuade markets to accept lower interest rates by tying their level to decreasing rates of inflation, thus leading markets to believe that the real rate of interest is already at its equilibrium level. This opinion is further reinforced by connecting easier monetary policies to planned reductions in public deficits aimed at increasing the overall saving rate.

If the economic policy adopted during a recession turns out to be based on the recognition of real forces determining the rate of interest in a full employment equilibrium, it is no wonder that financial markets come in handy in this game, which provides speculators with some certainty to cling to. However, the game is not rewarding for economic policy makers because it gives financial markets unnecessary power, which they are at present fully using by resisting the reduction of long-term real interest rates.

Rereading Joan Robinson's essay on the rate of interest today helps to point out what can be considered a fundamental contradiction of present economic policy in Europe. It is in fact self-contradictory to rely on easy money policies to recover from a recession and at the same time to enforce that policy with a 'full employment convention' implying that real rates of interest are already at their natural equilibrium level.

NOTE

1 Financial support from the Italian Ministry of University and Scientific Research (MURST 40%) is gratefully acknowledged.

REFERENCES

Carabelli, A. (1991) Comment on S. Dow. In R. M. O'Donnell, ed., *Keynes as Economist-Philosopher*. London: Macmillan.

Committee on the Working of the Monetary System (1959) *Report Presented to Parliament by the Chancellor of the Exchequer by Command of Her Majesty*. London: HMSO.

Dow, S. (1991) Keynes's Epistemology and Economic Methodology. In R. M. O'Donnell, ed., *Keynes as Economist-Philosopher*. London: Macmillan.

Harrod, R. (1973) *Economic Dynamics*. London: Macmillan.

Kaldor, N. (1939) Speculation and Economic Stability, *Review of Economic Studies*, 7: 1–27.

——— (1986a) Recollections of an Economist, *Banca Nazionale del Lavoro Quarterly Review*, 39: 3–26.

——— (1986b) *Ricordi di un economista*, a cura di M. C. Marcuzzo. Milan: Garzanti.

Kahn, R. (1954) *Some Notes on Liquidity Preference*, Manchester School, reprinted in *Selected Essays on Employment and Growth*. Cambridge: Cambridge University Press, 1972.

Keynes, J. M. (1936) *The General Theory of Employment, Interest and Money*. In D. Moggridge, ed., *The Collected Writings of John Maynard Keynes*, vol. VII. London: Macmillan, 1972.

——— (1937) The General Theory of Employment. In D. Moggridge, ed., *The Collected Writings of John Maynard Keynes*, vol. XIV. London: Macmillan, 1972.

Robinson, J. (1952) *The Rate of Interest and Other Essays*. London: Macmillan.

8

BEGGAR-MY-NEIGHBOUR POLICIES

The 1930s and the 1980s[1]

Annamaria Simonazzi

The relationship between the external equilibrium and the objective of a high level of employment is the leitmotiv in Joan Robinson's contributions to international economics. In her analysis of the propagation of economic fluctuations she extended the theoretical framework developed by Keynes to the open economy. Starting from Keynes' critique of the working of the gold standard, in her early papers[2] she focused on developing the tools required to generalize the new theory. The monetary experience between the wars provided the background for her critique of the premises of the 'old orthodoxy', so vehemently opposed by Keynes himself. The aim of this paper is to consider how Joan Robinson's analysis might be applied to analyse Europe's experience with the system of fixed exchange rates of the 1980s.

In the 1920s, the stability of the exchange rate had been singled out as a crucial target on the road to stability, after the excesses of war finance and post-war inflationary adjustments. The return to the gold standard reflected the priority given to financial stability and distrust of discretionary policies in favour of automatic rules of adjustment. When the *Essays in the Theory of Employment* were published, in 1937, the few countries still on gold had finally devalued. But the process that led to the demise of the gold exchange standard had been marked by deflation, unemployment and competitive devaluations.

Several explanations have been offered for the collapse of the system:[3] failure to play by the rules of the game, inadequate international economic leadership by the United States, absence of international cooperation, and the intrinsic instability of a gold exchange (as distinct from a pure gold) standard.

The failure to play by the rules of the game has been attributed a prominent role among the causes of the collapse of the gold exchange standard.[4] Sterilization of gold inflows by surplus countries prevented the price mechanism from working, while exerting ever-increasing pressure on the deficit countries' reserves and prices. With the expected inflation in the USA failing to materialize, the British decision to return to gold at the pre-war parity meant that the Bank rate was given the impossible and unprecedented task of bringing about a *substantial* fall in prices and wages.[5] Given the high mobility of capital and the US commitment to the gold standard, high rates in London had to be met with high rates in the USA, imposing a constraint on the US monetary policy. When the United States entered the Great Depression, its turn came to transmit deflation to Europe. Finally, with a crisis of confidence, the liquidation of foreign exchange reserves led to a sort of domino effect, with speculative capital flights putting each currency under pressure in turn (sterling first, then the dollar, and, eventually, the franc).

Determined defence of the fixed exchange rates, together with a different capacity, or willingness, to endure the deflationary costs entailed by this policy, resulted in inability to coordinate any reflationary initiatives.[6] In the absence of cooperation, the gold standard represented a binding constraint even for the largest surplus countries: the United States and France.[7] In these conditions, the only way to ease the external constraint was by devaluation and/or beggar-my-neighbour policies.

It was against this background that Joan Robinson set out to analyse the effects of competitive policies. Approaching the question, as usual, from the standpoint of the highest possible employment level, she condemns these policies. In 'Beggar-My-Neighbour Remedies for Unemployment' Joan Robinson stresses the different consequences of an increase in income brought about by an increase in exports and an increase in home investment:

> an increase in home investment brings about a net increase in employment for the world as a whole, while an increase in the balance of trade of one country at best leaves the level of employment for the world as a whole unaffected.
>
> (Robinson 1973a: 229)

Yet beggar-my-neighbour policies may be necessary to keep the reward of greater investment at home or to prevent other countries from taking advantage of an increase in domestic money wages (ibid.: 240). This qualification is prompted by experience in the 1930s when resort to coordinated reflationary policies was barred while, at the same time, compliance with the rules of the game made it impossible, for any single country, to pursue reflationary policies.[8]

In her analysis of the effects of beggar-my-neighbour policies Joan Robinson focuses on the effects on employment of an improvement in the trade balance, while neglecting the effects on domestic reflation made possible by the easing of the external constraint. Thus, she does not explicitly consider here the possibility that competitive devaluations might exert positive effects on the system as a whole.[9] This may be due to the fact that in *Essays in the Theory of Employment* the point was to show how a surplus in the balance of trade could favourably affect domestic employment, against

'Marshall's pure theory of international trade, in which the balance of trade *ex hypothesi* is always zero' (Robinson 1937b: 700).

A positive systemic effect is acknowledged the same year in her review of *Exchange Depreciation* by S. E. Harris, where she writes:

> Professor Harris attributes the increase in activity which follows exchange depreciation to the general relief from deflationary pressures rather than to the direct effect of an increase in the balance of trade... Exchange depreciation, in itself, merely gives a competitive advantage to one country at the expense of the rest, but it also opens the way to expansionist policies (cheap money in Great Britain, public expenditure in the United States) which are impossible so long as each country is struggling to preserve a fixed exchange rate, and Professor Harris' survey leaves no doubt that the effects of exchange depreciation have been beneficial to the world as a whole.[10]
>
> (Robinson 1937b: 700–1)

This analysis anticipates modern interpretations of the competitive devaluations occurring in the 1930s,[11] where the stress is on the systemic deflationary effects of the gold standard and the need to remove the constraint on domestic reflationary policies represented by the exchange rate.

Looking back to the real functioning of the gold standard for a guide to the new order, Joan Robinson (1947) singles out two problems:

1 The flaw in the classical adjustment mechanism and the consequent deflationary bias derived from the asymmetric functioning of the system. Surplus countries are under no necessity to check the inflows, while those who lose gold are under the obligation to check the outflows. Hence the need to provide safeguard clauses against any deflationary bias deriving from the working of the system or from the policies of surplus countries.[12]

2 Asymmetry in the adjustment of prices and nominal incomes. A loss of gold does not automatically lead to the fall in prices required to stimulate exports and reduce imports. Although devaluation and deflation of domestic prices have similar effects upon the balance of trade,[13] the deflationary process can be very painful.

> For a country in which money wages do not readily yield to the pressure of unemployment the gold standard can be maintained, in an era of rapid change, only by means of recurrent periods of severe unemployment, and it is the realisation of this fact which has in recent years so much impaired the popularity of the gold standard.
>
> (Robinson 1973b: 227–8)

If the 'classical' mechanism fails, the income mechanism takes over; in reality, for the deficit countries the mechanism of adjustment worked through a reduction in demand rather than in prices. But if domestic deflation is transmitted to foreign countries through the international trade multiplier, a country may be unable to reduce its *relative* prices and wages. The reduction of imports can throw into deficit other countries previously in equilibrium, and can worsen the conditions of surplus countries. Deflation can become general, and the pressure to bring down wages can become general 'and much else, including the gold standard itself, may give way under the strain long before equilibrium has been restored' (Robinson 1947: 343).

For all these reasons Robinson subscribed to Keynes' plea for a policy of adjustable exchange rates designed to preserve national monetary independence and to avoid the need for deflation in the face of persistent external deficits.

The European experience with the European Monetary System (EMS) in the 1980s has many features in common with inter-war experience with the gold exchange standard and it is worth examining just how relevant Joan Robinson's analysis and proposals prompted by that experience may still be today.

The EMS reflects a turnabout in both theory and policy priorities. On the one hand, reactions to the inflationary pressure and financial disorder of the 1970s led to the demand for fiscal and monetary discipline, and this has brought price stability once again to the forefront. On the other hand, the theory of inflation and output determination based on the concept of the 'equilibrium' rate of unemployment has left price stability as the only legitimate policy goal. Against this background, the exchange rate has resumed its role as an instrument for price stability.

In the remaining part of the paper, I shall briefly consider the policies pursued respectively by Germany and the other member countries within the system of fixed exchange rate. It is argued that these policies have resulted in a deflationary bias for the system as a whole and are largely responsible for the poor employment and growth record of Europe in the 1980s.

In the 1980s, Germany adopted a disinflation policy based on the nominal appreciation of the exchange rate, complemented by a policy of reduction of domestic costs.[14] With such a strategy, the exchange rate takes care of inflation and monetary policy takes care of competitiveness. This approach, subscribed to by the Council of Economic Experts (Sachverstandigenrat), stresses the role of supply factors. It rests on three propositions.[15]

First, in the medium term, output and employment are capacity constrained: their rate of growth depends on the rate of investment. The level of profits, together with the rate of interest and the state of expectations, determine the volume of investment. The low level of profits is responsible for the capacity constraint resulting in low employment. Say's Law applies, so demand has no role to play.

Secondly, the state of public finances affects inflationary expectations and hence confidence in the DM. Fiscal discipline is required in order to sustain the exchange without having to resort to high interest rates that, by crowding out investment, would worsen medium-term employment prospects.

Thirdly, the nominal appreciation of the exchange rate allows a reduction in the rate of increase in import prices. In order to keep competitiveness constant, the nominal appreciation has to be compensated for by a reduction in the rate of change in domestic prices relative to foreign prices. Defence of the export surplus therefore requires flexible money wages so as to allow for the stability of the real exchange rate *vis-à-vis* the currencies of the export markets. Monetary policy is given the double task of maintaining wage discipline while sustaining the external value of the DM.

While in Germany the EMS may have served to prevent a strong exchange rate policy from leading to real appreciation and loss of competitiveness *vis-à-vis* the other European countries,[16] the system of fixed exchange rates, pegged to the DM, has been used by the other European countries as a disinflationary mechanism.

There are two different versions of this approach. According to the credibility hypothesis, inflation differentials are not accounted for by institutional or structural differences among countries, but are the consequence of government policies. The commitment to peg the exchange rate to the currency of the central bank with the strongest anti-inflationary bias signals the policy maker's determination to refrain from producing surprise inflation. By voluntarily sacrificing monetary independence, the member countries can achieve the anti-inflation credibility of the anchor-country and reduce inflation at no cost.

Despite the popularity enjoyed by the credibility hypothesis among economists, it was the 'discipline' effect of the EMS that was relied upon by policy-makers. With fixed exchange rates, countries whose inflation rates exceed that of the anchor-country must endure real appreciation of exchange and steady decline in competitiveness. The result is higher unemployment, further aggravated by rationalization introduced to reduce the loss in competitiveness. According to the discipline approach to exchange rate stability, an increase in unemployment would put pressure on the nominal wage rate, thus triggering the disinflation process. With nominal inflexibilities conquered and inflation decreasing beyond the lower rate set by the anchor-country, the ensuing real depreciation would entail an improvement in the trade balance and a consequent decrease in unemployment.

Here we shall disregard the difficulties involved in the downward rigidities of nominal values, in order to concentrate on the consequences of these policies for the level of aggregate income and employment.[17] Both models rest on the pursuance of an export surplus, achieved by improving relative prices. In fact, the German model of growth without inflation rests on the existence of an export surplus, necessary to guarantee a level of reasonably full employment and a low degree of conflict on income distribution.[18] But in the disinflation phase, for the other European countries a net reduction in domestic demand is required. For the system as a whole the net effect is not zero but negative. Both Germany, with its austerity policy, and the other European countries, with their competitive disinflations, have underestimated the effects deriving from the interdependence of their policies. European deflation undermined the German model, reinforcing the vicious circle between German austerity and European deflation.

In the early 1980s the deflationary effects of these policies were mitigated by two factors. First, there were periodical realignments within the EMS to offset, in full or in part, the inflation differentials, thus mitigating the exchange discipline and allowing varied degrees of deflation to the various countries.[19] Secondly, gains of competitiveness over the dollar area were achieved. The EMS was meant to ensure a *coordinated* floating of the European currencies against the dollar. As it turned out, each European currency remained linked to the dollar through the DM. During the early 1980s a high dollar and American expansion allowed the European countries to enjoy an export surplus towards the non-EC area.

With the fall of the dollar, starting from 1985, the European currencies moved up with the DM, appreciating towards the dollar, while suffering a downward pressure on the bilateral exchange rate with the DM. This resulted in two cumulative deflationary impulses for the non-DM European countries: a loss of competitiveness towards the non-European area, owing to the exchange rate appreciation *vis-à-vis* the dollar area; and a domestic deflationary impulse via the increase in the interest rate differential required to offset the downward pressure on the bilateral exchange rate exerted by a stronger DM.

They had to persevere in restrictive monetary policies, keeping interest rates high even when the rise in Germany's rate of inflation (resulting from the post-unification boom) eased the process of inflation convergence. In fact, Germany's policy to contain inflation was based on two decisions: it enabled the pressure from domestic demand to be eased by the external account without, however, renouncing the strong DM as an anti-inflationary device. Hence, further monetary tightening was needed to defend – through the inflow of capital – the value of the DM, which might otherwise have been jeopardized by the disappearance of the trade surplus. Thus, export-led growth in other European countries, induced by the rise in German domestic demand, might have been accompanied by tensions among the European currencies provoked by Germany's monetary policy. Determination to defend the exchange led the other countries to follow Germany along the road of monetary rigour, preventing them from taking full advantage of the German expansion by reflating their economies. With the post-unification boom over, the tight monetary policy resulted in a low level of domestic demand,[20] while endeavours to secure an export surplus were thwarted by competitive disinflations.

Thus we come to the conclusions we saw in the first part of the paper. Improvement in relative prices can be achieved only if one country reduces its prices (or their rate of increase) faster than its competitors. But, as Joan Robinson had already pointed out, when all countries are pursuing the same disinflationary policy, as in our case by pegging the exchange rate to the DM, individual attempts to reduce relative prices can lead only to a fall in the global demand. Moreover, if the anchor-country itself is successfully engaged in a disinflationary policy, it will keep the other countries in the condition of diminishing competitiveness and increasing unemployment. The country that is most successful in reducing inflation can achieve a competitive advantage, and attain the targets of a minimum inflation rate and a trade surplus, but within a context of increasing recession. The positive effects on net exports deriving from the improved competitiveness could then be wiped out by the worsening of the income effect.[21] These effects combined to determine increasing rates of unemployment throughout Europe.

In these conditions, it is difficult for *any single* country to find a way out of the global recession by policies of domestic demand management while defending the parity. As in the 1930s, the cure lies in abandoning the aim of stable exchanges, not so much for the sake of competitive advantages as, rather, to increase the degrees of freedom of domestic policy. Given the impossibility of reaching agreement on coordinated reflation policies, *coordinated* devaluations against the DM (or the unilateral appreciation of the DM), by easing the external constraint, could have opened the way to an expansion in domestic demand.[22] Rather than being competitive, these devaluations could have had a virtuous effect on the system as a whole. The expenditure-increasing effect due to domestic reflation could outweigh the competitive expenditure-switching effect due to devaluation. Given the weight of investment goods in total German exports, the income effects of a higher European growth rate could have outweighed the negative (price) effects of a real appreciation of the DM, so that Germany too could have benefited from a general expansion.[23]

In the 1980s the exchange rate was given the task of encouraging, through competitive disinflations, the restructuring of the economy and the upgrading of the structure of production. The conclusion that an easing of exchange-rate constraint is now indispensable for increase in the growth rate to resume does not imply that the exchange rate can solve 'deep-seated causes of disequilibrium'. Rather, it reflects the conviction that a process of industrial restructuring is best achieved in a context of growth, rather than deflation. It is on this point that Joan Robinson's warning is still most relevant today:

> The main reason for making exchange rates variable is not to correct the deep-seated causes of disequilibrium, for which, I have argued, more far-reaching policies are required, but simply to offset differences in the

cost structure of various countries. When Lord Keynes used to maintain that Bretton Woods was not the gold standard, but just the opposite, it was this that he had mainly in mind.

(Robinson 1966: 224)

NOTES

1 This work has benefited from helpful comments from Antonia Campus, Anna Carabelli and Andrea Ginzburg. The usual disclaimers apply. Financial support from the Italian National Research Council (NCR) and the Italian Ministry of University and Scientific Research (MURST) is gratefully acknowledged.

2 With the exception of the 1950 article, I intend to concentrate here on Robinson's pre-war writings on international economics.

3 See Eichengreen (1989).

4 See Nurkse (1944).

5 See Keynes' *Evidence to the Macmillan Committee* (Keynes 1981: 56). This task was made all the more difficult by the radical changes that had taken place in the mechanisms determining wages and prices at the turn of the century. On this point see Sylos Labini (1993).

6 Diverging interests made cooperation on a common exchange rate policy impossible. For instance, in addition to the problem of relative prices *vis-à-vis* its competitors, the UK faced a problem of absolute prices: a higher level of prices (in relation to money wages and nominal liabilities) was absolutely needed in order to deal with the debt problem. In contrast, the European countries had already partially or fully solved this problem, thanks to the inflation of the early 1920s. See Keynes (1982b: 278).

7 The USA had to raise the discount rate in the final months of 1931, following the devaluation of the pound. Domestic credit expansion (through open market purchases) in the spring of 1932 led to a loss of gold and was promptly suspended. In France, reflationary policies attempted by two successive governments (Flandin in November 1934 and Laval in April 1936) had to be reversed owing to loss of reserves. When opposition against deflation mounted and led to the victory of the popular front, in the 1936 spring election, '[a] new reflationary program was adopted. When its operation again compelled the authorities to choose between abandoning their recovery program and devaluing the currency, this time they opted for the latter' (Eichengreen 1989: 34).

8 On the prospects of having to resort to beggar-my-neighbour policies as last-ditch self-defence given the lack of international cooperation, see also Keynes, 'The Means to Prosperity': 'Currency depreciation and tariffs were weapons which Great Britain had in hand until recently as a means of self-protection. A moment came when we were compelled to use them, and they have served us well. But competitive currency depreciations and competitive tariffs, and more artificial means of improving an individual country's foreign balance such as exchange restrictions, import prohibitions, and quotas, help no one and injure each, if they are applied all round' (Keynes 1972: 352).

9 Reference to this problem was made by Keynes in his 'Notes for a Speech to the Political Economy Club' (11 November 1931). Having stressed the indisputable benefits accruing to UK competitiveness with the end of the gold standard, he continues: 'Would this benefit be lost if *everyone* came off gold? This raises a curious and important point often overlooked. Suppose every country had

simultaneously devalued 50 per cent including the creditor countries who are exerting the deflationary strain, the benefit would have been problematic' (Keynes 1982a: 14).

10 By comparing the increase in exports going to depreciating countries with those going to gold countries Harris finds that the increase in imports induced by the increase in general prosperity following devaluation far outweighs the protective effect of devaluation itself (Harris 1936: xxii–xxvi).

11 See Eichengreen and Sachs (1990), Eichengreen (1989, 1990), Broadberry (1989).

12 In the immediate aftermath of World War II, the economic pre-eminence of the United States was seen as particularly threatening for the smooth working of the international economic system. If the external equilibrium of all countries apart from the US was obtained with the USA at full employment, any reduction in the level of activity in the USA would have created a deficit elsewhere. If deficit countries resorted to measures aimed at reducing the deficit, unemployment would have been aggravated in the USA. Thus 'the policies which restore equilibrium "without resort to measures destructive of national or international prosperity" are policies which surplus countries, not deficit countries, can pursue' (Robinson 1966: 224).

13 The difference derives not only from the existence of obligations that are fixed in terms of home currency but, above all, from the fact that 'a fall in money wages is never spread evenly over all industries and relative prices inside the home country are never unaffected by it' (Robinson 1973b: 226–7).

14 With the system of fixed exchange rates of the 1960s, the German authorities' attempts to check inflation through increases in the interest rate led to capital inflows and a loss of control over money supply. Floating was the answer to the imported inflation of the 1970s.

15 See Carlin and Jacob (1989).

16 On this point see Simonazzi and Vianello (1994).

17 Note, however, that the larger the inflation differential, the greater the cost of disinflation, and the lower the growth rate of the economy, the stronger wage resistance is likely to be.

18 This model had been successfully pursued by Germany in the expansionary environment of the 1950s.

19 Deflation has been most severe in France and in the smaller Northern countries, where monetary restraint has been accompanied by fiscal discipline, while it has been less strict in Italy, where monetary restraint has been tempered by fiscal accommodation. This difference waned towards the end of the 1980s, when fiscal restraint became general, with the possible exception of post-unification Germany.

20 And in an increasing burden of debt, particularly onerous for those countries with a high debt/income ratio.

21 The French experience is emblematic. As a result of the deflationary policies and institutional reforms of the labour markets, the rate of increase in money wages fell behind inflation. The consequent increase in the mark-up and in profits did not lead to greater investment, but went to reducing corporate indebtedness and into foreign investments. The improvement in competitiveness led to an improvement in the external accounts, but was not sufficient to sustain employment. Among the European countries, France now has one of the lowest inflation rates and one of the highest unemployment rates. See Blanchard and Muet (1993).

22 It is worth stressing the need for a *coordinated* policy because a country pursuing

a devaluation policy in the context of serious world recession can expect only very limited advantages, while the risks for the system of sliding into competitive devaluations are indeed great.

23 At any rate, the need to avoid too large a loss of competitiveness on European markets would have shifted the burden of defending the parity within the EMS onto Germany's shoulders, and would have made German interest rate policy more observant of its partners' needs.

REFERENCES

Blanchard, O. and Muet, P. (1993) Competitiveness through Disinflation: An Assessment of the French Macroeconomic Strategy, *Economic Policy* 16: 12–66.

Broadberry, S. N. (1989) Monetary Interdependence and Deflation in Britain and the United States between the Wars. In M. Miller, B. Eichengreen and R. Portes, eds, *Blueprints for Exchange-rate Management*. London: Academic Press.

Carlin, W. and Jacob, R. (1989) Austerity Policy in West Germany: Origins and Consequences, *Economie Appliquée*, 42: 203–38.

Eichengreen, B. (1989) International Monetary Instability between the Wars: Structural Flaws or Misguided Policies? *CEPR Discussion Paper*, no. 348.

——— (1990) Relaxing the External Constraint: Europe in the 1930s, *CEPR Discussion Paper*, no. 452.

Eichengreen, B. and Sachs, J. (1990) [1985] Exchange Rates and Economic Recovery in the 1930s, *Journal of Economic History*, 65: 925–46; reprinted in B. Eichengreen, *Elusive Stability*. Cambridge: Cambridge University Press.

Harris, S. E. (1936) *Exchange Depreciation*. Cambridge, Mass.: Harvard University Press.

Keynes, J. M. (1972) [1933] The Means to Prosperity. In D. Moggridge, ed., *The Collected Writings of John Maynard Keynes*, vol. IX. London: Macmillan.

——— (1981) [1930] Evidence to the Macmillan Committee. In D. Moggridge, ed., *The Collected Writings of John Maynard Keynes*, vol. XX. London: Macmillan.

——— (1982a) [1931] Notes for a Speech to the Political Economy Club. In D. Moggridge, ed., *The Collected Writings of John Maynard Keynes*, vol. XXI. London: Macmillan.

——— (1982b) [1933] Shall we Follow the Dollar or the Franc? In D. Moggridge, ed., *The Collected Writings of John Maynard Keynes*, vol. XXI. London: Macmillan.

Nurkse, R. (1944) *International Currency Experience*. League of Nations, London: Allen & Unwin.

Robinson, J. (1937a) *Essays in the Theory of Employment*. London: Macmillan.

——— (1937b) Review of S. E. Harris, *Exchange Depreciation*, *Economic Journal*, 47: 699–701.

——— (1947) [1943] The International Currency Proposals, *Economic Journal*, 53: 161–75; reprinted in S. E. Harris, ed., *The New Economics*. London: Dobson.

——— (1966) [1950]. Exchange Equilibrium. In *Collected Economic Papers*, vol. I. Oxford: Blackwell.

——— (1973a) [1937] Beggar-My-Neighbour Remedies for Unemployment. In *Collected Economic Papers*, vol. IV. Oxford: Blackwell.

——— (1973b) [1937] The Foreign Exchanges. In *Collected Economic Papers*, vol. IV. Oxford: Blackwell.

Simonazzi, A. and Vianello, F. (1994) Modificabilità dei tassi di cambio e restrizioni alla libertà di movimento dei capitali. In F. R. Pizzuti, ed., *Pragmatismo, disciplina e saggezza convenzionale. L'economia italiana dagli anni '70 agli anni '90.* Milan: McGraw-Hill.

Sylos Labini, P. (1993) Long-run Changes in the Wage and Price Mechanisms and the Process of Growth. In M. Baranzini and G. C. Harcourt, eds, *The Dynamics of the Wealth of Nations*. London: Macmillan.

Part III

FOLLOWING MARX, KALECKI AND SRAFFA

9

JOAN ROBINSON ON MARX'S THEORY OF VALUE

Marco Lippi

Joan Robinson's contributions on economic and social Marxian theory can produce quite different feelings in the reader. In some cases it appears that she did not find sufficient interest and concentration to achieve a thorough insight into the conceptual and analytic apparatus of *Das Kapital*. In other cases, instead, I believe that her style as a historian of economic thought, consisting of a fairly ironic 'translation into prose' of major classic and neoclassical economists, is very effective. In particular, her method yields very interesting results for those *loci* of Marxian theory of value that are overloaded with aims and meanings, and that have been the foundation of so many orthodox developments. Moreover, although her rendering of Marx's thought is sometimes definitely inaccurate, Joan Robinson takes Marx's theory 'seriously' and gets into details of *Das Kapital* that many modern readers have completely overlooked. Not only does she discuss the main theme of labour value as a first step for the determination of the rate of profit; she also takes into consideration Marx's presentation of labour value as an autonomous principle at the opening of *Das Kapital*, labour value in socialist economic systems, issues such as the value of agricultural products or the production of value in the circulation of commodities. I believe that this attentive and detailed reading takes us a long way from the image of Marx as an intermediate step between David Ricardo and Piero Sraffa that we get from some neo-Ricardian interpretations.

I shall try to justify my preference for Joan Robinson as an interpreter of Marx, as compared first with Marxian orthodoxy, secondly with a mathematically sophisticated orthodoxy to which I shall return below, and finally with neo-Ricardian interpretations.

JOAN ROBINSON AND MARXIAN ORTHODOXY

By using 'translate into prose' for Joan Robinson's style of interpretation I wish to emphasize the contrast between her way of reading Marx and all the versions in which the complexity of the original text is kept, if not increased, rather than dissolved into a sequence of clear statements.

First of all, it should be recalled, Marx is rather a difficult author. His philosophical background is often mentioned as an explanation. However, a more direct explanation lies in the fact that Marx did not limit himself to building a science of capitalism, namely to establishing the specific laws of motion of capitalism. He wished at the same time to offer a theory of the self-consciousness of economic agents under capitalism. Moreover, in his view, capitalism was bound to give rise to a different and superior social system, in accordance with a necessary law regulating historical development.

Within this most impressive construction, labour embodied plays a multiplicity of roles. Naturally, labour embodied is the basis for the determination of prices and the rate of profit. This means, in particular, that labour values are not proportional to prices; they are not first approximations to prices nor are they ever presented by Marx as correct prices in special circumstances. However, in the first volume of *Das Kapital*, the only one published during Marx's life, labour value is presented through an argument that is completely autonomous from the price problem. As is well known, the labour socially necessary to produce different commodities emerges as the only quality that such different things have in common. For that matter, there are very important passages in Marx's writings in which labour value is presented as nothing other than the historically specific manifestation of a more general 'natural' law. In the same way, in my opinion, his idea of a general law influenced the strenuous defence of labour value against what Marx considered a blameworthy lack of firmness in Ricardo's thought.

Lastly, let me recall Marx's treatment of the value of agricultural products and circulation costs. As Joan Robinson clearly points out in *An Essay on Marxian Economics* (1966), Marx's arguments look more like consequences of a general principle than necessary steps aimed at understanding the actual phenomena taking place in real markets.[1]

These are the aspects of the Marxian theory of value that I had in mind when I said that labour embodied is overloaded with too many aims and meanings. Now, I think that a good definition of the Marxian orthodoxy may be the following. Marxian orthodoxy is the interpretation and constructive position in which those aspects of Marxian theory cannot be disentangled from one another. If any one of them falls, everything falls.

In my opinion, one of the most important founding fathers of orthodoxy was Rudolph Hilferding [1904] (Böhm-Bawerk 1949), who defended Marx's labour value from Böhm-Bawerk's (1949) attack by sticking to all of the labour-value aspects and functions. I would not even dare to speculate how many times since Hilferding the superiority of Marxian theory with respect to any other theory has been argued on the basis that Marxian theory gives an explanation not only of economic facts but also, and at the same time, of social and historical phenomena. And let me add that the argument has often been employed by authors ignoring even the most elementary statistics on capitalist systems, or by scholars hiding the weakness of their standpoint behind unnecessary mathematical intricacies.

Pointing out the distance separating Joan Robinson from Marxist orthodoxy is not even necessary. Rather, it would be interesting to measure this distance in the general context represented by the contrast between the Anglo-Saxon analytical approach and the persistence in continental Europe of the important influence of Hegelian idealism and faulty logic. Joan Robinson is interested in all aspects of Marxian theory, but not with the aim of keeping them together, as Marx did. On the contrary, she is interested in singling out what might be interesting for the construction of an economic model, what yields a historical characterization of capitalism, what could be useful to discuss socialist economies, etc.

The difference between Joan Robinson's point of view on Marx and economics in general and the above-mentioned 'mathematical orthodoxy' deserves some attention. Here I label as mathematical orthodoxy the work ranging from the countless transformations of values into prices to the various discoveries of a 'Fundamental Marxian Theorem', the measurement of the exploitation rate by means of Sraffa's standard commodity, etc. To make clear what I think about this branch of literature, I shall begin by quoting a beautiful passage by the mathematician Paul Halmos:

> The best notation is no notation; whenever it is possible to avoid the use of a complicated alphabetical apparatus avoid it. A good attitude to the preparation of written mathematical exposition is to pretend that it is spoken. Pretend that you are explaining the subject to a friend on a long walk in the woods, with no paper available; fall back on symbolism only when it is really necessary.
>
> (Quoted in Knuth 1984: 183)

Halmos is treating an issue in a very particular field here. He recommends parsimony in the use of symbols when presenting mathematical results. However, I think this recommendation can be extended to the use of mathematics in economics, and maybe to more general considerations.

As an example consider the following statement: if the rate of profit is positive then the rate of exploitation, as measured by the ratio of surplus labour to the labour embodied in the real wage, must be positive. This is the famous Fundamental Marxian Theorem.

For Marx this statement is utterly trivial, since profit is nothing other than redistributed surplus value. Joan Robinson is aware that Marx's redistribution does not lead to production prices (actually Joan Robinson does not take Marx's argument much into consideration), and of course she knew Sraffa's *Production of Commodities by Means of Commodities* (1960) when she was writing the Preface to the second edition of *An Essay on Marxian*

Economics in 1965. Her argument in the Preface is the following: prices are not proportional to values unless we make assumptions that are not warranted by economic reality. However, the statement that positive profits imply a positive rate of exploitation can be presented without even mentioning prices in a one-commodity economy, e.g. an economy in which corn is produced by means of corn and labour, and labour is paid in corn. Joan Robinson concludes:

> Now, it seems obvious that this analysis cannot be affected, in essence, by allowing for a variety of commodities. The commodities may be supposed to be sold at prices which yield a uniform rate of profit on all capital. This introduces some troublesome problems of measuring net output and the stock of capital, since relative prices will change with the real-wage rate, but it does not alter the main line of the argument.
>
> (Robinson 1966: vii)

To take 'parsimony' and 'translation into prose' first of all. There are aspects of a multi-commmodity economy that can be understood by resorting to a one-commodity simplification. I think that the effect of this way of reasoning on orthodox Marxists can be fully appreciated only by someone who has for some time been himself a priest in that church. This is the case with myself, as far as my recollection is concerned, few things would annoy orthodox Marxists more than such trivializations of value problems: 'Here we again have Robinson Crusoe's economies, about which Marx himself used to warn. How can you think you would understand a complex economic and social system such as the capitalist economy by resorting to a one-commodity model.'

To me, it is now evident that such orthodox reactions were almost always motivated by the lack of any experience in dealing with scientific problems, and therefore with the method consisting in first treating the simplest case and leaving to subsequent steps the introduction of all the complications. This having been established, I must also say that Joan Robinson could have written more on the point in an effort to obtain, perhaps, the effect of blocking the route to 'mathematical orthodoxy'. I am talking about the possibility of extending the one-commodity result to a multi-commodity model without losing clarity and parsimony. If there are many commodities, first of all we must assume that the system produces a surplus, i.e. that, for any commodity, the quantity produced is not less than the quantity employed as a means of production, and is greater for at least one commodity. This means assuming that the system is viable. We are also assuming for simplicity that the system is not 'traversing' from one configuration to another, so that some commodity might not be entirely reproduced. If under given prices all profits are non-negative and positive in at least one industry (notice that we do not need to assume a uniform rate of profit), then the aggregate profits can buy a portion of the surplus. This is equivalent to saying that aggregate wages cannot buy the whole surplus. As a trivial consequence, the labour embodied in the portion of the surplus bought by wages is smaller than the labour embodied in the whole surplus. The latter is equal to the new labour added to the labour embodied in the means of production; therefore the rate of exploitation is positive.

The only statement in the above reasoning that perhaps deserves a formula is the one asserting that labour embodied in the surplus is equal to the new labour added to the means of production. We have:

> Labour embodied in total production = Labour embodied in the means of production + Labour embodied in the surplus = Labour embodied in the means of production + New labour added.

The first equality is trivial, the second is the definition of labour embodied. As a consequence:

> Labour embodied in the surplus = New labour added.

As soon as the Fundamental Marxian Theorem has been presented in this way, namely according to the Robinson–Halmos style, the link between profit and exploitation emerges as rather trivial, first for Marx, secondly for the one-commodity model, and lastly for the multi-commodity model.

Moreover, in my opinion, exploitation does not need any labour measurement. I think that the core of Marx's definition is the following: exploitation of labourers simply means that they cannot command the whole surplus (command, not consume). The *differentia specifica* of capitalist exploitation with respect to feudal exploitation lies in the fact that, under capitalism, labourers do not yield a visible part of the product of their labour; rather, they sell beforehand the right to use their labour power, while the price of their labour power is determined by the reproduction costs. This implies, among other consequences, the illusion of a fair exchange.[2]

Naturally, I am not claiming that Marx's theory is indisputable. I maintain only that such a theory can be reformulated without even mentioning the concept of labour embodied. We are not interested in knowing how long labourers work in excess with respect to what is necessary to reproduce the means of subsistence, nor are we interested in whether such a calculation is possible. Rather, we are interested in the fact that, as soon as labourers sell their labour power (not the product of the application of the labour power), appropriation of a portion of the surplus by capitalists becomes possible. In Joan Robinson's words:

> First of all, Marx shows that the development of the capitalist system is founded on the existence of a class of workers who have no means to live except by selling their labour power.... The possibility of exploitation depends upon the existence of a margin between net output and the subsistence minimum of the workers.... This idea is simple, and

can be expressed in simple language, without any apparatus of specialised terminology.

(Robinson 1966: 17)

I have mentioned above the Marxian theory of wages, which is based on Ricardo's theory, modified in order to allow the inclusion of historical and social elements. I will not expand on this point. Let me observe only that the discussion about what determines wages does not naturally depend on acceptance or rejection of the labour theory of value. Lastly, I wish to recall that, in line with Joan Robinson's view that Marx's theories can be better appreciated by getting rid of labour value, most of *An Essay on Marxian Economics* deals with the theories of accumulation, employment, crises, monetary and real wage.

JOAN ROBINSON AND MARXIAN ORTHODOXY: CONCLUSIONS

Before I conclude on orthodoxy let me point out some cases in which Joan Robinson's analysis of Marx is definitely inaccurate. Neither in the *Essay* nor in the Preface does Joan Robinson show any interest in Marx's idea that profits result from a redistribution of surplus value, to the point that one may even wonder whether she has given it any thought. Let me recall that Marx assumed that the rate of exploitation was equal across industries; this was equivalent to assuming a uniform hourly wage, after reduction of different skills to simple labour. This is quite reasonable. Total surplus value, i.e. the sum of industry surplus values, was then redistributed in proportion to the magnitude of capitals advanced in order to achieve a uniform rate of profit. The ratios between profit and wage were therefore different across industries, although the ratios between surplus values and wages were uniform. The redistribution idea was proved wrong by Bortkiewicz [1907] (Böhm-Bawerk 1949) among others (but not by Böhm-Bawerk, who did not go much beyond insisting on the difference between prices and values). Nevertheless, it is not nonsense and deserves attention as an ingenious, though naive, attempt at solving a system of simultaneous equations. The point is completely missed by Joan Robinson, who insists in confusing the ratio between profits and wages with the ratio between surplus values and wages. Thus, creating a uniform rate of profit, competition necessarily causes different exploitation rates: 'The push and pull of competition then tends to establish a common rate of profit, so that the various rates of exploitation are forced to levels which offset differences in the ratio of capital to labour' (Robinson 1966: 17; see also the Preface: xi).

I think that other interpretative inaccuracies may be found in Joan Robinson's writings on Marx. Nevertheless, I believe that overall the 1942 *Essay on Marxian Economics*, the 1965 Preface to the second edition of *An*

Essay on Marxian Economics, and the 1950 comment on the volume edited by Paul Sweezy (Böhm-Bawerk 1949) in which the works on Marx's labour value by Böhm-Bawerk, Hilferding and Bortkiewicz are republished, contains arguments that could have been sufficient to free scholars interested in Marx's point of view from the curse of labour value.

First, the notions that are conveyed by the idea of capitalist exploitation do not require any measurement. For that matter, insistence on the labour measurement of exploitation implies a very poor understanding of Marx's thought. According to Marx, capitalism consists not in the appropriation and *consumption* of surplus product but in the allocation of most of it to accumulation and technical progress. Capitalism is bound to fall and to be replaced – but not by a system in which surplus product is given back to labourers so that they can individually decide what to do with it. On the contrary, socialism is a system in which surplus product is rationally and collectively employed. Like it or not, the heart of Marx's theory lies in the explanation of how crises are the inevitable consequence of capitalist systems and the prelude to the final crash. The explanation of fluctuations and crises is indeed the centre of Joan Robinson's interest in Marx's theory.

Secondly, after *Production of Commodities by Means of Commodities*, transformation of values into production prices becomes an exercise devoid of any interest. It should be recalled that, in Marx's transformation, labour value is needed to determine some crucial aggregate magnitudes (total profits, total capital, constant and variable) that remain invariant under the transformation (total value = total price). This is Marx's mistake: we can use labour embodied as a measure only of single commodities, not of aggregates (apart from particular cases that are void of economic interest). As a consequence, labour embodied is nothing other than a special physical measure of commodities, while the transformation of values into prices is a special presentation of the system of production prices. This is Joan Robinson's conclusion in her 1950 comment on Sweezy (here again, she pushes her criticism somewhat too far: the final page, where she claims that prices are the logical basis of values, is rather confused and decidedly mistaken).

In conclusion, apart from some inaccurate passages, Marx's interpretation by Joan Robinson consists of a very useful analysis of the function of labour values in *Das Kapital* and in the statement, which I fully share, that nothing important is lost if labour values are dropped. All the work trying to solve or restate the transformation problem is misleading and derives either from a misunderstanding of the role played by labour values in Marx or from an approach to Marx entirely dominated by fashion.

TAKING MARX SERIOUSLY: THE ULTIMATE ROOT OF ORTHODOXY

I mentioned Hilferding above as one of the most important orthodox defendants of labour values. This may be true, but only if we limit ourselves to considering the followers of Marx. I am convinced that Marx himself was responsible for the strenuous defence of labour embodied. Joan Robinson is in no doubt about it. Let me quote from her comment on Sweezy:

> Mr. Sweezy hints that this [i.e. assuming a uniform ratio between labour and capital] is how he would like us to take it. But it is not the way Marx looked at the matter. For him *value* and prices were important, and were connected with each other in a fundamental way. He did not think of exchange-values as a relationship between commodities which has no significance when the total of output is considered, but as a quality inherent in each of them – a quality analogous to weight or colour.
>
> (Robinson 1950: 360)

The same interpretation emerges in the long footnote to the *Essay*, already quoted, where Joan Robinson reports and criticizes Marx's distinction between labour that produces value and labour that does not (for instance, part of the labour necessary to circulation), and the determination of value for agricultural products as average labour embodied, instead of marginal.

In 1978, I claimed that the source of the rigid orthodoxy that we have known must be found in Marx himself, and in particular in the fact that Marx, unlike Ricardo, established the identification of value and labour not as a mere instrument for the theory of prices. My arguments were partly similar to Joan Robinson's, and partly based on other important passages in Marx's works. I would observe incidentally that, in spite of my explicit intention, some othodoxy can be clearly detected in my book. Indeed, I do not find any mention of Joan Robinson's work in it: either I had not even read it or I must have considered Joan Robinson too extraneous to Marxism to be taken into consideration.

Naturally, this is not the place to go back to my arguments. Rather, I wish to compare the interpretation of Marx that I am attributing to Joan Robinson with two neo-Ricardian interpretations. I shall consider two passages by Maurice Dobb and Pierangelo Garegnani respectively. Let me begin by quoting from Dobb:

> It will be clear . . . that the nature of his approach required him to start from the postulation of a certain rate of exploitation or of surplus-value . . .; since this was *prior* to the formation of exchange-values or prices and was not derived from them. In other words, this needed to be expressed in terms of production, *before* bringing in circulation and exchange. How then to express the rate of surplus-value as initial *datum*? It would not have been satisfactory to express it in terms that

> were themselves relative to changes in the ratio itself. It could have been expressed, as we have seen that Ricardo initially did, in terms of a single commodity such as Corn, thus rendering it a *product*-ratio unaffected by changes in exchange-value or prices. Alternatively, if the notion had been invented by then, it could have been in something like Sraffa's standard composite commodity.... But much better for his immediate purpose than a single commodity... was its expression in terms of Labour.... The rate of exploitation could then be unambiguously expressed as a ratio between two quantities of (average) labour, as well as the source of surplus-value being simultaneously revealed. If things were exchanged in proportion to labour expended, changes in this rate could not *per se* affect relative exchange-values, nor could changes in the latter react upon the exploitation-ratio when represented in this way.
> (Dobb 1973: 148)

Here Dobb disentangles a very important function of labour embodied, which makes it different from measurement in any commodity taken as a standard. Labour embodied measures the crucial aggregates invariantly with respect to changes in distribution. However, I believe that, if Marx had adopted labour embodied to measure the exploitation rate without being certain that labour embodied would have led to the determination of prices and the rate of profit, he would not have deserved any attention from economists. This implies that Marx's labour values cannot be taken as a development of Ricardo's corn. In fact, if a corn–corn industry existed, we could determine both the rate of exploitation and the rate of profit within that industry, and no price problem would arise. In Marx's construction, instead, labour embodied leads to the measurement of the exploitation rate; however, the whole building stands or crashes according to whether the Volume III solution to the price problems stands up.

One could argue that Marx deemed that his solution – the calculation of the profit rate by means of the redistribution of surplus value – was warranted. If so, why not give it immediately, in Volume I? Why not make it clear at the beginning that labour values were an auxiliary instrument? Why, on the contrary, was value introduced in Volume I by an autonomous argument, without even mentioning the measurement problem on which Dobb insists? And why – if value was introduced only to carry out a measurement function – was the treatment of circulation costs and the value of agricultural products based on arguments that bear no relationship to any measurement problem? Lastly, why not use the first criticisms of *Das Kapital* to clarify the nature of labour values as mere instruments? On the contrary, in a much-quoted letter to Kugelmann, Marx gave an even stronger version of labour value as a self-sufficient principle with respect to *Das Kapital*.

For that matter, in Dobb's elegant chapter on Marx we find no mention of the argument of Volume I. By contrast, Joan Robinson takes it very seriously, even though she is in sharp disagreement. For Joan Robinson, what Marx really meant about labour values is first of all what he wrote in his published work. I fully agree.

Let me now quote and comment on a passage by Pierangelo Garegnani:

> the labour-theory of value played essentially the same role in Marx as it did in Ricardo. This role was to determine the rate of profit (and hence relative prices) thus overcoming the inconsistencies and ambiguities of Adam Smith and his immediate followers in the only manner which the state of theoretical development allowed at the time. In the phrase often used by Marx, the role of that theory of value was to reveal the '*inner connection* ... of the bourgeois system' – i.e. the 'inverse relation between the wage and the profits of capital', which shows how 'the interests of capital and the interests of wage labour are diametrically opposed' – in contrast with the '*apparent connection*' we witness in Adam Smith when he 'constructs the exchange value of the commodity from the values of wages, profit and rent, which are determined *independently* of one another'.
>
> (Garegnani 1981: 55–6)[3]

In spite of a considerable difference between this presentation and Dobb's, I think that the argument raised against Dobb applies here as well. There is no doubt that the role of the labour theory of value stressed by Garegnani was a most important aim in Marx's construction, and the most important from our point of view. However, the argument provided in Volume I of *Das Kapital* for labour values, and insisted upon in many other *loci* of his work, was completely autonomous from the 'inverse relation'. Therefore, even if the latter must be considered as the centre of a modern economic theory based on classical and Marxian thought, the stubborn defence of labour values cannot be taken as a weakness of the followers, but is a consequence of a mistake deeply rooted in Marx himself.

NOTES

1 On agricultural products and circulation costs, see the footnote to p. 20 and the Preface to the second edition, dated 1965 (Robinson 1966). For a discussion of labour values in socialist systems see the Appendix to Chapter III and the Preface.

2 The fact that under joint production the paradox of a negative rate of exploitation may occur (see Steedman 1977: 177) should have been a major stimulus to get rid of labour embodied.

3 The translation from the Italian text has been provided by Pierangelo Garegnani; the quotations are, in order, from *Theories of Surplus Value* (vol. II, London, 1968: 165), *Capital and Wage Labour* (in Marx and Engels, *Selected Works*, vol. I, London, 1950: 90), *Theories of Surplus Value* (vol. II: 217); italics by Garegnani.

REFERENCES

Böhm-Bawerk, Eugen von (1949) [1896]. *Karl Marx and the Close of his System*; Rudolf Hilferding. *Böhm-Bawerk's Criticism of Marx* [1904]; Ladislaus von Bortkiewicz. *On the Correction of Marx's Fundamental Theoretical Construction in the Third Volume of Capital* [1907], edited with an Introduction by Paul M. Sweezy. New York: M. Kelly.

Bortkiewicz, L. von (1949) [1907] *On the Correction of Marx's Fundamental Theoretical Construction in the Third Volume of Capital*; in Böhm-Bawerk, E. von, *Karl Marx and the Close of his System*, edited by P. M. Sweezy, New York: M. Kelley.

Dobb, M. (1973) *Theories of Value and Distribution since Adam Smith: Ideology and Economic Theory*. Cambridge: Cambridge University Press.

Garegnani, P. (1981) *Marx e gli economisti classici*. Turin: Einaudi.

Hilferding, R. (1949) [1904] *Böhm-Bawerk's Criticism of Marx*; in Böhm-Bawerk, E. von, *Karl Marx and the Close of his System*, edited by P. M. Sweezy, New York: M. Kelley.

Knuth, D. (1984) *The TeXBook*. Reading, Mass.: Addison Wesley.

Lippi, M. (1978) *Value and Naturalism in Marx*. London: New Left Books.

Robinson, J. (1966) *An Essay on Marxian Economics*, 2nd edn. London: Macmillan.

——— (1950) Review of E. Böhm-Bawerk, *Karl Marx and the Close of His System*; R. Hilferding, *Böhm-Bawerk's Criticism of Marx*; L. Bortkiewicz, *On the Correction of Marx's Fundamental Theoretical Construction in the Third Volume of Capital* (ed. by P. M. Sweezy), *Economic Journal*, 60: 358–63.

Sraffa, P. (1960) *Production of Commodities by Means of Commodities*. Cambridge: Cambridge University Press.

Steedman, I. (1977) *Marx after Sraffa*. London: New Left Books.

Sweezy, P. M., ed. (1949) Eugen von Böhm-Bawerk, *Karl Marx and the Close of His System* [1896]; Rudolph Hilferding, *Böhm-Bawerk's Criticism of Marx* [1904]; Ladislaus von Bortkiewicz, *On the Correction of Marx's Fundamental Theoretical Construction in the Third Volume of Capital* [1907]. Edited with an Introduction. New York: M. Kelley.

10

JOAN ROBINSON ON NORMAL PRICES (AND THE NORMAL RATE OF PROFITS)[1]

Fernando Vianello

In 1962 Joan Robinson published an essay entitled 'The Basic Theory of Normal Prices' (Robinson 1962a), which was reprinted in the same year – with the title of *Normal Prices* (Robinson 1962b) – as the first of her *Essays in the Theory of Economic Growth* (Robinson 1962c). The prices referred to in the essay are those appearing in Piero Sraffa's (1960) price equations. Adding to these equations the idea that the rate of profits 'is determined by the rate of accumulation of capital' (Robinson 1962b: 12) is Joan Robinson's way of 'closing the system' (ibid.: 11). 'Postulating a real-wage rate governed by conventional standard of life' was Ricardo's and (less consistently) Marx's (ibid.). As to Sraffa, he allegedly 'offers no observation on the subject' (ibid.). His view of the rate of profits as 'susceptible of being determined from the outside of the system of production, in particular by the level of the money rates of interest' (Sraffa 1960: 33) is not mentioned.

In this paper I wish to analyse, in order, (1) the concept of normal prices and the related concept of the *normal rate of profits* (Robinson 1962b: 11); (2) Joan Robinson's view of normal prices and the normal rate of profits as the (market) prices and the uniform rate of profits obtaining 'in a state of tranquillity, when expectations are realised' (Robinson 1962b: 8), i.e. in economies growing in steady-state conditions; (3) the concept of the *realized rate of profits*, put forward by Joan Robinson in another of her *Essays* (Robinson 1962d: 29), and the determinants of this rate (which are by no means the same as those of the normal rate of profits); (4) the misleading nature of the steady-state assumption, which rules out the possibility of over- and under-utilizing productive capacity; once this possibility is allowed for, I shall maintain, the existing wage and its corresponding normal rate of profits turn out to be compatible with the pace at which accumulation happens to be carried on, however fast or slow it may be.

THE NORMAL PRICE AS THE PRICE NECESSARY TO BRING THE COMMODITY REGULARLY TO MARKET

Normal prices are those prices that Adam Smith calls 'natural prices', or 'prices of free competition' (Smith 1961, bk. 1, ch. 7: I, 62 and 69). According to Smith, the natural price, which affords no more than the 'ordinary or average' rate of profits, is 'the lowest [price] at which [a dealer] is likely to sell [his goods] for any considerable time; at least where there is perfect liberty, or where he may change his trade as often as he pleases' (ibid.: I, 62 and 63). Malthus expresses the same concept by describing the natural price as 'the price necessary . . . to bring the commodity regularly to market', or 'the necessary condition of the supply of the object wanted' (Malthus 1951: 49 and 53). The idea of the natural price (or 'price of production') as the 'necessary condition of the supply' is taken up by Marx (1981: 300), who also refers to the price of production as 'the guiding light of the merchant or the manufacturer in every undertaking of a lengthy nature' (Marx 1976: 269, n24). This should be taken in the sense that investors are not prepared to buy capital goods and to employ them in a particular trade unless they are satisfied that over the relevant time-span they will receive no less than the normal rate of profits on the value of investment.

Thus, Joan Robinson has good reason to associate Marx's price of production (and, indeed, Smith's natural price) with Marshall's 'normal long-run supply price' (Robinson 1962b: 8), which is that price 'the expectation of which is sufficient and only just sufficient to make it worthwhile for people to set themselves to produce that aggregate amount' (Marshall 1964: 310) – an association that loses none of its significance on account of the fact that the idea of a downward-sloping demand curve, and thus the idea of an equilibrium price determined by the intersection of this curve with the supply curve, are quite alien to the approach of the classical economists and Marx.

If we take the normal price as the price necessary to bring the commodity regularly to market – or the price the expectation of which over the relevant time-span is just sufficient to make a particular trade attractive to investors – and if we allow for the existence of durable instruments of production, then it becomes apparent that the normal price is the price affording the normal rate of profits *when the commodity is produced with the normal method of production*, i.e. with the method that utilizes the capital goods normally purchased by investors and produced in the respective industries. Along with those capital goods there may be newly devised ones, affording an opportunity for extraordinary profits (which are doomed to cease once the new method of production has become normal), and others that, 'having been in active use in the past, have now become superseded but are worth employing for what they can get' (Sraffa 1960: 78). To this it must be added that the price and the rate of profits the expectation of which is regarded as just sufficient to make a trade attractive to investors cannot be conceived of as implying a degree of capacity utilization different from the *normal*, or *desired* one, i.e. from *the rate of capacity utilization planned by investors* (particularly – though not only – in the light of the expected fluctuations of demand; see Steindl 1977: ch. 2 and Ciccone 1986: 26–32).

Clearly, where competition is unrestricted, the market price of a commodity will not be allowed to stay either permanently above or permanently below that price the expectation of which is just sufficient to make the producing industry attractive to investors – and to make it worthwhile to replace the capital goods that reach the end of their economic life.

JOAN ROBINSON'S VIEW OF NORMAL PRICES AND THE NORMAL RATE OF PROFITS AS PERTAINING TO ECONOMIES GROWING IN STEADY-STATE CONDITIONS

Joan Robinson appears to regard the concept of normal prices and that of the normal rate of profits as devoid of any meaning unless commodities are actually sold at normal prices and a uniform rate of profits actually obtains all over the economy (see Ciccone 1984: 101–2; 1986: 21), as can happen only if 'there has been correct foresight in the past about what today would be like, so that the composition of the stock of capital today is appropriate to . . . the composition of output obtaining today' (Robinson 1962b: 16). Accordingly, she confines the analysis of normal prices and of the normal rate of profits to the case of economies set on a steady-state path, along which the productive capacity installed in each industry and the demand for the corresponding product keep growing *pari passu*.

This is at variance with her own qualification of normal prices as normal long-run supply prices, since the significance of the latter prices and of the rate of profits entering them (the normal rate of profits) is not impaired by the fact that commodities are not usually sold at such prices, or that the normal degree of capacity utilization usually fails to prevail all over the economy. However high or low the market price of a commodity or the degree of capacity utilization obtaining in the producing industry may in fact be, the normal price and the normal rate of profits retain their quality of being the lowest price and, respectively, the lowest rate of profits the expectation of which is regarded by investors as sufficient to make it worthwhile to employ capital in production.

The normal rate of profits is also the rate actually expected (as a rough approximation) over the relevant time-span by an investor employing the normal method of production and not anticipating persistently high or low market prices for the commodity produced or those used up in production – nor buying the plant at an exceptionally high or low price. (As to the expected rate of capacity utilization, it should not be forgotten that, since it is the investors themselves who decide on the amount of productive capacity to be installed, they cannot expect such capacity to be systematically over- or under-utilized. Indeed, the future degree of capacity utilization is a question not of expectation but of requirement and planning. See above and Vianello 1989: 174–5 and 180.)

REALIZED VS. NORMAL RATE OF PROFITS

The 'realized', or 'current', rate of profits is defined by Joan Robinson as 'the ratio of current gross profits, minus depreciation, to the value of the stock of capital at current replacement costs' (Robinson 1962d: 29). In order to give this 'vague and complex entity' (ibid.: 29) a somewhat more precise and simpler form, I shall assume that only one method of production is used in each industry, that the capital goods employed do not wear out with use, that they are confidently expected not to become obsolete and that they are commonly valued at their normal prices. The realized rate of profits can then be expressed as P/K, where P denotes the amount of profits realized in the economy and K the value of the economy's capital at normal prices.

As shown by Kalecki (1954: ch. 3), if profits are entirely saved and wages entirely spent on the purchase of consumer goods, then (in a closed economy where both government expenditure and taxation are negligible) the amount of profits received in the economy is equal to the value of the current output of capital goods ($P = I$). It follows that the realized rate of profits is equal to the rate of accumulation of capital ($P/K = I/K$). (If capitalists save a proportion $s_c < 1$ of their profits, it will be $s_cP/K = I/K$. The discussion that follows can easily be adapted to this more familiar hypothesis.)

Consider a simplified, two-industry economy in which all the assumptions made above hold good. As in John Hicks' well-known example (Hicks 1965: ch. 12), one of the two industries produces a number of tractors, T, and the other a quantity of corn. Let T_t and T_c be the number of tractors employed in the tractor and corn industry, respectively, tractors being the only means of production in both industries. The quantities produced can be increased and decreased both through changes in the degree of capacity utilization (which leave output per unit of labour unaffected) and through changes in the productive capacity installed. The relationship between the wage in terms of corn, w, and the normal rate of profits, r, holding in the simplified economy is the one represented graphically by the curve shown in Figure 10.1.

Initially the wage is equal to Ow_1 and the normal rate of profits to Or_1. All tractors are operated normally and products sell at normal prices. The realized rate of profits, equal to the rate of accumulation, is also equal in this case to the normal rate of profits, or

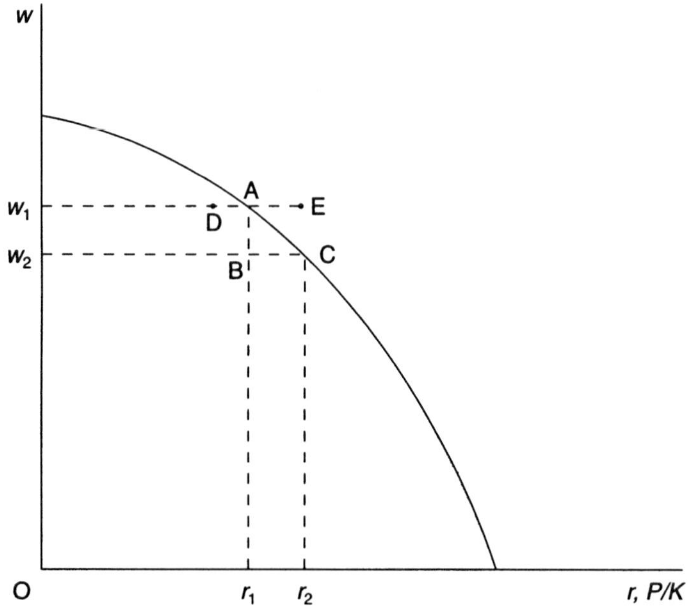

Figure 10.1 Relationship between the wage in terms of corn (w) and the normal rate of profits (r). Points A, B, C, D and E refer to the realized rate of profits (P/K), which is measured on the horizontal axis alongside r

$$\frac{P}{K} = \frac{T}{T_t + T_c} = r.$$

Point A in Figure 10.1 shows the realized (and normal) rate of profits corresponding to the wage Ow_1 in the above-described situation. Suppose now that the wage falls from Ow_1 to Ow_2, the reduced demand for corn resulting in lower employment and in a lower-than-normal degree of capacity utilization in the corn industry. As the number of tractors employed in the two industries, T_t and T_c, and the number of tractors produced, T, remain unchanged, the realized rate of profits remains equal to Or_1 (point B) although the normal rate of profits has risen to Or_2. This constancy of the realized rate of profits in the overall economy results from a rise in the profits obtained in the tractor industry – where tractors continue to be run at their normal degree of capacity utilization – and an equivalent fall in the profits obtained in the corn industry.

THE NORMAL RATE OF PROFITS AND THE RATE OF ACCUMULATION OF CAPITAL: THE SHORTCOMINGS OF THE STEADY-STATE ASSUMPTION

In a previous paper (Vianello 1985) I proposed describing as a 'fully-adjusted situation' a situation such as the one in which the simplified economy referred to above finds itself before the fall in the wage; namely, a situation in which all tractors are operated normally and products sell at normal prices. Departing from the premises of that paper (which have been convincingly criticized by Committeri 1986), here I am not maintaining that sooner or later the tendency to produce under normal conditions will necessarily prevail, so that the economy – after having shifted from the original fully adjusted situation to a situation characterized by the under-utilization of productive capacity in the corn industry – will eventually move to a new fully adjusted situation. What I am asking the reader is simply to concede, for the sake of argument, that such a situation is reached by accident after a certain period of time (say, ten years), the wage having remained equal to Ow_2. If a tractor operated normally continues to be manned with the same number of workers and to produce the same number of tractors or the same quantity of corn as in the original fully adjusted situation, both r and P/K will be equal to Or_2 (point C in Figure 10.1).

The equation on the previous page may be conveniently rewritten as

$$\frac{P}{K} = \frac{\dfrac{T}{T_t}}{1 + \dfrac{T_c}{T_t}} = r,$$

thus making apparent that, because the T/T_t ratio has remained unchanged, the $T/(T_t + T_c)$ ratio and the realized rate of profits must have been brought into line with the new, higher, normal rate of profits by a fall in the T_c/T_t ratio. This shows that the rate of accumulation observable in a fully adjusted situation tells us nothing about the speed at which accumulation is actually being carried on. Indeed, the higher rate of accumulation observable in the new fully adjusted situation implies not that the stock of capital is now growing faster than before, but only that – owing to the lower wage in terms of corn – the corn industry has fallen in size relative to the tractor industry.

Let us turn, now, to the case of *continuous* full adjustment, or, in more familiar terms, of steady-state growth. In our simplified economy continuous full adjustment requires that T and $(T_t + T_c)$ keep growing *pari passu*, as can happen only if both grow at the fully adjusted, or 'warranted', rate r (and the same must be true of T_t and T_c taken separately). As long, then, as one confines oneself to comparing different steady-state paths, it comes as no surprise that one finds that faster (slower) accumulation goes hand in hand with a higher (lower) normal rate of profits and a lower (higher) wage.

The ultimate reason for this lies in the fact that, thanks to the steady-state assumption, a definite relationship comes to be established between the rate of accumulation and the T_c/T_t ratio – and between the latter and the wage. This is the same relationship we have arrived at above by comparing two fully adjusted situations. The difference is, however, that – whereas the rate of accumulation observable in a fully adjusted situation was shown to have nothing to do with the speed at which accumulation is carried on through time – *accumulation is now assumed to be actually carried on at the fully adjusted rate peculiar to each steady-state path.*

In order to elucidate further the misleading nature of the above assumption, let us go back to the beginning of the story, when the economy found itself in a fully adjusted situation belonging to the family of such situations described by point A in Figure 10.1. Suppose that, were accumulation carried on at the fully adjusted rate $r = Or_1$, the stock of capital ($T_t + T_c$) would double in size in ten years' time. If the inducement to invest is weaker than required to keep the economy growing at that rate, so that after ten years the stock of capital turns out to have less than doubled in size, what one can reasonably expect to have happened is that, with the normal rate of profits and the 'warranted' rate of growth remaining unchanged, productive capacity has been under-utilized and P/K has been lower than r for at least a part of the decade. Point D in Figure 10.1 illustrates the case of $P/K < r$ with $w = Ow_1$. But the above argument is compatible with a temporary fall in the price of corn relative to the money wage due to a delay in reducing the level of output, as well as with a temporary rise in the price of corn relative to the money wage, as might result from the attempt to 'protect' profits from the negative consequences of the fall in output (see Kalecki 1954: 17).

Suppose once more that the tendency to produce under normal conditions prevails, leading the economy back to point A, namely to a fully adjusted situation characterized by the same w and r as the situation at the outset. In the new fully adjusted situation the $T/(T_t + T_c)$ ratio is again equal to the fully adjusted rate of accumulation $r = Or_1$. This, however, should not be taken to mean that the stock of capital is growing at the same speed as ten years before, but that the cumulative effect of the lower investments made along the way happens to have been such that T and ($T_t + T_c$) *fall short by the same proportion* of the level they would have reached had the economy grown all the time at the fully adjusted rate.

Obviously, there is nothing wrong with tying the economy to never over- or under-utilizing productive capacity, and with investigating the constraints that this condition imposes on the relative size of the consumer goods sector, and through it on the wage and the normal rate of profits – providing, however, that this innocent exercise does not mislead one into disregarding the fact that the possibility of over- and under-utilizing productive capacity is an all-important feature of real-world economies, and into maintaining that in the real world slower accumulation entails a higher real wage. (Which is what Joan Robinson claims when writing: 'Whatever the ratio of net investment to the value of the stock of capital may be, *the level of the prices* [relative to the money wage] *must be such as to make the distribution of income such* that net saving per unit of value of capital is equal to it' – Robinson 1962b: 11–12; italics added.)

The situation resulting from an inducement to invest stronger than required to keep the economy growing at the fully adjusted rate r is symmetrical to the one considered above (the case of $P/K > r$ with $w = \text{O}w_1$ is illustrated by point E in Figure 10.1) whenever over-utilization of productive capacity in the corn industry can be relied upon in order to meet the increase in the demand for corn due to the increased production of tractors. It is only when a bottleneck is reached in the corn industry that the task of balancing savings (realized profits) and investment can no longer be discharged by the increase in the production of corn, and instead devolves – as claimed by Joan Robinson – upon the rise of the price of corn relative to the money wage. The fall in w cannot, however, but share the temporary character of its cause. As soon as the bottleneck is removed, the long-run factors affecting the wage or the normal rate of profits will reassert their influence.

Among these factors – which, in Joan Robinson's words reported at the beginning of this paper, provide a suitable way of 'closing the system' – I include both the 'conventional standard of life' (acting on the wage, mostly by setting a limit below which it cannot fall) and the 'level of the money rates of interest' (acting on the normal rate of profits), but not the 'rate of accumulation of capital', whose influence vanishes, as I have endeavoured to show, as soon as one achieves freedom from the steady-state assumption.

Indeed, if investors are assumed to choose the fully adjusted rate of accumulation (i.e. the steady-state path) that suits them best, then it is to the rate of accumulation that the task of determining the normal rate of profits is *ipso facto* entrusted. But what real-world investment decisions do in fact determine, year after year, is the *level* of investment, whose ratio to the stock of capital will usually be higher or lower than the fully adjusted rate of accumulation. Once this is recognized, it becomes apparent that the resulting pace of accumulation has no influence on the normal rate of profits (a temporary fall in the wage being, however, required, as pointed out above, whenever the productive capacity installed in the consumer goods sector proves insufficient to meet a rise in demand).

NOTE

1 I am deeply indebted to the editors of this volume for helpful collective criticism, to which Alessandro Roncaglia added further stimulating comments. I also

benefited very much from discussion with Antonietta Campus, Edward Nell and Annalisa Rosselli. Mistakes and deficiencies that may remain are my responsibility alone. Financial assistance from the Italian Ministry of University and Scientific Research (MURST) is gratefully acknowledged.

REFERENCES

Ciccone, R. (1984) La teoria della distribuzione nell'analisi di Joan Robinson, *Note economiche*: 99–123.

——— (1986) Accumulation and Capacity Utilisation: Some Critical Considerations on Joan Robinson's Theory of Distribution, *Political Economy. Studies in the Surplus Approach*, 2: 17–36.

Committeri, M. (1986) Some Comments on Recent Contributions on Capital Accumulation, Income Distribution and Capacity Utilisation, *Political Economy. Studies in the Surplus Approach*, 2: 161–80.

Hicks, J. R. (1965) *Capital and Growth*. Oxford: Clarendon Press.

Kalecki, M. (1954) *Theory of Economic Dynamics: An Essay on Cyclical and Long-Run Changes in Capitalist Economy*. London: Allen & Unwin.

Malthus, T. R. (1951) [1820] *Principles of Political Economy Considered with a View to their Practical Application*, 1st edn. In Piero Sraffa with M. H. Dobb, eds, *Notes on Malthus. The Works and Correspondence of David Ricardo*, vol. II. Cambridge: Cambridge University Press.

Marshall, A. (1964) [1920] *Principles of Economics*, 8th edn. London: Macmillan.

Marx, K. (1976) [1867] *Capital. A Critique of Political Economy*, vol. I. Harmondsworth, Middx: Penguin Books.

——— (1981) [1894] *Capital. A Critique of Political Economy*, vol. III. Harmondsworth, Middx: Penguin Books.

Robinson, J. V. (1962a) The Basic Theory of Normal Prices. *Quarterly Journal of Economics*, 76: 1–19.

——— (1962b) Normal Prices. In *Essays in the Theory of Economic Growth*. London: Macmillan, 1–21.

——— (1962c) *Essays in the Theory of Economic Growth*. London: Macmillan.

——— (1962d) A Model of Accumulation. In *Essays in the Theory of Economic Growth*. London: Macmillan, 22–87.

Smith, A. (1961) [1776] *An Inquiry into the Nature and Causes of the Wealth of Nations*, edited by E. Cannan. London: Methuen.

Sraffa, P. (1960) *Production of Commodities by Means of Commodities. Prelude to a Critique of Economic Theory*. Cambridge: Cambridge University Press.

Steindl, J. (1977) [1952] *Maturity and Stagnation in American Capitalism*. New York: Monthly Review Press.

Vianello, F. (1985) The Pace of Accumulation, *Political Economy. Studies in the Surplus Approach*, 1: 69–87.

——— (1989) *Effective Demand and the Rate of Profits: Some Thoughts on Marx, Kalecki and Sraffa*. In M. Sebastiani, ed., *Kalecki's Relevance Today*. London: Macmillan.

11

JOAN ROBINSON, PIERO SRAFFA AND THE STANDARD COMMODITY MYSTERY[1]

Giorgio Gilibert

'Our Women are Straight Lines'
(A. Square, *Flatland*, 1884)

The intellectual relations between Joan Robinson and Piero Sraffa are not an easy subject to deal with in a short space. They are two of the most prominent economists of our century, and they were close friends for over fifty years. This, together with various other factors, makes it particularly difficult to compare their respective works.

Sraffa did not particularly like writing. Indeed, his legendary conciseness, which has fascinated so many readers, has also contributed to persistent discussions about the 'true' meaning of his theory. Joan Robinson (JR) on the contrary, has been a prolific and impulsive author. Even if we take into account recyclings and overlappings, her books surely number more than a dozen, and her articles one hundred.

Sraffa worked untiringly on a text and would publish it only when it matched the extraordinarily high standards he set himself as regards the compactness of its exposition ant the tightness of its logic. JR liked provocative language and was fond of discussion: a remarkable intellectual honesty led her readily to admit any imprecisions and errors and, not infrequently, to change her mind about a whole argument. Significantly enough, her articles most often concluded with Postscripts and Post-postscripts – true corrections 'in real time' owing to the discussions that followed the submission and preceded the publication of the paper.

It seems therefore advisable here to trim the subject so that it becomes sufficiently narrow and clearly defined to allow a fruitful discussion. And I will begin by pointing out the topics that I shall not discuss.[2]

I will not deal with the pre-war writings. This obviously excludes an important topic such as 'the famous paper by professor Sraffa that was destined to produce the English [Robinsonian] branch of the theory of imperfect competition' (Schumpeter). But this is in fact a topic that has already been largely explored by historians of economic analysis.

I will not concentrate on the analytical ground that is common to our two authors regarding scientific interests and theoretical approach; a common ground that has justified frequent reference to an 'Anglo-Italian School' of political economy.

Equally, I will neglect those differences between her and Sraffa or the Sraffian disciples that have been underlined by JR herself: on the relation between the rates of profit and interest,[3] for instance, or on the meaning of the so-called pseudo-production function and the importance of the whole reswitching affair. Moreover, these topics form the subject of a separate paper.

What remains for us?

ROBINSON'S CORN MODEL

In the beginning – so the Annals of the Cambridge Controversies tell us – was Joan Robinson's famous 1953 paper on 'The Production Function and the Theory of Capital'. The fundamental point raised was that 'the value of the stock of concrete capital goods is affected by [the] rate of profit and the amount of "capital" that we started with cannot be defined independently of it' (1960a: 127)[4] – a fact that can lead to 'perverse' behaviours such as the capital-reversing phenomenon, described a few years later under the name of 'Ruth Cohen Curiosum'.[5]

JR has always readily acknowledged the Sraffian origin of her reflections on capital theory:

> it was not till I found the 'corn economy' in his *Introduction* to Ricardo's *Principles* that I saw a gleam of light on the question of the rate of profit on capital. This led to a new upheaval in ideas, comparable in excitement, though not in immediate practical importance, to the Keynesian revolution itself.
>
> (Robinson 1978: xvii; see also 1973a: 125)

She went so far as to maintain: 'For me the Sraffa revolution dates from 1951, the *Introduction* to Ricardo's *Principles*, not from 1960. The thought experiment is simple and robust – the corn model' (Robinson 1979b: 2).

These rather striking statements deserve some attention. The corn model is presented by JR as describing a one-commodity economy:

> When corn is the only wage good, and the corn-wage is given, the rate of profit on capital is determined by the technical conditions of production of corn. Output per man on marginal, no-rent land is a particular quantity of corn per annum; given the wage, the profit on employing a man is a particular quantity of corn. The investment required to employ a man is a quantity of corn in the barn after one harvest, sufficient to pay out the wage until the next harvest, along with the seed that is to be planted by a man (no other inputs are required).

> Then the corn profit per man over the corn invested per man is the annual rate of profit on capital.
>
> (Robinson 1979c: 132)

> Ricardo himself got lost when he departed from a one-commodity economy in which all inputs and outputs are quantities of corn.
>
> (Robinson 1979d: 212–13)

This model is highly suggestive, and certainly shows extremely clearly the working of a surplus theory of profits, as contrasted with the usual equilibrium theory.[6] However, it is difficult to see how it could lead to the arguments used by JR to question the possibility of finding a suitable unit for measuring capital, this being made of a heterogeneous collection of goods.

It is true that Sraffa mentions in his Introduction the difficulties we encounter in measuring the amount of capital, and quotes the following remarkable passage from a letter from Ricardo to McCulloch (21 August 1823): 'These capitals are not the same in kind . . . and if they themselves are produced in unequal times they are subject to the same fluctuations as other commodities. Till you have fixed the criterion by which we are to ascertain value, you can say nothing of equal capitals.'

But the argument appears in connection with the Ricardian search for an 'invariable standard of value' (§V of the Introduction) and not in connection with the corn theory of profits (§IV). We all know today that the corn model can be considered as a first step on the way towards the standard system, but we do have the benefit of *Production of Commodities* (1960), which was to be published years later.

And indeed JR's attitude towards the search for an invariable standard is not particularly enthusiastic:[7] 'Ricardo's theory of profits was not well understood until Piero Sraffa disinterred the simple "corn" model from the complications with which it was overlaid in the course of Ricardo's search for an invariable standard of value' (Robinson 1979c: 132). Moreover, when she describes the possible variation in the price of capital goods corresponding to changes in the rate of profit, she names the phenomenon 'price Wicksell effect': a rather questionable (though successful) term, from the historical point of view, if we keep in mind the letter of Ricardo just mentioned.[8]

SRAFFA'S CORN THEORY

JR's mistrust towards the importance (and meaning) of the search for a suitable standard of value is deep rooted and is common, with small variations, to other Cambridge economists. A closer examination of this attitude may prove interesting.

As we have seen – according to JR – the corn model describes a one-commodity economy. At first sight, this is inconsistent with the original

Ricardian proposition that 'it is the profits of the farmer that regulate the profits of all the other trades'.

But it could be easily answered that the corn industry is a sort of core of a multi-commodity economy, and that it is therefore analytically legitimate to consider it provisionally as a self-sufficient sub-economy. Using Sraffa's notation, we could write the following equation:

$$C_c p_c (1 + r) = C p_c,$$

where the wage, consisting of the corn necessary for subsistence, is included in the stock of corn advanced for production. The price in the equation proves the existence of other commodities in the economy, but does not play any role in the determination of the profit rate. Once r has been determined, we can easily calculate the relative prices, assuming a uniform profit rate.

Let us now consider the reference to the Corn Theory that can be found in *Production of Commodities* (Sraffa 1960): the idea 'is that of singling out corn as the one product which is required both for his own production and for the production of every other commodity... Another way of saying this, in the terms adopted here, is that corn is the sole "basic product" in the economy under consideration' (Appendix D).

Following this suggestion, we can rewrite the equation:

$$C_c p_c (1 + r) + L_c w = C p_c.$$

We can divide this by the price, *which is no longer pleonastic*:

$$C_c (1 + r) + L_c (w/p_c) = C,$$

where the wage does not necessarily *consist of* corn, but is *measured in terms* of corn. The relationship between r and w is *not* independent of prices, but depends on only one price, which can – so to speak – be sterilized by making it equal to unity. So the 'simple' corn model has landed us directly in the abstract realm of value standards.

A DIGRESSION ABOUT ACCOUNTING

Value accounting in an economic system means that every point in the k-dimensional commodity space has an image on a one-dimensional line passing through the origin. This mapping operation is performed by means of a system of weights.

In other, more familar, words, any point in the space – net output, capital, etc. – is a collection of items, which can be reduced to a common measure, or evaluated, by means of a system of prices. The common measure is its purchasing power in terms of a commodity, or basket of commodities, used as standard.

The choice of the standard of value is precisely the identification of one accounting line from among the infinite possible lines passing through the origin, in order to guarantee the accounting system certain desired characteristics. Only the unit of length along the line is really arbitrary. If the economist has no precise requisite in mind for his accounting system, he will probably be induced to consider the choice of the standard as an irrelevant matter. And out of laziness he will choose any coordinate axis as his accounting line.

We are now able to understand the full potentiality of the archetypal Corn Theory of Profits for Sraffa. It is definitely not a one-commodity model; because other (non-basic) commodities are produced and priced. Neither is it necessarily an economy with a one-commodity industry, in which the profit rate can be seen as a simple physical ratio between two homogeneous quantities. There is in fact no reason why wages should be spent on corn.

It is indeed a most ingenious example, in which the 'right' choice of the accounting line is immediately evident to the observer. Because we wish to obtain a simple, possibly linear, relation between wages and the profit rate, the right line is the corn axis. The ensuing accounting system is able to make the economy wonderfully 'transparent' to our eyes.

In general, we cannot make use of a Corn Theory of Profits; i.e. we cannot utilize a commodity axis as a suitable accounting line for our purposes. The standard system was devised precisely to identify in general the desired accounting line in the positive quadrant.

A NOTE

The peculiar way used here to present the problem of the standard of value may call to mind Goodwin's 'principal' or 'general' coordinates (other names, such as 'normalized' coordinates, are somewhat unfortunate because the axes – as it will be obvious – can no longer be orthogonal). But the two approaches do not coincide.

Goodwin suggests transforming the present system of coordinates by which we describe our commodity space into a new system of principal coordinates. In this new system, *k* different types of 'corn' (or of standard commodity) are measured on each axis, and we can use any coordinate axis as our accounting line. For every type of corn we can indeed write the following equation (in the notation that is usual for linear models):

$$l_i p_i (1 + r) + l_i w = p_i,$$

where l_i is the corresponding eigenvalue.

What we face here is a curious U-turn: the Ricardian corn example was used by Sraffa for singling out the general problem of finding a correct standard of value. The Sraffian solution – the standard commodity – is now used by Goodwin to reconstruct a sort of artificial corn economy that is valid generally.

The difference between the two approaches would be of a merely aesthetical character if the two problems could be proved to be equivalent, but they aren't. It can be shown that the conditions for the existence of a meaningful system of principal coordinates are much more restrictive than those usually required for the existence of one 'standard' accounting line in the positive quadrant.[9]

JOAN ROBINSON, PIERO SRAFFA AND THE STANDARD COMMODITY

In the three volumes that collect JR's economic papers written after 1960, the standard commodity is mentioned twice, but only once in some detail. This might seem surprising, given the great admiration attested by JR for the theory presented in *Production of Commodities*. After all, Sraffa dedicated, directly or indirectly, more than half of his efforts to the problem of the standard (that is, if we confine our attention to the part on single-product industries, the only one that really interested her).

But we have already noted the mistrust reserved by JR for the whole search for the standard. Let us consider how the subject is presented in her enthusiastic 1961 review of *Production of Commodities*:

> When the wage is not given by technical conditions, what do prices mean? A change in the division of the surplus between wages and profits alters relative prices. But we need to know the prices to value the surplus that is to be divided. This was the problem that flummoxed Ricardo.
>
> Sraffa's solution is ingenious and satisfying. He isolates those *basic* commodities which enter directly or indirectly into the production of all commodities and, from the technical equations which show how each enters into the production of the others, he constructs a standard of value in the form of a composite commodity into which each particular item enters, as means of production, in the same proportion as it appears as output.
>
> The beauty of this is that, as the wage reckoned in terms of this standard rises, the prices of some of the commodities composing it (in which wages are a high proportion of cost) fall, to just such an extent as to balance each other, and leave the ratio of the value of the surplus to the value of the means of production unchanged. This provides a technically determined ratio of surplus to means of production which is independent of the division of the surplus between wages and profits.
>
> (Robinson 1965: 10)

This exposition is not very felicitous for two reasons. First, the nature of the standard commodity as a unit of measure is neglected, and the stress is completely on its property of being produced in a surrogate one-commodity economy. On the other hand, it is misleadingly suggested that the choice of the standard commodity as numéraire does have something to do with a 'desirable' behaviour of prices (which 'balance each other'). This suggestion has led generations of (superficial) commentators – not JR, to be fair – to maintain obstinately and erroneously that, thanks to the adoption of the standard commodity as numéraire, the value of the surplus stays constant as distribution changes.

Seventeen years later, JR has become more impatient: 'Sraffa takes great trouble to provide a foolproof numeraire in which prices can be expressed, but the Keynesian wage unit serves as well' (Robinson 1979a: xx).

And finally, in her 'Spring Cleaning': 'The definition of the standard commodity takes up a great part of Sraffa's argument but personally I have never found it worth the candle' (Robinson 1985: 163).

CONCLUSION

This lack of understanding for the Sraffian (and Ricardian) search for an 'invariable standard of value' can be a useful clue to understanding (and an index for following) her increasing perplexity and even dissatisfaction with the operational meaning of Sraffa's equations.

At first, she seemed to interpret them as determining the equilibrium prices for a steady-state economy, during some metallic age. However, a quotation from the 1961 review reveals some uncertainty.

> We are concerned with equilibrium prices and a rate of profit uniform throughout the economy, but we are given only half of an equilibrium system to stand on. We need a fence to prevent us plunging off into the abyss. The author suggests as a helpful (but not necessary) provisional assumption that constant returns prevail. I, for one, found that this only made me all the more dizzy. It seems better to assume that changes in the share of wages do not affect the composition of output.
>
> (1965: 9)

However, it can equally be said that 'the system of prices of production (as set out by Sraffa) is a stylized picture of competitive capitalism' (Robinson 1973b: 57).

A few years later, Sraffa's prices are still equilibrium prices, but of a somewhat less tangible character. 'These models [von Neumann or Sraffa] are systems of equations expressing equilibrium relationships. They cannot be used to discuss the behavior of the human beings who inhabit them' (Robinson 1971: 72). 'The specification of a self-reproducing or self-expanding system such as that of Sraffa or von Neumann exists in logical time, not in history' (Robinson 1979c: 50).

The time is ripe for metaphors: 'In Sraffa's model . . . [we] are presented with, so to speak, a snapshot of a process of production going on in a particular industrial economy . . . These calculations must be regarded purely as an intellectual experiment' (Robinson 1979f: 64–5).

'The equations of production represent a formalized picture of a supposed actual economy, in which actual production is going on – as it were, an x-ray showing its bones' (Robinson 1979g: 285; see also 1973c: 118).[10]

These attractive metaphors (snapshots, intellectual experiments, etc.) were – as is well known – to become very popular, but they are of little use to overcome analytical difficulties. A snapshot, by its nature, records external reality, and the reality is made up of produced quantities, utilized inputs and current (market) prices. It is difficult to see how our snapshot can give a different treatment to quantities and prices.

In her last writings, JR eventually matured a clearer and more disenchanted attitude towards Sraffa's 'somewhat cryptic manner' of theorizing and towards his 'enigmatic book': 'Only in Sraffa's intellectual experiment does the rate of profits have an exact meaning, for it is a *postulate* of the system that prices are such as to make the rate of profits uniform over the whole value of capital reckoned at these prices' (Robinson 1979b: 7; italics in original).

> Sraffa did not need to ask whether his system was growing or not. Net output may or may not include some physical items to be added to stock, and the workers receive a share in the value of net output, not a supply of specific wage goods.
>
> (Robinson 1980: 66)

'Sraffa's model is too pure to make a direct contribution to formulating answerable questions about reality but it makes a very great contribution to saving us from formulating unanswerable questions' (ibid.: xii).

These are truly remarkable statements. Indeed, in the abundant and growing literature on Sraffa, it is difficult to find statements that express more clearly the purely logical nature of his contribution.

What Sraffa does is a sort of linguistic cleaning up, thanks to which the central notions of the theory of value are *defined* with the utmost rigour. Though important for the construction of an explanatory model, this operation does not coincide with the construction of the model itself.

It should be noted that for JR, who was so passionately interested in building models with the purpose of throwing light on the real working of capitalism, it was particularly difficult to accept this attitude.[11]

'This is where Sraffa leaves us and hands us over to Keynes' (Robinson 1985: 165).

POSTSCRIPT

The post-Sraffian literature shows a somewhat favourable disposition to the use of analogies and metaphors – snapshots, X-rays, virtual movements and gravitation centres being just a few instances. The most popular amongst these metaphors is probably the description of Sraffa's equations as a 'photograph of the system at a given moment of time'; and it was repeatedly used (under successive guises: snapshot, radiograph, etc.) by JR.

Professor Roncaglia, who twenty years ago originally invented this successful metaphor, has recently strongly argued that my criticism on the subject is misplaced. His proposal was merely intended to underline and illustrate the conclusions of a fully developed analysis. It cannot be denied that the use of metaphors and analogies is legitimate, and often very useful, for didactic and expository purposes.

Of course, I completely agree. I did not object to the use of metaphors as such, but only to their misuse in analysis, i.e. when they are utilized – more or less consciously – to disguise and conceal unsolved difficulties (a fault to which JR is not always immune).

The same point was made more than sixty years ago by Piero Sraffa in his 'negative and destructive criticisms' of Robertson's 'poetry' (intended to rehabilitate Marshallian orthodoxy):

> It is with some diffidence that I attempt to criticise Mr. Robertson's concluding paragraph; for the difficulties which he warns us to expect are not diminished, for students of economics, by the use he makes of analogies. At the critical points of his argument the firms and the industry drop out of the scene, and their place is taken by the trees and the forest, the bones and the skeleton, the water-drops and the wave – indeed all the kingdoms of nature are drawn upon to contribute to the wealth of his metaphors.
>
> (Sraffa 1930: 90–1)[12]

NOTES

1 I am grateful to Pier Luigi Porta and Alessandro Roncaglia for their stimulating comments and criticisms.

2 I should also add that I will not normally use arguments of a biographical or anecdotal character, not because I think these arguments to be necessarily irrelevant or even futile – on the contrary; simply, I have no special knowledge apart from what is already well known to scholars.

3 The concept – says JR – that the rate of interest governs the rate of profit is 'unnatural (though Sraffa himself flirted with it)' (Robinson 1979a: xxii).

4 'The student of economic theory . . . is hurried on to the next question, in the hope that he will forget to ask in what units *C* is measured. Before ever he does ask, he has become a professor, and sloppy habits of thought are handed on from one generation to the next' (Robinson 1960a: 114). But 'a quantity has no meaning unless we can specify the units in which it is measured' (Robinson 1960b: v).

5 JR convincingly argues the logical (and chronological) priority of the capital-reversing phenomenon with respect to reswitching: 'double switching is associated with perversity. The interesting point, however, is the perversity, not the duplicity' (1973d: 75).

6 'These essays [*On Re-reading Marx*] were written in a hilarious mood after reading Piero Sraffa's Introduction to Ricardo's *Principles* [Sraffa 1951], which

caused me to see that the concept of the rate of profit on capital is essentially the same in Ricardo, Marx, Marshall and Keynes; while the essential difference between these, on the one side, and Walras, Pigou and the latter-day textbooks on the other, – is that the Ricardians are describing an historical process of accumulation in a changing world, while the Walrasian dwell in timeless equilibrium where there is no distinction between the future and the past' (Robinson 1973e: 246).

7 Or very perspicuous: 'When you read *Absolute Value and Exchangeable Value* you get the funny feeling. What does this remind me of? And then you say: Of course – Volume I of *Capital* (though two prose styles could not be more different)' (Robinson 1973e: 250; see also 1960c: 51).

8 Of course, the explanation is that JR was influenced as much by reading Sraffa's Introduction as by discussions that preceded and followed its publication. We know that, as early as October 1936, Sraffa wrote a letter to JR explicitly arguing the inconsistency of the very concept of a quantity of capital, measured independently of distribution and prices. In another letter, to President Einaudi, written immediately after the publication of Ricardo's first volume (18 August 1951) he says he is on vacation in the Austrian Alps 'with other economist friends (Joan Robinson, Kaldor, Kahn)'; it is not difficult to imagine the subjects discussed.

9 The proof of this has been produced by Andrea Carboni (unpublished dissertation, Modena, 1992).

10 It can be observed that the transparency is here attributed to the equations and not, as in Sraffa, to the particular standard used to measure wages and prices.

11 Compare the incipit of her last 'model of accumulation and exploitation' (written with A. Badhuri): 'Piero Sraffa was completely successful in his aim of providing a basis for the critique of neoclassical theory but the model in *Production of Commodities* (1960) provides a very narrow basis for constructive analysis' (Robinson 1980: 64).

12 I am indebted to Alessandro Roncaglia for having reminded me of this delightful quotation.

REFERENCES

Robinson, J. (1960a) [1953] The Production Function and the Theory of Capital. In *Collected Economic Papers*, vol. II. Oxford: Blackwell.

——— (1960b) *Exercises in Economic Analysis*. London: Macmillan.

——— (1960c) [1954] The Labour Theory of Value. In *Collected Economic Papers*, vol. II. Oxford: Blackwell.

——— (1965) [1961] Prelude to a Critique of Economic Theory. In *Collected Economic Papers*, vol. III. Oxford: Blackwell.

——— (1971) *Economic Heresies*. London: Basic Books.

——— (1973a) [1970] Economics Today. In *Collected Economic Papers*, vol. IV. Oxford: Blackwell.

——— (1973b) [1968] Value and Price. In *Collected Economic Papers*, vol. IV. Oxford: Blackwell.

——— (1973c) [1971] The Relevance of Economic Theory. In *Collected Economic Papers*, vol. IV. Oxford: Blackwell.

——— (1973d) [1967] The Badly Behaved Production Function. In *Collected Economic Papers*, vol. IV. Oxford: Blackwell.

——— (1973e) *Collected Economic Papers*, vol. IV. Oxford: Blackwell.

——— (1978) *Contributions to Modern Economics*. Oxford: Blackwell.

——— (1979a) *The Generalisation of the General Theory and other Essays*. London: Macmillan.
——— (1979b) Misunderstandings in the Theory of Production, *Greek Economic Review*, 1: 1–7.
——— (1979c) [1974] Reflections on the Theory of International Trade. In *Collected Economic Papers*, vol. V. Oxford: Blackwell.
——— (1979d) [1978] Keynes and Ricardo. In *Collected Economic Papers*, vol. V. Oxford: Blackwell.
——— (1979e) [1974] History versus Equilibrium. In *Collected Economic Papers*, vol. V. Oxford: Blackwell.
——— (1979f) [1977] The Meaning of Capital. In *Collected Economic Papers*, vol. V. Oxford: Blackwell.
——— (1979g) [1977] The Labour Theory of Value. In *Collected Economic Papers*, vol. V. Oxford: Blackwell.
——— (1980) *Further Contributions to Modern Economics*. Oxford: Blackwell.
——— (1985) [1980] The Theory of Normal Prices and Reconstruction of Economic Theory. In G. R. Feiwel, ed., *Issues in Contemporary Macroeconomics and Distribution*. London: Macmillan; originally entitled 'Spring Cleaning'.
Sraffa, P. (1930) Increasing Returns and the Representative Firm. A Criticism, *Economic Journal*, 40: 89–93.
——— (1951) Introduction to vol. 1 of *The Works and Correspondence of D. Ricardo*. Cambridge: Cambridge University Press, xiii–lxii.
——— (1960) *Production of Commodities by Means of Commodities*. Cambridge: Cambridge University Press.

Part IV

GROWTH, DEVELOPMENT AND DYNAMICS

12

JOAN ROBINSON'S CONTRIBUTION TO ECONOMIC DEVELOPMENT

Siro Lombardini

JOAN ROBINSON'S SCIENTIFIC CURIOSITY

Let me report a personal anecdote that may help in understanding Joan Robinson's personality and rightly assessing the place of *The Economics of Imperfect Competition* (1933) in the development of her thought.

In the spring of 1949, when I was a student at the London School of Economics, I went to see her in Cambridge. I had submitted to her a note on the main points of my research on 'Monopoly'. There were two main points in it: the *rigidities* of monopolistic situations[1] and the *internal* factors of development that characterize a monopolistic firm, affecting the development of the entire economy.[2] As was her wont, she reacted strongly while I was trying to present my points. At the end she said: 'I realize, I am too Marshallian.' In 1951 I met Joan Robinson at the conference held by the International Economic Associations in Talloires (Haute Savoie) on 'Monopoly and Competition and Their Regulation'. Quite a few economists used to talk of 'Monopolistic Competition alias Imperfect Competition whose father is Chamberlin and whose mother is Joan Robinson'. That did not please Chamberlin and irritated Joan Robinson. Chamberlin was trying to *differentiate* his product from Joan Robinson's. According to Chamberlin, Joan Robinson had elaborated the theory of monopoly whereas he had produced the theory of a new market form overcoming the competition–monopoly dichotomy.[3] Joan Robinson, on the contrary, no longer identified with the theory of imperfect competition. She was striving to clarify problems of accumulation and economic development.

The most striking feature of Joan Robinson's personality was her curiosity – a curiosity that is the necessary vice of any real scientist. When considering what is labelled as scientific activity, we must distinguish *thinkers* from *technicians*. Joan Robinson was a thinker.

All of us start our research with some prejudices. The thinker always tries to discover them, in order to discuss them. For a thinker, economic theories are simply *tools*; thinking over the social system is a much tougher challenge than building and using formalized models. However, models are useful. *The Accumulation of Capital* (1969) was intended to offer new *tools*, their use being clarified in the *Essays in the Theory of Economic Growth* (1962).

THE TOOL OF 'IMPERFECT COMPETITION' FOR THE ANALYSIS OF ECONOMIC DEVELOPMENT

Robinson's aim in writing *The Theory of Imperfect Competition* was different from both Sraffa's and Chamberlin's. Sraffa tried to demonstrate the inconsistency of marginalist theories and revive classical theory. Thus he showed how the size of firms is set not by costs but by limitations imposed by demand in markets where products are differentiated. Chamberlin was trying to overcome the monopoly–competition dichotomy. The theory of perfect competition is not a theory of competition: the firms, all being price takers, do not compete with one another; they simply adjust supply (products being the same as supplied by other firms) according to signals coming from the market (prices). True competition results from inter-firm relationships that can be seen more easily when we assume product differentiation. Monopoly implies market power; competition, according to the definition above, destroys market power.[4] Thus, the most realistic assumption about market structure is *monopolistic competition*.[5] In contrast, Robinson was more inclined to think that, as a result of increasing returns and firms' strategies, only a few firms would remain in the market, whereas Chamberlin, emphasizing the role of product differentiation, was able to retain the assumption of a large number of firms, more akin to marginalist philosophy. Joan Robinson's approach is completely different.[6]

The main peculiarity of Joan Robinson's theory of market forms is her interest in the analysis of economic development. Market behaviour can affect development mostly through the effects on income distribution. According to Sraffa, marginalism appears to be incapable of explaining the interactions between price structure and income distribution even if we assume the economy to be composed of different industries producing homogeneous products.[7] In Joan Robinson's *The Economics of Imperfect Competition* (1933), neoclassical analysis appears inadequate since the normal structure of the economy is not the competitive one. When we think of a *world of monopolies*, a new link is established between market performance, income distribution and growth. The main effect of monopolies is labour exploitation, which depends on price elasticity for individual commodities: the lesser the elasticity, the greater the exploitation. In a world of monopoly, full employment may not be ensured; nor is competition a sufficient condition for the elimination of involuntary unemployment. In *The Economics of Imperfect Competition*, Joan Robinson still seems convinced that marginalism has something to say about technical efficiency (Robinson 1933: 316); she notes that, apart from the complications represented by Pigou's externalities, 'the optimum distribution of resources between industries is achieved under conditions of perfect competition' (ibid.). But this is a corollary of a theory that is just a tool. In a world of monopolies we cannot compare market structures with those of an ideal competitive world. As Joan Robinson pointed out, changes in market structures produce changes in income distribution, which affect the structure of demand (demand for products for the affluent is favoured) and therefore the structure of production. She is well aware that 'if technical economies can be gained from growth in the size of the firms the monopolies would reorganize industries in fewer and larger productive units and the average physical productivity of the factors would be increased' (ibid.: 321).[8] Assessment of a world of monopolies cannot be made in a static context. This is also Schumpeter's view. However, there is a difference. Schumpeter deals with oligopoly: oligopolistic competition is the engine of development. But the engine of development is not a subject for analysis in Joan Robinson's work. Development entails specific phenomena (capital accumulation being the central one) but it is too complex to be caged in *economic theory*. Personally, Joan Robinson was more interested in the cultural–social–institutional conditions for development, as is shown by her interest in the developments in China (see Robinson 1962: 94–116). But she felt it her duty, as an economist, to supply *tools* to those who wanted to venture upon thinking about development.

EFFICIENCY AND MARKET BEHAVIOUR

Eventually, Joan Robinson's interest in economic growth superseded her interest in market structures. It is for this reason that she never took Pareto optimality seriously. Joan Robinson was more interested in the efficiency of growth. In fact she was impressed by the golden rule: 'When the conception of the rate of profit determined by the rate of accumulation of capital and thriftlessness conditions is combined with the conception of a choice of techniques from a given spectrum of possibilities, it can be seen that the highest rate of output of consumption goods is achieved when the rate of profit on capital is equal to the rate of accumulation' (Robinson 1962: 120). Her final comments on the theorem show that for Joan Robinson we cannot frame the problem of efficiency while ignoring the problem of distribution.[9] In spite of the change of context, the most striking result of *The Theory of Imperfect Competition* still applies.[10]

ASYMMETRIES IN ECONOMIC GROWTH

New tools were provided by Joan Robinson's *The Accumulation of Capital* to analyse the factors accounting for growth.

We have seen that Robinson seems to share some Schumpeterian views. She wrote: 'The persistence of competition must depend upon a tension between the desire for profit on the one hand and countervailing factors on the other, such as love of independence, mutual distrust, and so forth; and this balance may be essentially precarious' (Robinson 1954: 245). Anyway, competition is unstable:

> When a large number of firms are in competition, any one which gets a good start may easily knock out or absorb small neighbours; as the size of the survivors grows and their number is reduced the cost of further competitive warfare grows greater and its outcome less certain, so that industries often persist indefinitely with a few firms, none of which attempts to fight its way to complete monopoly.
>
> (ibid.: 246)

The marginalist tools that were still utilized in *The Economics of Imperfect Competition* have already become obsolete. Robinson criticizes some interpretations of *mark-up* theory by stressing certain asymmetries in the evolution of the economy. When demand increases, and the increase is not perceived as a temporary one, investment increases; for a certain interval of time the rate of profit increases; after investments have been completed, having, *because of competition*, overshot the target, there is a decline in profits.[11] When demand decreases, we do not have any such spontaneous reverse in the evolution of profits.[12] In an expansion, *mark-ups* are adjusted. If that does not occur, because expansion makes it possible to increase productivity and decrease costs, prices would decrease. But that is unlikely. 'Rather, it seems, the normal procedure is to maintain "full cost" at at least its old level, by taking the opportunity of conditions of strong demand to write capital off faster than was originally intended and by taking a more optimistic view than formerly about what rate of profit is "reasonable"' (Robinson 1954: 249). When the economy declines, entrepreneurs may abide by the *mark-up* theory. 'If each producer believes that prices ought to be maintained at the level corresponding to notional average cost, and if he believes that his competitors will act on this belief, then, in fact, the price will be maintained, and the disastrous losses predicated by the orthodox theory will be avoided' (Ibid.: 250).[13]

ACCUMULATION AND MONOPOLY IN THE EVOLUTION OF THE ECONOMY

Joan Robinson was among the few who clearly realized the difference between the equilibrium path and the Walrasian equilibrium, which is essentially static: in every period conditions are created – with regard to consumers' savings and firms' expectations – such as to make it possible for the economy to grow. An equilibrium path of development implies that equilibrium has been realized in all previous periods, so that it will occur in all future periods (alternatively we can say that an equilibrium path of growth requires specific initial conditions).[14] In point equilibrium, congruence among agents' decisions is assured only at the end of the period on the basis of the agents' expectations concerning successive periods. Initial conditions, too, depend on such expectations.[15]

To analyse how thriftlessness, capital and labour coefficients affect growth, we need to explore all possible equilibrium paths (essentially with the method of comparative dynamics). Comparison can help us understand which techniques are actually chosen, given certain structural conditions (with regard, for instance, to thriftlessness) and which relations are established between rate of growth, rate of profit and real wages. Robinson's contribution lies not only in the peculiarity of her representation of the equilibrium path in its technological features, but also in her analysis of how changes in external conditions affect the economy's evolution.

Robinson's analysis differs from that of the neoclassical economists in spite of some formal similarities. Robinson is well aware that the equilibrium path characterized by full employment is 'a mythical state of affairs not likely to obtain in any actual economy' (Robinson 1969: 99); it is for this reason that she coined the nickname *golden age*.

Robinson's model, built to represent the economy in evolution along equilibrium paths, resembles von Neumann's. It accepts an essential premise for marginalism: the availability of alternative techniques. However, Robinson is well aware that the choice of techniques cannot be interpreted in the neoclassical way.

> In reality techniques are not fully blue-printed before they are about to be used. The spectrum of techniques is a real phenomenon, but a very amorphous one. The possibility of using less or more mechanized techniques than those actually being operated is known only in a vague and general way. When a new technique is to be applied it requires adaptation and a period of 'teething troubles' quite as much when it is introduced in response to a change in costs as when it follows from a new discovery.
>
> (Robinson 1969: 156)

Robinson's analysis of accumulation is applied to analyse the effect of both widespread monopoly and changes in real wages. Two economies are compared: Alaph and Beth, similar in every respect except in the real wage rate, which has always been lower in Beth.

Robinson assumes that Alaph entrepreneurs gradually set up a collective monopoly. The price rise causes a reduction in demand (or in the rate of growth). Demand for capital goods decreases too; there is unemployment. After a transition phase, a new process of growth may eventually materialize in Alaph, having the same features (concerning, in particular, the ratio of accumulation to the stock of capital) as that occurring in Beth. This result has been produced by a reduction in Alaph of both the stock of capital and the labour force. 'This illustrates an essential paradox of capitalism. Each entrepreneur individually gains from a low real wage in terms of his own product, but all suffer from the limited market for commodities which a low real-wage rate entails' (Robinson 1954: 77–8).

We can come to similar results if we start from an economy in which capital increases at a rate lower than that at which population is increasing; the consequence can be a reduction in wages (through the mechanism already pointed out by Adam Smith). In fact, the evolution of the economy depends on entrepreneurs' reaction to the fall in wages. If a constant rate of accumulation is maintained in physical terms, employment is not reduced in the investment sector; however, the wages paid are reduced. A general fall in demand is induced, causing a reduction in price:

> so that, in spite of the weak position of the workers, the real wage remains constant. Since the rate of accumulation has failed to respond to the increase in the surplus supply of labour, the reserve of unemployed workers continues to increase and the ratio of unemployment to employment to rise.
>
> (Robinson 1954: 79)

Income distribution is affected by the evolution of market structures; exogenous changes in income distribution may cause changes in market structures. This is an issue that has been very little explored. The relationship between market structure and income distribution in an evolving economy is a complex one. It depends on the way in which monopoly (or oligopoly) emerges. If non-competitive (in the neoclassical sense) market situations are the result of innovation – as in Schumpeter's model – then it is difficult to make any clear-cut statement. In fact, for both Smith and Schumpeter, there is no unique relationship between development and income distribution. It is only in the Ricardian context that, with growth induced by the growth of population and curbed by the limited availability and heterogeneity of land, we can visualize a clearly defined pattern of evolution in income distribution: income distribution changes in favour of landowners, checking the process of growth. In Joan Robinson's theory, monopoly plays a role resembling that of land limitation. Unlike land scarcity, it causes a decrease not in profit but in real wages; however, the effect on growth is similar.

In *The Accumulation of Capital*, the novelty concerning income distribution is not so much the relationship between market structures and real wages, but rather, and much more, the denial of a fundamental dogma of neoclassical philosophy – i.e. that initial conditions and competition determine not only relative prices but also both distributive variables: rate of profit and real wages. With a given set of technical conditions we can associate a set of equilibrium paths having the same rate of profit and different wage rates. Such a result comes close to Sraffa's findings. In Joan Robinson it has a different meaning and different implications. It enlarges the scope for comparative dynamics, whereas in Sraffa it is intended to bring out into the open the ideological character of neoclassical analysis.

ENTREPRENEURS AND ACCUMULATION

The Accumulation of Capital, as Joan Robinson recognized, 'was found excessively difficult'. It was not clear how Joan Robinson stood *vis-à-vis* the new neoclassical approach, on the one hand, and the neo-Keynesian line, on the other. This is why she published, in 1962, *Essays in the Theory of Economic Growth*, which she regarded as an introduction rather than as a supplement to *The Accumulation of Capital*. The evolution of the economy is no longer conceptually constrained by the cage of equilibrium. However, equilibrium can be a benchmark to visualize actual processes better. It may help in clarifying Joan Robinson's position to recall her definition of *the desired rate of accumulation*. In accordance with Schumpeter's approach, Joan Robinson does not consider accumulation as resulting from *rational choices* in the neoclassical sense. As she noted: 'the inducement to invest is conceived in terms of a desired rate of growth rather than a desired stock of capital. The natural rate of growth permits but does not cause actual growth. The actual trend of growth is generated from within by the propensity to accumulate inherent in the system' (Robinson 1962: 87). This propensity reflects, as Joan Robinson suggests, the entrepreneurs' *animal spirits*.

There is in fact a two-way relation between rate of profit and accumulation that must be considered also in visualizing equilibrium paths (see Figure 12.1): expected rates of profit are a function of the rate of accumulation that generates them (curve A); the rate of accumulation is a function of the rate of profit that induces it (curve I).

In the situation represented in the figure at point D, the rate of accumulation generates such expectations of profit as are required to cause it to be maintained. We can speak of the *desired* rate of accumulation being 'the rate which makes the firms satisfied with the situation in which they find themselves' (Robinson 1962: 49).

This rate is different from the rates that will actually occur, because of lags between profit realization and investments and the coexistence of different technologies: the effect on the structure of the economy (not compatible with equilibrium) is accentuated by fluctuations in final demand. It is true that, if the fundamental conditions remain unchanged, the system can be conceptually brought to its long-run equilibrium of which the relation represented in the figure is a necessary condition. However, Joan Robinson is not convinced of the realism of such a conception (as a tool). It is for this reason that she rejected, *ante litteram*, the idea of rational expectations as it had been developed by Lucas. Rational expectations are possible only when the system moves along an equilibrium path of development. (Expectations are also of the adaptive type, but they are merely trivial.) In a process of growth induced

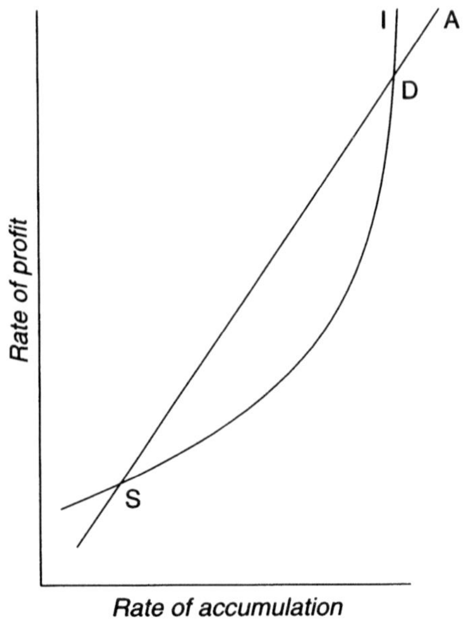

Figure 12.1
Source: Robinson (1962: 48)

by entrepreneurial innovations – even in a mere process of accumulation – rational expectations are impossible. In fact, the desired rate of accumulation reflects the propensity to growth that affects innovations, as well investments.

A VARIETY OF EVOLUTIONARY PATHS

Conceptual visualization of self-sustainable growth can also lead to different growth paths, to which Joan Robinson has given expressive nicknames. We have already recalled the *golden age* path, which is a highly unlikely path, indeed an ideal one. 'A steady state of accumulation of capital may take place below full employment. The stock of plant has the composition appropriate to the desired rate of accumulation, but there is not enough of it to employ the whole labour force' (Robinson 1962: 53). Such a growth path is labelled the *limping golden age*. It resembles, in a different context, Malinvaud's *classical unemployment* (Malinvaud 1980). As long as reduction of wages is possible, the limping golden age may be converted into a golden age. I have suggested another possible remedy: the appearance of *breaking monopolies* that can cause an increase in accumulation (Lombardini 1971: 242).

> When Malthusian misery checks the rate of growth of population, then, in the absence of technical progress, a situation might be reached in which the rate of accumulation and the rate of growth of the labour force were equal, the ratio of non-employment being great enough to keep the latter down to equality with the former.
>
> (Robinson 1962: 54)

This is a *leaden age*. A 'more cheerful scene' occurs when 'with induced technical progress, it is impossible to maintain as high a rate of growth as firms are willing and anxious to carry out' (Robinson 1962: 54). Two possible outcomes are visualized by Joan Robinson in such a *restrained golden age*. Wages rise or firms, adopting the Smithian strategy in the labour market, reduce the increase in productive capacity by what could be qualified as *unconscious parallelism*. Such dynamics remind us of Malinvaud's *repressed inflation* (Malinvaud 1980). The desired rate of growth may be hampered because of lack of demand for the final products. Then remedies can be provided both by sales promotion activities that, by reducing savings, change the rate of growth aimed at by firms, or by a rise in wages that has similar effects on final demand.

Special dynamics occur when the stock of capital is not congruent with the desired rate of growth (*galloping platinum age* and *creeping platinum age*). When, because of inflationary pressure (caused by the refusal of real wages to be depressed below a particular level), 'the rate of accumulation is being held in check by the threat of rising money wages due to a rise in prices (as opposed to rising money wages due to a scarcity of labour)' we have a situation that may be described as a *bastard golden age* (Robinson 1962: 58). Such dynamics bear some resemblance to Malinvaud's *Keynesian unemployment* (Malinvaud 1980); in this case it is not so much the high level of wages as the low level of demand that may be caused by *pessimistic self-fulfilling expectations*. Various remedies can be conjectured: increases in wages, increases in public expenditure, reduction in the rate of interest. All these remedies may fail to hit the objective if they have a positive feedback on inflation. Investments can increase relative to consumption if technical progress reduces the amount of labour required to produce the minimum acceptable real wage; then we have a *bastard platinum age*.

These various patterns of growth have not been properly analysed, because the modern growth models have been mostly conceived as equilibrium models. The convergence of one growth path with a different one has not been adequately explored (an interesting contribution is in Cozzi 1966). I shall confine myself to a few remarks on unemployment. Population growth is not a rigid constraint on growth, nor are population dynamics the main factor that can explain non-golden age paths. In fact, if the rate of growth of the economy is higher than the rate of growth of population, labour can come from outside (think of the United States); in the opposite case, labour can migrate. When neither of these possibilities exists, we must avoid the fallacy concerning the macroeconomic assessment of the firms' reduction in employment. For each firm, a reduction in employment can increase efficiency; the sum of the firms' reductions in employment may entail a reduction in efficiency for the whole economy, because the unemployed have to be fed, in one way or another. To conceive possibilities of a *limping golden age* – which can occur not only in *classical conditions*, but also when technological progress occurs at a rate higher than that at which consumption can increase (see Pasinetti 1993) – means raising a problem of the proper interaction between economic policies and firms' strategies. Economic policies can no longer be conceived merely in aggregate terms as, essentially, monetary and fiscal policies.

EVOLUTION: ANALYSIS OR PROPHECY?

Joan Robinson was, as is well known, very sympathetic towards China, engaged as it was in building a new social and economic system. I was myself much interested in the venture, so we had several talks on the subject. She was convinced of China's success: a new system completely different from the capitalistic one would emerge in China after a difficult transition. I too was convinced of China's success in promoting industrialization. However, I was, and still am, convinced that a new social and economic system will not be possible until the ratio between social consumption and private consumption is completely reversed.[16] Joan Robinson was not in substantial disagreement. However, she deemed the prospect very likely in China, because Chinese culture could make possible what had not been achieved in the West: the integration of ethical values with rational economic criteria – the reason being that Chinese culture does not encourage neglect of the earth's problems in the expectations of heaven's solutions. From these talks, I discovered a different Joan Robinson, closer to prophecy than to the economist's activity in producing *tools* to be used to understand the economy and its evolution. I must say that my appreciation of Joan Robinson has increased. As Hayek himself has recognized, prophecy may help the evolution of society. Prophecy may exploit our knowledge by surpassing it. However, that is not the scientist's job. In fact, it concerns all men. Economists, before being scientists, are men or women.[17] Joan Robinson's contributions are the scientist's. But she was also well aware that to be a person means accepting others as persons too.

NOTES

1 This point was developed in Lombardini (1954).
2 These problems are analysed in Lombardini (1953).
3 The 'monopolistic competition revolution' has been commented on by Paul Samuelson (1954), who clarified the interaction between structure and processes,

taking into account the role of uncertainty.

4 In fact, this is true if it is assumed – as Chamberlin did in the first edition of his *The Theory of Monopolistic Competition* and most economists do in their presentation of his theory – that the equilibrium of monopolistic competitive markets is characterized by the demand curve being tangent to the average cost curve. This assumption – that 'the tangency of cost and demand curves is the central principle involved' – is in fact abandoned in subsequent editions by Chamberlin who, however, recognizes that the interpretation 'may perhaps be accounted for by the over-prominence given to this solution in my own statement of the theory' (1962: 195).

5 In fact, Chamberlin states the purpose of his book in the following manner: 'The theory of pure competition could hardly be expected to fit facts so far different from its assumptions. But there is no reason why a theory of value [which Chamberlin considers to be the marginalistic theory of general equilibrium] cannot be formulated which will fit them – a theory concerning itself specifically with goods which are not homogeneous' (Chamberlin 1962: 10).

6 'Among the persons interested in economic analysis [she writes in the Introduction to *The Economics of Imperfect Competition*] there are tool-makers and tool-users. This book is presented to the analytical economists as a book of tools' (Robinson 1933: 1). The tools have to be used to build those models required to understand the real world and to solve problems of economic policy. Unfortunately there is a distressingly wide gap between the tool-makers and the tool-users, which may account for the poor, sometimes misleading, information provided to businessmen and politicians.

7 Robinson frequently refers to Sraffa, although I am afraid she was not properly aware of his aims. In contrast with Sraffa, she emphasizes the heterogeneity of factors of production, which makes it impossible to keep costs constant even in the presence of unlimited demand. She does not think that interdependences between demands for various commodities, resolving in a cluster of surrogates, create serious problems (Robinson 1933: 116–19). Sraffa's analysis – at least in his essay of 1926 – seems to justify the classical assumptions of constant average costs (except in some peculiar cases): it was not competition (with free entry) that was required to ground such an assumption, but simply product differentiation and the associated sales promotion activities. To resort to competition was to justify marginalistic tools (which, anyhow, Joan Robinson does not despise). Sraffa's aim was indeed to bring into the open the inconsistencies of marginalism. The assumption of product differentiation soon appeared to Sraffa inadequate and unnecessary for radical criticism of marginalism. Sraffa, indeed, has become a reference point in the debate on value theory for his *Production of Commodities by Means of Commodities* (1960).

8 In my *Il monopolio nella teoria economica* (1953) I outlined how the strategy of monopolistic firms may induce growth because of learning by doing so, of research activities, of the evolution of relations with financial market and banking system, of consolidation of results of sales promotion activity (Chapter 6, dealing with the dynamics of monopolistic firms, was translated into English in 1994).

9 In fact, Joan Robinson was well aware of the scant relevance of the theorem. She wrote: 'When we think of the proposition in terms of the condition that the workers consume the whole wage and capitalists save the whole profit, it appears somewhat mysterious. When we realize that it does not matter at all who does the saving so long as the rate of profit is equal to the rate of growth, it seems fairly obvious' (Robinson 1962: 136).

10 Chamberlin's view of the efficiency problem is completely different. Pareto,

convinced that competition is not a realistic assumption, mentions a situation very close to the one that will be labelled as *monopolistic competition*. However, he is convinced that only by assuming competition can we isolate the effects of *logical actions* and define equilibria that represent both normal and optimal structures of the economy. The evolution of the system can then be analysed by the method of comparative statics. Chamberlin, by integrating competition and monopoly, thought he had provided a realistic scheme to explain how markets work: the problem of efficiency has to be rethought afresh. For Chamberlin, indeed, 'The explicit recognition that product is differentiated brings into the open the problem of variety and makes it clear that *pure competition may no longer be regarded as in any sense an "ideal" for purposes of welfare economics*' (Chamberlin 1962: 214). A similar view is held by Schumpeter, who goes further in assessing the scant relevance of consumers' tastes, since new products are imposed on them.

The problem raised by Chamberlin is still largely unsolved. Most economists think that variety reflects individual *potential tastes*. I argued against this view by pointing out that for efficient situations, when competition is assumed away, some forms of cooperation are required to make it possible to exploit certain results of technical progress making the production of standardized commodities more convenient. In fact, each firm tries to exploit its market better by differentiating the product; this creates a taste for variety that may become an obstacle that, added to others, makes it no longer economical for new firms to exploit possible innovations that could greatly reduce their prices through standardization of final product (Lombardini 1953: 302–6). What I then had in mind was a situation similar to those that, in successive years, have been analysed by what was called the Prisoner's Dilemma scheme.

11 'Now, supposing that the new, higher level of demand is expected to last, investment in new capacity is being planned. High profits last during the gestation period of new plant, and begin to fall as new capacity comes into operation' (Robinson 1954: 249).

12 'The process of adjustment to an increase in demand is likely to include a period of subnormal profits to offset the period of supernormal profits, whereas there is no such offset the other way round' (Robinson 1954: 252).

13 This is in line with Zimmerman's (1952) remarks on the increased propensity to monopolize in depression.

14 See Lombardini and Nicola (1974).

15 'User cost therefore depends upon a mixture of technical facts and subjective estimations of future market condition' (Robinson 1954: 248).

16 When I speak of social consumption I do not mean services and consumption goods produced by public administrations. I refer to consumption that is decided after collective decisions, no matter who is the producer of the services and commodities required.

17 Joan Robinson does not believe in economists' neutrality towards value judgements: 'Every human being has ideological, moral and political views. To pretend to have none and to be *purely objective* must necessarily be either self-deception or a device to deceive others. Value judgements differ; economists have no superior capacity in making them. But just as there are some basic elements which set limits to the possible structures of languages so there is a core of common values in all moral codes' (Robinson 1970: 122–3).

REFERENCES

Chamberlin, E. H. (1962) [1933] *The Theory of Monopolistic Competition*, 8th edn. Cambridge, Mass.: Harvard University Press.

Cozzi, T. (1966) *Movimenti in equilibrio nell'analisi macroeconomica*. Turin: Giappichelli.

Lombardini, S. (1953) *Il monopolio nella teoria economica*, Milan: Vita e Pensiero.

——— (1954) Monopoly and Rigidities in the Economic System. In E. H. Chamberlin, ed., *Monopoly, Competition, and Their Regulation*. London: Macmillan.

——— (1971) Modern Monopolies in Economic Development. In Robin Marris and Adrian Wood, eds, *The Corporate Economy*. London: Macmillan.

——— (1994) The Development of the Monopolistic Firm, *Italian Economic Papers*, vol. 2: 69–86.

Lombardini, S. and Nicola, P. C. (1974) Income Distribution and Economic Development in Ricardian and Walrasian Models, *Proceedings of 11th Polish–Italian Conference on Applications of Systems Theory to Economic Management and Technology*, Pugnochiuso, Italy, 1–6 May.

Malinvaud, E. (1980) *Réexamen de la théorie du chômage*. Paris: Calman-Lévy.

Pasinetti, L. L. (1993) *Structural Economic Dynamics*. Cambridge: Cambridge University Press.

Robinson, J. (1933) *The Economics of Imperfect Competition*. London: Macmillan.

——— (1954) The Impossibility of Competition. In E. H. Chamberlin, ed., *Monopoly, Competition, and Their Regulation*. London: Macmillan.

——— (1962) *Essays in the Theory of Economic Growth*. London: Macmillan.

——— (1969) [1956] *The Accumulation of Capital*, 3rd edn. London: Macmillan.

——— (1970) *Freedom and Necessity. An Introduction to the Study of Society*. London: Allen & Unwin.

Samuelson, A. A. (1954) The Monopolistic Competition Revolution. In E. H. Chamberlin, ed., *Monopoly, Competition, and Their Regulation*. London: Macmillan.

Sraffa, P. (1926) The Laws of Returns under Competitive Conditions, *Economic Journal*, 36: 535–50.

——— (1960) *Production of Commodities by Means of Commodities*. Cambridge: Cambridge University Press.

Zimmerman, L. J. (1952) *The Propensity to Monopolize*. Amsterdam: North-Holland.

13

DEGREE OF MECHANIZATION OF TECHNIQUES AND SCALE OF MECHANIZATION OF THE ECONOMY[1]

Salvatore Biasco

Joan Robinson spent part of her academic life attempting to establish a conceptual reference framework that would blend together a theory of growth and a theory of income distribution. It would probably be more exact to say that the attempt was mainly concerned with how to establish a framework for analysing the conditions of income distribution consistent with indefinitely sustainable (exogenous) growth. In fact, Joan Robinson never tackled the construction of a theory of growth in the strict sense of the term and argued forcibly that only conditions of equilibrium growth could be treated analytically, because otherwise it was impossible to know what unrealized expectations were embedded in the economy, what the historical conditions had been at the start and what type of reaction the gap between expectations and actual results would generate.

In this Joan Robinson was strongly influenced by the Swedish school and always maintained the distinction between historical time and logical time. Within the framework of logical time, the state of continuous growth had to be presupposed and presupposed in equilibrium terms, without investigating how the economy arrived at it: the economy had always been and would always be in this state. Nor was it possible to say anything about the shift from one growth condition to another brought about by changes in exogenous conditions. Today's equilibrium logically presupposed all those that had been and all those to come. It also presupposed expectations consistent with maintaining the growth path. Nonetheless, the effect of different exogenous conditions could be analysed in connection with different growth equilibria because by comparing these it was possible to understand the different (endogenous) consequences to which they would give rise.

Every rate of equilibrium growth obviously implies a consistency of the real sector (the technique chosen, the proportion between the sectors and the amount and composition of investment) and a consistency of the expenditure flows. The latter consistency is regulated by the distribution of income, insofar as it determines the flows of total savings in the economy.

The context in which Joan Robinson moves is the disaggregated one in which every distribution of income is associated – for a given technique – with various relative price ratios between the goods produced and hence with different relative values of the heterogeneous set of consumer and investment goods produced. The combination of profit and wage rates also determines the selection of efficient techniques.

Coupling Kalecki with Sraffa and von Neumann with Kaldor, Joan Robinson arrives at the synthetic conceptualization of growth paths in conditions to which she gives the name of 'golden age'. From the comparison of the characteristics of golden age economies she derives a series of substantive propositions on a set of characteristics (concerning production, consumption, capital and labour inputs, and sectoral proportions, etc.) that differentiate economies with more or less growth and with different income distributions and propensities to save.[2]

This essay explores some insights into Joan Robinson's theory of economic growth by comparing specific features of various economies, each in a state of long-run equilibrium at different points on a given spectrum of techniques. Steady-growth paths differ because of one of two exogenous conditions – saving behaviour and the growth rate. The range of techniques is assumed to permit re-switches in profitability.

The focus is on the relative mechanization of golden age economies. At the rate of money wages prevailing in each of them, economies may find it more advantageous to sustain a given rate of growth with the relatively more or relatively less mechanized of two techniques belonging to the known range of technological options. However, the relative capital intensity of the technology adopted does not allow any *a priori* inference about the relative capital intensity that results for the economy as a whole in comparison with the alternatives discarded.[3] When, with a given rate of money wages, the less mechanized of two techniques is found, for instance, to be advantageous, the ensuing equilibrium path of a growing economy is not necessarily the one that provides the least capital-intensive output; the equilibrium path associated with the inferior (more mechanized) technique could entail less use of capital per unit of output and of capital per man.[4]

The point at issue is that *the ranking of different technical alternatives with regard to the capital intensity of output needed to maintain steady growth varies with the rate of growth.*

Hence when economies grow at a different pace and are fully adjusted at that pace, a full range of possibilities can occur. The faster growing of two economies on a golden age path can present features (compared with the slower-growing economy) that can be represented in a double entry table concerning techniques used and how they fare in the economy as a whole: (a) it can present a different or a similar technical choice compared with the other; (b) that choice can rank similarly or differently as far as capital intensiveness for the economy as a whole is concerned. (Any of the four alternatives split into another two once it is specified whether it refers to the combination of the more or the less capital-intensive choice for the economy and for the technique.)

It follows that we must keep claims referring to features of techniques strictly separate from claims referring to features of economies using them for steady-growth equilibrium.

SPECIFICATION OF THE TECHNIQUES

A technique is an interrelated set of production activities, each of which is defined by its production coefficients. A *net* unit of any good can be produced with different techniques. This means – when every activity has a constant return to scale – that the good in question can be obtained with different arrangements of activity, and hence with different physical stocks of capital goods and levels of employment.[5]

Known techniques will be classified as relatively more or relatively less mechanized (or, using a different terminology, more or less capital intensive) depending on whether, for any scale of operation, they require more or less capital per worker and capital per unit of output. Because capital and output can be measured only in value terms and the comparison can be made only with the same price system, the classification of techniques pair by pair refers to the levels of the profit and wage rates at which the choice is indifferent.[6]

A technique that is found to be more mechanized for the production of a net unit of any good is more mechanized for all the other goods that are a part of its activities and for their combinations. Hence, if the net product extracted from the two techniques has exactly the same commodity composition,[7] and both are operated at a scale given by the availability of labour,[8] the more mechanized technique will allow more per capita units of the basket of commodities in the net product. If the unit of this basket is also the unit of measurement for the system of relative prices, net products are measured in physical terms.

With this specification, the characteristics of the techniques are fully described by the relative positions of the curves that give the *wage/profit rate* relationship that corresponds to each of them.

Let the curves be A and B of Figure 13.1, obtained from two fully specified techniques that will be called A and B and referred to accordingly in all the reasoning of this paper. The example is as general as possible.[9] Technique A is chosen in two non-contiguous intervals of the profit rate, r, from 0 to r_1 and from r_2 to R (the maximum profit rate). There is, therefore, a double switch of techniques. At the points r_1 and r_2 the choice between A and B is indifferent.

Technique A is more mechanized than B because at the points of coexistence r_1 and r_2 – i.e. at the levels of the profit rate that produce an

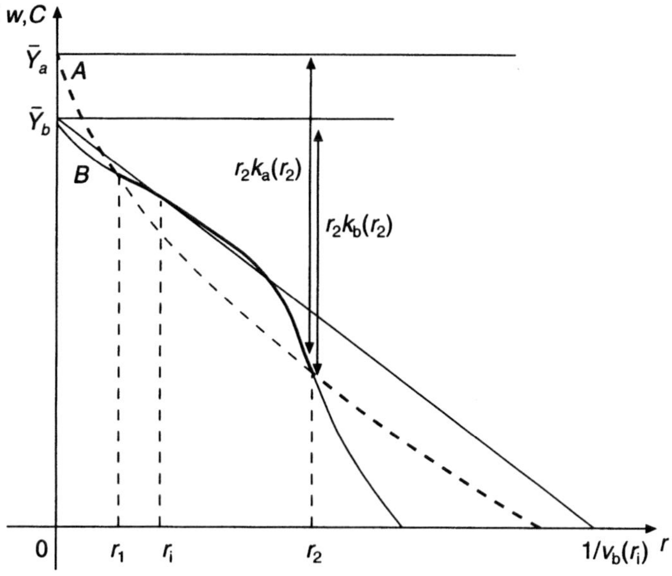

Figure 13.1

identical price system – it has a higher capital/output ratio. The same technique, with an equal amount of labour employed, requires a larger amount of capital and gives a higher income.

It is sufficient to give a simple graphical demonstration of the relationships described.

(a) Per capita income, *Y*. This coincides with the net product and, by the choice of the unit of measurement, net product will not change in value as reference prices vary with *r*. Hence, it is determined at the intersections of curves A and B with the *y* axis (where the share of wages is 100% of the net product and wages coincide with it) and represented by two straight lines parallel to the *x* axis because it is invariant with respect to *r*. In this case $Y_a > Y_b$ always.

(b) Per capita capital, $K(r)$. After subtracting the part of income taken by wages, $w(r)$, the rest – equal to the difference between the straight line and its frontier – is the share of profits, i.e. $rK(r)$. At the points of coexistence *r* and *w* are identical: necessarily at those points $K_a > K_b$.

(c) Capital income ratio, $v(r)$. For every technique this is the inverse of the length of the segment cut off on the *x* axis by the straight line that joins the point Y on the *y* axis with any point of its frontier.[10] At the points of intersection of the frontiers it is the straight line with the highest intersection of the *y* axis to have the shortest intersection on the *x* axis. Hence $v_a > v_b$.

The relative amount of per capita income produced is enough to identify the relative degree of mechanization of a technique; the other properties follow.

EQUILIBRIUM WITH ZERO GROWTH

In Joan Robinson style, we can imagine that any point of the curves in Figure 13.1 corresponds to a different economy and fully depicts its long-run growth. Equilibrium paths are maintained because expectations are fulfilled and the current situation is projected.[11]

The hypothesis of a uniform net product obtained in economies presenting a different income distribution and using alternative techniques calls implicitly for a comparison of how the latter influence the equilibrium position in a stationary state. In other words, everything that is produced is consumed, so that the growth rate, g, is equal to zero. This is the only condition in which the hypothesis that the net product is made up of an identical basket of commodities is logically sound. In fact, if the two techniques are compared in relation to a positive *equilibrium* growth rate, it is inconceivable that they would give rise to the same composition of the surplus. Income per capita can no longer be measured in physical terms.

There is nothing against taking the purest case of $g = 0$ as a benchmark and assuming that the net product consists only of a fixed basket of consumer goods – in practice, just one consumer good – which is assumed to be the only non-basic good of the system.

The situation corresponding to Figure 13.1 will therefore be redefined in analytical terms. It is assumed that there are still fixed coefficients and single-product industries. The latter assumption is made to simplify the notation and exposition, but it can be shown that the conclusions are independent of it and remain valid in the more general case of joint production.[12]

For the more mechanized technique, A, let the input matrix be matrix $\bar{A}$ of order $n \times n$; for the less mechanized technique, B, let the matrix be $\bar{B}$ of size $n \times n$.

$$\bar{A} = \begin{vmatrix} A & \mathbf{a}_c \\ \mathbf{l}_a & l_{ac} \end{vmatrix} \quad (1) \qquad \bar{B} = \begin{vmatrix} B & \mathbf{b}_c \\ \mathbf{l}_b & l_{bc} \end{vmatrix} \quad (2)$$

The columns of $\bar{A}$ give the requirements of each activity when it is performed at the unit level; A of order $(n-1) \times (n-1)$ is the sub-matrix of the inputs of basic goods, while a_c is the *input* column vector of the non-basic goods (the basket of consumer goods); $[\mathbf{0}_a l_{ac}]$ is the row vector of the labour coefficients in the basic and non-basic activities. $\bar{B}$, B, $\mathbf{b}_c$ and $[\mathbf{0}_b l_{bc}]$ have analogous meanings.

If the net product includes only consumer goods and for the rest output makes good what is used, the former's composition coincides, in the case of technique A, with the solutions of system (3):

$$\begin{aligned} |A - \mathbf{0}|\mathbf{X}_a + \mathbf{a}_c C_a &= 0 \\ \mathbf{l}_a \mathbf{X}_a + l_{ac} C_a &= 1 \end{aligned} \qquad (3)$$

and, for technique B, with the solutions of system (4):

$$\begin{aligned} |B - \mathbf{0}|\mathbf{X}_b + \mathbf{b}_c C_b &= 0 \\ \mathbf{l}_b \mathbf{X}_b + l_{bc} C_b &= 1 \end{aligned} \qquad (4)$$

In the systems (3) and (4) **X** is the vector of the level of activity of the basic sectors, *C* is a scalar regarding the consumption goods sector and *1* is the total amount of labour available. The systems have solutions that are all positive if the conditions of Hawkins and Simon are satisfied for the matrices $|A - \mathrm{I}|$ and $|B - \mathrm{I}|$.[13]

The dual systems of prices are Sraffa systems. If p_c is put equal to 1 in both systems of prices, where p_c is the unit price of consumer goods, C_a coincides with Y_a and C_b coincides with Y_b. The whole product is by assumption equal to the demand for consumption as the propensity to save (out of both wages and profits) is zero and the sum of incomes equal to the net production.

On passing from a rate of profit of 0 to one of *R* we encounter economies differing as regards the distribution of income. By assumption, however, they are all equilibrium alternatives: as consumption out of wages decreases (because the wage rate declines), it is replaced by consumption out of profits (because these rise correspondingly).

In all other respects the arguments of the previous section hold good: as far as the technical possibilities of Figure 13.1 refer to economies producing a net output with identical commodity composition, the comparative features of the economies coincide with the comparative features of the techniques themselves. The intervals of the profit rate in which the more mechanized technique A is preferred to the less mechanized technique B correspond to a choice of greater relative capital intensity for the economy as a whole.[14] And vice versa in the opposite case.

EQUILIBRIUM WITH POSITIVE GROWTH

One is justified in asking what happens when the same range of techniques gives rise to a problem of choice in economies that grow at a positive and identical rate. When $g > 0$, it is necessary to renounce a part of the consumer goods that it would be technically possible to produce with each unit of labour, because some of that unit of labour is used to produce a surplus of investment goods in the proportion and physical form needed to permit the growth rate, *g*, to be constant.[15] Here again, we must imagine systems that are in equilibrium, i.e. that have achieved a composition of stocks that is entirely suited to the rate of growth considered and to the technique being used as well as having the composition of their surpluses that is equally suitable.

Once the hypothesis of stationary equilibrium is abandoned, it can no longer be assumed that alternative golden age paths based on techniques A and B have a net product of identical physical characteristics. If alternative paths are compared at the rate of growth $g = \bar{g}$, (where $0 < \bar{g} < R$), they are nonetheless identified by a point belonging to the same $w - r$ relationship because the form of the curves does not depend on the composition of the net product, provided there are constant returns to scale and the numéraire does not change.

When the rate of growth is positive, it is no longer certain that the choice of (more mechanized) technique A corresponds to the choice of greater capital intensity for the economy as a whole; and vice versa for the (less mechanized) technique B.

Before discussing the features that emerge for golden age economies, it is necessary to analyse in a more formal and less intuitive way how Joan Robinson's golden age paths must be represented.

First, the physical characteristics. The composition of the net product and of the levels of activity that enable an economy to grow in a balanced manner at the rate $\bar{g}$ and with technique A are obtained from the solution of system (5):[16]

$$\left| A - \delta_{ij} \frac{1}{1 + \bar{g}} \right| \mathbf{X}_\mathrm{a} + \mathbf{a}_\mathrm{c} C_\mathrm{a} = 0 \tag{5}$$

$$\mathbf{l}_\mathrm{a} \mathbf{X}_\mathrm{a} + l_\mathrm{ac} C_\mathrm{a} = 1$$

in the analogous case of technique B, from the solutions of system (6):

$$\left| B - \delta_{ij} \frac{1}{1 + \bar{g}} \right| \mathbf{X}_\mathrm{b} + \mathbf{b}_\mathrm{c} C_\mathrm{b} = 0 \tag{6}$$

$$\mathbf{l}_\mathrm{b} \mathbf{X}_\mathrm{b} + l_\mathrm{bc} C_\mathrm{b} = 1$$

where the symbols have the same meaning as in the previous section and where δ_{ij} is Kronecker's constant, which is equal to 1 if $i = j$ and equal to zero if $i \# j$.[17]

In conclusion, for every rate of accumulation g there is only one relative composition of the net product and of the capital goods used that is compatible with g being constant; the absolute composition depends on the actual amount of labour. The physical flows implied by the solutions of system (5) are common – for a given g – to all economies identified by a point in the w-r relationship and using the technique involved. The same holds true for system (6) and the economies using technique B.

Second, expenditure flow conditions. Underlying equilibrium positions are also implied from the demand side, in the dual system of prices. The logical consistency of the analytical scheme requires that for any set of normal prices the value of investment goods (the final surplus of basic goods) be matched by a corresponding (*ex ante* and realized) saving, and the value of the basket of consumer goods (the final surplus of non-basic goods) be matched by the flow of consumption expenditure. In the simplest hypothesis that all wages are consumed ($s_w = 0$) and that a share of profit, s_p, is saved ($1 \geq s_p \geq 0$),[18] demand equilibrium is represented by

$$s_p rK(r) = I(r),$$

which amounts to constraining the dual Sraffa system of prices with the equation

$$rs_p = g \tag{7}$$

in perfect neo-Keynesian style.[19]

Golden age economies associated with points on the curves in Figure 13.1 and growing at a rate $g = \bar{g}$ differ because of a different saving propensity out of profits[20] and because of the technique used. They are fully adjusted, with inputs and output consistent with the growth rate $\bar{g}$. The economically significant range of variation of r is now bounded by $\bar{g}$ and R. For an economy to be in equilibrium with a profit rate less than $\bar{g}$, it would have to maintain a level of s_p permanently greater than 1, which obviously has no economic significance.[21]

As far as the technical possibilities of Figure 13.1 were referred to economies producing a net output with identical commodity composition, the comparative features of the economies coincide with the comparative features of the techniques themselves. This coincidence may not apply at $g > 0$ and a reverse in the ranking of the relative capital intensiveness of equilibria reached with technique A rather than with technique B may occur.[22]

In correspondence with a switch point (where the system of prices is identical for the two economies using technique A and technique B) we know nothing about the reciprocal position of Y_a with respect to Y_b. For instance, there are no grounds for excluding *a priori* that, at the point r_2, $Y_a(r_2) < Y_b(r_2)$ and consequently $K_a(r_2) < K_b(r_2)$ or that the capital/income ratio also behaves in the same way. If this were to happen, the situations in which an economy uses B, the less mechanized technique, would entail – compared with the alternative of using A – the employment of more capital per worker and per unit of product (and vice versa).[23]

It can be shown that, if techniques admit a re-switch point, this reverse in the ranking of techniques for capital intensiveness occurs. Although the demonstration refers to the example of Figure 13.1, it is general.

Let the accumulation rate lie between a switch and a re-switch point, $r_1 < \bar{g} < r_2$. The information available on primary and dual systems indicates that, with $r = \bar{g}$ and $s_p = 1$, all the consumer goods are consumed by wage-earners:

C_a and C_b necessarily coincide in equilibrium with $w_a(\bar{g})$ and $w_b(\bar{g})$.[24] It is consequently easy to determine in Figure 13.2, which reproduces the curves of Figure 13.1, the amount of consumer goods that the two techniques make it possible to produce in the two systems (5) and (6). Since consumer goods are measured in terms of themselves, their value remains unchanged for all the price systems corresponding to the combinations of w and r, characterizing an equal number of golden age economies; i.e. the value of consumer goods is independent of r. Two straight lines of constant height can therefore be drawn, C_a for economies using technique A and C_b for economies using technique B. In the figure, $C_a < C_b$.

The following theorem can now be demonstrated:

> *for any viable rate of accumulation the one of two techniques that permits the highest per capita consumption gives rise, at the (economically significant) points of indifference, to the highest per capita investment and, consequently, to the highest per capita income.*

At the point where two techniques coexist they have the same values of r and w. Necessarily, in an economy for which they are possible alternatives, the level of s_p is the same. It follows that if $s_p < 1$, the condition for equilibrium, the mirror image of that between saving and investment,

$$w + \frac{1 - s_p}{s_p} I(r) = C, \tag{8}$$

is always satisfied with the highest value of I for the alternative that permits the highest value of C, Q.E.D.[25]

It follows from the theorem above that, in order to establish the relative degree of capital intensity entailed in golden age economies by the use of two alternative techniques at a given rate of growth, it is enough to compare the relative amounts of consumer goods that each technique includes in the net product appropriate to the equilibrium that it sustains. And this is true at whatever rate of accumulation between 0 and R the comparison is carried out.[26]

From the proof of the theorem above it follows that if $C_a < C_b$, as in the example of Figure 13.2, $Y_a(r_2)$ is also less than $Y_b(r_2)$ and consequently $r_2K_a(r_2) < r_2K_b(r_2)$, which implies $K_a(r_2) < K_b(r_2)$. It can also be shown that $v_a(r_2) < v_b(r_2)$.[27]

In relation to the growth rate $\bar{g}$, lying between r_1 and r_2, it has to be concluded that when an economy adopts the more mechanized methods of production corresponding to technique A it is actually producing its equilibrium output with a relatively lower use of capital equipment. In fact, capital per worker and capital per unit of output are less than would have derived from use of the less mechanized alternative technique, B.

The result is disconcerting in some respects: the ranking that is established

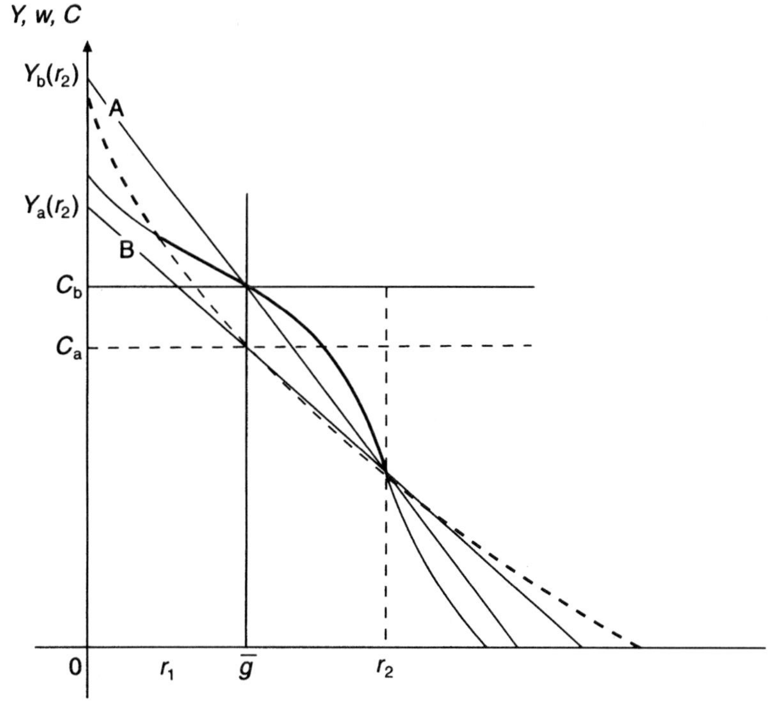

Figure 13.2

between two techniques on the basis of the degree of mechanization, and which refers to the physical production relationships (3) and (4), does not in itself permit us to establish a ranking of the capital requirements needed to maintain a steady proportional growth in economies faced with the two technical possibilities. And yet – as is well known – if a technique is more mechanized than another, it is so univocally for the production of all the goods involved in its matrix.

Obviously, the possibilities that correspond to any one spectrum of techniques are numerous. The perverse effect encountered occurs every time the spectrum allows a double switch. This point will now be clarified, with full details set out in the Appendix.

If there is a switching of techniques, then some rates of growth permit a higher flow of per capita consumption when technique A is used; while other rates of growth permit a higher flow of per capita consumption when technique B is used. This result is obtained from (5) and (6), but it is possible to test it graphically by observing Figure 13.1, or alternatively Figure 13.2. In these figures the differences between the ordinates necessarily represent the difference in per capita consumption obtained by using A and B when the growth rate coincides with the value of the abscissa. When $\bar{g} = r$, necessarily $s_p = 1$ and the per capita wage coincides with per capita consumption. The relative performance of golden age economies in terms of consumption goods at different rates of growth can be identified by the intercept of a vertical line at any point of the abscissa.[28] With s_p always equal to 1, it is the growth rate that varies with r along the x axis and the w–r relationship.

Moving along the scale of growth rates, $(C_a - C_b)$ changes sign. When $0 < g < r_1$, use of technique A (the more mechanized one) involves a higher capital/output ratio; when $r_1 < g < r_2$, this is true for technique B, which is the less – xx mechanized of the two. The curves of Figure 13.1 are simultaneously compatible with the two cases and are also compatible with a third case, that of equal capital intensity for A and B. This is the case of $g = r_1$ and of $g = r_2$, when the two techniques permit the same level of consumption and, at the economically significant points of switch, have the same levels of income and capital and capital/income ratio in nominal terms.

For any given rate of growth, an analysis of Figure 13.1 makes it possible to test the following general propositions:

(a) that the more capital-intensive alternative for the economy (based sometimes on A and sometimes on B in the example) is always chosen for values of the profit rate equal to the rate of accumulation;
(b) that the first economically significant switch of profitability goes always from the more to the less capital-intensive alternative and from the higher to the lower *real* wage rate (whether the switch is from A to B or from B to A);
(c) that the case $g = 0$ (adopted as the point of departure in the 'Specification of the Techniques' section) is no more than a special case in which (a) and (b) hold good.

It is worth noting that point (a) above, together with the theorem on page 156, gives a more general formulation of the neo-neoclassical theorem of Joan Robinson, i.e. that even when there is heterogeneous capital, the highest consumption per head is achieved when the profit rate is equal to the rate of accumulation.[29]

Drawing the threads together, it can be concluded that *the degree of relative capital intensity ensuing for an economy from the choice of a technique in a given range of possibilities is not based on any element of identification that is an attribute of the techniques as such.* It depends not only on the difference in production methods but also on the different relative levels of their operation needed to sustain the rate of balanced growth.

Depending on the level of the rate of growth, it is possible to classify in our example as the more capital-intensive choice for the economy the one based on (the more mechanized) technique A or the one based on (the less mechanized) technique B, or assign both the same degree of capital intensiveness.

The only case in which it is possible to associate the relative attributes of a technique with those of relative capital intensity per worker and per unit of output of an economy using that technique is when the w–r relationship has only one intersection at the frontier; in other words, when there are no re-switch points.[30]

EQUILIBRIUM AT DIFFERENT RATES OF GROWTH

Any of the profit rates allowed by a given spectrum of techniques correspond to a golden age economy presenting that rate as an equilibrium one. So far we have compared the capital requirements of golden age economies when producing first an identical net product and then a different net product able to maintain a constant and given growth rate, g. Economies will now be compared for different rates of growth obtained from the same spectrum of techniques. The features of economies fully adjusted at a different pace of accumulation are a typical concern of Joan Robinson.

When s_p is kept constant at a level $\bar{s}_p$ for all economies, any viable profit rate is an equilibrium rate provided the corresponding golden age economy has the appropriate rate of growth, in accordance with the formula $r = (1/\bar{s}_p)g$. Even with the same technique, the composition of the net product is different for the various levels of r and is that obtained from (5) or (6), solved for all values of g from 0 to $R/\bar{s}_p$.[31] Solutions concerning the physical compositions of inputs and outputs vary, of course, according to g. But, given the hypothesis of constant returns to scale, such solutions do not influence the price system: the relationship between w and r remains unchanged with its usual switch points. Nevertheless, only one of the alternative distributions of income is compatible with any particular rate of growth.

Passing from 0 to R, the spectrum underlies economies growing at different growth rates, and hence different points imply a different net product and capital equipment. Any particular profit rate is the one that warrants the equality between aggregate saving at normal prices and the value of investment goods produced to maintain the associated rate of growth; i.e. it is the rate of growth derived from $r\bar{s}_p = g$.

A surprising range of possibilities can occur. For example, two economies – fully adjusted at the growth rates g_I and g_{II} (with $g_I < g_{II}$) – may find it profitable to use the same technique (say, the more mechanized one) even though they adopt it, in the one case, as the technique requiring more capital per worker in the economy as a whole and, in the other, as the technique requiring less capital per worker, in comparison with the equilibrium that would be reached with an inferior (less mechanized) available technique. Alternatively, the two economies can effectively make use of two different techniques, but we may find that the slower-growing economy finds it more advantageous to use the more mechanized one and in this way chooses the

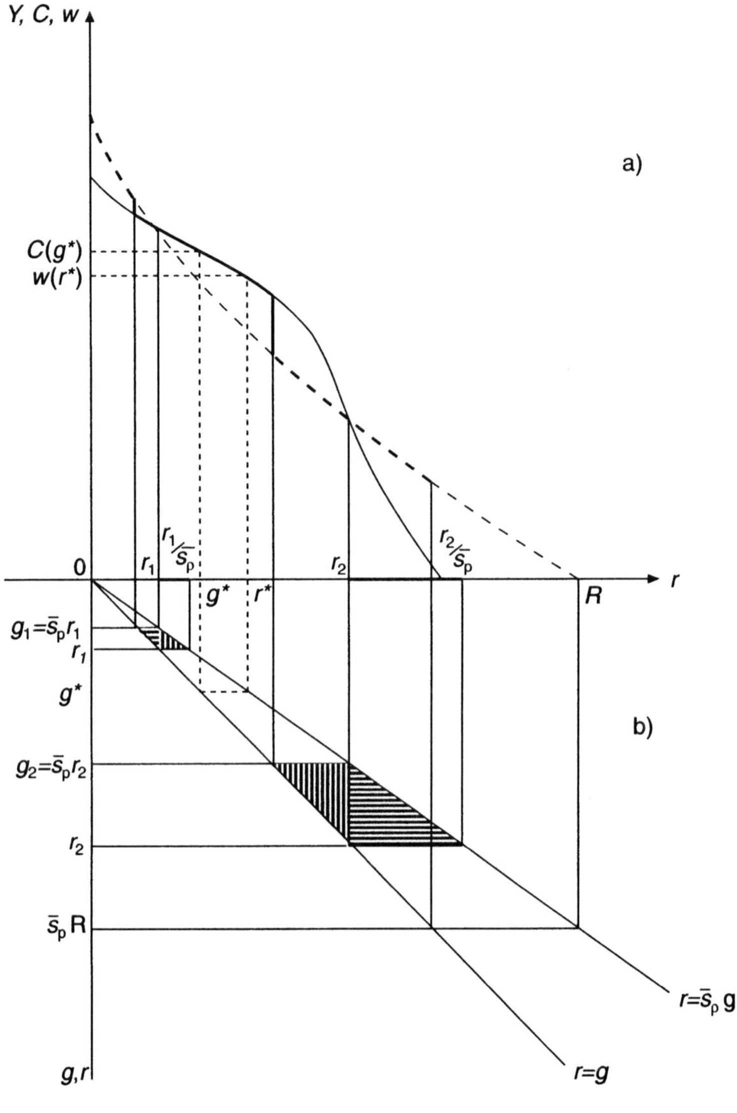

Figure 13.3

lower relative intensity of capital; or that it is the faster-growing economy to make a similar choice.[32]

It is again possible to have a graphical view of the properties of the individual accumulation paths representing golden age economies ranked according to their profit rates, from 0 to *R*. An economy in which the rate r^*

prevails can immediately be associated graphically – by means of quadrant (b) of Figure 13.3[33] – with the rate of accumulation g^* that determines it as the equilibrium profit rate. Knowing g^*, it is immediately possible to determine $C(g^*)$. By means of the straight line joining $(g, C(g^*))$ and $(r, w(r^*))$, one can also determine the values of $Y(r^*)$, $K(r^*)$ and $v(r^*)$.[34]

We know from the previous paragraph that the relative capital intensity of golden age economies, compared pair by pair, is fully identified by the relative production of consumption goods.

When an economy's growth rate is between the levels $g = \bar{s}_P r_i$ and $g = r_i$ (where r_i is a switch point), the technique chosen is not the one of the two that would permit the highest level of per capita consumption.[35] Hence, the technique chosen in correspondence with the equilibrium profit rate is not the one that gives rise – compared with the alternative – to a higher degree of capital intensity for the economy.[36]

Let us refer to the graphical example maintained throughout the paper. If, in Figure 13.3, the rate of growth of the corresponding economy lies between the levels of $\bar{s}_P r_1$ and r_1, the technique adopted in that economy is B, while the technique that would allow higher per capita consumption at the same growth rate is A. The levels of consumption associated with the various growth rates are shown in bold in Figure 13.3, as an envelope of sections of the frontiers of the techniques. To avoid confusion, it should be remembered that in this case the reference axis is the bisector of quadrant (a). The intervals of the profit rate in correspondence with which the less capital-intensive alternative for the economy is chosen are marked in black on the x axis. To these intervals correspond growth rates (see the shaded part of quadrant (b)) for each of which the ranking of techniques as regards the value of C allowed does not correspond to their ordering as regards relative profitability.

Now a few points have to be made that are liable to complicate Robinson's analysis of capital accumulation. Joan Robinson, for example wrote:

> Comparing two economies in the same phase of technical development, one with higher real wages than the other (whether because the degree of monopoly in the past has been lower and the bargaining power of workers greater, *or because the urge to accumulate capital has been greater*), the economy with higher real wages is using more mechanized methods of production and consuming more relatively capital-intensive products. High wages, therefore, are associated with high output per man employed.
>
> (Robinson 1960b: 154; italics added)

A similar concept is expressed in Robinson (1962):

> Since the cost of labour, in terms of their own product, to the firms is lower in the economy with the higher rate of growth, the degree of

mechanization is less (except in some very cranky cases).

(ibid.: 96–7)

It does not need to be recalled that in the more general case of double switching the more mechanized technique can be advantageous when growth is slower, and vice versa. The point that needs to be made is above all another: that these choices do not necessarily coincide with those of greater or lesser capital intensity (compared with the alternatives that each economy faces *at its own growth rate*). Thus, it is possible to have an economy that grows more slowly, finds it more advantageous to use the more mechanized technique and in this way chooses the lower relative intensity of capital for the economy as a whole. In practice, what Robinson says is correct, precisely because the *very cranky cases* – in other words, reswitching of techniques – are excluded. It is, however, worth examining in detail what happens when reswitches occur.

Let I and II be two distinct golden age alternative equilibria with corresponding growth rates g_{I} and g_{II}, and $g_{\mathrm{I}} < g_{\mathrm{II}}$. It is assumed that $\bar{s}_{\mathrm{p}} r_1 < g_{\mathrm{I}} < r_1$ and $r_1 < g_{\mathrm{II}} < \bar{s}_{\mathrm{p}} r_2$. Both economies base their growth on technique B, which is the less mechanized technique. In the first case this technique corresponds to the choice of a lower capital intensity in the economy and in the second of a higher. With the terms inverted, the same would happen with technique A if $0 < g_{\mathrm{I}} < \bar{s}_{\mathrm{p}} r_1$ and $\bar{s}_{\mathrm{p}} r_2 < g_{\mathrm{II}} < r_2$.[37] This is the case in which the same technique is the most profitable alternative for different rates of balanced growth, though it is the alternative that makes greater relative use of capital in one case and less in the other.

Another paradox occurs when the two alternatives really involve two different techniques and for both, nonetheless, it is a question of the technique that requires the more (or less) intensive capital choice at the relative rate of growth. This, for example, is the case when $0 < g_{\mathrm{I}} < \bar{s}_{\mathrm{p}} r_1$ and $r_1 < g_{\mathrm{II}} < \bar{s}_{\mathrm{p}} r_2$ (or, conversely, when $\bar{s}_{\mathrm{p}} r_1 < g_{\mathrm{I}} < r_1$ and $\bar{s}_{\mathrm{p}} r_2 < g_{\mathrm{II}} < r_2$).

The case postulated by Joan Robinson of an inverse relationship between the rate of growth and capital intensity implied in golden age economies by the choice of the most profitable technique occurs only if g_{I} lies between 0 and $\bar{s}_{\mathrm{p}} r_1$, while g_{II} lies between $\bar{s}_{\mathrm{p}} r_1$ and r_1; or else if g_{I} lies between r_1 and $\bar{s}_{\mathrm{p}} r_2$ and g_{II} between $\bar{s}_{\mathrm{p}} r_2$ and r_2. Although they are special cases, they do not even fit Joan Robinson's example very well (and the neoclassical condition depicted in the production function even less), because the two techniques can interchange their role. In the first case, the higher relative intensity of capital for the economy that grows more slowly and has a lower profit rate and a higher real wage rate is associated with technique A, and in the second case with technique B.

Another effect now needs to be emphasized. When one goes along the scale of growth rates (from the lowest to the highest) and there is a change of technique, the switch is always to a less capital-intensive alternative. If we take the switch points of Figure 13.3, technique A is adopted up to the growth rate $g_1 = \bar{s}_p r_1$, after which technique B is adopted. The value at normal prices of per capita income, of per capita capital and of the capital/income ratio shift downwards. Starting from the point r_2, i.e. at the rate of growth $g_2 = \bar{s}_p r_2$, it is again the (more mechanized) technique A that is eligible. Nonetheless, we again have the same situation as in r_1: per capita income, per capita capital and the capital/income ratio reckoned at normal prices show another downward shift. In both cases, furthermore, per capita consumption falls in a non-continuous manner. This means that, in the interval between r_1 and r_2, technique A has become the technique corresponding to the less capital-intensive choice after being the more capital-intensive choice. At an intermediate profit rate, the techniques A and B are indistinguishable with regard to the degree of capital intensity to which they give rise.[38]

CONCLUSIONS

This paper has tackled some of Joan Robinson's exercises by comparing specific features of various economies, each in a state of long-run equilibrium at different points on a given spectrum of techniques.

The starting point taken in this paper is the question whether the alternation of profitability from a more to a less mechanized technique and vice versa means an equal alternation of advantageousness from a more to a less capital-intensive output and vice versa in economies adopting those techniques as an equilibrium choice at each point of the spectrum.

It has been found that the relative attributes of the production methods – i.e. of the techniques – that an economy is using do not in themselves make it possible to establish those of the economy, because the latter depend on the operating level of the production methods in the technique. In the final analysis, they depend on the rate of growth of the economy.

The relationships become even more complicated when a choice within the same range of techniques is made in order to sustain different rates of balanced steady growth. A more rapid growth may require a different technique from that needed for a slower growth and nonetheless always involves the choice of a higher (or, depending on the case, lower) relative capital intensity at the corresponding rate of growth as compared with the inferior alternative. Conversely, the more advantageous technique may always be the same, but the economies may be producing their output with a greater use of capital in one and with a lesser use of capital in the other – 'greater' or 'lesser' compared with how the technique discarded would fare.

Everything considered, if it is wished to establish *a priori* a correspondence between the relative degree of mechanization of techniques and the relative degree of capital intensity of golden age economies, it is necessary that reswitches should not occur in the range of technical possibilities, or that the economy's rate of expansion be zero, or if it is positive that it be below the level of the profit rate that gives rise to the first switching of profitability. Beyond these three alternatives no association is possible.

The reversing of the technological effect is not unexplainable: it occurs when it is dominated by the composition effect.

Taken individually, every net unit of all the goods produceable with two sets of production methods *always* requires a higher capital intensity – with normal values and at the points of indifference – in one case than in the other. Hence, there is a clear distinction between the two techniques as regards the capital intensity of their methods, a distinction that is derived on the basis of the physical specification of these methods.

Given the set of normal prices, the composition effect can indifferently be understood as working in either of two ways. We can either say that the composition of net output is heavily weighted with capital-intensive goods in the economy using the less mechanized technique; notwithstanding it can produce these goods, taken separately, with less capital inputs, it nonetheless has to produce 'too many' of them to maintain steady growth. Or else we can say that the composition of net output forces the same economy to use more of the more expensive capital goods and less of the less expensive capital goods; if the economy had used the other (more mechanized) technique, the *same* output would cost still more in terms of capital inputs, but with the other technique a different arrangement of production is suitable, and that arrangement implies a lower capital cost.

If the composition effect (in whatever direction it works) is stronger than the technology effect, the growing economy ends up with an average use of capital per worker (at normal prices) that is higher when it is organized on the less mechanized technique.

APPENDIX
CONDITIONS FOR CAPITAL INTENSIVENESS OF THE ECONOMY TO REVERSE THAT OF TECHNIQUES

We first have to establish how the values of per capita income, per capita investment and the capital output ratio associated to a permanent rate of growth, g ($0 \leq g \leq R$), and reckoned at normal prices can be determined on the w–r diagram. Consumption is given by the intercept of the vertical line with the w–r curve and is invariant with respect to r. Reference will be made to a generic situation represented by Figure 13.4.

We shall start from a national accounts identity, incomes equal the value of net production, that a Sraffa system must respect at any rate of profit:

$$rK(r) + w(r) = C + I(r)$$

From this, when the net product is such as will sustain a permanent rate of growth, g, it is possible to derive:

$$\frac{r-g}{g} I^g = C^g - w, \tag{9}$$

and hence (omitting the superscript g)

$$I = \frac{C-w}{r-g} g.$$

Let V denote the intercept on the y axis of the straight line passing through the points (C, g) and $(r, w(r))$ of the w–r curve and Z the intercept on the x axis. Similar triangles give

$$\frac{C-w}{r-g} = \frac{V-C}{g}$$

By substitution it is possible to obtain $I = \mathrm{O}V - C$ and hence

$$Y^g(r) = I^g(r) + C^g = \mathrm{O}V.$$

Having established this, it can easily be shown that: $1/v^g(r) = Z$.

The result is general. Hence the theorem on page 156 has a graphical proof in the fact that the slope of the straight lines passing through a switch point between two techniques, r_i, and respectively (C_a, g) and (C_b, g) is steeper for the technique that permits a higher consumption at the rate of growth g, provided $g < r_i$. These lines cut the y axis in such a way as to determine the

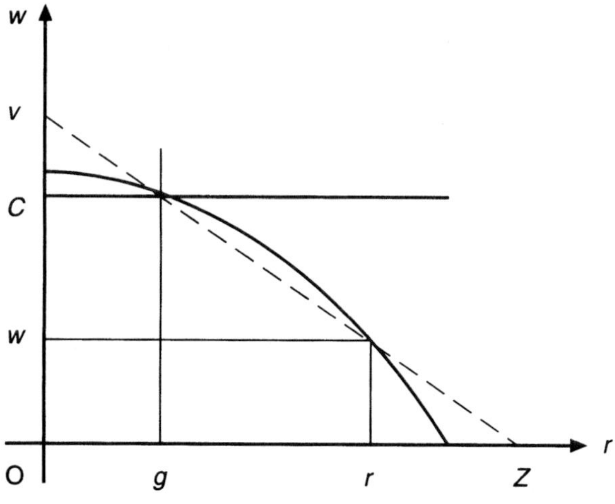

Figure 13.4

higher investment for the technique that involves the highest consumption.

When $g = r_i$, the consumption baskets permitted by the two techniques are identical. If the value of the investment goods needed in the two situations in order to permit growth at the rate r_i is measured using the $p(r_i)$ price system, resulting at the switch point r_i, we have in correspondence $s_p = 1$. The national accounts identities expressed by (9) still hold, since for both systems total consumption (coinciding with total wages) is equal to the output of consumer goods, and what remains of national income is the value of investment goods, equal to total profits. In this case, however, $I_a(r_i)$ # $I_b(r_i)$, because both are determined on the *y* axis by the tangent to the *w*–*r* curve at the point $(r_i, w(r_i))$, which is steeper for technique A than for technique B.

At the rate of growth r_i, however, if we measure the same physical aggregates using the $p(r_{ii})$ price system, where r_{ii} is another switch point and $r_i < r_{ii}$, $I_a(r_{ii})$ is necessarily always equal to $I_b(r_{ii})$.

It is desirable to arrive at a more general formulation of these points. Reference will continue to be made to an exogenously given growth rate, *g*. The condition for growth at this rate to occur with the (more mechanized) technique A rather than with technique B is that:

$$w_a(r) > w_b(r),$$

that is,

$$C_a + I_a(r) - rK_a(r) > C_b + I_b(r) - rK_b(r). \tag{10}$$

Given that C_a and C_b remain unchanged in value, the key to the determination of the relative advantageousness between the two techniques lies in the relative cost of the investment (measured in terms of consumer goods) at the various rates of profit and related price systems.

With $C_a - C_b$ known, the frontier of the possible values of $I_a - I_b$ in correspondence with indifference in the choice between the two techniques is given by:

$$I_a(r) - I_b(r) = \frac{g}{1+g}(C_a - C_b). \tag{11}$$

Equation (11) delimits the locuses of Figure 13.5 (constructed assuming $C_a - C_b > 0$) and of Figure 13.6 (constructed assuming $C_a - C_b < 0$) where techniques A and B are respectively chosen. The white region includes the set of points for which (10) is satisfied (technique A is chosen) and the shaded region the set of points for which it is not satisfied (technique B is chosen).

Although *a priori* the value of $I_a - I_b$ can behave in all the possible ways when *r* varies, some general properties can be derived by examining the two diagrams. Reference will be made to Figure 13.5, but the same propositions hold, *mutatis mutandis*, for Figure 13.6.

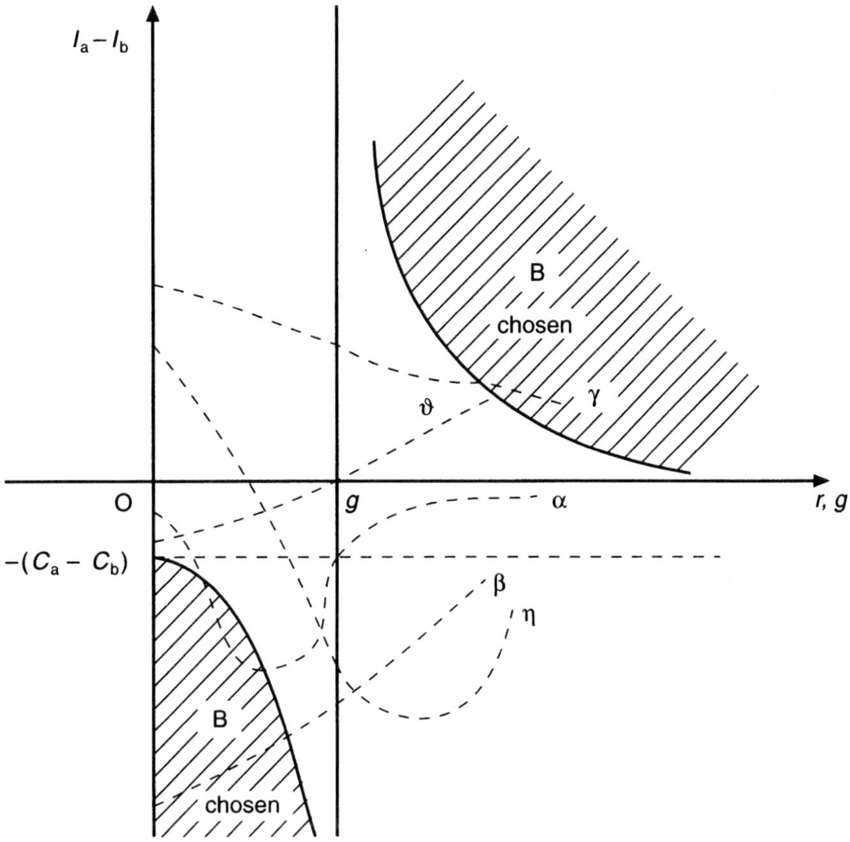

Figure 13.5

(a) The technique that permits the highest consumption at the growth rate g is always chosen when the rate of profit is equal to the rate of growth, $r = g$. No shapes of $I_a(r) - I_b(r)$ can reverse this result.

(b) Since technique A (the more mechanized one) is always more advantageous when $r = 0$, if there are inversions of advantageousness before $r = g$, their number will be even if $C^g_a < C^g_b$ and odd if $C^g_a > C^g_b$.

(c) At the inversion points in the economically significant stretches (to the right of $r = g$) the sign of $I_a(r) - I_b(r)$ is always the same as the sign of $C_a - C_b$; in fact, the curve passes from one region to the other with positive values in Figure 13.5. It may nonetheless happen that the cost of the investment implied by technique A decreases constantly compared with the cost of the investment implied by technique B (valued, however,

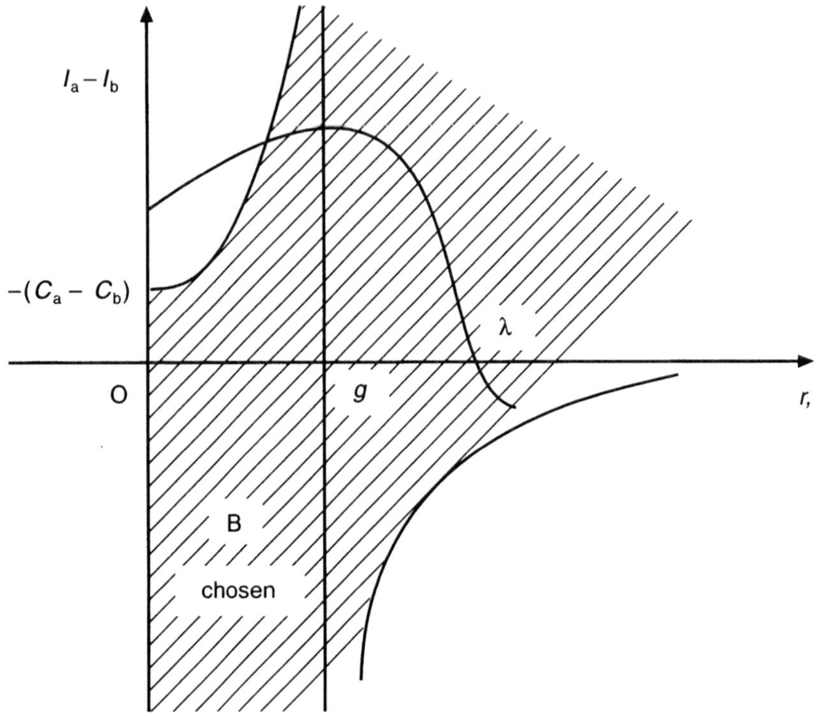

Figure 13.6

with different systems of prices) without an inversion of advantageousness occurring. The converse holds for Figure 13.6, where the switch at $r_i > g$ occurs with negative values of $I_a(r) - I_b(r)$.

In the case where g is exactly equal to a rate of profit corresponding to indifference with respect to the advantageousness of the two techniques, Figures 13.5 and 13.6 collapse to Figure 13.7. Because the curve $I_a - I_b$ starts from the white region, $I_a(0) - I_b(0) > 0$, the value of $I_a(r) - I_b(r)$ is definitely positive at the point of inversion $r = g$ if this is from A to B; it is definitely negative if the switch is from B to A . Nonetheless, if there are other inversion points to the right of g, at each such point the curve must cross the x axis on passing from one region to the other. Hence, at such points $I_a(r) - I_b(r) = 0$.

NOTES

1 This paper is based on the results reached in chapters 5 and 6 of Biasco (1968). Written on my return from Cambridge under the influence of Robinson's and Pasinetti's lectures, the article lay on my desk pending some refinement. As time

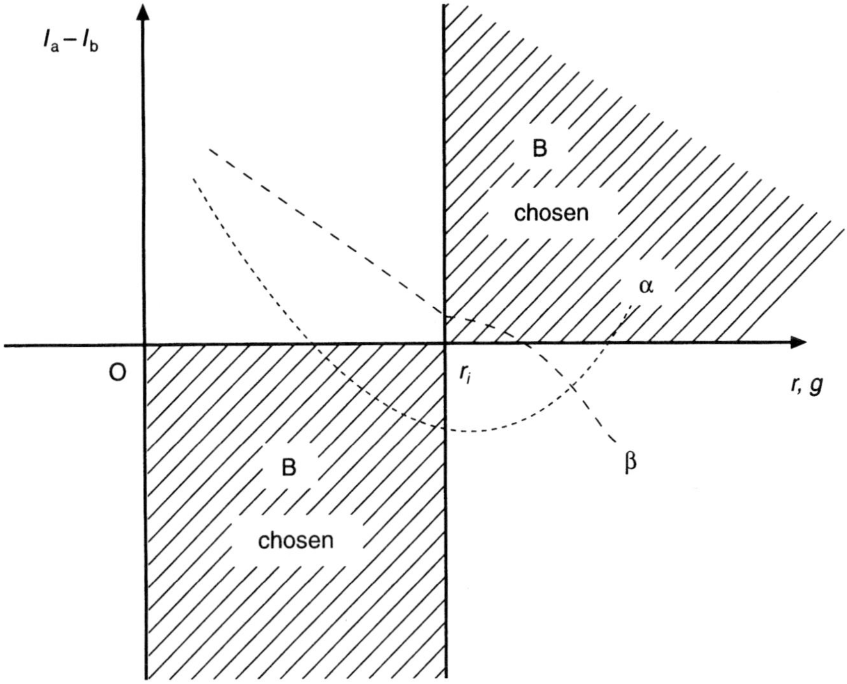

Figure 13.7

passed, my interests radically changed and the article was forgotten. In the meantime, Pasinetti's *Theory of Production* (1974) came out and some of the arguments of the paper were addressed in his last chapter; this was a further incentive to forget the paper. At the time it was written, the essay received useful comments from Professors P. Garegnani, L. Spaventa and P. Sylos Labini. Recently it has benefited from comments by Professor Lippi and by the editors of this volume.

2 The main contribution of Joan Robinson to the theory of economic growth is to be found in Robinson (1956 and 1962). For the concept of 'golden age', see in particular Robinson (1960a).

3 For the definition of concepts such as 'technique', 'relative mechanization' and 'relative capital intensity', see the next section. The difference in the values of the two sets of different physical goods has an unambiguous meaning only if calculated on the basis of an identical set of prices.

4 This can be an equilibrium path only if the economy following it does not know or cannot adopt the other technique. The path corresponding to the inferior technique is a purely hypothetical one.

5 It is implied here and hereafter that the techniques do not differ as regards the number and physical characteristics of the goods they involve.

6 It is well known that, at these levels of the profit and wage rates, the system of equilibrium prices obtained on the basis of the matrix of the two techniques is identical.

7 This means that, if there is more than one good, each good is present in identical proportions in the net product allowed by the two techniques.

8 If the latter is put equal to 1, the values obtained will be per capita values. 'Per capita' refers to workers employed, not to population.

9 The choice is limited to two techniques to simplify thc cxposition, but nothing would change if there were any discrete number of alternatives.

10 Calling x the extremity of this segment, the similarity of triangles gives $Y/x = rK(r)/r$, from which one obtains: $x = Y/K(r)$. In other words, the length of the segment cut off by the straight line in question is the income/capital ratio valued with the price system associated with the combination (w, r) of the point through which the line passes.

11 It has to be assumed that the growth: (a) takes place with unchanged production coefficients (i.e. that the given techniques are maintained) and unchanged tastes and habits; and (b) reflects a hypothetical rate of growth of natural forces. In what follows only the growth of labour force is considered.

12 The crucial assumption here is that the consumer good be produced by only one industry and be the only non-basic good of the system.

13 The condition requires that $|A - I|$ and $|B - I|$ have all the principal minors greater than zero. In economic terms this is equivalent to requiring that the production of a unit of good j does not use, directly or indirectly, more than a unit of good j itself.

14 We have still to refer to the ranking of relative capital intensities for the economies at the profit rate (or rates) yielding the same price system for both techniques, r_1 and r_2 in the example of Figure 13.1.

15 The assumptions of note 11 need to be remembered; i.e. the rate of growth of the economy reflects the growth rate of natural forces. Because the latter concerns only the growth of the labour force, the per capita ratios of the growing golden age economy do not change.

The conclusions reached in the text remain valid even with the introduction of an exogenous technical progress of the neutral Harrod type. This point is beyond the scope of this essay but for a discussion, see Biasco (1968: Appendix).

16 Written out, the production of good j that permits a surplus $(1 + g)$ times the amount used is:

$$(a_{j1}X_1 + a_{jj}X_j + a_{jn}X_n + a_{jc}C_a)(1 + g) = X_j.$$

17 The condition that a portion $g/(1 + g)$ of every unit of good j and of its means of production should be set aside to obtain the required surplus of investment goods is mathematically equivalent to multiplying all the terms of matrix A of the *inputs* by a scalar $(1 + g)$. For a given A the conditions of Hawkins and Simon are more restrictive if referred to a matrix $|A - \delta_{ij}/(1 + g)|$ than if referred to a matrix $|A - I|$, and all the more restrictive the higher g is. In economic terms, as part of the production has to be put aside when g rises, the quantity of good j needed to produce directly or indirectly a unit of the same good j increases as g rises. A technology that would satisfy the conditions for the reproduction of the system – which occurs when $|A - I|$ satisfies the conditions of Hawkins and Simon – may nonetheless not permit the achievement of a net product with the composition necessary for balanced growth at a predetermined rate g. It is easy to test that this happens when $g > R$.

18 Nothing would change if the propensity to save out of wages were greater than 0. It would only be necessary to take account of some validity constraints. For the rest, there would be no change in either the conclusions or the procedure for reaching them. Cf. Pasinetti (1962), Modigliani and Samuelson (1966). An analysis of the case in which $s_w > 0$, conducted in terms that make it comparable

with this paper, is to be found in Biasco (1968: chapters 7 and 8).

19 If we call $\mathbf{K}^g$ the row vector of the physical stock of capital that is in harmony with the rate of growth g and $\mathbf{I}^g$ the row vector of physical components of investment, the equality $S(r) = I(r)$ can be written as

$$s_p r\mathbf{K}^g\mathbf{p}(\mathbf{r}) = \mathbf{I}^g\mathbf{p}(\mathbf{r}),$$

where $\mathbf{p}(\mathbf{r})$ is the column vector of normal prices. The solutions of systems (5) and (6) guarantee that $\mathbf{I}^g = g\mathbf{K}^g$. From now on we will omit the superscript g, unless strictly necessary. It should be obvious that I, K, C, etc., are functions of the rate of growth and refer to some level of the latter.

20 Given g, every level of r is associated with the level of s_p – obtained as a residual from (7). That saving ratio is the one at which the flow of expenditure on capital (consumption) goods and the output of capital (consumption) goods (calculated at normal values, $p(r)$) are equal. By allowing s_p to vary, the Sraffa system has its degree of freedom restored.

21 As an example, it is possible to take the case in which $r = 0$. To imagine an equilibrium situation in which investment has a positive value, $I(0)$, while there is no saving financing it, is contrary to economic logic. The part of the frontier to the left of $r = g$ is of no interest.

22 What was said in note 4 needs to be kept in mind; i.e. the existence of a superior technique must not be known in one of the two economies.

23 Because capital goods are measured in physical terms and do not change in value, it is the value of investment that changes when r varies. Correspondingly, the value of income changes compared with the income there could be if consumer goods only were produced. (The unproduced part of consumer goods – the part it was potentially possible to obtain on the basis of systems (3) and (4) – makes room for the amount of investment goods required, because the two aggregates directly and indirectly incorporate the same quantity of labour.)

24 Whereas C_a and C_b are obtained from the primary systems (5) and (6) of quantities, w_a and w_b are obtained from the dual systems of prices. The condition $r = g/s_p$, which implies equality between saving and investment at normal prices, also implies that consumption expenditure is equal to the value of consumption goods production at normal prices.

25 From $r = (1/s_p)g$ and from $I/K = g$ it follows that $rK(r) = (1/s_p)I(r)$. It should be noted that the level of the rate of accumulation does not affect the demonstration of the theorem, which is valid within the limits $g < r_i \leq R$ if r_i is a point of switch. When $\bar{g} = r_i$ the condition (8) holds in the form $w_a^g - w_b^g = C_a^g - C_b^g = 0$, as $s_p = 1$, and $I_a^g(r_i) - I_b^g(r_i) \# 0$. However, for any successive point of switch, r_{ii} (implying $s_p \# 1$), it is $I_a^g(r_{ii}) - I_b^g(r_{ii}) = 0$. For conditions attached to the satisfaction of the (8) see the Appendix.

26 Actually, for growth rates higher than the profit rate of the last switch there is no basis for comparison between the techniques because it is as if there were only one that dominates the others in the interval of economically significant profit rates.

27 A graphical proof of the relationship is given in the Appendix. It shows that, for any technique, the value of $I^g(r)$, $Y^g(r)$, C^g is fully specified by the straight line passing through the points (C, g) and $(r, w(r))$ of the w–r curve. The intercept of the same line on the x axis is equal to the income, $Y^g(\mathrm{r})$, hence $I^g(r) = Y^g(r) - C^g$, and the intercept on the y axis is equal to the inverse of the capital/income ratio reckoned at normal prices. Having established this, it can easily be derived that the position of the straight lines passing through the intersection of the two w–r relationships and, respectively, through $(C_a, \bar{g})$ and $(C_b, \bar{g})$ is such as to warrant a greater intercept on the x axis for the technique that involves the lowest

consumption. Hence, in Figure 13.2, $v_a(r_2) < v_b(r_2)$.

28 It should be remembered that, with a growth rate $\bar{g}$ the significant segment of the x axis goes from $\bar{g}$ to R for $\bar{g} \leq R$.

29 Cf. *A Neo-neoclassical Theorem* in Robinson (1962). Joan Robinson proves the theorem by taking as a starting point two golden age economics, Aleph (with greater s_p) and Beth (with lower s_p), where techniques Alpha (more mechanized) and Beta (less mechanized) are respectively in operation. No reswitch exists between the two techniques.

> On the basis of prices corresponding to the rate of profit (where the two techniques are equally eligible) we can value the two stocks of capital goods. In Aleph we find that the value of capital on this basis is greater than in Beth. This follows from the general principles of choice of technique
>
> (Robinson 1962: 122)

From here Joan Robinson derives that:

> so long as the rate of profit on capital at which the calculation is made exceeds the rate of accumulation, the physical output of consumption goods is higher in Aleph than in Beth.
>
> (ibid.: 122)

The point at issue is the following. If Robinson assumed a more general case of double switching between two techniques, at appropriate rates of growth, the economies Aleph and Beth with all the characteristics described by Robinson could very well use the first, the Beta technique, and the second, the Alpha technique. The 'golden rule' (the neoclassical theorem) would in any case be verified, because the value of capital stock would still be greater in Aleph than in Beth. The inclusion of this case broadens and generalizes the field of verification of the 'golden rule'.

30 Account must be taken of the limits set in note 26, i.e. that for some growth rates comparison is impossible.

31 Here again it has to be assumed that the various growth rates correspond to hypothetical rates of expansion of natural forces. The maximum rate of expansion allowed is that which in equilibrium results in the maximum allowed rate of profit, and is therefore, $R/\bar{s}_p$.

32 A parallel range of possibilities would result if the exercise were repeated for a given rate of profit, $\bar{r}$, identical for all golden age economies (where $\bar{r}$ is a switch point) and s_p and g were allowed to vary along the spectrum of the w–r relationship.

33 Quadrant (b) gives the relationship between g and r, which is expressed by the straight line of slope $\bar{s}_p$. The bisector of the quadrant makes it possible to return g to the same axis as r.

34 See note 27 and the Appendix.

35 From any value of g between $\bar{s}_p r_1$ and r_1 on the bisector $g = r$ of quadrant (b) we can draw a vertical line that indicates in quadrant (a) the flows of consumption goods allowed by the two techniques at that rate of accumulation. To that level of g corresponds, on the straight line $g = \bar{s}_p r_1$ in quadrant (b), an equilibrium profit rate. The vertical line from that point meets the w–r curves in quadrant (a) when they have inverted their mutual position.

36 However, capital intensiveness is compared not with systems of prices resulting from that profit rate, but with the system of prices resulting at the switch point(s).

37 Actually, for the rates of accumulation between $\bar{s}_p r_2$ and $\bar{s}_p R$, technique A is the only one that exists.

38 This happens at $r = r_1/\bar{s}_p$. As we already know, the techniques A and B produce the same degree of capital intensity in the economy when the growth rate is equal to the switch-point profit rate.

REFERENCES

Biasco, S. (1968) *Problemi di dinamica comparata*. Rome: Edizioni Ateneo.

Modigliani, F. and Samuelson, P. (1966) Reply to Pasinetti and Robinson, *Review of Economic Studies*, October.

Pasinetti, L. L. (1962) Rate of Profit and Income Distribution in Relation to Rate of Growth, *Review of Economic Studies*, October.

——— (1974) *Theory of Production*. London: Macmillan.

Robinson, J. (1956) *The Accumulation of Capital*. London: Macmillan.

——— (1960a) *Exercises in Economic Analysis*. London: Macmillan.

——— (1960b) The Theory of Distribution. In *Collected Economic Papers*, vol. II. Oxford: Blackwell.

——— (1962) *Essays in the Theory of Economy Growth*. London: Macmillan.

14

THE ACCUMULATION OF CAPITAL AND STRUCTURAL ECONOMIC DYNAMICS[1]

Roberto Scazzieri

Even a casual look at the *General Index* of Joan Robinson's *Collected Economic Papers* (Robinson 1980) shows that her interest in capital accumulation and growth is not matched by an explicit, theoretical consideration of structural economic dynamics. More precisely, Joan Robinson's analysis of the pure logic and historical features of capitalist economic history seemingly leaves no room for the special blend of history and theory that characterizes classical and modern contributions to the *theory* of an economic system undergoing structural change.

This paper aims at providing an assessment of Joan Robinson's contribution to the theory of an expanding economy, by especially considering whether her lifelong interest in growth, development and capital accumulation might not suggest a definite conceptual approach to the analysis of structural economic dynamics. The paper is organized as follows. First, I consider the fundamental structure of Joan Robinson's *theory* of capital accumulation and growth. Then I examine a number of contributions Joan Robinson made to the analysis of the uneven growth and development of a modern capitalist economy. Finally, I suggest an interpretation of structural economic dynamics in the light of Joan Robinson's approach to the pure logic and historical actuality of an expanding economy characterized by capitalist institutions.

ACCUMULATION OF CAPITAL AND ECONOMIC DYNAMICS: A THEORETICAL FRAMEWORK

Joan Robinson's early attempt to cope with the theory of long-run economic expansion may be considered as arising from 'an attempt to apply the principles of Mr. Keynes' *General Theory of Employment, Interest and Money* to a number of particular problems' (Robinson 1947: v; Foreword to a reprint of the first edition). Especially interesting in this connection is the paper on 'The Long-Period Theory of Employment', which was originally published in the Viennese *Zeitschrift für Nationalökonomie* (1936) and reprinted as chapter 5 of *Essays in the Theory of Employment* (1947).

At the very beginning of the above contribution, we find the statement that 'Mr. Keynes' General Theory of Employment has been developed mainly in terms of short-period analysis, and the background of equilibrium theory which corresponds to it is largely unexplored' (Robinson 1947: 75). In particular, Joan Robinson argues that 'Mr. Keynes' system of analysis may be extended into the regions of the long period [so that] it may become possible to examine the long-period influences which are at work at any moment of time' (ibid.: 75). This paper also provides a useful insight into the early application of what was to become the characteristic Robinsonian approach to dynamic theory. This approach consists in considering a simplified case at the beginning of the analysis, then moving on to more complex and realistic cases in a sequence of steps.

Joan Robinson's starting point in the formulation of a theory of the long period is to consider 'a closed community, living under a capitalist system, with population stable in respect to numbers and to age distribution, and with given tastes and technical knowledge' (ibid.: 75). Under such conditions, and provided that 'a certain rate of interest has been established and is maintained at an unvarying level' (ibid.) for a sufficiently long period, the accumulation process (that reflects the entrepreneurs' decisions to undertake investment) *has come to an end*, and only replacement investment takes place.[2] Against this analytical background, Joan Robinson considers first 'the change in the position of long-period equilibrium corresponding to an alteration in the rate of interest' (Robinson 1947: 79), then the effects of 'an alteration in the thriftiness of the community', as well as of 'movements in population' and 'changes in technique' (ibid.: 94). The general conclusion reached by Joan Robinson at this stage of her analytical development is that '[t]he effect of an increase in thriftiness . . . is to reduce the equilibrium level of employment and the stock of capital' (ibid.). On the other hand, population increase and technical progress may be generally associated with positive net investment: '[s]ince an increase in population requires an increase in capital equipment, to provide for a higher level of consumption, a continuous increase in the population would prevent investment from ever falling to zero' (ibid.: 95). And,

> [i]n general we may suppose that, except when inventions are highly capital-saving, a period of positive net investment will result from them, even when the equilibrium stock of capital (reckoned in wage units) is not increased, for all except the most capital-saving require an increase in capital per head, while the reduction in total output which results from increased thriftiness will not be immediately foreseen.
>
> (Robinson 1947: 98)

The analytical and methodological foundations of Joan Robinson's later approach to dynamic analysis are clearly expounded in the Introduction to *The Generalisation of the General Theory and Other Essays* (Robinson 1979: ix–xxviii). There it is argued that

> dynamic analysis . . . cannot explain how an economy behaves, in given conditions, without reference to past history. . . . My generalisation of the General Theory was an attempt to treat the analysis of accumulation according to Keynes' prescription. I worked out the internal relationships of a capitalist economy in steady growth – a golden age – omitting the large fields of foreign trade and government action which, however, are susceptible to be treated in the same manner. I used it as the background to analyse departures from it – that is to study the effect upon a growing economy of various types of vicissitudes that it may meet with.
>
> (Robinson 1979: xvii–xviii)

The bulk of *The Generalisation of the General Theory and Other Essays* had already appeared in 1952 under the title of *The Rate of Interest and Other Essays*. Remarkable features of that contribution to the theory of capital accumulation are the explicitly Marshallian standpoint, the interpretation of Keynes' *General Theory* as 'an application to output as a whole of the analysis developed by Marshall of the short-period equilibrium of a particular industry' (Robinson 1979: 3), and the belief that '[t]o extend Marshall's long-period theory to output as a whole is by no means such a simple matter' (ibid.). The main difficulty with an *aggregative* theory of the long period is found in Marshall's own conception that an industry in long-run equilibrium 'on balance, is making no change in its capital equipment' (ibid.). Such a conception, when applied to the economic system as a whole, entails stationary conditions, and this is considered to be 'contrary to the spirit of Marshall's system, which is obviously intended to apply to an expanding economy' (ibid.). Indeed, as Joan Robinson points out, 'the main difficulty is that, as soon as we envisage an economy in equilibrium with zero net investment, we are plunged into an imaginary world, for the institutions of capitalism, in actual experience, are closely bound up with the process of accumulation' (ibid.: 4–5). Moving from the above premise, Joan Robinson maintains that a 'generalization' of Keynes' theory to the process of capital accumulation should first of all be based on dropping the Marshallian view of long-period equilibrium: 'let us boldly throw away the notion of long-period equilibrium and see how we get on without it' (ibid.: 5). This attempt leads her to examine the conditions for the steady expansion of an economic system in which 'accumulation of capital is going on continuously' (ibid.: 24). Steady growth is examined 'in order to see what conditions are required to make such a state of affairs possible' (ibid.). It is worth considering Joan Robinson's characterization of steady economic expansion in some detail:

> The position that we are looking for cannot correctly be described as 'equilibrium' for it has not the property of restoring itself in the face of a chance shock. It is, rather, a position which is free from 'internal contradictions' in the sense that it can perpetuate itself continuously provided that no shock ever occurs. Let us imagine that in our ideal world land and labour are always available as required, that the supply of potential finance is continuously renewed as it is used up, and that the monetary system functions in such a way as to keep the rate of interest constant. Then the initial position of full capacity working can perpetuate itself provided that the following conditions are fulfilled: (1) Technical progress goes on at a steady pace, and the age composition of the stock of capital is such as to require renewals at a regular rate. Amortisation allowances are set at the level appropriate to the rate of obsolescence and wear and tear which is being experienced, and, taken as a whole, are being continuously reinvested as they accrue. (2) The gestation period of capital goods, on the average, is constant, so that there is a regular relationship between investment and the rate at which new capital goods become available for use. (3) Technical progress is neutral on balance, in the sense that the cost in terms of wage units of capital per unit of output falls at the rate at which output per man-hour rises. (4) Competition between entrepreneurs keeps constant the normal rate of profit, that is, the rate of profit obtainable when effective demand is such as to keep capital working just at capacity . . . (5) The proportion of net income saved remains constant.
>
> (Robinson 1979: 26–7)

The self-replacing features of an economic system in which the five conditions above are satisfied essentially reflect a correspondence between the structure of flows on the production side and that on the demand side:

> In the initial position we assumed that (steady development having occurred in the past) the stock of productive equipment was divided between consumption and investment industries (including in investment both the construction of capital equipment and the building up of stocks and work-in-progress) in the proportion in which gross income is divided between consumption and gross saving. The investment which was going on was in course of increasing the stock of capital in each sector. The five conditions set out above ensure that this situation is free from any 'internal contradiction', that is to say it has no inherent tendency to upset itself. For if the stock of capital continues to increase at the same proportionate rate (reckoned in terms of product) as in the initial position, capacity, output, investment and consumption all increase at that proportionate rate. The stock of capital, as it grows, is continuously worked at capacity; it finds demand for its product growing at the same rate as output and yielding the same rate of profit.

> The expectations of profit in the light of which investment was planned are continuously fulfilled, and therefore renewed, as time goes by. *The initial position continuously reproduces itself upon a gradually expanding scale.*
>
> (Robinson 1979: 27–8; italics added)

The fundamental analytical structure of Joan Robinson's theory of long-run accumulation and growth is clearly expressed in the above passages (dating back to the 1952 edition of *The Rate of Interest and Other Essays*). This logical structure may be considered as a natural theoretical development of some of the main conclusions reached in the early paper on 'The Long-Period Theory of Employment' (Robinson 1936; see above). It is indeed a logical structure related to an important tradition of economic theorizing that emphasizes the *logical* possibility of steady accumulation and expansion of an economic system characterized by capitalist institutions (Karl Marx, Gustav Cassel, Roy Harrod and Evsey Domar being the authorities mentioned by Joan Robinson herself in her 1952 paper 'The Model of an Expanding Economy' published in the *Economic Journal*).

It is worth considering now in some detail the role assigned by Joan Robinson to the analysis of steady growth within the framework of dynamic theory. She explicitly admits that the model of a steadily growing economy 'does not correspond to the behaviour to be expected from any actual economy. It is nothing more than a piece of simple arithmetic' (Robinson 1979: 30). The role of steady growth is essentially that of providing 'a *standard of reference*, in order to classify the various types of disturbances to which actual economies may be subject' (ibid.; italics added).

In particular, Joan Robinson makes it clear that the logical conditions for continuous accumulation (see above) allow for identification of the *necessary* conditions for steady progress. However, she readily admits that,

> even when all the necessary conditions ... are fulfilled, its realisation depends upon faith. So long as entrepreneurs expect to find a profitable market for increased output they will maintain investment and so, at one stroke, maintain (expanding) effective demand and provide the equipment to meet it. Once they are smitten with doubt and each waits to see what the others will do, investment becomes insufficient to absorb potential saving and effective demand not only fails to expand but fails to remain at the level which makes the existing stock of capital profitable to operate. Thus *the given conditions are not sufficient to ensure continuous accumulation, but they are such as to make continuous accumulation possible*
>
> (Robinson 1979: 29–30; italics added)

As pointed out in the 1952 *Economic Journal* paper, the conditions for a 'continuously expanding capitalist economy' (Robinson 1960: 74) point to two distinct features of an economic system with capitalist institutions: on the one hand, steady growth cannot be excluded; on the other hand, it may be shown that it can take place only under very special circumstances. The 'simple piece of arithmetic' (ibid.) that expresses the common core of steady dynamics in the variety of theories mentioned above leads economists to the discovery that,

> [w]hen a constant proportion of income is added to capital every year and capital bears a constant ratio to income, then income expands continuously at a constant proportional rate. Thus, when 10 per cent of net income is invested every year, and the stock of capital is 5 years' purchase of net income, then the stock of capital, the rate of investment per annum, consumption per annum and net income per annum all expand cumulatively at 2 per cent per annum.
>
> (ibid.)

The objections raised against the possibility that the correct 'proportions' be satisfied in most historical circumstances make it quite explicit that steady expansion has to be considered as a special case, a 'reference path' useful in order to disentagle the logic of capitalist dynamics, but not a growth pattern explaining (even only in a 'stylized' fashion) the actual course of economic history. The logical possibility of steady expansion has a twofold implication: on the one side 'it contradicts the view that there is an inescapable necessity for capitalism to run down' (ibid.); on the other hand, 'it contradicts the view that there is, in general, an automatic tendency for capitalism to keep going' (ibid.).

To sum up, the fictive path of steady accumulation may be considered as 'an analytical device to permit us to discuss unsteady development' (Robinson 1979: 32). It may also be considered as a benchmark ensuring that some rationale for effective economic policy may indeed be found within the logic of a capitalist economy.

VICISSITUDES OF ECONOMIC PROGRESS AND UNSTEADY GROWTH

Joan Robinson often recognized the irregular pattern followed by the historical, long-run development of a capitalist economy. On the other hand, the careful consideration of steady accumulation is a characteristic feature of her contribution to dynamic theory. In this section, I shall examine where exactly the consideration of historical developments breaks the fulfilment of conditions for steady dynamics. If we consider a fictive economy that has been growing according to a steady pattern indefinitely in the past, it will be found that 'there is a certain stock of physical equipment, adapted to the demands which have been ruling for various commodities' (Robinson 1979: 24). In particular, the composition of the existing capital stock must be compatible with the current division of purchasing power between consumption and non-consumption uses: 'the division of capacity between investment-goods and consumption-goods industries [must be] in the same ratio as the division of gross income between gross saving and consumption' (ibid.). Under such conditions, '[e]ffective demand is such as to secure full capacity working of the stock of equipment, in both sectors' (ibid.). The assumption that continuous accumulation takes place implies that the capital stock in each sector is increasing. However, a steady increase of the capital stock in each sector entails that the original proportion between the productive capacity in the investment goods industries and the productive capacity in the consumption goods industries is maintained through time. This *proportional expansion* of sectoral capacities makes it possible for productive capacity to expand in line with the expansion of effective demand, on the assumption that the shares of consumption and gross saving in gross income remain constant through time. Technical progress is compatible with steady accumulation provided it is assumed that it goes on at a steady pace and that it affects all productive sectors in a uniform way. As a matter of fact, technical progress of this type entails, under conditions of constant population, that

> [t]he division of the labour force (and of the productive capacity of capital goods) between the investment sector and the consumption sector... remains unchanged as time goes by. A given number of workers in the investment sector produce plant (for both sectors) of an ever increasing productive capacity, and a given number of workers in the consumption sector operate it to produce an ever increasing output.
>
> (Robinson 1965: 88)

Proportional expansion of this kind may be considered to be free from 'internal contradictions' (ibid.: 99). The 'logical feasibility' of proportional expansion entails that, in the absence of external disturbing influences, and of changes in entrepreneurs' attitudes and beliefs, there is no inherent obstacle for the economic system to divert from the steady-accumulation and steady-growth path.[3]

The idealized character of such an expansion pattern is emphasized by Joan Robinson with the phrase 'golden age', which denotes that 'mythical state of affairs not likely to obtain in any actual economy' (ibid.: 99) in which a continuous process of capital accumulation is compatible with the absence of structural bottlenecks and structural change.

The actual historical course followed by the expansion of an economic system characterized by capitalist institutions shows a variety of disturbing factors at work, which make steady expansion extremely unlikely (even if *not logically impossible*). Among such factors, Joan Robinson mentions changes in thriftiness (that is, changes in saving propensities), changes in the rate of population growth, a variation in the supply of land (or of other non-produced resources), factors that may ease finance or put a check upon it, 'direct effects of changes in the rate of interest' (Robinson 1979: 54).[4]

Joan Robinson briefly considers 'other vicissitudes' as well, although maintaining that they are 'well known and obvious in their effects' (Robinson 1979: 55). These are changes in the general level of prices (which may have important redistributive effects, as well as influencing expectations on which investment decisions depend), changes in tastes (which require switching productive capacity from one form of utilization to another), and changes in technique (considered to be the most important factor that may disturb the smooth course of capital accumulation).

ON THE EVOLVING STRUCTURE OF A CAPITALIST ECONOMY: NOTES ON METHODS OF DYNAMIC ECONOMICS

The foregoing argument entails that, in Joan Robinson's view, economic dynamics (of an economic system with capitalist institutions) lend themselves to a purely theoretical study of the fictive case in which the accumulation process proceeds free from internal contradictions and steady expansion is achieved. However, it is also admitted that 'a private-enterprise economy is subject to so many vicissitudes' that 'it can never in fact enjoy steady progress' (Robinson 1979: 58). The critical theoretical implication of the above proposition is that a capitalist economy may be analytically reconstructed in terms of the model of steady accumulation (the 'golden age'). The golden age pictures a 'mythical' capitalist economy whose internal relationships may accurately be investigated by economic theory (see, in particular, Book II of *The Accumulation of Capital*, which considers 'Accumulation in the Long Run' and concludes with a 'Synopsis of the Theory of Accumulation in the Long Run'). The role of the golden age is *not* that of providing (directly or indirectly) an explanation of the actual course of economic history. It is rather that of providing a benchmark (a 'standard of reference') in terms of which the actual 'vicissitudes' of a real economy may be *classified* (see Robinson 1979: 30).

It may be worth considering some implications of the above perspective for what concerns the role of economic theory (and of dynamic theory in particular) in providing what may be called an 'analytical understanding' of economic history. There is, first of all, one important consequence of the unrealism of the steady state, which Joan Robinson is ready to acknowledge. This is the fact that, if an actual (capitalist) economy cannot be assumed to have 'a history of smooth development behind it' (Robinson 1979: 58), then the steady state cannot be a reference path in the study of transitions (or 'traverses', if we were to use the terminology later adopted by John Hicks in his 'Neo-Austrian' analysis; see Hicks 1970 and 1973). In particular, if past economic history is characterized by an alternation of booms and depressions (as is often the case), then the capital stock existing at any given time bears the mark of its own past history, and the renewals of capital stock cannot follow a steady pace. On the contrary 'renewals … come in sudden rushes, divided by periods when the accumulation of amortisation funds exceeds current expenditure on replacement, and "echoes" of the original speeding up or retardation of the rate of investment repeat themselves several times before dying out' (Robinson 1979: 58). Another difficulty (also related to the 'material side' of capital accumulation) is that changes in the physical characteristics of capital goods generally entail a change in the gestation period of capital equipment. This contradicts one important assumption of the model of steady accumulation, and has the implication that abrupt changes in the rate of change of the capital stock may take place from one year to another. A similar obstacle to steady expansion comes from rigidities in labour supply due to the received structure of working skills or to the existing territorial distribution of the labour force.

In conclusion, '[t]he fossils embedded in the stock of capital (and in the supply of labour trained to various occupations or settled in various districts) destroy the possibility of perfectly smooth development' (Robinson 1979: 59). And the most effective 'fossil' (that is, the most important mark on the present coming from the past) is the character of expectations. For a past experience of uneven growth tends to be associated with the expectation that the future course of economic activity will also be troubled (and vice versa): '[e]xperience of prosperity in the past creates conditions favourable to prosperity in the present, and fear breeds the disaster which it fears' (ibid.).

Finally (last but not least), the relatively *narrow scope* one could associate with entrepreneurial expectations makes it even more likely that a historical experience of troubled business life will be reflected in the belief that 'tranquillity' (an essential feature of the golden age) will not prevail in the future:

> entrepreneurs are looking back over a disturbed past which teaches them that anything may happen in the future. This is even more true for any one line of industry than it is for the system as a whole. Entrepreneurs do not (and have no business to) think globally. Each is interested in a narrow range of markets. And each section of the economy has all sorts of vicissitudes even when the whole is developing fairly steadily. Thus it is not rational to expect a steady future, and, what cuts much deeper, it is not rational to expect anything in particular with great assurance, for experience teaches that expectations generally turn out to be mistaken.
>
> (Robinson 1979: 59)

In conclusion, Joan Robinson finds that the 'historical heritage' linking the past and the future of any given economic system makes the utilization of the golden age as a *reference path* highly problematic. History leaves 'fossils' behind it, and a troubled history makes it untenable to use the structural and behavioural features of the steady state as the starting point in the investigation of dynamic processes brought about by actual 'impulses' (Joan Robinson's 'changes of fortune'). However, it is possible to use the model of steady accumulation in order to assess in which way the actual characteristics of dynamic paths may *distance* the economic system from the ideal features of a golden age.[5]

Joan Robinson's approach to the analysis of an expanding economy is characterized by the view that dynamic investigations are best carried out by considering the relationship between broad, overall movements of the economy (such as those involving demographic changes, capital accumulation and technical change), rather than detailed transformations of the economic structure (see, for instance, the Preface to *The Accumulation of Capital*).

This perspective is probably influenced by the Keynesian roots of Joan Robinson's approach to the analysis of long-run dynamics. Indeed, Keynes' influence upon Joan Robinson's attitude is perhaps deeper than one might think. For the Robinsonian approach to economic dynamics is associated with Keynes' view that economic analysis has to deal with 'relationships that cannot be reduced to a system of axioms' (Robinson 1979: xvi). Joan Robinson quotes approvingly Keynes' statement that '[t]he object of [economic] analysis is, not to provide a machine, or method of blind manipulation, which will furnish an infallible answer, but to provide ourselves with an organised and orderly method of thinking out particular problems' (J. M. Keynes, *General Theory*, p. 297; quoted in Robinson 1979: xvi). In Joan Robinson's view, the above perspective entails that the aim of economic theory may be that of providing a conceptual framework within which the rational discussion of particular issues may be conducted, rather than that of formulating a direct (even if simplified) map of dynamic processes. To use a somewhat casual expression, a 'theory of economic history' is a feasible intellectual endeavour according to John Hicks, but not according to Joan Robinson.

Economic theory, according to Joan Robinson, should be able 'to set up a highly simplified *model* of an economy, which is intended to bring into an orderly scheme of ideas the main movements that may be expected to occur in reality, while ruling out innumerable detailed complications' (Robinson 1965: 63–4).

In this connection, the task of dynamic theory is not to suggest a realistic interpretation of actual processes. It is rather 'to [map out] a large area of the problems that should be investigated in the light of contemporary history' (Robinson 1979: xvii–xviii).

There is a sense in which the above viewpoint shifts economic theory away from the theoretical reconstruction of actual processes and turns it into an experiment in instrumental inference, which is, using Adolph Lowe's words, an attempt 'to discover the particular set of causes that are suitable for the realization of some postulated effect' (Lowe 1965: 264). And a pupil of Joan Robinson, Gautam Mathur, has admitted that '[t]he analysis [of post-Keynesian macrodynamics] is relevant to reaching broad conclusions about the tendencies which are, on the average, *instrumental* in maintaining steady growth' (Mathur 1965: 4; italics added).

It may be worth examining at this point a feature of Robinsonian theory that is especially useful in considering a number of subsequent contributions to the theory of structural economic dynamics.

A useful starting point may be Joan Robinson's view that the model of steady accumulation is best formulated by considering broad aggregates only, thus 'abstracting from relative movements, [and conducting the] argument in terms of simple quantities' (Robinson 1965: 64). This opinion is presented by Joan Robinson as a way of avoiding the index number problem (ibid.). It may, however, be argued that this perspective has far-reaching implications as far as the treatment of structural change is concerned. In particular, changes in the composition of aggregates are generally overlooked as a specific theoretical issue in dynamic analysis, and important sources of rigidities in the productive structure may ultimately be reduced to temporary frictions not to be assigned autonomous theoretical relevance.

A case in point is Joan Robinson's treatment of the implications of 'changes in tastes'. In this connection, it is argued that

> changes in the objects of consumption, if gradual, need produce no disturbing effects (provided that they are neutral between capital and labour) for productive capacity can be switched from one line to another by changing its character as it is renewed in the normal course out of amortisation funds, and the supply of skilled labour can be adapted to requirements (though this may be a more troublesome process) by normal wastage and recruitment.
>
> (Robinson 1979: 57)[6]

In other words, the smooth operation of dynamic factors involving changes in the composition of aggregates is not considered *per se* a sufficient reason for dropping the model of steady accumulation, and ultimately the aggregative approach to long-run dynamics. This perspective is remarkably different from the course taken by a number of subsequent writers in the 'new classical' or post-Keynesian traditions, who have explicitly emphasized the theoretical interest of an analysis of structural economic dynamics carried out within the framework of multi-sectoral, complex representations of the economic system (see, for example, Goodwin 1976, Leon 1967, Pasinetti 1981, 1993, Quadrio Curzio 1986, 1995).

NOTES

1 This paper is based on my contribution to the conference 'The Passion of Reason: Joan Robinson (1903–1983)', Luigi Einaudi Foundation, Turin, 13–14 December 1993. Research support from the Italian Ministry of University and Scientific Research (Project 'Economic Dynamics, Structural Change and Growth Paths') is gratefully acknowledged.

2 It may be interesting to follow Joan Robinson's argument on this matter:

> [t]he marginal efficiency of capital corresponding to zero net investment is equal to the rate of interest and if, by chance, positive or negative investment were to occur, the marginal efficiency of capital would cease to be equal to the given rate of interest. If new investment were to take place capital would be increased and its earnings at the margin would fall. The marginal efficiency of capital would then be less than the rate of interest. The investment would turn out to have been unprofitable, capital goods would not be worth replacement and a movement back to equilibrium would set in with a decline in the stock of capital. On the other hand, if, in equilibrium, the stock of capital goods were allowed to deteriorate the marginal efficiency of capital would rise above the rate of interest and investment would take place until the stock of capital was restored to its former level.
>
> (Robinson 1947: 76)

3 In Joan Robinson's words,

> [p]rovided that political events cause no disturbances, and provided that the entrepreneurs have faith in the future and desire to accumulate at the same proportional rate as they have been doing over the past, there is no impediment to prevent them from continuing to do so. As long as they do, the system develops smoothly without perturbations. Total annual output and the stock of capital (valued in terms of commodities) then grow together at a constant proportionate rate compounded of the rate of increase of the labour force and the rate of increase of output per man.
>
> (Robinson 1965: 99)

4 An example of the latter could be a fall in the rate of interest that 'transfers demand to more capital-using types of consumption (as when a fall in house rents increases outlay on living space from a given family income)' (Robinson 1979: 54).

5 This characteristic of Joan Robinson's dynamic theory may be considered to be an important distinguishing feature with respect to the approach to economic dynamics proposed by the late Hicks. In the latter case, the steady state is defined as the situation in which 'the particular characteristics of the initial position cease to have much effect upon the [dynamic] path – when it comes to be determined by the *current* determining elements only' (Hicks 1973: 62). The steady state (a situation in which the past history of the economic system *does not matter*) is then used by Hicks in order to investigate the dynamic path followed by a given economic system on certain simplifying assumptions (the fixwage assumption or the full employment assumption) when the actual economy is not a steady state. The reason for Hicks' approach is that, when the economic system is out of the steady state, *history does matter*, so that a definite starting point must be selected. Hicks recognizes that it would ideally be better to start from an initial state that is 'itself a mixed state, itself the result of a transition which is still incomplete'

(Hicks 1973: 81). But the analytical difficulties associated with the consideration of an incomplete transition make Hicks prefer consideration of a steady state as the starting point in the analysis of historical dynamic paths (which are analytically represented as 'traverses' from one steady state to another). Joan Robinson's utilization of the model of steady accumulation is clearly different from Hicks's. In particular, Joan Robinson's view seems to be that it is irrational to conceive of fictive processes taking place in 'historical' time (as in Hicks' traverse analysis), and that a *comparison* between steady accumulation and unsteady development (perhaps associated with a *classification* of the main disturbances in a real economic system) is what economic theory may achieve in the analysis of dynamic processes.

6 It is, however, acknowledged that 'a sudden and large switch of demand from one commodity to another' may be a source of unsteady dynamics (see Robinson 1979: 57). It is also remarkable that Joan Robinson admitted, to a certain extent, the greater realism of a disaggregated model in investigating the actual dynamics of any given economic system, but found this an insufficient reason for abandoning the steady-state model. For example, in discussing Paolo Leon's contribution to the analysis of structural change, Joan Robinson maintains that 'as Paolo Leon has argued, the notion of a uniform rate of profit in a growing economy is somewhat anomalous, but it is just as well to get the analysis settled at this stage before going on to the next' (Robinson 1973: 67).

REFERENCES

Goodwin, R. M. (1976) The Use of Normalized General Coordinates in Linear Value and Distribution Theory. In R. Polenske and J. V. Skolka, eds, *Advances in Input–Output Analysis*. Cambridge: Ballinger, 581–603.

Hicks, J. R. (1970) A Neo-Austrian Growth Theory, *Economic Journal*, 80(June): 257–81.

——— (1973) *Capital and Time. A Neo-Austrian Theory*. Oxford: Clarendon Press.

Leon, P. (1967) *Structural Change and Growth in Capitalism*. Baltimore, Md.: Johns Hopkins University Press.

Lowe, A. (1965) *On Economic Knowledge. Toward a Science of Political Economics*. New York: Harper & Row.

Mathur, G. (1965) *Planning for Steady Growth*. Delhi: Oxford University Press.

Pasinetti, L. L. (1981) *Structural Change and Economic Growth. A Theoretical Essay on the Dynamics of the Wealth of Nations*. Cambridge: Cambridge University Press.

——— (1993) *Structural Economic Dynamics. A Theory of the Economic Consequences of Human Learning*. Cambridge: Cambridge University Press.

Quadrio Curzio, A. (1986) Technological Scarcity: An Essay on Production and Structural Change. In M. Baranzini and R. Scazzieri, eds, *Foundations of Economics. Structures of Inquiry and Economic Theory*. Oxford and New York: Blackwell, 311–38.

——— (1995) *Production and Efficiency with Global Technologies*, with an Appendix by C. F. Manara and M. Faliva. In M. A. Landesmann and R. Scazzieri, eds, *Production and Economic Dynamics*. Cambridge: Cambridge University Press, forthcoming.

Robinson, J. V. (1936) The Long Period Theory of Employment, *Zeitschrift für Nationalökonomie*, 7: 74–93.

——— (1947) [1937] *Essays in the Theory of Employment*, 2nd edn. Oxford: Blackwell.
——— (1952) *The Rate of Interest and Other Essays*. London: Macmillan.
——— (1960) [1952] The Model of an Expanding Economy. In *Collected Economic Papers*, vol. II, Oxford: Blackwell.
——— (1965) [1956] *The Accumulation of Capital*, 2nd edn. London: Macmillan.
——— (1973) [1970] Harrod after Twenty-One Years. In *Collected Economic Papers*, vol. IV. Oxford: Blackwell, 67–73.
——— (1979) *The Generalisation of the General Theory and Other Essays*. London: Macmillan.
——— (1980) *Collected Economic Papers. General Index*, edited by M. Milgate and P. Kerr. Oxford: Blackwell.

15

HARROD'S DYNAMIC ECONOMICS AND JOAN ROBINSON'S GENERALIZATION OF THE GENERAL THEORY[1]

Paolo Varri

The generalization of the *General Theory* (Keynes 1936) was the main objective of Joan Robinson's programme of scientific research in economics. By this she meant the construction of a theoretical scheme to analyse the growth of capitalist economies in the long run, compatible with Keynesian short-period analysis and, therefore, liable to be considered an extension of that theory. The objective is very similar to what Harrod was trying to achieve in his attempt to develop dynamic economics as a way out of the internal contradictions of static analysis.[2] In his opinion, the *General Theory*, from this point of view, was as open to criticism as was traditional theory (Harrod 1948: 10–11). The fact of aiming at the same target did not prevent them from following quite different theoretical routes in their elaborations, with an almost total absence of any cooperation and with much explicit reciprocal criticism.

In this paper, I shall try to compare both approaches synthetically and to examine how the relations between them developed over the years.

Both of them assisted Keynes, and took part in the preparation of the *General Theory*, but their roles were quite different. Joan Robinson, being in Cambridge together with Austin Robinson, Sraffa and Kahn, was part of the Circus, and participated at first hand in the whole process. Harrod, on the other hand, was in Oxford and, though he was destined to become Keynes' official biographer (Harrod 1951), he was only an external correspondent and remained rather isolated.

Though Harrod was only a few years older than Robinson, their relationship was certainly uneven. Joan Robinson was explicitly concerned with Harrod's works in at least three publications: the review of *The Trade Cycle* (Harrod 1936), a long review article of *Towards a Dynamic Economics* (Harrod 1948) and the anniversary article 'Harrod after 21 Years'. Harrod, in contrast, has largely ignored not only Joan Robinson's work but also the contributions of the other post-Keynesian economists in Cambridge.[3] His remarks are always in the form of a defence of his own theory and against what he considered misinterpretations of his ideas.

However, Joan Robinson's concern for Harrod's ideas was not limited to reviews or comments on his contributions. In each successive version of her theory of growth she increasingly acknowledged her intellectual debt to Harrod for his fundamental concepts of dynamic analysis. Nevertheless, while sharing with Harrod, as we shall see later, a common general view of the working mechanism of capitalist economies, which derives from Keynes, she never agreed with Harrod's dynamic analysis.

THE REVIEW OF *TOWARDS A DYNAMIC ECONOMICS*

The disagreement is already very clear in her review article of *Towards a Dynamic Economics* (Robinson 1949). This starts with two critical remarks about the abstraction of aggregate analysis and the oversimplifications of considering dynamics in terms of assuming constant rates of change of economic variables, an assumption that, in her opinion, excludes any role for history.

She then carefully reports Harrod's argument. There is a constant rate of growth of output that is possible in order to maintain the full employment of a steadily growing population and a constant rate of neutral technical progress. This is the 'natural rate of growth', G_n, and represents the maximum rate of steady growth that the system can achieve. The rate of capital accumulation that is required to allow the system to grow at the natural rate of growth is the same (but Harrod is aware that to consider capital requirements as a linear function of income is an oversimplification). This leads directly to the basic question of the analysis: is there any tendency for savings to adjust to capital requirements?

This is the same problem of the *General Theory*, even if the shift from short-period to long-period analysis has reversed the role of variables and constants. The propensity to save becomes the variable, and investments, in the form of the rate of accumulation, become the constant.

The answer that comes from Harrod's analysis is negative: there is no tendency for savings to adjust to capital requirements, either in the case of a constant rate of interest, or when the rate of interest is variable. The analysis tries to discover the origins of net saving supply in terms of individual choices, distinguishing three categories of savings: (a) hump savings, (b) savings for heirs and (c) business savings. In general, it comes out that the influence of the rate of interest on savings is open and may go in either direction. Harrod is also sceptical about the influence of the rate of interest on the choice of methods of production. Moreover, the flexibility of wages and prices is shown to increase the imbalances rather than create harmony.

The general conclusion is, therefore, that the Keynesian thesis of short-period disequilibrium between savings and investments remains valid even in long-period dynamic analysis.

Since this review in 1949, the main criticism that Robinson has made is that Harrod totally disregarded changes in income distribution as a way of obtaining the amount of savings required to finance the natural rate of growth.

Two additional critical remarks regard instability and the concept of a warranted rate of growth. Robinson, of course, agrees with Harrod's idea that long-run equilibrium (if it exists) is unstable, and she considers his analysis as a rough sketch of a theory of the trade cycle. In her view, however, the acceleration principle is insufficient to give a complete account of business cycles. If investment, in a certain period, falls below (or is above) the steady rate, the expansion of output will be insufficient (or excessive) in the usual self-propelling way. But the turning points require a different explanation. Whereas the end of a boom with price or wage inflation is reasonable, the end of a slump is not an easy problem to solve using Harrod's categories.

The concept of a *warranted growth rate* is openly considered baffling and mysterious, being defined as such that, if maintained, producers will be content with what they are doing and will continue to maintain it. She suggests that, to be content, producers should have their stock of capital working at normal capacity. But this is not sufficient. The income produced when capital is fully utilized should determine an amount of savings that has to be equal to the investment. In her words: 'the *warranted* rate of growth is that rate of growth of output $\Delta Y/Y$ which would result from continuous operation at full capacity of the stock of capital, when the stock of capital is continuously growing at a rate dictated by the investment which just absorbs the rate of saving corresponding to full-capacity income' (Robinson 1949: 80).

The interpretation of the warranted rate of growth that Robinson gives here is obviously rather anti-Keynesian and will be modified very soon, as we shall see in the following, omitting the requirement of full-capacity utilization.

The theoretical relevance of the concept is that it introduces a distinction between the actual rate of capital accumulation and a different rate, which is the reference for the analysis. We could say the 'equilibrium' rate; but this is a word that both Robinson and Harrod try not to use because they do not want to use traditional definitions and because, in their view, it could be misleading, owing to instability.

The comment Robinson makes on Harrod's conservative prescriptions for policy is of course totally negative: 'we cannot take Mr. Harrod's proposals as more than a *jeu d'esprit*, but that does not detract from the interest and importance of his analysis upon its own plane' (Robinson 1949: 85).

ROBINSON'S SOLUTION OF HARROD'S PROBLEM

Yet only three years later, in *The Rate of Interest and Other Essays*, the comment is more favourable, at least as regards the method of analysis: 'I have profited very greatly from Harrod's *Towards a Dynamic Economics* – indeed the central point of the foregoing analysis is taken from it – and I have been much impressed by the subtlety of his theoretical analysis. All the same I totally disagree with his application of it' (Robinson 1952: 159).

Though Joan Robinson is ready to acknowledge her debt to Harrod, she is also very proud to recognize that her model of steady accumulation is equivalent to Marx's schemes of expanded reproduction. The scope of her analysis is to show which conditions are required to make it possible for the system to grow at a constant rate in time – something that Marx considered possible in principle, but not realistic, unless by an accident, in a capitalist economy.

The model is therefore used as a reference in order to classify actual situations as deviations from it. In conditions of steady accumulation, the rate of growth of the capital stock has to be equal to s/c, the saving ratio divided by the capital–output ratio. It is interesting to notice that she is now giving a revised interpretation of Harrod's warranted rate of growth as the rate of accumulation of capital that, in combination with the capital–output ratio, is warranted by the thriftiness of the economy. Full-capacity utilization is no longer explicitly required.

In the *Accumulation of Capital* (1956) Robinson reaches her most complex analytical vision of the dynamics of a capitalist economy in the long run. The description of accumulation in the long run precedes the short-period behaviour of the economy,[4] which corresponds to Harrod's suggestion of considering Keynesian short-period analysis as a particular case of a truly general dynamic long-period theory.

Though considering her analysis an elaboration of Harrod's theory, she does not face the problem of Harrod. The reason is that she gives an explanation of savings different from the one given by Harrod, which she had already criticized.

She divides income between wages and profits and follows the classical assumption that all profits are saved and all wages are spent. In this way, the rate of profit is equal to the rate of growth and, if it is also equal to the rate of population growth plus the rate of neutral technical progress, the system is said to be in conditions of golden age, a mythical situation able to maintain full employment and full-capacity utilization in time.

At this stage of the analysis Robinson does not need the Harrodian concept of a warranted growth rate, which she simply goes on to interpret as the growth rate of income warranted by the thriftiness of the economy given the capital–output ratio.[5] She denies, in other words, the theoretical relevance of a third growth rate as a concept different from the natural and the actual one.

A COMMON KEYNESIAN VISION OF ECONOMIC DYNAMICS

The argument is further developed in the *Essays in the Theory of Economic Growth* (1962). She regards them as an introduction, rather than a supplement, to the *Accumulation of Capital* but, as a matter of fact, the content is considerably different and in many ways closer to Harrod. Almost all the analysis of the choice of techniques is ignored, and a third concept of rate of accumulation is introduced – the desired rate of accumulation. This is defined as the rate of accumulation that makes firms satisfied with the situation in which they find themselves.

Robinson has no difficulty in admitting that '[t]his concept is very similar to Harrod's *warranted rate of growth* and has a similar role in the analysis. Harrod, however, has never removed the ambiguity as to whether the firms are supposed to be content with the stock of productive capital that they are operating, or with the rate at which it is growing. To avoid confusion, it seems better to use a different term from his' (Robinson 1962: 49n). Her solution is to link the desired rate of accumulation to the rate of profit and, at the same time, to consider the rate of profit a consequence of the rate of accumulation. In this way she is able to introduce a variety of steady-growth states in addition to the golden age.

At this stage, having offered multiple solutions to the problem that Harrod suggested had no solution, Robinson and he seem to be poles apart. But to me these differences remain on the surface of their theories. Both conclusions show a large compatibility with the Keynesian vision of capitalism. In long-period as well as in short-period analysis, full employment is only a possibility, and the market mechanism alone cannot guarantee it will be achieved. Dynamic imbalances are the rule and unemployment may persist in time.

I think that, having realized that steady-growth models may be only a first simplified approximation of reality and that the Keynesian vision requires a different approach to the analysis of dynamic economics, Robinson was eventually led to the more positive consideration of Harrod's dynamic theory that emerges from the short article 'Harrod's Knife-Edge' (1965)[6] and from the article written to celebrate the twenty-first anniversary of *Towards a Dynamic Economics* published in 1970.[7]

Unfortunately, Harrod was not prepared to recognize the common features of their analysis and maintained the discussion at the surface of a useless struggle of principles.

As a matter of fact, if we try to leave these polemics out of the picture, we can see that, in the same period, the early 1970s, Harrod was writing the final formulation of *Economic Dynamics* (1973) and was ready to accept that the warranted rate of growth is not necessarily constant in time, that entrepreneurs will not necessarily behave in a way to keep it constant and that, therefore, the warranted rate of growth is simply the ratio between the propensity to save and the capital–output ratio. He was also ready to introduce in his analysis the concept of special (or temporary) warranted growth rates, which Keynes had originally introduced to criticize his original idea of a warranted growth rate constant in time. Moreover he was finally prepared to weaken the effects of his principle of instability, allowing that the parameters of his fundamental equation might change in the ups and downs of the business cycle (Harrod 1973).

Robinson and Harrod were at opposite extremes ideologically, but they shared a common scientific vision that derives directly from Keynes. It is a real pity that, by trying to amplify the distance between their schemes of analysis, rather than focusing on strengthening and developing their common Keynesian backgrounds, they ended up rather isolated in post-Keynesian and neoclassical debates about the theory of economic growth in those years.[8] Their relationship is, perhaps, a living example of the struggle between ideas and ideologies, which Robinson felt very deeply and was so keen and effective in describing.

NOTES

1 Financial support from the Italian Ministry of University and Scientific Research (MURST 40%) is gratefully acknowledged.

2 Recent literature on the scientific contributions of Harrod to economics is considerable: see Young (1989), Varri (1990), and Pugno (1992). Biographical essays have been written by Blake (1970), Hinshaw (1978), and Phelps Brown (1980). A bibliography of the works of Harrod is contained in Eltis, Scott and Wolfe (1970) and in Varri (1990).

3 The only relevant exception is the very short review of Sraffa's *Production of Commodities by Means of Commodities* (Harrod 1961). Harrod also wrote a review of Robinson's *Essays in the Theory of Employment* (Harrod 1937), and a review of Kaldor's *Essays on Economic Policy* (Harrod 1965).

4 It is interesting to note that the second edition of *The Rate of Interest and Other Essays*, published in 1979 with the title *The Generalization of the General Theory and Other Essays*, reverses the order of the parts, putting the model of growth at the beginning.

5 The capital–output ratio may itself be variable as a function of the rate of profit, both in the case of a single technique and in the case of a *spectrum* of techniques to be chosen, but, in principle, this does not prevent the equality between the two growth rates.

6 In the four pages of this essay, she explicitly exposes her vision of long-run growth in terms of Harrod's categories, suggesting that it is not so much from the variability of v as a function of the rate of interest, which might be weak and in the wrong direction, but from the variability of s that the logical possibility of steady growth may come. It was the uniqueness of g that created the problem of the knife-edge and not the question of stability.

7 This paper is interesting because Robinson, arguing about the variability of v on a number of factors, to cut out complications, takes it as a constant, independent of both the rate of profit and the rate of growth. She also tries to accommodate

the variability of the propensity to save as a function of the distribution of income with the determination of the rate of profit in terms of the degree of monopoly.

8 More detailed critical assessments of the evolution of the theories of Harrod and Robinson may be found in Young (1989), Varri (1990), Pugno (1992) and Marcuzzo (1991).

REFERENCES

Blake, R. (1970) A Personal Memoir. In W. Eltis, M. Fg. Scott and J. N. Wolfe, eds, *Induction Growth and Trade: Essays in Honour of Sir Roy Harrod.* Oxford: Clarendon Press.

Eltis, W., Scott, M. Fg. and Wolfe, J. N., eds (1970) *Induction Growth and Trade: Essays in Honour of Sir Roy Harrod.* Oxford: Clarendon Press.

Harrod, R. F. (1936) *The Trade Cycle: An Essay.* Oxford: Clarendon Press.

——— (1937) Review of J. Robinson *Essays in the Theory of Employment*, *Economic Journal*, 47: 326–30.

——— (1948) *Towards a Dynamic Economics: Some Recent Developments of Economic Theory and Their Applications to Policy.* London: Macmillan.

——— (1951) *The Life of John Maynard Keynes.* London: Macmillan.

——— (1961) Review of P. Sraffa, *Production of Commodities by Means of Commodities*, *Economic Journal*, 71: 782–7.

——— (1965) Review of N. Kaldor, *Essays in Economic Policy*, *Economic Journal*, 75: 794–803.

——— (1970) Harrod after Twenty-one Years, A Comment, *Economic Journal*, 80: 737–41.

——— (1973) *Economic Dynamics.* London: Macmillan.

Hinshaw, R. (1978) Sir Roy Harrod, *Journal of International Economics*, 8: 363–72.

Keynes, J. M. (1936) *The General Theory of Employment, Interest and Money.* London: Macmillan.

Marcuzzo, M. C. (1991) Joan Robinson e la formazione della scuola di Cambridge. In *Joan Robinson, occupazione, distribuzione e crescita.* Bologna: Il Mulino.

Phelps Brown, E. (1980) Sir Roy Harrod: A Biographical Memoire, *Economic Journal*, 90: 1–33.

Pugno, M. (1992) *Roy F. Harrod: dall'equilibrio dinamico all'instabilità ciclica.* Bologna: Il Mulino.

Robinson, J. V. (1936) Review of R. F. Harrod *The Trade Cycle*, *Economic Journal*, 46: 691–3.

——— (1949) Mr. Harrod's Dynamics, *Economic Journal*, 59: 68–85.

——— (1952) *The Rate of Interest and Other Essays.* London: Macmillan.

——— (1956) *The Accumulation of Capital.* London: Macmillan.

——— (1962) *Essays in the Theory of Economic Growth.* London: Macmillan.

——— (1965) Harrod's Knife-Edge. In *Collected Economic Papers*, vol. III. Oxford: Blackwell.

——— (1970a) Harrod after Twenty-one Years, *Economic Journal*, 80: 731–7.

——— (1970b) Harrod after Twenty-one Years, A Reply, *Economic Journal*, 80: 741.

——— (1979) *The Generalization of the General Theory and Other Essays.* London: Macmillan.

Varri, P. (1990) Introduzione a *Harrod, Dinamica economica.* Bologna: Il Mulino.

Young, W. (1989) *Harrod and his Trade Cycle Group: The Origins and Development of the Growth Research Program.* London: Macmillan.

16

'THE GOLDEN AGE' AND JOAN ROBINSON'S CRITIQUE

Pierluigi Ciocca

In the August of 1983 Federico Caffè (1990: 22) bade goodbye to Joan Robinson, calling her 'indestructible' – indestructible in 'her constant combativeness, her biting criticism of any ideological cover-up of conservative ideas, her use of analytical instruments for the advancement of society'.

An indomitable critical spirit was the most immediately striking of Joan Robinson's qualities. We students of economics in the 1960s were struck by it too. Indeed, it was during the 1950s and 1960s that her critique of the *modus operandi* of market economies was most creative. Today – after living through the two so-called oil crises and the current recession, the longest in the post-war period – those twenty years stand out as the 'golden age' of industrial capitalism, if there ever was one. Between 1955 and 1973 the OECD economies performed remarkably well: stable growth at an annual average rate of 4.8 per cent; real interest rates of 2 per cent on average and investment equal to 20 per cent of GDP; unemployment that fell as low as 2.3 per cent of the labour force and average inflation of 3.5 per cent; balanced budgets and fixed exchange rates (Table 16.1).

Faced with capitalism's mediocre performance today – marked by a rate of growth that fails to create employment and is not even half the real rate of interest – and the cold arrogance and critical immobility of much of the economics profession, Joan Robinson's criticism appears even more exceptional.

For Joan Robinson (1985: 159), competition is 'imperfect', instability 'real', full employment beset by 'obstacles', distribution conflictual and 'unfair', and foreign trade 'neo-mercantilist'. As to the elusive equilibrium, 'Jam tomorrow but never jam today'. At various times economics appeared to her to be caught between 'ideology' and 'heresy', at 'an awkward corner', and, if not 'disintegrated', at least in need of 'spring cleaning'.

Thus, of the many possible questions, the one I want to raise is: why was Joan Robinson so critical? Why was she so critical even then, in the midst of an apparently golden age? What is the source, the underlying motivation for her having played the part of the critical economist, a role that has almost

Table 16.1 Selected macroeconomic indicators for the OECD countries and the United Kingdom (annual average rates of change, %, 1955–73)

Indicator	*OECD*	*United Kingdom*
Gross product	4.8	3.1
Investment/gross product[a]	20.8	17.0
Productivity (output per employee)	3.7	2.8
Consumer prices	3.5	4.4
Unemployment rate[b]	2.3	0.8
Long-term real interest rate[a]	2.1	2.3
Budget deficit/gross product[c]	–0.2	–0.8
External current account balance/gross product[a]	0.4	0.3

Sources: OECD and national bulletins.
[a]Average value for the reference period.
[b]Minimum value in the reference period; 1966 for the OECD and 1955 for the UK.
[c]Average value for the period 1960–73

disappeared and for which there is a great need today?

Rather than seeking to arrive at the right answer at any cost, I shall suggest several answers in an attempt to clarify the nature of the question and evoke a number of aspects of the context in which Robinson worked. I hope the issue is of interest to those who were close to Joan Robinson, and to those who have studied and developed her thinking and can answer the question better than I.

The first hypothesis is that not everything really worked so well even in the 1950s and 1960s: there were cyclical downturns, albeit limited to growth rates; bouts of inflation, especially in connection with the Vietnam War; and balance-of-payments disequilibria in some countries. In particular, the United Kingdom continued the strategic retreat from its position as the leader of the world economy; although this was managed in a dignified and orderly manner, British growth was lower and its inflation higher than the average for the industrial countries (Table 16.1). However, it would be an injustice to Robinson to ascribe her criticism to minor flaws in the performance of the system, especially when these concerned a single country, even if it was her own. At the same time, she was not alone among the distinguished economists of the period in underestimating the seeds of instability that the 'Triffin dilemma' and the fall in the relative price of oil introduced into the monetary system and the entire world economy, thus preparing the ground for the crisis of the 1970s.

The second hypothesis is perhaps less obvious. Having lived through the depression of the 1930s and the birth of Keynes' General Theory, Joan Robinson's criticism may in the end have been rooted in fear of a repetition of 1929, although I do not believe she was a stagnationist. Under the tranquil surface of the first twenty post-war years, capitalism would thus have harboured the risk of recession, which then materialized in the 1970s. In 1977, Robinson noted, 'The present situation raises new questions. The long boom of twenty-five years after 1945, interrupted only by shallow and local recessions, blew up into a violent inflation in 1973 and collapsed into a world-wide slump. The economists ... now do not know what to say' (1979: 29). Nevertheless, the stagflation of the 1970s was very different from the crisis of the 1930s, perhaps closer to a model of disproportions than to one based directly on the General Theory. Faced with the recession of the 1970s, Robinson seems to concentrate her criticism on mainstream theory and the system in general rather than specifically analysing the historical fact of the recession with inflation: 'what is growth for? ... These questions involve the whole political and social system of the capitalist world; they cannot be decided by economic theory, but it would be decent, at least, if the economists admitted that they do not have an answer to them' (ibid.: 29–31).

The third possibility is that Robinson's criticism of advanced market economies stemmed from the favour with which she looked on planned economies, China more than Eastern Europe. Her interest in the economies of the Third World was active and constant, beginning with her stay in India from 1926 to 1928 and continuing with her frequent visits to China from 1953 onwards. She was especially sympathetic to Mao's economic experiment, which was not particularly successful. I do not know what her reaction was to that initiated by Deng in 1978, which was to double the per capita income of 1.2 billion people in barely a decade. Convinced of the central importance of capital accumulation for development, Robinson saw a potential advantage for centrally planned economies in their special ability to resolve the problems of saving and effective demand: to extract the surplus from disposable income and centralize the decision to invest it, without having to rely on the 'flagging "animal spirit"' of entrepreneurs (1964: 97). She reached the point of identifying a 'high level of morality (or "political consciousness")' in the Chinese system of production, convinced as she was that 'when everyone has enough to eat today and hope of improvement tomorrow, when there is complete social security ... and employment for all, then it is possible to appeal to the people to combat egoism and eschew privilege' (1973: 7–13). And yet, even though she studied Marx in search of valid points of strictly economic analysis, Robinson was not a Marxist. Above all, she clearly distinguished advanced from backward economies, and she does not appear to have suggested central planning for the former. Her criticism was directed more at the market than at capitalism. It was aimed at the limits of the market in economies that had overcome backwardness through capitalism and that would continue to use the market – corrected of its imperfections and guided by economic policy – as the basis for the organization of production. For backward economies, however, she saw planning as potentially offering a way to overcome underdevelopment faster and less traumatically. In her 'Notes' of 1957, she predicted that the two economic systems – the market economy for rich countries and the planned economy for poor countries – would coexist for a long time (1964: 106).

The fourth hypothesis, already hinted at, is that her criticism was concerned not so much with the negative aspects of actual capitalism, past or present, as with the neoclassical theory of the market, notably as regards its application to the key themes of value, distribution, growth and instability. Robinson tirelessly and polemically opposed the neoclassical position with that 'in the classical tradition, revived by Sraffa, which flows from Ricardo through Marx, diluted by Marshall and enriched by the analysis of effective demand of Keynes and Kalecki' (1974: xii). She devoted enormous energy to this clash of views and schools of thought. Much of it went into *pars construens*, but no less into *pars destruens*. In the latter, she was driven by the conviction that the ideological and apologetic element predominated in the opposing theory. To bring this out, she often accepted to fight on her opponents' preferred terrain, that of the mathematical consistency of neoclassical theory. In her analyses, the frequent references to history, chronological time and initial conditions did not always translate into a solid empirical foundation on which to base the realism of her hypotheses and confirm the validity of her conclusions.[1] In the heat of battle, she may have exposed herself to the charge of having adopted an 'approach which did not limit itself to privileging a given conception, but considered it indispensable to destroy once and for all those, such as marginalism, that have been an integral part of the development of economics' (Caffè 1984: 17).

The objection to this superficially attractive interpretation of the critical force of her work – as being due to her involvement in theoretical and academic disputes – stems, of course, from her having been a great disciple of Keynes. Economics for Keynes and his Cambridge group was not a technique but a moral science. Persuasion is its instrument, rather than any supposedly irrefutable formal logical proof purporting to resolve all theoretical controversies. Its end is the greatest good for the greatest number, through the satisfaction of what Keynes called 'absolute' needs (1952: 365), for a better relationship between freedom and necessity (Robinson 1970). In this conception of economics, tearing down is less important that constructing. More than correct or incorrect, economic theories are rated according to their ability to contribute to the development of truer and more general propositions that promote the advance from necessity to freedom. Keynes never claimed that earlier theory was absurd or incoherent or fallacious; indeed, he acknowledged that it was 'broadly correct' (1973: 489). He simply went further, considering it a special case of his General Theory. Joan Robinson was not perhaps the great philosopher, as well as great economist, that her mentor had been, with a G. E. Moore behind him. However, she was also unlucky in having to contend not with Marshall, Pigou and Robertson, but with the worst of neo-positivism applied to economics.

There remains one other answer to my initial question. It may well be the most accurate, but it is also the least exciting on an epistemological plane and the least useful for the purpose of identifying ways to revive the critical energy of the economics profession. It is almost a Manzonian response: like courage, a critical spirit 'cannot be acquired'. In Joan Robinson, it coincided with moral tension. Harcourt was right: 'She passionately hated injustice ... All her life she searched for ways of creating a more just and equitable society, in the process analysing and trenchantly criticizing the societies she knew and the theories of other people about them' (1992: 455–6).

NOTE

1 Robinson's tendency to shy away from historical analysis and empirical testing was noted early on as a shortcoming by a leading Italian economist, Umberto Ricci, who was one of the first to review her work.

> What is even more serious, she always remains in the midst of her collection of instruments, never or hardly ever putting them to use.... In any case we are justified in expressing the hope that, after guiding us through the showroom of instruments, she will take us into the workshop where their power can be demonstrated by applying them to material made up of facts and figures, and gradually producing results that make us gasp with admiration at the ingeniousness of the instruments.
>
> (Ricci 1933: 840)

REFERENCES

Caffè, F. (1984) *Lezioni di politica economica*. Turin: Boringhieri.

——— (1990) 'Indistruttibile' Joan Robinson, addio. In *La solitudine del riformista*. Turin: Boringhieri.

Harcourt, G. C. (1992) Joan Robinson (1903–1983). In P. Arestis and M. Sawyer, eds, *Biographical Dictionary of Dissenting Economists*. Aldershot: Elgar.

Keynes, J. M. (1952) Economic Possibilities for our Grandchildren, *Essays in Persuasion*. London: Hart-Davis.

——— (1973) *Collected Writings*, vol. XIII. London: Macmillan.

Ricci, U. (1933) Review of 'The Economics of Imperfect Competition', *Giornale degli Economisti*, 48, November.

Robinson, J. (1964) Notes on the Theory of Economic Development. In *Collected Economic Papers*, vol. II. Oxford: Blackwell.

——— (1970) *Freedom and Necessity. An Introduction to the Study of Society.* London: Allen & Unwin.

——— (1973) *Economic Management – China 1972*. London: Anglo-Chinese Educational Institute.

——— (1974) Foreword to J. A. Kregel, *The Reconstruction of Political Economy.* London: Macmillan.

——— (1979) What Are the Questions? In *Collected Economic Papers*, vol. V. Oxford: Blackwell.

——— (1985) The Theory of Normal Prices and Reconstruction of Economic Theory. In G. R. Feiwel, ed., *Issues in Contemporary Macroeconomics and Distribution*. London: Macmillan.

17

ECONOMIC GROWTH AND THE THEORY OF CAPITAL

An evaluation of Joan Robinson's contribution

Amit Bhaduri

A theoretical scheme, by definition, involves simplification. However, whether the simplification is illuminating or misleading can be judged only by applying it to specific problems. For at least the last three decades of her working life, the problem of economic growth in a capitalist economy had continued to engage Joan Robinson. She preferred to describe it as the 'generalization of the General Theory'. In this search for a satisfactory scheme for analysing economic growth, she rejected the neoclassical paradigm, based on the idea of 'capital' as a factor of production. She recognized that this was an oversimplification that misled rather than illuminated our understanding of the process of capitalistic growth.

It is not always emphasized that Robinson's critique of neoclassical capital theory had two distinct, although interrelated, aspects. The first aspect concerns the problem of value or relative prices and distribution. The second aspect, which has been less emphasized in the literature, concerns the structure of production, i.e. the pattern of existing capacities in relation to the composition of aggregate demand in the process of economic growth. And, unlike most other major participants in the debate on capital theory, she became increasingly more concerned with the latter aspect and saw the problem of distribution associated with capital theory as a derived problem, namely, a problem arising from the evolution of the structure of production in relation to the changing composition of aggregate demand. In her somewhat cryptic formulation, it was the problem of accumulation in 'historical time' that lay at the heart of the entire debate.

In *The Accumulation of Capital* (1956) and even earlier (e.g. Robinson 1953–4), Joan Robinson's main criticism of neoclassical capital theory was directed at pointing out that it did not have a coherent macroeconomic theory of the rate of profit. In order to demonstrate this she emphasized in particular the so-called 'negative Wicksell effect', where a higher value of capital per worker is associated with a higher rate of profit. This destroys logically a central idea of neoclassical macroeconomics that the rate of profit is a sort of barometer of the relative scarcity of 'capital as a factor of production'. It is a proposition without any logical foundation outside a one-commodity world.

However, the full impact of this criticism came to be realized over the 'reswitching debate', forced upon conventional economic thinking by Sraffa's work (1960) and Pasinetti's further demonstration (1966) of the generality of the reswitching problem. In her *Accumulation*, Joan Robinson had tended to treat the reswitching of techniques as a 'curiosum'. Since reswitching meant that the same technique of production could be most profitable both at a relatively low (high) and at a relatively high (low) real wage rate (profit rate) while being dominated by other techniques of production for the intermediate ranges of values of the real wage rate (profit rate), the most awkward conclusion for neoclassical macroeconomic models now became inescapable (cf. Samuelson 1966). The rate of profit could be explained neither in terms of the notion of the 'productivity' of a technique of production nor in terms of the relative scarcity of capital as a factor of production. The fact that neoclassical economics did not have any coherent macroeconomic theory of profit had become logically established.

The significance of Joan Robinson's attempt 'to generalize the General Theory' can be appreciated only against this background. The fact that there is no logically coherent neoclassical macro theory of profit made her turn to the principle of effective demand for an explanation of profits. In this, the intellectual lead of Kalecki (1971) was probably more important than that of Keynes of the *General Theory* (1936). Like Kaldor (1955–6), she made use of the multiplier mechanism to derive the relation between the rate of economic growth and the rate of profit. Assuming all savings come from profit, any exogenously given level of investment (I) generates that matching level of saving through the multiplier relation, i.e.

$$I = S = s_p R,\ 1 \geq s_p > 0. \tag{1}$$

Or, dividing both sides by the value of capital K, we obtain the celebrated Cambridge equation of the rate of profit as:

$$I/K = g = s_p r,\ r = R/K, \tag{2}$$

where $g = I/K$ = rate of accumulation, $r = R/K$ = rate of profit and, s_p = propensity to save out of profit.

However, the multiplier mechanism through which an autonomous level of investment (or rate of accumulation) generates its matching level of saving (or rate of profit) can operate in two distinct ways – *either* by raising the level of capacity utilization and output *or* by redistributing income from wages to profits. In the *General Theory* (1936), Keynes made use of the former route, following Kahn's (1931) classic analysis of the multiplier; whereas in his earlier *Treatise on Money* (1930) he had made use of the latter route in his theory of the 'profit inflation', which is also the core of Kaldor's so-called

Keynesian theory of distribution. To show these two routes explicitly, we may rewrite (1) as,

$$I = S = s_p \cdot \frac{R}{Y} \cdot \frac{Y}{Y^*} \cdot Y^*,$$

where Y = actual GDP and Y^* = potential GDP (i.e. full capacity output).

Thus, assuming $Y^* = 1$ as the procedure for normalization, we have corresponding to (1),

$$I = s_p \cdot h \cdot z, \tag{3}$$

and, corresponding to (2),

$$g = s_p \cdot \frac{R}{Y} \cdot \frac{Y}{Y^*} \cdot \frac{Y^*}{K} = s_p \cdot h \cdot zv, \tag{4}$$

where $Y/Y^* = z$ = degree of capacity utilization, $1 > z > 0$; $R/Y = h$ = profit share; and $Y^*/K = v$ = ratio of full capacity output to book value of capital.

Equations (2) or (4) show that, either through an increased degree of capacity utilization (i.e. higher z) or through a higher profit share (i.e. higher h), investment could 'finance' itself by raising the level of savings correspondingly.

Joan Robinson's classification of steady-state growth paths in her various writings, starting with the *Accumulation of Capital*, follows easily from the underlying equation (4). For any exogenously given rate of growth, we have the rate of profit determined from (2) as,

$$r = g/s. \tag{5}$$

But this rate of profit determined by (5) may be associated with a lower or higher degree of capacity utilization and employment, provided the profit share (and the Kaleckian 'degree of monopoly') moves in the opposite direction in a compensating manner, in accordance with equation (4). Moreover, given the value of capital at that rate of profit determined from (5) along a steady-state growth path, she could use the Harrodian classification of technical progress to determine how the parameter v in equation (4) would behave. This scheme provided the foundations of her remarkable analysis of alternative growth paths of a capitalist economy in the *Accumulation*. The classification required neither the postulate of full employment nor full capacity utilization, because capacity utilization (z) was a variable of the system. At the same time, she could incorporate the influence of income distribution and technical progress in the analysis, through the parameters h and v respectively in equation (4), without having to have any recourse to the logically unsound neoclassical intellectual apparatus of an aggregate production function. She had set up not only an alternative framework, but also a more flexible scheme of analysis. It was a less deterministic scheme with considerable flexibility to compare properties of alternative steady-state growth paths.

This flexibility in the scheme could not have been achieved without rejecting the neoclassical capital-theoretic paradigm. Without an aggregate production function and the usual marginal productivity conditions for distribution at profit-maximizing equilibrium, profit share (h), output–capital ratio (v) and the degree of capacity utilization (z) could be treated as relatively independent variables in equation (4).

It was, for example, no longer necessary to restrict the analysis to perfect competition and precise profit maximization by price-taking firms. The theory of capitalistic growth had to be liberated from the unrealism of perfect competition. Broadly speaking, she considered profit share, h, to be determined by the bargaining power of the contending classes, paralleling Kalecki's idea of the 'degree of monopoly'. The full-capacity output to the value of capital ratio, i.e. the parameter v, was largely determined by the nature of technical progress according to the Harrodian classification. She inverted Harrod's original definition (Harrod 1948) to avoid capital-theoretic valuation problems and defined technical progress as neutral, if at a *given* rate of profit (determined from equation (5) at an exogenous steady rate of growth) the value of output to the value of capital, both evaluated at the given profit rate, remained constant. Nevertheless, she was also the first to recognize that this scheme of analysis of comparative steady states was highly fragile because one could examine the implications of the analysis only along given steady-state paths of growth at which the rate of profit and the corresponding relative prices remained constant.

The second aspect of Joan Robinson's contribution to capital and growth theory followed precisely from this recognition. Her concern with the problem of economic growth required her to analyse the changing structure of production and technology under changing expectations of profit. In this respect, she found not only the neoclassical capital-theoretic paradigm totally misleading but the capital valuation problem as the tip of the iceberg of a far more complex problem. Although the marginal productivity theory of distribution was logically incoherent outside a one-good model, the one-good model itself was hopelessly inadequate to deal with any of the problems of structural change in the process of growth.

Even the Keynesian condition for flow equilibrium between investment and savings could not be appreciated properly without going beyond the one-good model. As she very often pointed out, 'saving' was in terms of consumables but 'investment' was in terms of (immediate) non-consumables, so that the economic consequences of the equilibrium condition needed to be analysed in the context of at least corresponding two-good classification.

In most of her writings, she relied on Marx's two departmental scheme for analysing growth. In that context, the essence of her criticism becomes transparent by restating equation (1) in terms of saving investment equality. Assuming for simplicity that all of profits and no wages are saved, the equality between investment and saving can be written as,

$$wL_i = (x_c - w)L_c, \tag{6}$$

where w = real wage rate in terms of consumption goods; x_c = labour productivity in the consumption sector (department II); and L_i and L_c are workers engaged in the investment (department I) and in the consumption sector (department II) respectively.

From equation (6), the proportion in which labour needs to be employed in the two sectors in order to avoid problems relating to aggregate demand is determined as,

$$L_i/L_c = (x_c - w)/w. \tag{7}$$

Note in passing that (7) is only a restatement of the Keynesian 'employment multiplier'. Given the number of workers in the investment sector, L_i, as an independent or autonomous variable in any short period, the 'equilibrium' number of workers in the consumption sector, L_c, needed to provide just enough surplus of wage goods to support those L_i workers depends on the 'savings propensity' or surplus per worker in the consumption goods sector given by $(x_c - w)/w$ in equation (7). Thus, when labour is employed in the proportion given in (7), the 'surplus' of consumption goods represented on the right-hand side of equation (6) finds a 'market' or effective demand just large enough through the consumption demand of workers employed in the investment goods sector, which is represented by the left-hand side of equation (6). As a result, the surplus of consumption goods is realized into monetary profits without unplanned inventory changes. Consequently, equation (7) may be said to represent the realization proportion. However, and this was Joan Robinson's main point to engage labour in this right proportion, historically inherited capacities in the two sectors must be in the same right proportions. Otherwise, there would be either structural excess capacity in one of the sectors or imbalance between the demand and supply of consumption goods (i.e. $I \neq S$) at that given real wage rate. Therefore, unless we assume that the initial condition is one of structural equilibrium in terms of inherited capacities, there would be a mismatch between the inherited productive structure and the productive structure that resolves the problem of realization of surplus into profit at the given real wage rate.

This simple but insightful demonstration by Joan Robinson had at least three far-reaching implications. First, it showed how the Marxist 'crisis of proportionality' was related to the 'crisis of realization', because the historically inherited proportions of sectoral capacities could be out of line with the market-clearing saving–investment flow equilibrium (Bhaduri and Robinson 1980). This focuses on the crucial distinction between the stock equilibrium and the flow equilibrium (cf. Hicks 1985) when attempts are made to 'generalize the General Theory'. Secondly, it destroyed the mechanistic notions of 'stability of equilibrium', which failed to distinguish between movement in space and movement in time. The assumption that the initially inherited stock proportions (e.g. sectoral capacities) are consistent with the flow equilibrium (e.g. saving–investment equality) amounts to assuming that expectations are being fully realized and that the economy – assumed in equilibrium – can continue to be in equilibrium. But this 'equilibrium dynamics' must not be confused with 'moving towards an equilibrium' from an arbitrary initial condition, because in the latter case expectations are continuously changing during the process of adjustment. The mechanical notion of stability does not distinguish between a relatively small perturbation of equilibrium and moving towards an equilibrium from an arbitrary initial position in the neighbourhood of equilibrium. But this distinction is crucial in the treatment of capital as a stock in the process of economic growth. Because, adjusting stocks (capacities) from an arbitrary initial configuration to the equilibrium configuration (consistent with flow equilibria over time) entails expectations that are altogether different from the unsettling of expectations when an ongoing equilibrium is perturbed (Robinson 1974). Thirdly, she brought back into the debate on capital valuation in relation to distribution theory the importance of the 'structure of capital', i.e. non-malleable capacities given in arbitrary historical proportions at any point of time.

Joan Robinson's critique of the neoclassical model had this wider dimension because she realized that the aggregative production function not only ignored all problems of capital valuation in relation to distribution but also led to a habit of thinking that ignored the problem of historically inherited arbitrary proportionality, which is crucial for analysing economic growth through structural change. Indeed, standard surveys and neoclassical models (e.g. Hahn and Mathews 1964; Solow 1970) could not even see the significance of the problem. Joan Robinson was always candid enough to admit that she did not solve the problem either. But her polemics was intended to make the economics profession recognize that structural changes through time as the essence of economic growth cannot be analysed through any production function based analysis. That approach is incapable of posing even the right questions in this respect because it assumes away the very problem it is supposed to discuss! It was too inconvenient a problem to face openly and still maintain that conventional neoclassic economics has a 'theory' of economic growth. The mainstream profession chose the soft option of pretending that her criticisms never existed!

REFERENCES

Bhaduri, A. and Robinson, J. (1980) Accumulation and Exploitation: An Analysis in the Tradition of Marx, Sraffa and Kalecki, *Cambridge Journal of Economics*, 4: 103–15.

Hahn, F. H. and Matthews, R. C. O. (1964) The Theory of Economic Growth: A Survey, *Economic Journal*, 74: 779–902.

Harrod, R. F. (1948) *Towards a Dynamic Economics*. London: Macmillan.

Hicks, J. (1985) *Methods of Dynamic Economics*. Oxford: Clarendon Press.

Kahn, R. F. (1931) The Relation of Home Investment to Unemployment, *Economic Journal*, 41: 173–98.

Kaldor, N. (1955–6) Alternative Theories of Distribution, *Review of Economic Studies*, 23: 83–100.

Kalecki, M. (1971) The Determinants of Profits. In *Selected Essays on the Dynamics of the Capitalist Economy*. Cambridge: Cambridge University Press.

Keynes, J. M. (1930) *A Treatise on Money*, vol. 1. London: Macmillan.

——— (1936) *The General Theory of Employment, Interest and Money*. London: Macmillan.

Pasinetti, L. L. (1966) Changes in the Rate of Profit and Switches of Techniques, *Quarterly Journal of Economics*, 80: 503–17.

Robinson, J. (1953–4) The Production Function and the Theory of Capital, *Review of Economic Studies*, 21: 81–106.

——— (1956) *The Accumulation of Capital*. London: Macmillan.

——— (1974) History versus Equilibrium, *Thames Papers in Political Economy*, autumn.

Samuelson, P. A. (1966) A Summing up, *Quarterly Journal of Economics*, 80: 568–83.

Sraffa, P. (1960) *Production of Commodities by Means of Commodities*. Cambridge: Cambridge University Press.

Solow, R. M. (1970) *Growth Theory: An Exposition*. Oxford: Oxford University Press.

Part V

CAPITAL THEORY AND TECHNICAL PROGRESS

18

JOAN ROBINSON AND 'RESWITCHING'[1]

Luigi L. Pasinetti

For two decades, after her *Review of Economic Studies* article 'The Production Function and the Theory of Capital' (1953–4; hereafter RES) and her book *The Accumulation of Capital* (1956; hereafter AC), Joan Robinson relentlessly and consistently wrote articles, delivered lectures and gave seminars, in universities all over the world, criticizing, and drawing attention to the weaknesses of the theory of marginal productivity of capital. Joan Robinson must be given ample credit for her courage and determination.

Joan Robinson's criticisms concerned many points. I mention only two major ones: (a) the impossibility of conceiving an aggregate magnitude, called *K* (capital), that is independent of the rate of profits and income distribution; (b) the impossibility, in practice, of a process of capital accumulation through 'deepening' of capital, since techniques are changing continuously as time passes.

In her critique, however, Joan Robinson consistently avoided making use of 'reswitching of techniques' arguments. Paradoxically, she anticipated the existence of 'reswitching', at the same time always taking an ambiguous attitude towards it.

This is a sort of mystery on which I should like to concentrate.

A 'CURIOSUM'

At the very end of an Appendix to her 1953–4 RES article, Joan Robinson adds a strange paragraph, which is unconnected with all the rest:

> The geometry reveals a curious possibility. It may happen that, over a certain range, a reduction in the rate of interest produces a larger reduction in the capital cost of the equipment for a lower than for a higher technique, so that successive wage tangents become steeper as the rate of profit falls. They may then find contact with productivity curves at successively lower points, so that a lower rate of profit (and higher wage rate) results from the use of a less mechanized

> technique . . . This 'perverse' behaviour of the factor-ratio curve, where it occurs at all, can be only over a certain range.

She adds in a footnote that: 'This was pointed out to me by Miss Ruth Cohen', and concludes:

> A good deal of exploration of the possible magnitude and behaviour of the interest effect is needed before we can say whether the above is a mere theoretical rigmarole, or whether there is likely to be anything in reality corresponding to it.
>
> (Robinson 1953–4: 106)

This case sounds no doubt very curious. Joan Robinson leaves the question of its relevance entirely open. She claims she was alerted by 'the geometry', but the description she gives of curves and tangents in the above quotation does not provide a clear picture at all. In any case, no geometrical representation is given.

A diagram showing the 'perverse case' appeared two years later, in AC. It is added to all the other diagrams that had already appeared in the RES article. All of them are placed in an appendix to AC (the relevant diagram, her figure 5, is reproduced as Figure 18.3 in the appendix; two other diagrams are added, referring to the 'normal' case, Figures 18.1 and 18.2). In the book, hints at the 'perverse case' become a little more prominent, but more sceptical. In the middle of a presentation – along Wicksellian lines – of the 'technical frontier', a short section is inserted, called 'A Curiosum':

> As a general rule the degree of mechanization of the technique brought over the frontier by a higher wage rate is higher than that corresponding to a lower wage rate, but it is possible that within certain ranges there may be a perverse relationship.
>
> (Robinson 1956: 109)

The same earlier footnote is added, but is lengthened:

> This was pointed out to me by Miss Ruth Cohen. The following paragraphs are concerned with a somewhat intricate piece of analysis which is not of great importance.
>
> (ibid.: 109, n1)

She goes on to give further details and concludes: 'It seems on the whole rather unlikely that cases of this kind should be common' (ibid.: 110).

She returns to the 'curiosum' 40 pages later, in an incidental paragraph called 'The Perverse Case'. Again she warns in a footnote: 'This paragraph is recommended only to readers who take a perverse pleasure in analytical puzzles' (ibid.: 147, n3).

It must be mentioned that David Champernowne had written a critical 'Comment' on Joan Robinson's RES article (1953–4, same issue), in which he suggested the construction of a 'chain-index', meant to evaluate physical capital, in such a way as to avoid Joan Robinson's criticisms. For logical consistency, he was compelled to make the *assumption* that a technique of production, once discarded on the scale of variation of the rate of profit, would never return. He candidly admitted that 'there is no justification for the assumption' (ibid.: 118), but claimed that 'intuition suggests that the excluded case is unrealistic' (ibid.: 119).

Comment The phenomenon of 'switches of techniques' was favourable to Joan Robinson's arguments and fatally damaging to those of her critics. It was understandable that Champernowne should try to minimize it – his chain-index would otherwise break down. It is far less understandable that Joan Robinson should minimize it. One might suggest that, by becoming convinced that the case was 'unlikely', 'unimportant', and even 'perverse', she thought that it was not worth relying on it for her critique. But if this was so, why should she have mentioned it all?

THE 'BADLY BEHAVED PRODUCTION FUNCTION'

The reswitching phenomenon, as is well known, was presented very clearly four years later in Part III of Sraffa's book *Production of Commodities by Means of Commodities* (1960). This Part III of Sraffa's book is extraordinarily short (one single chapter of 6½ pages; as against six chapters – 40 pages – in Part I and five chapters – 36 pages – in Part II), and is devoted to the 'switch in methods of production', which is the title *both* of Part III *and* of its only chapter. Sraffa simply states the reswitching possibility. He draws absolutely no implication. Very few people took any notice of it.

But a debate blew up five years later at the Rome Congress of the Econometric Society (September 1965). There followed a well-known symposium in the *Quarterly Journal of Economics* (QJE; November 1966).

Joan Robinson reacted positively. She sent the QJE (November 1967) her own contribution to the debate, written with Naqvi. In it, she makes absolutely no claim for herself. She softens her earlier unsympathetic attitude and gives the impression of (reluctantly) moving towards appreciation:

> double switching is associated with perversity. The interesting point, however, is the perversity, not the duplicity. In order to avoid prejudice, let us call the 'perverse' case a *backward* switch, and the 'normal' one a *forward* switch.
>
> (Robinson 1973a: 75)

> Evidently multiple switching is the general case ... But there is no point in discussing which is most 'likely to be found in reality' ... the argument is concerned with a point of logic.
>
> (ibid.: 86)

The focus of her analysis remains on the value of capital – on how it changes and on how it compares for different techniques. She even finds Sraffa's example unhelpful because, by assuming that each of the two techniques yields the same physical output per man, 'there is no meaning in asking whether the production function they compose is well or badly behaved' (ibid.: 74).

She tries to link it up with her previous analysis: 'There is already afloat a terminology for this discussion. In a forward switch . . . there is a positive real Wicksell effect: a backward switch is a negative real Wicksell effect' (ibid.: 77). Her explanation is thus in terms of 'Wicksell effects' (see also Pasinetti 1978).

Later on, in a long review of Ferguson's book, Joan Robinson (1973b) opens herself up and reveals further details on her personal acquaintance with reswitching:

> Incidentally, I found that over certain ranges of the pseudo-production function the technique that becomes eligible at a higher rate of profit (with a correspondingly lower real-wage rate) may be less labour-intensive (that is, may have a higher output per man employed) than that chosen at a higher wage rate, contrary to the rule of a 'well-behaved production function' in which a lower wage rate is always associated with a more labour-intensive technique. (I attributed this discovery to Ruth Cohen – a private joke.)
>
> I had picked up the clue from Piero Sraffa's Preface to Ricardo's *Principles* and my analysis (errors and omissions excepted) was a preview of his. When his own treatment of the subject was finally published in *Production of Commodities by Means of Commodities* (in 1960) the 'Ruth Cohen case' (which I treated as a *curiosum*) was seen to have great prominence; the striking proposition was established that it is perfectly normal (within the accepted assumptions) for the same technique to be eligible at several discrete rates of profit. It was from this that the sobriquet 'reswitching of techniques' was derived.
>
> (ibid.: 144–5)

Comment This is very interesting indeed, but even more puzzling. Joan Robinson reveals that the discovery was not due to Ruth Cohen after all. She says that she picked it up from Sraffa's Preface (I take it she means Introduction) to Ricardo's *Principles* (Sraffa 1951), and that her analysis was a preview of his! She also admits to having made errors, but does not say *which* errors. Most of all, she does not specify *which* page or expression in Sraffa's (rather long!) Introduction to Ricardo's *Principles* gave her the clue to reswitching.

'THE UNIMPORTANCE OF RESWITCHING'

'Reswitching' kept on stimulating papers for years. In another QJE article, in 1975 (after the publication of Geoffrey Harcourt's book, *Some Cambridge Controversies in the Theory of Capital*, 1972, which contributed a lot to drawing attention to her anticipation), Joan Robinson swings back to a harder position – reswitching is 'unimportant':

> The story of what is known as the debate over the reswitching of techniques is a sad example of how controversies arise between contestants who confront the conclusions of their arguments without examining their respective assumptions.
>
> How is it possible to have a controversy over a purely logical point? When various theorists each set out their assumptions clearly, after eliminating errors, they can agree about what conclusions follow from what assumptions. They have then prepared the ground for a discussion, not a controversy, about the relevance of various models to an explanation of whatever situation it is that they are trying to explain.
>
> (Robinson 1979: 76)

She repeats various earlier arguments. Basically her point is that:

> there is no such phenomenon in real life as accumulation taking place in a given state of technical knowledge. The idea was introduced into economic theory only to give a meaning to the concept of marginal productivity of capital, just as the pseudo-production function was constructed in order to show that it has no meaning.
>
> (ibid.: 82–3)

Therefore, 'reswitching' is 'unimportant' because it can never be observed, as no process of capital accumulation takes place at a given technology.

Comment I find these propositions unconvincing, if not inconsistent. Joan Robinson says herself, in the same article, that *there was* an analytical point to be settled:

> in 1965 a fortunate accident occurred. A disciple of Professor Samuelson claimed [etc.] . . . It was fortunate because, after his argument had been challenged by a counterexample presented by Luigi Pasinetti at the Rome Congress of the Econometric Society in September 1965, the mathematical error in the supposed proof was a bait that attracted several others to the field, which they explored from various points of view.
>
> (ibid.: 81)

In fact the disproof of the non-switching theorem was carried out, not only by producing a counter-example, but also by actually showing *where* the logical argument had gone wrong (see Pasinetti 1966, 1969).

If it was justified to construct a pseudo-production function in order to show that the concept of marginal productivity of capital has no meaning, it is not clear why one should not use reswitching for the same purpose. In fact – once the analytical point was settled – there was indeed a controversy, which was about the *implications* of reswitching *for capital theory*. But on this subject, inexplicably, Joan Robinson always avoided taking any stand.

PROVISIONAL CONCLUSION

The attitude of Joan Robinson to 'reswitching' remains an intriguing and incomplete puzzle (if I may use a word she liked so much).

I hope the participants to the discussion may help me in placing correctly the existing pieces of this puzzle, and in looking for the missing ones.

POSTSCRIPT

The discussion that took place at the Turin conference threw up many conjectures but very few further useful elements for a solution of the riddle. Jack Birner (who, with a brave effort, tried hard) was unable to rely on new, or first-hand, evidence (see Chapter 20 in this volume). Stefano Zamagni (who tried to explain Joan Robinson's 'underestimation' of 'reswitching' as a consequence of her methodology) could not explain why she mentioned it at all in the first place (see Chapter 19 in this volume). Piero Garegnani (who enjoys the privilege of exclusive access to Sraffa's papers) has remained silent.

Let me try to assemble the pieces of evidence as I see them at the present stage.

It appears by now clear that general awareness of the relevance for capital theory of the reswitching phenomenon started only with the disproof of the Levhari–Samuelson non-switching theorem at the September 1965 World Congress of the Econometric Society.

The reswitching phenomenon itself, however, as a general property of production models, had unambiguously and clearly been presented by Piero Sraffa in Part III of his 1960 book. The intriguing point is that Joan Robinson anticipated it, presenting it as a 'curiosum' in her 1953–4 RES article and in her 1956 book.

How did this come about?

There can be little doubt that Joan Robinson and Piero Sraffa did discuss capital theory (presumably at length) at the time (early 1950s) that Robinson was writing her article on the production function. That was precisely the time of publication of the first volume (the *Principles*) of Ricardo's *Works*, containing Sraffa's famous 'Introduction'. Most probably the Joan Robinson/Sraffa discussions on capital theory intermingled with discussions on Sraffa's

'Introduction'. This may explain why Joan Robinson came to associate her picking up the clue to reswitching precisely with that 'Introduction'. But Sraffa's hints may have been incomplete or reticent. Joan Robinson must have made a lot of effort to try to grasp the point. As usual, she brought in Richard Kahn and – through him – David Champernowne, who was summoned from Oxford (see Champernowne 1953–4, and Champernowne and Kahn 1953–4).[2] Their perception of the reswitching phenomenon was in terms of an unusual, or abnormal, or 'perverse' case.

All this must have infuriated Sraffa.

It is clear (from evidence gathered independently by various people, besides myself, from conversations with Piero Sraffa) that he strongly disapproved of Joan Robinson's 'curiosum', and refused to have anything to do with it. I saw the letter,[3] with which Joan Robinson had accompanied a complimentary copy of her *Accumulation of Capital* to Piero Sraffa, in which she warned him that her Preface was a 'fraud' because it contained no acknowledgement to him, knowing that he did not want to be implicated.

Thus, Joan Robinson had a bad conscience about the reswitching phenomenon. This is more than sufficient to explain her emotional aversion and hostility to it, especially when the discussions began to show the generality (not the abnormality) of the phenomenon.

At this stage, what continues to remain unknown is the extent to which Joan Robinson's 'curiosum' may have had an impact on Piero Sraffa's book itself. The final, printed, version that Sraffa gave of the reswitching phenomenon, in what appears to me a ludicrously short six-page Part III of his book, cannot be taken as what he originally intended. One may ask: Has there ever been a more reasonably extended version of Part III ('Switch in methods of production') of *Production of Commodities*? This question remains open. To be able to return to the matter with the hope of some further evidence, one must wait for more liberal access to Sraffa's papers in Trinity College Library, Cambridge.

NOTES

1 Financial support from the Italian Ministry of University and Scientific Research (MURST 40%) is gratefully acknowledged.

2 There is independent evidence from conversations with Joan Robinson (by Geoffrey Harcourt and myself) that the Ruth Cohen joke was prompted by questions that Ruth put to Joan at a 'secret seminar' in Kahn's rooms at King's College, when Joan Robinson was struggling to give the 'curiosum' a diagrammatic form.

3 This letter – when I saw it, in Sraffa's Trinity College rooms, during a conversation with him – was kept in the book itself, on his shelves.

APPENDIX

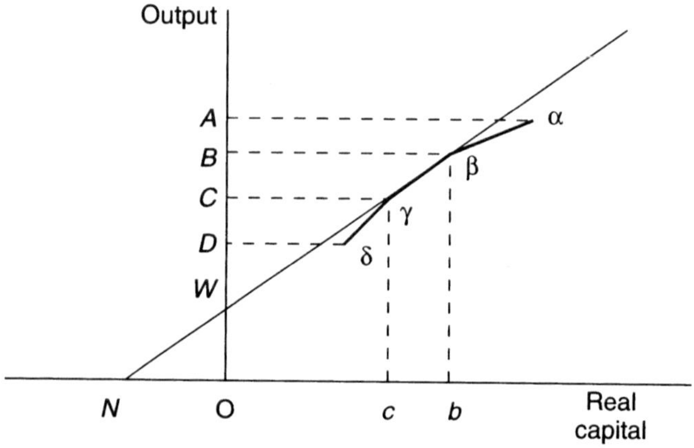

Figure 18.1
Source: Robinson (1956, appendix: 412, Fig. 1)

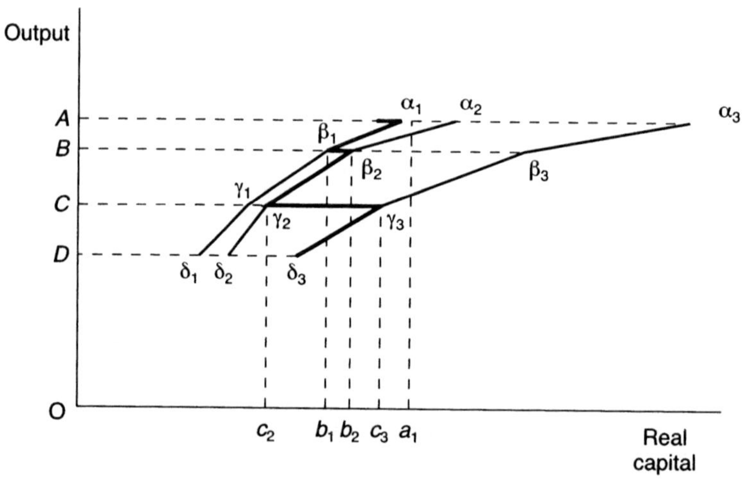

Figure 18.2
Source: Robinson (1956, appendix: 413, Fig. 2)

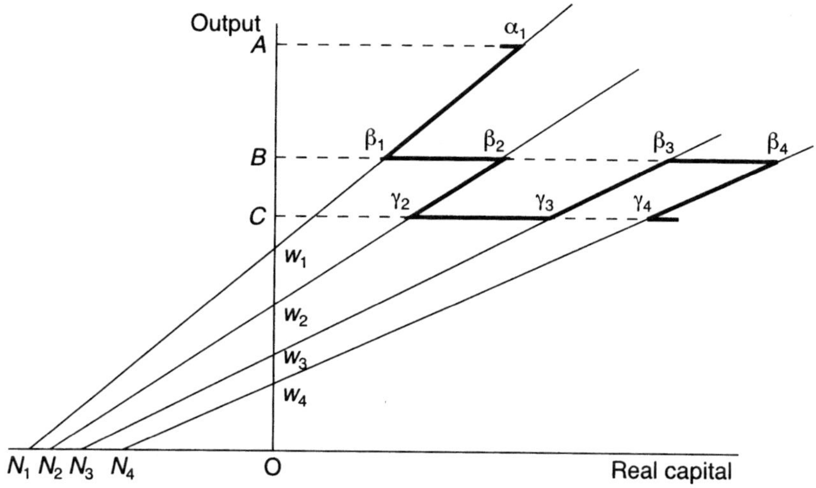

Figure 18.3
Source: Robinson (1956, appendix: 417, Fig. 5)

REFERENCES

Champernowne, D. G. (1953–4) The Production Function and the Theory of Capital: A Comment, *Review of Economic Studies*, 21(2): 112–35.

Champernowne, D. G. and Kahn, R. F. (1953–4) The Value of Invested Capital: A Mathematical Addendum to Mrs. Robinson's Article, *Review of Economic Studies*, 21(2): 107–11.

Harcourt, G. C. (1972) *Some Cambridge Controversies in the Theory of Capital.* Cambridge: Cambridge University Press.

Pasinetti, L. L. (1966) Changes in the Rate of Profit and Switches of Techniques (opening the symposium 'Paradoxes in Capital Theory'), *Quarterly Journal of Economics*, 80: 503–17.

——— (1969) Switches of Techniques and the 'Rate of Return', *Economic Journal*, 79: 508–31.

——— (1978) Wicksell Effects and Reswitchings of Technique in Capital Theory, *Scandinavian Journal of Economics*, 80: 181–9.

Robinson, J. V. (1953–4) The Production Function and the Theory of Capital, *Review of Economic Studies*, 21(2): 81–106.

——— (1956) *The Accumulation of Capital.* London: Macmillan.

——— (1973a) The Badly Behaved Production Function (with K. A. Naqvi). In *Collected Economic Papers*, vol. IV. Oxford: Blackwell.

——— (1973b) Capital Theory Up to Date. In *Collected Economic Papers*, vol. IV. Oxford: Blackwell.

——— (1979) *The Unimportance of Reswitching*. In *Collected Economic Papers*, vol. V. Oxford: Blackwell.

Sraffa, P. (1951) Introduction to vol. 1 of *The Works and Correspondence of David Ricardo*. Cambridge: Cambridge University Press.

——— (1960) *Production of Commodities by Means of Commodities. Prelude to a Critique of Economic Theory.* Cambridge: Cambridge University Press.

19

JOAN ROBINSON AND RESWITCHING

An interpretative note

Stefano Zamagni

THE POINT RAISED BY PASINETTI

After the publication of her 1953–4 article in the *Review of Economic Studies*, Joan Robinson took an active role in the debate on capital theory that characterized economic theory during the 1960s and 1970s. As is well known, this debate took a quite particular form, the 'famous' Cambridge (UK) vs. Cambridge (USA) controversy. At the heart of the debate was the critique of the marginalist theory of value, distribution and capital, based on the concept of marginal productivity of capital conceived as a factor of production on the same grounds and with the same characteristics as labour and land. The critique was directed both at the aggregate (i.e. macroeconomic) version of the theory as exemplified by the Solow–Swan–Meade parable of a one-commodity world[1] and at the disaggregated (i.e. microeconomic) version of the Walrasian (and neo-Walrasian) type. One aspect of the hot debate that deserves to be emphasized is that it was analytically framed within a comparative statics framework consisting of comparisons between long-period positions of the economy (i.e. long-period equilibria characterized by a uniform rate of profits on the supply price of capital goods and by a uniform rate of growth of quantities and employment).

In what follows, I will refer to the point raised by Pasinetti in Chapter 18 in this volume when he writes: 'In her critique, however, Joan Robinson consistently avoided making use of "reswitching of techniques" arguments. Paradoxically, she anticipated the existence of "reswitching", at the same time always taking an ambiguous attitude towards it' (p. 209). And he adds, 'this is a sort of mystery'. My purpose, here, is simply to elaborate a bit further Pasinetti's point. Specifically, I will argue that the "underestimation" by Joan Robinson of the reswitching possibility can be traced back to a typical methodological preoccupation of her entire work, i.e. the irrelevance of the comparative statics analytical framework for studying the process of capitalist accumulation going on in 'real time'.[2] In other words, according to Joan

Robinson, for a study of the process of accumulation of a capitalist economy, comparative statics, at best, is not the most convenient instrument to adopt, and, at worst, pushes the researcher to look for the wrong facts or to pose the wrong questions.

It is perhaps worth stating that this point is different from the one raised by neoclassical economists,[3] according to whom the irrelevance of the reswitching debate is due to the fact that the 'comparative statics' framework does not consider the economically relevant possibilities open to the economy. Burmeister, for example, writes: 'All the issues ... are predicated upon the completely unrealistic assumption that some steady-state equilibria always prevail; this assumption precludes an analysis of the economically feasible options, namely the set of dynamic paths that are technologically feasible from specified initial conditions' (Burmeister 1980: 102). As it can be seen, the question is here conceived as one of stability of the long-period equilibria and not as an 'analysis of processes' as Joan Robinson clearly put it.

A TENTATIVE, THOUGH LIKELY EXPLORATION

In several of her contributions, starting with the famous article on 'The Production Function and the Theory of Capital' (1953–4), Joan Robinson has underlined the impossibility of conceiving of capital as a quantity of a factor of production defined independently of the rate of profit, i.e. of income distribution. It is certainly possible to construct a pseudo production function for the economy as a whole relating the net output per man to the capital per man; however the hypothetical movement along such a curve need not be in the 'right' direction according to neoclassical theory. Furthermore, as Robinson writes in her contribution with Naqvi:

> The dramatic appearance of double switching has somewhat distracted attention from a more general point. While, at prices corresponding to any rate of profit, we can say that Alpha has a higher capital/labour ratio than Beta, we cannot say anything of the sort when we compare them at two different rates of profit.
>
> (Robinson and Naqvi 1967: 580)

The problem is that the prices of commodities are complicated functions of the rate of profit[4] and therefore the value of capital per man may increase or decrease with the rate of profit. As she notes:

> There is a special case in which Alpha is more capital-intensive in an unambigous sense. This is seen when, with each technique, there is a uniform capital/labour ratio, in the sense that, at any one rate of profit, the ratio of wages to net profits in value added is the same for all commodities and at all stages of the productive process, so that the relative prices of commodities are proportional to their wage costs.

> Within each technique a pure labour theory of value holds sway.
>
> (ibid.: 581)

In other words, this is the case when prices are technologically determined and do not depend (as in the case of labour values) on the rate of profit.[5] Double switching is a sufficient, even though not necessary, condition for the perverse behaviour of capital per man across steady-state equilibria; and perverse behaviour of capital per man is sufficient to deny that the rate of profit can be 'explained' according to the marginal productivity of capital and conceived as the price of a factor of production.

It must be pointed out that in the article on the 'badly behaved production function' Robinson writes:

> Evidently multiple switching is the general case. . . . But there is no point in discussing which is most 'likely to be found in reality'. First the argument concerns comparisons of equilibrium positions with different rates of profit and the same 'state of technical knowledge'. These are not found in nature and cannot be observed. Second, the argument is concerned with a point of logic, to which the number of instances has no relevance one way or the other. The benefit of the discussion is only to dispel illusions.
>
> (ibid.: 591)

So, the argument goes, the critique of neoclassical marginalist theory based on reswitching, and therefore on the perverse behaviour of capital per man, is in terms of the coherence of the theory, but its importance seems to be related to what Robinson writes a few lines later:

> But when the fog has lifted two great fields of inquiry come into view – the determination of the rate of profit on the stock of capital in existence, and the choice of techniques in a process of accumulation.
>
> (ibid.: 591)

It seems to me that this passage is particularly important because it clarifies another aspect that is relevant to understanding Joan Robinson's attitude towards reswitching.

In her 1975 article she writes, at the very beginning:

> The story of what is known as the debate over the reswitching of techniques is a sad example of how controversies arise between contestants who confront the conclusions of their arguments without first examining their respective assumptions.
>
> (Robinson 1975: 31)

and later on:

> When various theorists each set out their assumptions clearly, *after eliminating errors*, they can agree about what conclusions follow from

> what assumptions. They have then prepared the ground for a discussion, not a controversy, about the relevance of various models to an explanation to whatever situation it is that they are trying to explain.
>
> (ibid.: 31; italics in original)

There is no doubt that Robinson's target is here more methodological. The argument may be put in the following way. The model of the neoclassical parable has been developed to provide an explanation of the process of accumulation going on in a (competitive) capitalist economy; this model uses a comparative statics framework to analyse a process of accumulation but, as she remarks at the end of the paper,

> [t]here is no such phenomenon in real life as accumulation taking place in a given state of technical knowledge. The idea was introduced into economic theory only to give a meaning to the concept of the marginal productivity of capital, just as the pseudo production function was constructed in order to show that it has no meaning.
>
> (ibid.: 39)

In other words, reswitching is unimportant because the neoclassical model is irrelevant in analysing the evolution of a capitalist economy. It seems to me that the critique here is addressed to a method of analysis and not so much to a particular theory. Now it is certainly true that showing the possibility of reswitching is relevant in order to set out its implications for the foundation of a coherent capital theory. However, I believe that what Joan Robinson is aiming at is to assess the relevance of the theory and not so much its logical correctness.

To me, this explains why she 'underestimated' the reswitching possibility. The fact is that in a truly dynamic context – the context in which she was mainly interested – the methods of production are no longer given from the start. The methods that become available over time depend on the path taken by accumulation, in particular by the intensity and direction of investment. The latter, in turn, depends crucially on the rate of profit, as well as on other factors such as expectations. It follows that the distribution and production structures can no longer be kept separated, as is the case, for example, in the Sraffa system. Indeed, a certain pattern of distribution and investment has a direct effect on the availability of productive processes. This means that the change in productive techniques is related to the pace and pattern of accumulation.

To conclude, it is certainly true that – as Pasinetti writes – Joan Robinson 'avoided making use of reswitching of techniques arguments' in her critique of neoclassical theory, but this is because these arguments, although adequate for studying the relationships between relative prices and distributive variables, do not represent the right analytical framework within which to tackle the fundamental idea of Robinson's research programme: the idea of the link between division of labour, growth of markets and productivity increases.

NOTES

1 As well as at the generalization of this parable by Samuelson's 'surrogate production function' model developed in the article published in 1962.

2 Therefore the 'choice of technique' problem cannot be dealt with in the way it was framed by the participants to the debate on both sides, as a competitive choice within a given book of blueprints (i.e. the process of accumulation implies, realistically, a moving across wage–profit curves and not along a given curve or frontier).

3 See, for example, Burmeister's contribution summarized in chapter 4 of *Capital Theory and Dynamics* (1980).

4 Sraffa has a numerical example in his *Production of Commodities* (1960) that disproves the possibility of using the period of production as a satisfactory measure of the capital intensity of the economy. The Sraffian example has been used, in an amended form, by Pasinetti in his critique of Levahri's non-reswitching theorem. A general treatment of the relationship between prices of commodities and rate of profit can be found in Schefold (1976).

5 Of course, labour values do not depend on the rate of profit within a given technique; on the contrary, labour values of commodities, i.e. the direct and indirect labour embodied in them, depend on the rate of profit when we consider a spectrum of techniques (as for example Roemer 1982 has emphasized in his critique of the Marxian labour theory of value).

REFERENCES

Burmeister, E. (1980) *Capital Theory and Dynamics*. Cambridge: Cambridge University Press.

Dumenil, G. and Lévy, D. (1993) *The Economics of the Profit Rate*. Cambridge: Cambridge University Press.

Robinson, J. (1953–4) The Production Function and the Theory of Capital, *Review of Economic Studies*, 21(2): 81–106.

——— (1975) The Unimportance of Reswitching: A Reply, *Quarterly Journal of Economics*, 89: 53–5.

Robinson, J. and Naqvi, K. A. (1967) The Badly Behaved Production Function, *Quarterly Journal of Economics*, 81: 579–91.

Roemer, J. (1982) *A General Theory of Exploitation and Class*. Cambridge: Cambridge University Press.

Samuelson, P. (1962) Parable and Realism in Capital Theory: The Surrogate Production Function, *Review of Economic Studies*, 29: 193–206.

Schefold, B. (1976) Relative Prices as a Function of the Rate of Profit: A Mathematical Theorem, *Zeitschrift für Nationalökonomie*, 36: 21–48.

Sraffa, P. A. (1960) *Production of Commodities by Means of Commodities*. Cambridge: Cambridge University Press.

20

CAMBRIDGE HISTORIES TRUE AND FALSE

Jack Birner

PUZZLES AND MUDDLES ABOUT THE CAMBRIDGES

There is confusion about the history of the capital theory debate on the part of participants and commentators alike. One misconception is that Sraffa's *Production of Commodities by Means of Commodities* of 1960 was the immediate impulse that started the debate. True, Sraffa made reswitching a crucial part of his criticism of neoclassical economics. But this was not noticed until later, as I will show. I will also throw light upon some ironies of the history of the debate. One is that Robinson discovered reswitching and capital reversing at an early stage but dismissed them as curiosa instead of using them in her criticism of neoclassical production theory. It is another irony that, when Robinson had explained the apparent anomalies and proved that they could occur only over a limited range of the factor ratio curve, the neoclassics, who could have used these results in their defence, failed to notice them. Ironically, the critic Garegnani unintentionally alerted Samuelson to the consequences of reswitching. And if Samuelson had kept mum about reswitching, there just might have been no debate.

SRAFFA: CRITICISM

Sraffa was the first to use the reswitching of techniques explicitly as a criticism of neoclassical capital theory. This has wrongly rushed a number of authors into attributing the role of initiator of the debate to him. Dobb says that Sraffa's book 'provoked a famous, if recondite, discussion of the mid-1960s, commonly referred to as the "multiple-switching of techniques" debate' (Dobb 1973: 248). He also remarks that:

> In a sense its rigorous demonstration of the possibility of what came to be called the 'double-switching of techniques' with changes in the ratio of factor prices, came as an incidental corrollary of that work. But it represented, perhaps, its most important single contribution to 'a

Critique of Economic Theory' and occasioned a debate that will one day, no doubt, become celebrated.

(ibid.: 252)[1]

Lachmann claims that the debate entered a new stage with the publication of Sraffa's book, thus suggesting that there was a debate already. He observes that Sraffa's chapter XII 'gave rise to what became known as the "Reswitching Controversy"' (Lachmann 1973: 24), but fails to tell us how this happened. This again suggests Sraffa's direct involvement. Brown is even more explicit: 'The reswitching controversy [was] initiated by Piero Sraffa' (Brown 1973: 937). And Robinson writes: 'When his [Sraffa's] own treatment of the subject was finally published [in 1960] . . . the "Ruth Cohen Case" (which I had treated as a curiosum) was seen to have great prominence; the striking proposition was established that it is perfectly normal' (Robinson 1970: 309–10). By failing to point out *by whom* this was seen, Robinson suggests that it was seen quite generally. I will show later that this was not the case.

The above accounts of Sraffa's direct involvement are inconsistent with the historical evidence. None of the many reviews of Sraffa's book, including the two by Robinson (Robinson 1961, 1965), mentions reswitching. Harrod's review of 1961 is the only exception, but it dismisses Sraffa's conclusion that the quantity of capital is not independent of the rate of interest as 'one of Mr. Sraffa's subordinate propositions' (Harrod 1961: 786). Harrod considers reswitching to be of little consequence: 'While it is important to bear it in mind, it does not seem that it damages the usefulness of, still less that it creates ambiguity in, the concept of the period of production' (ibid.). Even Sraffa's crystal-clear reply failed to awaken the reviewers: 'This example [of reswitching] is a crucial test for the ideas of a quantity of capital and of the period of production' (Sraffa 1962: 478). Sraffa means that reswitching demonstrates the impossibility of defining the quantity of capital and the period of production independently of the rate of interest.[2] One of the reviewers later admits: 'certainly the importance of part III [of Sraffa 1960] in which double-switching and capital-reversing are discussed did not get the prominence which we can now see it merited' (Harcourt 1972: 178).[3]

So, Sraffa's book cannot have been the direct cause of the debate. Its role was more complicated, as I will argue later.

ROBINSON: CONSTRUCTION AND CRITICISM

Right from 1936 Robinson made it her explicit purpose to construct a theory of the long run that was to encompass the short-run *General Theory* of Keynes. Her 'The Production Function and the Theory of Capital' of 1953–4 marks a stage in this research programme. Robinson considers as crucial the relations among output, factor supply, and the state of technical knowledge.

She admits that the *intuitions* of neoclassical theory are correct: the availability of capital determines how much of it is used in production; some concept of equilibrium is needed; in the long run, the rate of real wages tends to a level at which all available labour is employed; and, finally, technical progress may be incorporated into the equilibrium conditions. But she criticizes the way in which neoclassics *translate* these intuitions *into theory*. They are wrong to think that the production function is a useful instrument, and they wrongly think of equilibrium as a state of affairs towards which the economy is tending. Robinson did not fully develop the second criticism until later. In the 1950s she concentrated on the production function. The production function contains the quantity of capital as an argument *and* it is used to determine the interest rate. This is circular, because measuring the amount of capital in economically sensible terms always involves the rate of interest. However, '[w]e cannot abandon the production function without an effort to rescue the element of common-sense that has been entangled in it' (Robinson 1953–4: 83). She is referring to the idea that the availability of capital determines its use.

Robinson discovers that the production function may be 'multi-valued', but she clearly considers this an anomaly. It is described in guarded terms such as 'apparently paradoxical' (Robinson 1953–4: 96), 'a curious possibility' (ibid.: 106), and a scare-quoted '"perverse"' (ibid.: 94). She is so cautious that she refrains from giving a final judgement: 'A good deal of exploration of the possible magnitude and behaviour of the interest effect is needed before we can say whether the above is a mere theoretical rigmarole, or whether there is likely to be anything in reality corresponding to it' (ibid.: 106).

In *The Accumulation of Capital* of 1956 Robinson is strongly inclined to give a negative answer to that question. The book is systematically organized according to the method of decreasing abstraction. To the bare and highly idealized 'core' model of the accumulation of capital is added layer after layer of 'complicating' factors. The book has the constructive purpose of providing a theoretical framework for organizing and disciplining our thinking about reality rather than generating precise predictions (Robinson 1969: 63). In addition, it has a critical purpose. For example, the analysis of a change in the capital–labour ratio in a constant state of technical knowledge 'has been set out with so much elaboration not to provide a model for actual economies but in order to guard against a confusion of thought into which it is only too easy to fall' (Robinson 1969: 151). The confusion is mistaking directions of change of variables in comparative static models for causal relationships.[4]

The first complication of the core model is the relaxation of the assumption of a single technique. This introduces the problem of the choice of techniques. It is here that the anomalies re-emerge. Quite literally, they are a complication of a complication of the core model. Robinson goes out of her way to emphasize that they are unimportant exceptions to the general rule that a lower rate of profit is associated with a more mechanized technique of production. The reader is warned off by the observation that the introduction of a spectrum of techniques 'very much complicates the foregoing analysis without altering its broad implications' (ibid.: 101) and involves a line of analysis that 'is difficult out of proportion to its importance' (ibid.: 101, n1). Robinson stresses that the anomalies are 'rather unlikely' (ibid.: 110) or exceptional, and, when she devotes a paragraph to 'The Perverse Case', the reader is told once more that the phenomenon described is of no relevance to the real world: 'This paragraph is recommended only to readers who take a perverse pleasure in analytical puzzles' (ibid.: 147, n3).

In view of the important role that reswitching and capital reversing were to play later, these remarks seem very puzzling. But are they really? The main purpose of Robinson's research programme was constructive, not critical: the development of the analytical apparatus for describing changes in the structure of capital. Also, she was sympathetic to some of the most important ideas underlying the neoclassical analysis of production. It seems both reasonable and rational that in that early phase of the development of her analytical apparatus Robinson did not feel too sure about its power or robustness. This is why she took seriously the possibility that the paradoxical results were due to her manner of modelling matters rather than being descriptions of states of the world. Remember that it was not her purpose anyway to construct an empirical theory.

But what are we to think of the fact that in 1956 Robinson *explains* the 'perverse' behaviour of the factor ratio curve? She shows that it may be caused by a great interest sensitivity of the value of capital due to a long gestation period or working life of the equipment (the different time structures of production processes) (Robinson 1969: 109). Moreover, she *proves* that the perverse behaviour can be found only over a certain range of the rate of interest (Robinson 1953–4: 106). If Robinson had been consistent, she would have had to conclude from her *explanation* of these effects that *they cease to be anomalies*! Why didn't she? I offer three explanations.

First, the fact that she did not draw this conclusion, and even seems to have forgotten her own explanation, testifies to her confusion and uncertainty about her own work, or her lack of a global grasp of it. These features are characteristic of most scientific work under construction, particularly at an early stage. Constructing a theory usually is a very complicated affair, and most of the time scientists are involved in solving local problems. They grope their way piecemeal through the maze of problems and analytical building blocks, often losing sight of the global connections and problems. These are more easily distinguished with hindsight. In the words of Arthur Koestler, scientists behave like sleepwalkers.[5] In the case of Robinson this effect is reinforced by the fact that she complicates her constructive task by criticizing neoclassical theory.

The second explanation has to do with Robinson's method. In practice, and contrary to what is often alleged, the method of starting with a highly idealized model that is assumed to contain the skeleton of the theory and gradually providing it with more 'factual flesh' makes it very hard to attribute the conclusions drawn from a model on a certain level of abstraction to changes in assumptions. One may easily be misled, as Robinson was.[6]

The third explanation is that she may have felt that an analysis in terms of the time structure of production brought her too close to the intertemporal general equilibrium theory that Friedrich Hayek had constructed on the basis of marginal value theory and that had served him to develop his disequilibrium growth theory. Hayek (who had been Keynes' main opponent) thought his business cycle theory encompassed Keynes' 'general' theory. Thus he would have achieved, with the help of rational choice theory, what Robinson set out to do in her research programme. However, Robinson explicitly denied that a theory of growth could be based on rational choice theory.[7]

SAMUELSON: DEFENCE, BUT AGAINST WHAT?

The year 1961 is an important step in the events leading up to the debate. It was the year of Robinson's 'memorable visit' to the Massachussetts Institute of Technology, as Samuelson calls it (Samuelson 1962: 193, n1). What happened?

> In 1961 I encountered Professor Samuelson on his home ground; in the course of an argument I happened to ask him: When you define the marginal product of labour, what do you keep constant? He seemed disconcerted, as though none of his pupils had ever asked that question, but next day he gave a clear answer. Either the physical inputs other than labour are kept constant, or the rate of profit on capital is kept constant.
>
> I found this satisfactory, for it destroys the doctrine that wages are regulated by marginal productivity.... The wage is determined by technical conditions and the rate of profit, as at a particular point on a pseudo-production function. The question then comes up, what determines the rate of profit?
>
> (Robinson 1970: 310)

Samuelson took this criticism seriously. He defended himself in 'Parable and Realism', published in 1962. In Robinson (1979) we are told that Samuelson's article is a reply to Sraffa, but this cannot be true. Had this been the case, it would have been natural, if not inevitable, for Samuelson to discuss reswitching. He did not. Samuelson (1962) reacts not to Sraffa but to Robinson.[8] At which point enters Garegnani.

In 1961–2 Garegnani was visiting MIT. Even before Samuelson's article was published, he pointed out to Samuelson, in a criticism not published until 1970,[9] that the latter's surrogate production model solved the problem it was designed to solve only under very restrictive conditions. Although reswitching is *mentioned* in one of the three paragraphs that were submitted to the *Review of Economic Studies* in April 1963 (Garegnani 1970: 407, n1), it is not *discussed* until the paragraphs that were apparently written later. Indeed, Samuelson recalls that reswitching was not part of Garegnani's original criticism.[10] Professor Garegnani was so kind as to send me copies of the original papers by both Samuelson and himself. Samuelson's paper does not mention reswitching. In Garegnani's hand-written original criticism (dated, apparently after it had been written, 'MIT Winter 1961?'), reswitching is mentioned, in a footnote. There he observes that 'The possibility of this seems sufficient to disprove any "Clark parable"'.[11] But the fact that Garegnani devotes almost all of the space of both his hand-written paper and the first three paragraphs of his 1970 article to criticizing Samuelson by means that do not involve reswitching, plus the fact that reswitching is only mentioned in a footnote of the manuscript strongly suggest that it did not play a part in Garegnani's criticism. What Garegnani did instead was to repeat the argument of his own 1960 book in Italian,[12] namely that the amount of capital cannot be determined independently of the rate of profit. However, he now puts his criticism in terms of the wage–profit frontier, which he had taken from Sraffa. But unlike Sraffa he does not assign a central part to reswitching. He just mentions it.

I suggest that the course of events was as follows. Garegnani's reference to Sraffa and possibly his mentioning of reswitching made Samuelson realize that reswitching was a counter-example threatening the neoclassical model.[13] It was via Garegnani's criticism and through Sraffa's book that one 'mainstream economist' realized that his 'orthodoxy' was at stake (see Robinson 1977: 174). I think that we have to take Robinson's observation quite literally: the *only* other economist apart from Sraffa who realized the importance of the reswitching result was mainstream, orthodox Samuelson. With the exception of Samuelson and Garegnani, it was apparently generally believed that Samuelson (1962) provided a satisfactory account of the neoclassical approach to distribution theory: 'For several years everyone (except Garegnani) was somewhat baffled by the surrogate production function' (Robinson 1975: 36).[14]

In the meantime, Samuelson did not sit still. He tried to find a way of saving his model. But instead of replying to Garegnani's main criticism, which did not make use of reswitching, *Samuelson changed the problem*. He turned it into: how can reswitching be avoided? He thought that the reswitching counter-example was not so strong as to render his surrogate production function model inapplicable in general. Samuelson sought the solution in the conjecture that indecomposable models are not affected by reswitching. Then 'sometime in 1964' (Solow 1983: 184) Samuelson told his PhD student David Levhari about his conjecture. In 1965, Levhari published his proof of Samuelson's conjecture. Pasinetti showed the mistake in Levhari's proof, and others followed suit (see Pasinetti et al. 1966). The 'Cambridge debate' had started.

IRONIES INSTEAD OF LESSONS FROM HISTORY

The picture of the capital debate that emerges from the above is full of ironies. Robinson later says she devised the pseudo production function in order to drive home her criticism of the neoclassical approach that comparative statics cannot substitute dynamics. This analytical device was taken over by the neoclassic Samuelson to defend his neoclassical model. But instead of clarifying matters, as had been Robinson's intention, she put defenders and critics of neoclassical theory alike on the wrong track: 'I confess that I was the first to draw [a pseudo production function]' (Robinson 1980: 221).

It is ironic, too, that Solow and other neoclassics much later reached the conclusion that the fundamental problem in the debate was that static models were used to make statements about processes in time (see Solow 1983 and Burmeister 1980: 154). Solow denies that it was Robinson who first recognized this. He is wrong. However, he is correct in thinking that she did not make this the main point of her criticism until the early 1970s.[15]

The recent rise of evolutionary economics also marks a historical irony. Economists are discovering that, in order to deal with processes, one has to take 'historical time' seriously; models that are based on 'logical time' cannot do the trick. This lesson could have been drawn much sooner from the Cambridge debate, or from Robinson's later insistence on this point (see, for example, Robinson 1974).

NOTES

1 Dobb is wrong twice over. Sraffa did not think that reswitching was an incidental corollary of the rest of his book. See the sequel of the text.
2 Sraffa had already said this explicitly in Part I of his book. There he gives an example of reswitching, and he concludes: 'The [concomitant] reversals in the direction of the movement of relative prices . . . cannot be reconciled with *any* notion of capital as a measurable quantity independent of distribution and prices' (Sraffa 1960: 38).
3 But the failure to read on to Part III cannot be the whole explanation of the oversight; see the previous note. Perhaps the readers took Sraffa's subtitle too literally, thinking that a prelude cannot be the thing itself.
4 Notice that Robinson's criticism of using comparative statics as a substitute for a dynamic theory is already more prominent here than in her 1953–4 article.
5 See Koestler (1964). The sleepwalker thesis is elaborated in Birner (forthcoming).
6 Again, the reader is referred to Birner (forthcoming).
7 See the Preface to *The Accumulation of Capital*.
8 This is confirmed by Samuelson in a letter to me of 25 August 1989:

> My Surrogate Capital effort . . . arose from my realization, as I listened to Joan talk about heterogeneous capital goods and separate pages of her blue-print book of techniques, that sometimes a model like hers would produce *aggregate* relations like those in the leets neoclassical parable. I quickly sketched an instance that looked like a 2 sector neoclassical model but was actually an n-good Sraffa model.

9 Garegnani (1970). In a conversation with me (13 June 1989), Garegnani mentioned as one of the reasons for the delay that he wanted to wait for Samuelson's revised version, in the light of Garegnani's criticism, of his 1962 article.

10 In an interview with me on 20 April 1989. This means that if it is the reswitching counter-example that Roncaglia means by 'Sraffa's results' that were 'destructive of Samuelson's efforts' (Roncaglia 1978: 100), it is doubtful whether he is right in putting the introduction of reswitching into the debate at this early a date. Apart from this detail, Roncaglia recognizes the complexity of the story as it is told here.

11 In the same note of the manuscript the possibility of reswitching is used to discuss the possibility of capital reversing (though this term is not used). It has 'been pointed out [to him, Garegnani] that this possibility is mentioned in J. Robinson, "The Accumulation of Capital" as a "curiosum"'.

12 Garegnani (1960). The book does not discuss reswitching.

13 Samuelson already knew Sraffa's book. Garegnani mentioned to me (16 January 1990) that at the time of his stay at MIT in 1961–2 Samuelson taught a course on it (though in Garegnani's memory it was more on matrices and Samuelson's own 'non-substitution theorem'). When asked (on 20 April 1989) whether he had read Sraffa's book, Samuelson replied that he did not want to say that (at that time) he understood all the things that were in this cryptically written book. But he was rather emphatic in his recollection that reswitching had not come up in Garegnani's oral criticism.

14 I suggest that we read 'everyone' as including Robinson herself.

15 Well before they themselves reached this conclusion.

REFERENCES

Birner, J. (forthcoming) *Strategies and Programmes in Capital Theory*. London: Routledge.

Brown, M. (1973) Toward an Econometric Accommodation of the Capital-Intensity-Perversity Phenomenon, *Econometrica*, 41: 937–54.

Burmeister, E. (1980) *Capital Theory and Dynamics*. Cambridge: Cambridge University Press.

Dobb, M. (1973) *Theories of Value and Distribution since Adam Smith*. Cambridge: Cambridge University Press.

Garegnani, P. (1960) *Il capitale nelle teorie della distribuzione*. Milan: Giuffrè.

——— (1970) Heterogeneous Capital, the Production Function and the Theory of Distribution, *Review of Economic Studies*, 90: 407–36.

Harcourt, G. C. (1972) *Some Cambridge Controversies in the Theory of Capital*. Cambridge: Cambridge University Press.

Harrod, R. F. (1961) Review of P. Sraffa *Production of Commodities by Means of Commodities*, *Economic Journal*, 71: 783–7.

Koestler, A. (1964) *The Sleepwalkers; A History of Man's Changing Vision of the Universe*. Harmondsworth: Penguin.

Lachmann, L. M. (1973) *Macro-economic Thinking and the Market Economy: An Essay on the Neglect of the Micro-Foundations and its Consequences*. London: Institute for Economic Affairs.

Levhari, D. (1965) A Nonsubstitution Theorem and Switching of Techniques, *Quarterly Journal of Economics*, 79: 98–105.

Pasinetti, L. L. et al. (1966) Paradoxes in Capital Theory: A Symposium, *Quarterly Journal of Economics*, 80: 503–67.

Robinson, J. (1936) *Essays in the Theory of Employment*, London: Hyperion Press (1980 reprint of 1947 Blackwell 2nd ed.).

——— (1953–4) The Production Function and the Theory of Capital, *Review of Economic Studies*, 21: 81–106.

——— (1961) Prelude to a Critique of Economic Theory, *Oxford Economic Papers*, 13: 53–8.

——— (1965) A Reconsideration of the Theory of Value. In *Collected Economic Papers*, vol. III. Oxford: Blackwell.

——— (1969) [1956] *The Accumulation of Capital*, 3rd edn. London: Macmillan.

——— (1970) Capital Theory up to Date, *Canadian Journal of Economics*, 3: 309–17.

——— (1974) History versus Equilibrium; reprinted in *Collected Economic Papers*, vol. V, Oxford: Blackwell, 1979.

——— (1975) The Unimportance of Reswitching, *Quarterly Journal of Economics*, 89: 32–9.

——— (1977) Qu'est-ce que le capital? *Revue d'économie politique*, 87: 165–79.

——— (1979) Misunderstandings in the Theory of Production, *Greek Economic Review*, 1: 1–7.

——— (1980) Time in Economic Theory, *Kyklos*, 33: 219–29.

Roncaglia, A. (1978) *Sraffa and the Theory of Prices*. London: Wiley.

Samuelson, P. A. (1962) Parable and Realism in Capital Theory: The Surrogate Production Function, *Review of Economic Studies*, 29: 193–206.

Solow, R. M. (1983) Modern Capital Theory. In M. Brown and R. M. Solow, eds, *Paul Samuelson and Modern Economic Theory*. New York: McGraw-Hill.

Sraffa, P. (1960) *Production of Commodities by Means of Commodities. Prelude to a Critique of Economic Theory*. Cambridge: Cambridge University Press.

——— (1962) Production of Commodities: A Comment, *Economic Journal*, 72: 477–9.

21

'PRODUCTIVITY CURVES' IN *THE ACCUMULATION OF CAPITAL*[1]

Neri Salvadori

> Two types of diagram have been used in this discussion. In Sraffa's diagram . . . a family of curves shows each technique at all rates of profit. In the other, a family of curves ('productivity curves') shows all techniques at each rate of profit, with the corresponding values of capital in terms of output.
>
> (Robinson and Naqvi 1967: 582–3)

In *The Accumulation of Capital* Joan Robinson (1956) developed a description of technology in terms of 'productivity curves'. After the publication of *Production of Commodities by Means of Commodities* by Piero Sraffa (1960), Joan Robinson seemed to abandon that description of technology. However she still maintained its use in 1967 – in a paper written with Naqvi where some productivity curves were drawn side by side with other diagrams, but not really used (see the epigraph to this paper) – and continued to use, for a number of years, a relationship between output per man and capital per man[2] that she called the 'pseudo-production function'. This relationship, in fact, can be obtained both from Sraffa's construction and from the Robinsonian productivity curves (see below). Finally, 'in 1974' Joan Robinson 'took the pseudo production function in pieces again' (Robinson 1980b: 138; see also Robinson 1980c: 133).[3]

In the four years between the publication of *The Accumulation of Capital* and that of *Production of Commodities by Means of Commodities* no mathematical formalization of the Robinsonian productivity curves was put forward. In the years afterwards the lack of interest by Joan Robinson herself certainly did not invite a job like that. This is a pity for at least one reason: the description of technology in terms of productivity curves is much more workable for economists with a neoclassical background and an interest in macroeconomics. This fact becomes especially relevant now that growth theory is again fashionable with endogenous growth. This is the reason why in this paper I will try to present a formalized version of the Robinsonian 'productivity curves'.

A 'productivity curve' is a sort of production function built upon the assumption that the rate of profit is kept constant. This assumption allows one to measure capital in terms of the consumption good correctly (consumption is assumed to be proportional to a given basket of commodities). Of course a productivity curve has interest only at the point(s) of the function where the slope equals the given rate of profit. Because this analysis can be performed for each feasible rate of profit, the wage rate–profit rate relationship, the capital–profit rate relationship, and the output–profit rate relationship can be determined.

The present paper can also be read as a comment on the first part of an appendix to *The Accumulation of Capital* called 'Diagrams' (1956: 411–23). Each of the following sections starts with references to this appendix, which are useful for grasping the relevant concepts as stated by Joan Robinson. These concepts are then analysed with the help of the mathematical tools that have been considered appropriate. The relevant concepts mentioned are those of a 'productivity curve', a 'family of productivity curves', and a 'pseudo-production function'. Joan Robinson (1956) considered the growth rate as given and I will follow her in doing so in this paper. Only in the appendix will I consider the growth rate as a(n independent) variable. This is done in order to stimulate possible uses of the Robinsonian 'productivity curves' outside the growth theory supported by Joan Robinson herself.

A PRODUCTIVITY CURVE

At the very beginning of the 'Diagrams' appendix we are informed that the diagrams to be dealt with illustrate what can be expressed 'in two dimensions' and therefore all relations 'can be illustrated in terms of comparisons of static positions' (Robinson 1956: 411). Then Joan Robinson adds:

> For this purpose we imagine that we are comparing positions in each of which the stock of capital goods is being maintained, item by item, and the flow of output is being consumed.... Output consists of commodities produced in fixed proportions, and is measured in units of a composite commodity consisting of a representative sample of production.
>
> (ibid.: 411)

Here there is a small problem. In these circumstances the problem of accumulation cannot be taken into consideration unless the 'capital goods' consist of the same 'composite commodity' as the product. In order to avoid this problem, in this paper it will be assumed that *consumption* 'consists of commodities' *consumed* 'in fixed proportions', whereas output will consist of units of the same 'sample of consumption' only if the growth rate equals zero. If, on the contrary, the growth rate is positive, the output will be measured in *value*, the 'sample of consumption' being the numéraire. The first diagram considered in the 'Diagrams' appendix (1956: 412, Figure 1)[4] is 'adapted' from a diagram used by Wicksell. 'The vertical axis represents output per annum measured in units of the composite commodity. The horizontal axis represents stocks of capital goods measured in terms of the labour time required to produce them, reckoned at a given notional rate of interest' (1956: 411). The measure of capital suggested by Joan Robinson implies that the numéraire consists of labour. Since it is convenient to measure the values of commodities in terms of the same numéraire, in this paper capital will be measured in terms of the 'sample of consumption' as well as the product.[5] The amount of labour is assumed to be unity, so that the vertical axis represents output per man and the horizontal axis represents the capital(–labour)[6] ratio. In Figure 21.1, OJ ($J = A, B, C, D$) is the output per man when all workers are employed with technique υ ($\upsilon = \alpha, \beta, \gamma, \delta$) and O$j$ ($j = b, c$) is the value of capital per man when all workers are employed with technique υ ($\upsilon = \beta, \gamma$). All these quantities are measured assuming that a given rate of profit and a given growth rate hold.

> Between O*c* and O*b* lie stocks of capital goods with a rising proportion of Beta outfits to Gamma outfits, so that *CB* represents the difference in output per man due to using Beta rather than Gamma technique, and *cb* represents the increase in the ... capital ratio involved by that difference. The curve $\delta\gamma\beta\alpha$ is a *productivity curve* showing the relation between output and the ... capital ratio.
>
> (1956: 411–12)

To formalize the concept of productivity curve as introduced and used by Joan Robinson some preliminaries are needed. Let us first assume that there are n commodities. For each commodity i there is at least one process ($\mathbf{a}$, $\mathbf{e}_i$, l) that is able to produce it: the n vector $\mathbf{a}$ is the material input vector, the i-th unit n vector $\mathbf{e}_i$ is the output vector, and the scalar l is the labour input. A collection of n processes, each producing a different commodity, is called a *technique* and is described by the triplet ($\mathbf{A}$, $\mathbf{I}$, $\mathbf{l}$), where $\mathbf{A}$ is the material input matrix, the identity matrix $\mathbf{I}$ is the output matrix, and $\mathbf{l}$ is the labour input vector. (In the following, matrix $\mathbf{I}$ will be dropped when no doubt could arise.)

If technique ($\mathbf{A}$, $\mathbf{l}$) holds, commodities are consumed in proportion to vector $\mathbf{d} \geq 0$, the growth rate equals $g \geq 0$, and one unit of labour is employed, then the intensity vector, $\mathbf{x}$, and the consumption per man, c, must be such that:

$$\mathbf{x}^{\mathrm{T}} = c\mathbf{d}^{\mathrm{T}} + (1+g)\mathbf{x}^{\mathrm{T}}\mathbf{A}$$

$$\mathbf{x}^{\mathrm{T}}\mathbf{l} = 1.$$

If technique ($\mathbf{A}$, $\mathbf{l}$) holds, the rate of profit equals $r \geq 0$, and the numéraire consists of the 'sample of consumption' $\mathbf{d}$, then the price vector, $\mathbf{p}$, and the wage rate, w, must be such that:

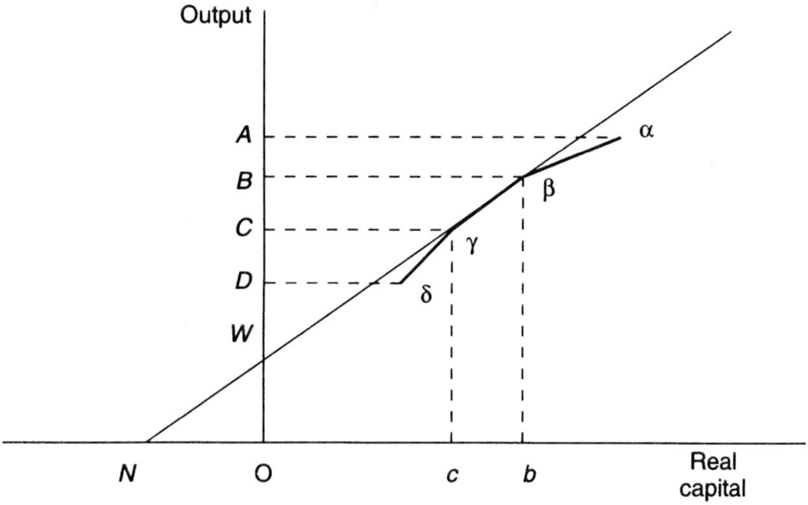

Figure 21.1

$$\mathbf{p} = (1 + r)\mathbf{Ap} + w\mathbf{l}$$

$$\mathbf{d}^{\mathrm{T}}\mathbf{p} = 1.$$

Hence at the growth rate, g, and at the rate of profit, r, the output per man, y, and the capital ratio, k, relative to technique $(\mathbf{A}, \mathbf{l})$ are:

$$y = \mathbf{x}^{\mathrm{T}}(\mathbf{I} - \mathbf{A})\mathbf{p} = w + r\mathbf{x}^{\mathrm{T}}\mathbf{Ap} = c + g\mathbf{x}^{\mathrm{T}}\mathbf{Ap}$$

$$k = \mathbf{x}^{\mathrm{T}}\mathbf{Ap}.$$

If there are several techniques, there is a pair (k, y) for each of them and all these k's and y's can be plotted in a diagram such as that provided by Joan Robinson because all k's (and all y's) are expressed in the same unit of measure, the 'sample of consumption'. In this way we get a set of points in the (k, y) plane. Appropriate assumptions may make this set dense. Let us first assume that if $(\mathbf{A}, \mathbf{l})$ is a technique, then $(\mathbf{B}, \mathbf{m})$ is also a technique provided that $\mathbf{B} \geqq \mathbf{A}$ and $\mathbf{m} \geqq \mathbf{l}$. The interpretation of this assumption is that waste is always possible. Of course, technique $(\mathbf{B}, \mathbf{m})$ is an inferior technique with respect to $(\mathbf{A}, \mathbf{l})$; nevertheless it is a technique. Secondly, let us assume that if $(\mathbf{A}_i, \mathbf{l}_i)$ and $(\mathbf{A}_j, \mathbf{l}_j)$ are techniques, then $(\lambda\mathbf{A}_i + (1 - \lambda)\mathbf{A}_j, \lambda\mathbf{l}_i + (1 - \lambda)\mathbf{l}_j)$ is also a technique provided that $0 \leq \lambda \leq 1$. That is, returns to scale are constant and it is possible to combine several techniques. The productivity curve relative to the rate of profit r (and the growth rate g) can now be defined as the function

$$y = f_r(k), \tag{1}$$

which is obtained by choosing for each k the maximum y such that (k, y) is the pair of the capital ratio and the output per man for a technique at the rate of profit r (and growth rate g).

Is it always possible to construct a productivity curve? Certainly not. If the rate of profit is too high there is no technique that would give non-negative prices at that rate of profit, and therefore no productivity curve can be built up at that rate of profit. However, it is possible to prove that, if the rate of profit is not too high, then the corresponding productivity curve can be constructed. In order to simplify the exposition, let us assume that all commodities are *basic* (in the sense of Sraffa 1960) in all techniques. As is well known, for each technique there is a maximum rate of profit, i.e. a rate of profit corresponding to a zero wage rate and positive prices. Moreover, for each positive rate of profit smaller than that, the wage rate and the prices relative to that technique are positive, whereas for each rate of profit larger than that, either the wage rate or some price relative to that technique is negative, some other prices being positive. Let R be the maximum of all these 'maximum rates of profit', i.e. R is a rate of profit corresponding to which no technique has both a positive wage rate and positive prices and at least one technique has both a zero wage rate and positive prices. It can be shown that if $g \leq r^* \leq R$, the productivity curve corresponding to r^* can be constructed.

Let r^* be not smaller than g but smaller than R. We know that a cost-minimizing technique at the rate of profit r^* $(\mathbf{A}^*, \mathbf{l}^*)$ is a technique that gives rise to a wage rate w^* such that no other technique allows a wage rate higher than w^* for $r = r^*$. This technique determines also the pair of capital ratio and output per man (k^*, y^*) as depicted in Figure 21.2, where $r^* = tg\ \alpha$. The property of w^* just mentioned implies that all pairs (k, y) relative to the available techniques must be either on the straight line WT or under it. As a consequence, the maximum problem that is involved in determining the productivity curve always has a solution, except for those k's that cannot be associated with any technique at the rate of profit r^*.

In order to show that the productivity curve is defined for $0 \leq k \leq k^*$, let us consider the technique $(\mathbf{A}^*, (1 + t)\mathbf{l}^*)$, $t > 0$. This is an inferior technique because it is obtained from technique $(\mathbf{A}^*, \mathbf{l}^*)$ by wasting a portion of labour for each unit of labour performed (workers 'twiddle their thumbs' so to speak for a portion of their work time). The capital ratio and the output per man associated with this technique at rate of profit r^* are $(1 + t)^{-1}k^*$ and $(1 + t)^{-1}y^*$, respectively. This is enough to assert that the productivity curve is defined for $0 \leq k \leq k^*$ and in this range it is not only not above the segment WA but also not below the segment OA. Similarly, let us consider the inferior technique $(\mathbf{A}^* + t\mathbf{l}^*\mathbf{d}^{\mathrm{T}}, \mathbf{l}^*)$, $0 < t \leq (1 + r^*)^{-1}w^*$. (If $t > (1 + r)^{-1}w^*$, the wage rate is negative.) The capital ratio and the output per man associated with this technique at rate of profit r^* are $k^* + t$ and $y^* - t$, respectively. This is enough

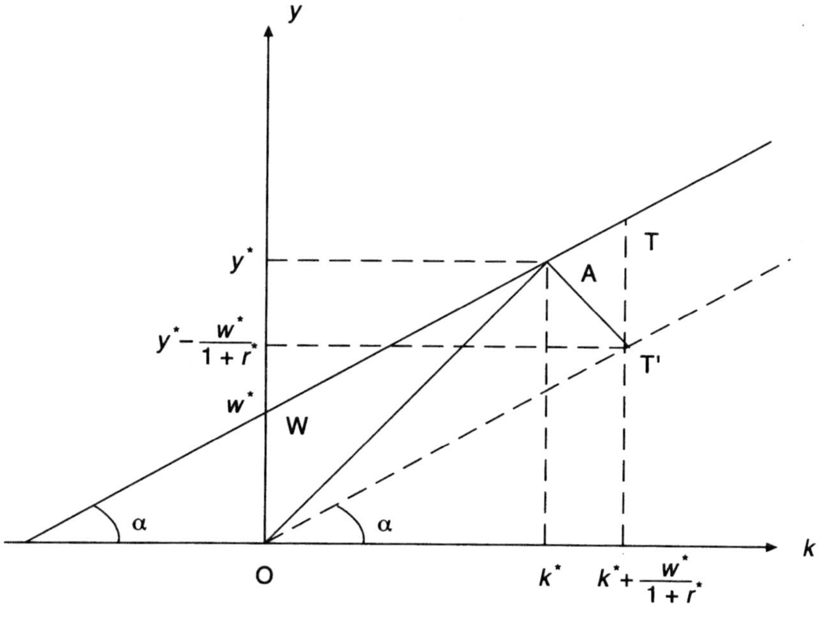

Figure 21.2

to assert that the productivity curve is defined for $k^* \leq k \leq k^* + (1 + r^*)^{-1}w^*$, and in this range it is not only not above the segment AT but also not below the segment AT′. We know enough to maintain that there is a $K > k^*$ such that the productivity curve is defined for $0 \leq k \leq K$ and it is concave and increasing on the left at $k = k^*$.

Let us now consider all the other relevant techniques. The corresponding pairs (k, y) are neither above the straight line WT nor under the straight line OT′ because at the rate of profit r^* these techniques give rise to wage rates that are not larger than w^* and not smaller than 0. If there are other cost-minimizing techniques, the corresponding pairs (k, y) are on the straight line WT, and the segments of the straight line WT joining two pairs (k, y) associated with two distinct cost-minimizing techniques are segments of the productivity curve because each point of this segment can be associated with a technique obtained by combining two cost-minimizing techniques. This is so because cost-minimizing techniques have the same wage rate and the same price vector.

In general it is not true that if (k_i, y_i) and (k_j, y_j) are two pairs associated with two distinct techniques, then the straight-line segment joining the two points consists of pairs (k, y) that can be associated with combined techniques. This difficulty does not allow us to use a well-known procedure that ensures that production functions relative to one-commodity economies are continuous, concave and not decreasing if returns to scale are constant. However, as has been shown, these properties hold at the points of the productivity curve that are on the straight line WT. Moreover, as will be shown in what follows, what happens at all other points is irrelevant in a static analysis. Then, in the following it will be assumed that there is a $K^*_r \geq k^*$ such that function (1) is defined, continuous, non-decreasing and concave for $0 \leq k \leq K^*_r$, where k^* is the larger capital ratio associated with a cost-minimizing technique. Hence, if function (1) is twice differentiable, then

$$f'_r(k) \geq 0, \quad f''_r(k) \leq 0 \quad 0 \leq k \leq K^*_r$$

If these assumptions hold, then the cost-minimizing techniques on the productivity curve are those and only those that have the property[7]

$$f'_r(k) = r.$$

In the limiting case in which $r^* = R$, the straight lines WT and OT′ coincide because $w^* = 0$. As a consequence, the productivity curve is $f_R(k) = Rk$, $0 \leq k \leq k^* = K^*_R$, which is increasing, differentiable and such that $f'_R(k) = R > 0$, $f''_R(k) = 0$. The *technically* inferior techniques in which there is a waste of labour are also cost minimizing because the wage rate equals zero.

A FAMILY OF PRODUCTIVITY CURVES

In the 'Diagrams' appendix Joan Robinson proceeds to compare positions with different rates of profit:

> The [consumption per man] corresponding to each technique is the same irrespective of the [rate of profit], and the outfits of capital goods required for each technique are the same from an engineering point of view.... The productivity curve therefore has to be redrawn for each rate of profit to exhibit the difference in the ... capital ratio due to a different element of interest in the cost ... of a given outfit of capital goods.
>
> (Robinson 1956: 413)

Figure 21.3, which is Figure 2 of the 'Diagrams' appendix, represents three productivity curves depicted as $\delta_i\gamma_i\beta_i\alpha_i$ ($i = 1, 2, 3$). 'The thick line represents all the positions of static equilibrium which are possible in the given technical conditions' (1956: 413–14) with a range of rates of profit. If the rate of profit is that relative to the slope of segment $\delta_3\gamma_3$, then two techniques, δ and γ, are cost minimizing. If the rate of profit is lower, but higher than that relative to the slope of segment $\gamma_2\beta_2$, then one technique, γ, is cost minimizing, and the change in prices related to changes in the rate of profit implies a relationship between k and y that is a straight-line segment with a slope equal to the growth rate. (In Figure 21.3 the growth rate is zero.) This is so because of the choice

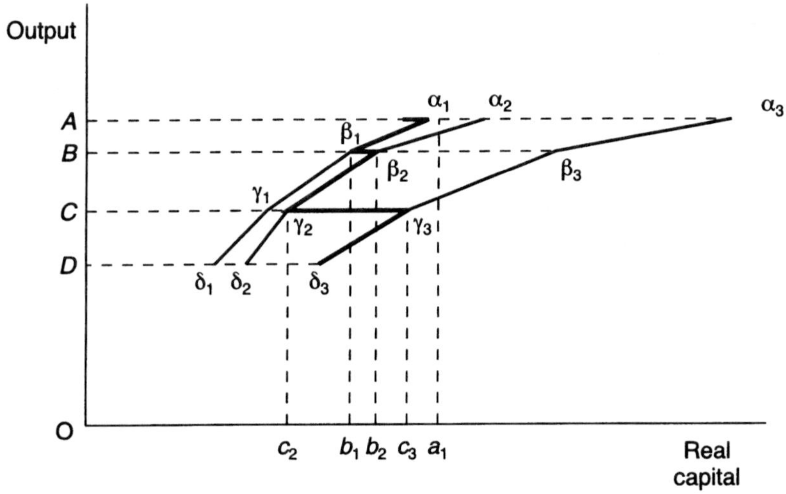

Figure 21.3

of the numéraire, which guarantees that consumption per man is unchanged for a given technique. If the rate of profit is that relative to the slope of segment $\gamma_2\beta_2$, then again two techniques, γ and β, are cost minimizing. And so on.[8]

From the results presented in the previous section, we get that the function

$$y = F(k, r) := f_r(k) \tag{2}$$

is defined for $g \leq r \leq R$ and $0 \leq k \leq K(r) := K^*_r$. Function (2) is called a 'family of productivity curves' (at the given growth rate g). Let us assume that $F(k, r)$ is continuous and twice continuously differentiable; moreover

$$\frac{\partial F}{\partial k} \geq 0, \quad \frac{\partial^2 F}{\partial k^2} \leq 0.$$

A simple argument will determine the relationship between the derivatives of the family of productivity curves. Let $\alpha := (\mathbf{A}, \mathbf{l})$ be a technique and let

$$k_\alpha(r) = \mathbf{x}_\alpha^{\mathrm{T}} \mathbf{A} \mathbf{p}_\alpha(r) \tag{3a}$$

$$y_\alpha(r) = \mathbf{x}_\alpha^{\mathrm{T}}(\mathbf{I} - \mathbf{A})\mathbf{p}_\alpha(r) = c_\alpha + g k_\alpha(r) = w_\alpha(r) + r k_\alpha(r), \tag{3b}$$

where $\mathbf{x}_\alpha$ and c_α are the intensity vector and the consumption per man of technique $(\mathbf{A}, \mathbf{l})$ (at growth rate g) and $\mathbf{p}_\alpha(r)$ and $w_\alpha(r)$ are the price vector and the wage rate of technique $(\mathbf{A}, \mathbf{l})$ at rate of profit r. Let (k^*, r^*, y^*) be a point on the family of productivity curves such that $k^* = k_\alpha(r^*)$ and $y^* = y_\alpha(r^*)$, i.e. $y_\alpha(r^*) = F(k_\alpha(r^*), r^*)$.

Finally, consider the function

$$z(r) := F(k_\alpha(r), r) - y_\alpha(r).$$

In the range in which function $z(r)$ is defined it is non-negative because of the definition of the family of productivity curves. Since $z(r^*) = 0$, if $r^* < R$, the function $z(r)$ has an internal minimum at $r = r^*$. Since function $k_\alpha(r)$ is differentiable and since function $F(k, r)$ has been assumed to be so, then, at (k^*, r^*),

$$\frac{\partial F}{\partial k} k'_\alpha(r) + \frac{\partial F}{\partial r} - y'_\alpha(r) = 0.$$

Thus

$$\frac{\partial F}{\partial r} = \left(g - \frac{\partial F}{\partial k}\right) k'_\alpha(r), \tag{4}$$

since $y'_\alpha(r) = gk'_\alpha(r)$. Let us add that, for $k = k^*$ and $r = r^*$,

$$\text{if } \frac{\partial F}{\partial k} = r, \text{ then } \frac{\partial F}{\partial r} < k, \tag{5}$$

since $w'_\alpha(r) < 0$ and, because of (3b), $w'_\alpha(r) = (g - r)k'_\alpha(r) - k_\alpha(r)$.

If capital and product consist of the same commodity, then $k'_\alpha(r) = 0$ for each α and each r and, as a consequence, all the productivity curves of the family are identical to each other and the derivatives of any order of function $F(k, r)$ with respect to r equal zero.

As has been shown in the previous section, costs are minimized when

$$\frac{\partial F}{\partial k} = r. \tag{6}$$

Equation (6) defines implicitly a relationship between k and r. This relationship is a correspondence because it is possible that, for some pair (k, r) in which equation (6) is satisfied, it is also true that

$$\frac{\partial^2 F}{\partial k^2} = 0. \tag{7}$$

This is the case in which two techniques are simultaneously cost minimizing. If (k^*, r^*) is a pair satisfying equation (6) but not equality (7), then there is a neighbourhood of (k^*, r^*) in which equality (7) does not hold; in that neighbourhood the relationship between k and r is a differentiable function, and

$$\frac{\mathrm{d}k}{\mathrm{d}r} = \frac{1 - \dfrac{\partial^2 F}{\partial k \partial r}}{\dfrac{\partial^2 F}{\partial k^2}} \tag{8}$$

Equations (2) and (6) also define implicitly a relationship between y and r. This relationship too is a correspondence. If (y^*, r^*) is a pair for which there is a k^* such that y^*, r^* and k^* satisfy equations (2) and (6) but not equality (7), then there is a neighbourhood of (y^*, r^*) in which the relationship between y and r is a differentiable function and

$$\frac{\mathrm{d}y}{\mathrm{d}r} = \frac{\partial F}{\partial r} + r\frac{\mathrm{d}k}{\mathrm{d}r} = \frac{\partial F}{\partial r} + r\,\frac{1 - \dfrac{\partial^2 F}{\partial k \partial r}}{\dfrac{\partial^2 F}{\partial k^2}}. \tag{9}$$

Finally, since

$$w = F(k, r) - rk, \tag{10}$$

equations (6) and (10) define w as a function of r for $0 \leq r \leq R$. Moreover (see statement (5))

$$\frac{\mathrm{d}w}{\mathrm{d}r} = \frac{\partial F}{\partial r} - k + \left[\frac{\partial F}{\partial k} - r\right]\frac{\mathrm{d}k}{\mathrm{d}r} = \frac{\partial F}{\partial r} - k < 0.$$

A PSEUDO-PRODUCTION FUNCTION

The 'thick line' of Figure 21.3 is called 'real-capital-ratio curve' (p. 414) in the 'Diagrams', but it will be called here 'pseudo-production function', which is the name Joan Robinson (1979: 82, 1980b: 136, 1978b: 103) said she had borrowed from Solow (1963) and which she used in later publications.[9] A few pages of the 'Diagrams' are then utilized to move from the measurement of capital in terms of labour to the measurement in terms of the product and to introduce a continuum of techniques so that both the productivity curves and the pseudo-production function can 'be drawn as smooth continuous curves' (1956: 416). Finally Joan Robinson illustrates, with the help of two figures (Figure 5 on p. 417 and Figure 6 on p. 418, which are here Figures 21.4 and 21.5, respectively), 'a "perverse" relationship in which a lower rate of profit corresponds to a less mechanised technique' (1956: 418). This 'perversity' is recognized in Figure 21.4 as a 'reswitching' of techniques. This possibility was to become famous shortly after the publication of *The Accumulation of Capital*. Technique β, in fact, is cost minimizing for two disconnected ranges of the rate of profit, technique γ being cost minimizing in the range in between. Therefore, either in the first switch or in the second, 'a lower rate of profit corresponds to a less mechanised technique'. Joan Robinson adds that with 'discontinuities smoothed out the [pseudo-production function] would appear as in [Figure 21.5]' (1956: 418). As is well known, these 'perversities' were at the centre of the capital controversy during the 1960s. (A classical and almost complete account of the controversy has been provided by Harcourt 1972; see also Harcourt 1986, 1992, and Kurz and Salvadori 1995: Ch. 14.)

The main difference between equation (8) and the analogous equation that could be obtained from a usual neoclassical production function is the presence of $\partial^2 F/\partial k \partial r$ in the numerator on the RHS. As a consequence, whereas the capital ratio as a function of the rate of profit is certainly decreasing when $\partial^2 F/\partial k \partial r = 0$ – which, as we have seen above, is the case when capital and product consist of the same commodity – it is not so in general – as the debate during 1960s has proved. Similarly, equation (9) implies that the product per man as a function of the rate of profit is also not always decreasing. Neither need the two curves have the same sign slope.

The pseudo-production function, i.e. the locus of k and y for which there is an r satisfying both equations (2) and (6), is not actually a function as Joan Robinson recognized so clearly: it is a correspondence. However, if (k^*, y^*)

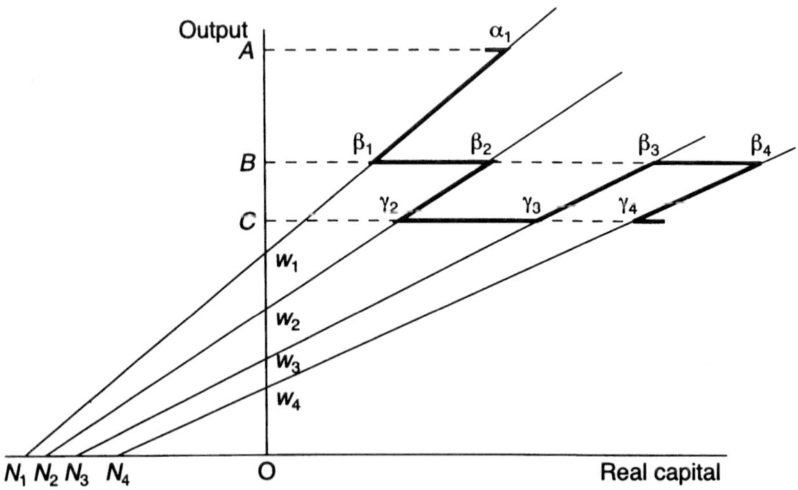

Figure 21.4

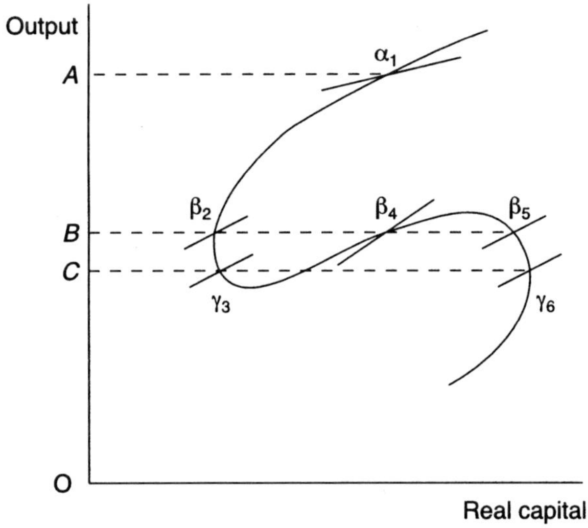

Figure 21.5

is a point of this locus, and if at this point $(\partial^2 F/\partial k\partial r) \neq 1$, then a segment of this locus including point (k^*, y^*) can be represented as a differentiable function. Moreover,

$$\frac{\mathrm{d}y}{\mathrm{d}k} = r + \frac{\partial F}{\partial r}\,\frac{\dfrac{\partial^2 F}{\partial k^2}}{1 - \dfrac{\partial^2 F}{\partial k \partial r}}. \tag{11}$$

It is interesting to analyse when $\mathrm{d}y/\mathrm{d}k = r$. This is obviously the case when either

$$\frac{\partial F}{\partial r} = 0 \tag{12}$$

or equation (7) holds. From equation (4) we obtain that equation (12) holds (i) when $k'_\alpha(r) = 0$ for each α and each r, i.e. when capital and product consist of the same commodity; (ii) when $k'_\alpha(r) = 0$ at the point considered, but not in general; (iii) when equation (6) is satisfied and $r = g$. Equation (7) holds (iv) when two techniques are cost minimizing. These four cases are well known to the participants in the reswitching debate. Case (i) has been investigated by Samuelson (1962), Bhaduri (1969) and mainly Garegnani

(1970); see also Robinson (1978b: 105) and Harcourt (1972: 131–54). Case (ii) is Ng's counter-example (see Harcourt 1972: 149–50). Case (iii) is related to the 'golden rule of accumulation': Bhaduri (1966) maintained that it was proved by von Weizsäcker (with no reference); Harcourt (1972: 149) referred to Koopmans (1965), Pearce (1962), Bhaduri (1966), Nell (1970), and Harcourt (1970) and maintained that the formulation presented by himself is due to Laing (with no reference); see also Robinson (1962). Case (iv) has been investigated by Solow (1967, 1970), whose interpretation of this result has been criticized by Pasinetti (1969, 1970); see also Robinson (1978a) and Harcourt (1972: 109–11, 157–69).

Finally, it is interesting to study when $\mathrm{d}y/\mathrm{d}k = g$. From equations (4) and (11) we obtain that this is the case when

$$(r-g)\left[1-k'_{\alpha}(r)\,\frac{\dfrac{\partial^2 F}{\partial k^2}}{1-\dfrac{\partial^2 F}{\partial k \partial r}}\right]=0. \tag{13}$$

Equation (13) holds when either $(r-g)=0$, as in case (iii) above, or $\mathrm{d}k/\mathrm{d}r = k'_{\alpha}(r)$ – see equation (8). The latter condition holds on each segment of the pseudo-production function where only one technique is cost minimizing.

The 'Diagrams' appendix goes on to deal with technical progress, the introduction of land and the value of invested capital. But we will not follow Joan Robinson in these analyses, since they are beyond the scope of this paper.

APPENDIX

At the beginning of this paper it was mentioned that the construction suggested by Joan Robinson might be useful to evaluate some recent contributions to growth theory known as 'endogenous growth'. But in order to do so comparisons of positions with different growth rates must be allowed. This necessitates taking more explicitly into consideration that productivity curves depend not only on the rate of profit but also on the growth rate. As a consequence, equation (1) becomes

$$y=f_{rg}(k),$$

equation (2) becomes

$$y=F(k,r,g),$$

equations (3) become

$$k_{\alpha}(r,g)=\mathbf{x}^{\mathrm{T}}_{\alpha}(g)\mathbf{A}\mathbf{p}_{\alpha}(r)$$

$$\mathbf{y}_\alpha(r,g)=\mathbf{x}^{\mathrm{T}}_\alpha(g)[\mathbf{I}-\mathbf{A}]\mathbf{p}_\alpha(r)=c_\alpha(g)+gk_\alpha(r,g)=w_\alpha(r)+rk_\alpha(r,g),$$

where $\mathbf{x}_\alpha(g)$ and $c_\alpha(g)$ are the intensity vector and the consumption per man of technique (**A**, **l**) at growth rate g. If (k^*, r^*, g^*, y^*) is a point on the family of productivity curves such that $k^* = k_\alpha(r^*, g^*)$ and $y^* = y_\alpha(r^*, g^*)$, i.e. $y_\alpha(r^*, g^*) = F(k_\alpha(r^*, g^*), r^*, g^*)$, the function

$$z(r,g) := F(k_\alpha(r,g), r, g) - y_\alpha(r,g)$$

has an internal minimum at the point (r^*, g^*). Since function $k(r, g)$ is differentiable, and if also function $F(k, r, g)$ is assumed to be so, then, at (k^*, r^*, g^*),

$$\frac{\partial F}{\partial k}\frac{\partial k_\alpha}{\partial r}+\frac{\partial F}{\partial r}-\frac{\partial y_\alpha}{\partial r}=0$$

$$\frac{\partial F}{\partial k}\frac{\partial k_\alpha}{\partial g}+\frac{\partial F}{\partial g}-\frac{\partial y_\alpha}{\partial g}=0$$

Thus

$$\frac{\partial F}{\partial r}=\left(g-\frac{\partial F}{\partial k}\right)\frac{\partial k_\alpha}{\partial r}$$

$$\frac{\partial F}{\partial g}=\left(r-\frac{\partial F}{\partial k}\right)\frac{\partial k_\alpha}{\partial g}$$

since $\partial y_\alpha/\partial r = g\,\partial k_\alpha/\partial r$ and $\partial y_\alpha/\partial g = r\,\partial k_\alpha/\partial g$. Hence, $\partial F/\partial g$ equals zero in equilibrium.

NOTES

1 This paper utilizes much of the material produced in preparing my Laurea dissertation, defended at the University of Naples in 1976. At the time I was not able to recognize that my 'family of production functions depending on the parameter r' was nothing less than the 'family of productivity curves' introduced by Joan Robinson. This was clear to me only a few years later when I read a paper by Don Harris (1973). This is perhaps the place to express my gratitude to Bruno Jossa and Augusto Graziani. The former was my supervisor in the preparation of my Laurea thesis. Suggestions and advice from both of them have been forthcoming ever since. My dissertation was also read, as far as I remember, by Pierangelo Garegnani, Giorgio Lunghini, Marco Lippi, Massimo Marrelli and Ian Steedman. I thank them all, as well as Enrico Bellino, Heinz Kurz and the editors of this book, who commented on a previous draft of this paper.

Financial support from the Italian Ministry of University and Scientific Research (MURST) and the Italian National Research Council (CNR) is also gratefully acknowledged.

2 The expressions output or capital 'per unit of labour' or 'per capita' would perhaps be more appropriate in modern literature, which prefers non-sexist expressions. Here, however, I have preferred to use expressions closer to those used by Joan Robinson in 1956 in order to avoid complications with quotations.

3 The quotation continues as follows:

> Obviously, stocks of equipment appropriate to different techniques cannot co-exist both in time and space. It should never have been drawn in a plane diagram in the first place. Different techniques are not isolated from each other on 'islands'. They succeed each other through time as new discoveries and inventions become operational. Normally, a new technique is *superior* to the one in use and does not have to wait for a change in the rate of profit to be installed.
>
> (Robinson 1980b: 138)

In the present paper the productivity curves are not utilized to study the procession of innovations. They are utilized as a description of a given set of techniques and a tool to determine the cost-minimizing technique(s) within this set. Hence this (self) criticism by Joan Robinson does not apply.

4 The figures from the 'Diagrams' appendix to *The Accumulation of Capital* by Joan Robinson are reproduced here by permission of Macmillan and Porcupine Press Inc. I should like to thank Macmillan and Porcupine Press Inc. for having granted free permission of the use of these figures; it should be noted that this permission is limited to the present edition of the paper, which is published in a book that is a tribute to Joan V. Robinson.

5 The measurement of capital in terms of the 'product' is also used by Joan Robinson herself (1956: 417 and Fig. 4 on p. 416) and by Pasinetti (1958) in an early note on Robinson's contribution.

6 The expression used by Joan Robinson is 'real-capital ratio'. The word 'real' is used because of the numéraire chosen for the capital goods, and is therefore dropped here. The word 'ratio' is connected with the fact that this variable measures the capital per unit of labour. I refrain myself from calling it 'capital–labour ratio' in the body of the paper and I use the expression 'capital ratio', which is closer to that used by Joan Robinson.

7 If $f_r(k)$ is not continuously differentiable, the property in the text can be stated as

$$[f'_r(k)]^- \leq r \leq [f'_r(k)]^+.$$

8 In Figure 21.3, to each increase in the rate of profit with no switch of technique there corresponds an increase in the capital ratio k. This is so since Fig 21.3 is nothing else than Fig 2 of the 'Diagrams' appendix, the capital ratio is measured in terms of labour and, therefore, an increase in the rate of profit determines an increase in all prices. With the measurement of the capital ratio used in this paper this fact does not need to hold. I am indebted to Enrico Bellino for this comment.

9 In 1977 Joan Robinson argued (see also Robinson 1978a: 92–3, 1978b: 103–4, 1979: 78–9, 1980c: 119–21):

> The pseudo-production function consists of the specification of a set of mutually non-inferior techniques, each requiring a particular stock of means of production per man employed. Each is eligible for at least one rate of profit, and none is superior to the rest at every rate of profit. When the techniques are listed in order of the flow per man employed of a homogeneous net output, it can be seen that a higher output is not necessarily associated with 'more capital', that a technique that is eligible

> at a higher rate of profit may require a larger value of capital at the corresponding prices, and that the same technique may be eligible at widely different rates of profit.
>
> (Robinson 1980a: 21)

This is exactly the way in which the pseudo-production function can be obtained from the Sraffa framework: just draw on the same (k, y) space all the values for k and y that (a) are relative to techniques that are cost minimizing for some rate of profit and (b) are calculated at the rate of profit at which the appropriate technique is cost minimizing.

REFERENCES

Bhaduri, A. (1966) The Concept of the Marginal Productivity of Capital and the Wicksell Effect, *Oxford Economic Papers*, 18: 284–8.

——— (1969) On the Significance of Recent Controversies on Capital Theory: A Marxian View, *Economic Journal*, 79: 532–9.

Garegnani, P. (1970) Heterogeneous Capital, the Production Function and the Theory of Distribution, *Review of Economic Studies*, 37: 407–36.

Harcourt, G. C. (1970) G. C. Harcourt's Reply to Nell, *Journal of Economic Literature*, 7: 44–5.

——— (1972) *Some Cambridge Controversies in the Theory of Capital*. Cambridge: Cambridge University Press.

——— (1986) *Controversies in Political Economy. Selected Essays of G. C. Harcourt*, edited by O. F. Hamouda. Brighton: Wheatsheaf.

——— (1992) *On Political Economists and Modern Political Economy. Selected Essays of G. C. Harcourt*, edited by C. Sardoni. London: Routledge.

Harris, D. J. (1973) Capital, Distribution, and the Aggregate Production Function, *American Economic Review*, 63: 100–13.

Koopmans, T. C. (1965) On the Concept of Optimal Economic Growth, in Pontificiae Academiae Scientiarum, *Scripta Varia*, Amsterdam: North-Holland.

Kurz, H. D. and Salvadori, N. (1995) *Theory of Production*. Cambridge: Cambridge University Press.

Nell, E. J. (1970) A Note on Cambridge Controversies in Capital Theory, *Journal of Economic Literature*, 7: 41–4.

Pasinetti, L. L. (1958) Il recente modello di sviluppo di J. Robinson e la teoria neoclassica del capitale: alcune osservazioni, *Rivista Internazionale di Scienze Sociali*, 66: 429–44.

——— (1969) Switches of Techniques and the 'Rate of Return' in Capital Theory, *Economic Journal*, 79: 508–31.

——— (1970) Again on Capital Theory and Solow's 'Rate of Return', *Economic Journal*, 80: 428–31.

Pearce, I. F. (1962) The End of the Golden Age in Solovia: A Further Fable for Growthmen Hoping to be 'One Up' on Oiko, *American Economic Review*, 52: 1088–97.

Robinson, J. V. (1956) *The Accumulation of Capital*. London: Macmillan.

——— (1962) *Essays in the Theory of Economic Growth*. London: Macmillan.

——— (1978a) [1964] Pre-Keynesian Theory after Keynes. In *Contributions to Modern Economics*. Oxford: Blackwell.

——— (1978b) [1970] Capital Theory up-to-date. In *Contributions to Modern Economics*. Oxford: Blackwell.

——— (1979) [1975] The Unimportance of Reswitching. In *Collected Economic Papers*, vol. V. Oxford: Blackwell.
——— (1980a) [1977] What are the Questions? In *Further Contributions to Modern Economics*. Oxford: Blackwell.
——— (1980b) [1979] Misunderstandings in the Theory of Production. In *Further Contributions to Modern Economics*. Oxford: Blackwell.
——— (1980c) *Further Contributions to Modern Economics*. Oxford: Blackwell.
Robinson, J. V. and Naqvi, K. A. (1967) The Badly Behaved Production Function, *Quarterly Journal of Economics*, 81: 579–91.
Samuelson, P. A. (1962) Parable and Realism in Capital Theory: The Surrogate Production Function, *Review of Economic Studies*, 29: 193–206.
Solow, R. (1963) Heterogeneous Capital and Smooth Production Functions: An Experimental Study, *Econometrica*, 31: 623–45.
——— (1967) The Interest Rate and Transition between Techniques. In C. H. Feinstein, ed., *Socialism, Capitalism and Economic Growth. Essays presented to Maurice Dobb*. Cambridge: Cambridge University Press, 30–9.
——— (1970) On the Rate of Return: Reply to Pasinetti, *Economic Journal*, 80: 423–8.
Sraffa, P. (1960) *Production of Commodities by Means of Commodities*. Cambridge: Cambridge University Press.

22

ON THE TRANSITION TO A HIGHER DEGREE OF MECHANIZATION

Ferdinando Meacci

CHOICE VS. CHANGE OF TECHNIQUE

Joan Robinson's treatment of the transition to a higher degree of mechanization deserves to be studied in the light of the distinction between *choice* and *change* of technique. This distinction was first highlighted by Pasinetti (1981: ch. IX) along with his parallel distinction between 'genuine production functions' and 'choice-of-technique functions'.

The first distinction relates to the second in the sense that the 'choice-of-technique functions' are to the problem of the choice of technique what the 'genuine production functions' are to the phenomenon of the changes of technique. Both the first and the second distinction reflect in the field of our discipline the most general distinction between *actus* and *actu*, i.e. between the *potentiality* that precedes the act of choice in the mind of the decision-making individual and the *actuality* that results from it in the economy as a *fait accompli* (i.e. as the set of irreversible outcomes of choices already made). In this sense the choice of technique is a (static) problem to be solved by forward-looking entrepreneurs (they act like a sieve through which potential techniques collapse into reality) whereas the change of technique is a (dynamic) phenomenon to be observed in the economy as moulded by the past decisions (actions) of entrepreneurs. In this very sense Pasinetti's 'genuine production functions' represent the techniques already *chosen* out of a given spectrum of potential techniques (they essentially consist of input–output relations and feature all the complementarities characteristic of actual production); while his 'choice-of-technique functions' (as well as, with regard to this specific aspect, neoclassical production functions in their micro-economic version) represent all potential techniques available to an entrepreneur *before* a choice is made.

THE BEHAVIOUR OF AN ENTREPRENEUR VS. THE ECONOMY AS A *FAIT ACCOMPLI*

The distinction between choice and change of technique is partly understood and partly misunderstood in Joan Robinson's work. This can be seen, implicitly and indirectly, in the intricate structure and arguments of Book II, 'Accumulation in the Long Run', of *The Accumulation of Capital* (henceforth TAC).[1] But it can also be seen, explicitly and more directly, in her brief introduction to the 1975 edition of Volume II of her *Collected Economic Papers* (henceforth CEP).

Let us start from this introduction. Here Joan Robinson (henceforth JR) repudiates her view of accumulation in a given state of technical knowledge (let alone with a single technique) previously expounded in Book II of TAC. This repudiation, however, is in some contrast with a distinction set out by JR herself in another article published in the same volume of CEP.[2] At the beginning of this article she notes that 'there are three quite distinct groups of questions involving capital regarded as means of production' and presents these questions as follows:

> 1. The choice which has to be made by an individual producer as to the form in which an investment should be embodied. (The *ex ante* production functions.)
> 2. The effect, in an economy considered as a whole, of having a larger or smaller quantity of capital, other things equal. (The *ex post* factor ratios.)
> 3. The reaction of an economy to a change in technical knowledge. (Accumulation and technical progress.)
>
> (Robinson 1975b: 159)

Now it should be noted that questions 1 and 2 can be viewed as an attempt to express with different words the very distinction between choice and change of technique highlighted above. For, irrespective of whether it occurs in logical or historical time, every decision is taken on the basis of what the decision-maker knows and expects up to the moment of the decision. However much his knowledge may have changed before and will change after it, the decision as such is a static problem that is studied by the tools of static analysis. The opposite, of course, holds *after* decisions have been made and, particularly, after techniques have been chosen. In this context a change of technique presents itself as a dynamic affair. Time is its central ingredient, for no change can occur without time. A change occurring in this context is a change in the outcome of choices or, to put it differently, is nothing but a *change in bygones*. The entrepreneur is not interested in this change (what he is interested in is only the choice of the techniques that will promote, if ever, the changes to come). This role is, accordingly, different from the role of an outside observer whose task is to study (nothing more is possible with bygones) the effects of decision-making in the economy as a *fait accompli*.

This should help us realize that question 3 is, on the one hand, in contrast with questions 1 and 2, and that the part of it which is put in brackets by JR is, on the other, badly worded. For, given the distinction between choice and change of technique highlighted in questions 1 and 2, it follows that question 3 should be reworded, to be consistent with questions 1 and 2, as follows:

> 3a: The reaction of entrepreneurs to a change in technical knowledge.
> 3b: The adjustment of the economy to the reaction (choices) of entrepreneurs.

Since, however, a change in technical knowledge has nothing to do with the accumulation of capital (if only because the former may occur without the latter, and vice versa), it follows that the problem of choice is faced by entrepreneurs irrespective of whether their choice will entail a change of technique (which is the case when accumulation occurs with technical progress or technical progress without accumulation) or will not (which is the case when accumulation occurs without technical progress). In this broader context JR's question 3 should be further reworded as follows:

> 3a: The reaction of entrepreneurs to a change in technical knowledge (without changes in the accumulation of capital).
> 3b: The reaction of entrepreneurs to a change in the accumulation of capital (without changes in technical knowledge).
> 3c: The adjustment of the economy to the reaction (choices) of entrepreneurs in cases 3a and 3b.

TECHNICAL PROGRESS: TWO CLASSIFICATIONS

The previous arguments may serve to introduce the difference, which is somewhat blurred in TAC, between changes in technical knowledge, on the one hand, and technical progress, on the other. Whereas a change in technical knowledge resolves itself in a change in the spectrum of *potential* techniques faced by entrepreneurs, the phenomenon of technical progress rather consists of changes in *actual* techniques (i.e. in the techniques already chosen by entrepreneurs). Technical progress, however, should be distinguished from technical change: the former consists of a reduction in technical coefficients, whereas the latter consists either of increases in these coefficients or of an increase in some and of a reduction in others. Now the sentence by which JR sums up her repudiation of her TAC view of accumulation, i.e. that 'there is no such thing as accumulation without technical change' (1975a: x), not only obscures the difference between technical change (or progress) and changes in technical knowledge (let alone the difference, to be discussed below, between the widening and the deepening of capital); it also runs against the idea of the rationality (however bounded) of the decision-making entrepreneur. For, again, one thing is the change of techniques, another their choice (which may or may not result in such a change). Furthermore, the idea that the accumulation of capital is one thing and technical change (let alone changes in technical knowledge) another is essential to go deeper into JR's well-known classification of technical progress in a two-sector and full-employment economy.[3] It should indeed be noted that this classification actually conceals *two* different classifications depending on whether technical progress is studied either (first classification) in the absence of, or (second classification) in conjunction with the accumulation of capital.

According to the first classification, technical progress may be said to be neutral or (if biased) capital using or capital saving depending on whether the productivity of labour *increases* in the capital goods sector in the same proportion, more slowly or more rapidly than in the consumption goods sector; or, which is the same, depending on whether the quantity of labour per unit of output (of productive capacity or of final output) falls in the same proportion, more slowly or more rapidly in the capital goods sector than it does in the consumption goods sector; or, which is the consequence of – rather than the same as – the above, depending on whether the division of a given labour force between the two sectors remains unchanged or is altered in favour of the capital goods sector or of the consumption goods sector, respectively. According to this classification, therefore, technical progress consists, whatever its form and whatever the sector, in a *reduction* of labour coefficients; it is not the result of – and does not require – an act of ad hoc accumulation. It can be viewed, in other terms, as the result of what the Austrians would call 'shortening' inventions. In this context *all* new techniques may be said to be (a) 'superior' to the techniques previously in use, and (b) 'eligible' with any configuration of prices and costs. The resulting improvements may consequently be called 'pure improvements'.[4]

According to the second classification, technical progress may be said to be neutral or (if biased) capital using or capital saving depending on whether the productivity of labour in the consumption goods sector increases *without* an increase, *with* an increase or *in spite of* a decrease of the labour employed (amount of investment) in the capital goods sector. The capital-using form of technical progress according to this classification is the result, to put it in Austrian terms, of 'lengthening' inventions: new techniques may accordingly be said to be (a) 'superior' to old ones (Böhm-Bawerk's 'wisely chosen' techniques) *only if* the extra labour they require in the capital goods sector is less than the labour they save in the consumption goods sector for a given level of output; and (b) 'eligible' *only with* a certain configuration of prices and costs (particularly, with a certain rate of interest). The resulting improvements may consequently be called 'partial improvements'.[5]

THE DEGREE OF MECHANIZATION AND THE DEEPENING OF CAPITAL

The gap between these two classifications of technical progress is essential to understanding (a) the notion of the degree of mechanization, and (b) the difference between the phenomenon of capital widening (which is compatible with the neutral form of technical progress of the first classification) and the phenomenon of capital deepening (which requires the capital-using form of technical progress contemplated by the second classification). Although the terms 'widening' and 'deepening' are not used in TAC,[6] these forms of accumulation are actually dealt with in this work in a way that helps us understand the similarities between the deepening of capital and the transition to a higher degree of mechanization.

For instance, although the titles of the two chapters of Section I of TAC ('Accumulation with constant technique' and 'Technical progress') reveal that it is a process of capital widening that this section deals with (although it is either its breakdown or the forms of technical progress of the first classification that here draw most of the attention), the very title 'Accumulation with one technique' of Section I (which implies that at any moment only one technique is known so that this is constant if technical progress is assumed away) indicates that this section is unconcerned with the particular changes of technique called for by a process of capital deepening, although it is still concerned with changes in the economy as a *fait accompli*. It is in perfect consistency with this approach, therefore, that JR here deals with (a) the relationship between capital accumulation and population growth *without* technical progress; and (b) the relationship between capital accumulation and technical progress *with* population constant.[7] On the other hand, it is the context of capital deepening that is brought to the fore when JR moves to her treatment of the degree of mechanization in Section II, Book II, of TAC. Indeed, it is in connection with the idea of a spectrum of techniques resulting from past changes in technical knowledge and ordered according to their different coefficients of investment per head and output per head that this treatment is carried out; while it is in connection with the form of technical progress relating to the second of the two forms of capital accumulation mentioned above (capital deepening) that the actual transition to a higher degree of mechanization takes place.

COST VS. AMOUNT OF INVESTMENT: THEIR DIFFERENT IMPLICATIONS

A relevant aspect of JR's analysis of capital deepening is that the notion of the degree of mechanization she puts forward at the centre of this analysis is constructed with regard to the point of view of an entrepreneur 'contemplating investment' (as she says). Now it should be noted that this has nothing to do with the point of view of an observer who contemplates from the outside the outcome of the choices of this entrepreneur. This is made unclear, however, in JR's definitions of the new notion and of the related concepts of 'hierarchy of techniques' and 'mechanization frontier'. These concepts are worded in such a way as to obscure the problem they are intended to solve:

> With given prices and wages, quasi-rent per man is greater the greater is the rate of output per man. A greater rate of output per man is offered by a greater investment in capital goods, that is to say, the higher is the *degree of mechanisation* of the technique the greater is the quasi-rent per man employed, and the greater also is the cost of the required investment per man.
>
> (Robinson 1965: 102)

> When the available techniques, Alpha, Beta, Gamma, etc. are arranged in a hierarchy, according to the rate of output per man, the technique with a higher rate of output requires a larger investment per man and the frontier lies at the technique which offers the highest rate of profit on investment at the ruling wage rate, or between the two techniques which are equally profitable at that wage rate.
>
> (ibid.: 106)

To be consistent with the point of view of an entrepreneur 'contemplating investment', the expression 'a larger investment' in the second passage above should be taken to stand for the 'greater cost of investment' of the first – an expression that must be understood, as JR herself admits and the very term 'cost' implies, as the *cost of investment to a particular entrepreneur*. Thus the problem of the choice of technique is solved in the sense that this choice is governed by the simple rule of the wage rate: the higher the wage (and therefore the lower quasi-rent per man) the higher the degree of mechanization (and therefore the greater investment and output per man) of the technique chosen by a forward-looking entrepreneur.

It should be noted, however, that if the notion of 'cost of investment' is quite appropriate to the point of view of an entrepreneur, speaking of this cost, as JR does, in terms of the wages of the labour embodied in the investment goods plus the interest charged during their gestation period is misleading in two different senses.

First, the *cost* of a piece of equipment however capitalized at a notional interest during the gestation period – not to speak of the *amount* of labour embodied in the equipment – is irrelevant to a forward-looking entrepreneur. It is true that in a golden age the capitalization of past costs of production of a particular stock of capital goods is equal to their future quasi-rents discounted back to the present at the notional interest rate. But the fact that, under these special conditions, one of these two magnitudes is equal to the other cannot signify in any circumstances that they represent the same *concept*. Indeed, the concepts that they represent are so different that when the economy is out of the golden age a particular change in the rate of interest will result in a change in the *same* direction in the first of those two magnitudes (capitalization) and in a change in the *opposite* direction in the other (discounting).

Secondly, the relationship between investment per head and output per head is, properly speaking, a 'technical' rather than a 'social' relation (a relation, that is, between man and nature rather than between man and man):[8] the productivity of direct labour (output per head) may rise only as a consequence of a greater amount (not of a greater cost) of indirect labour embodied in the equipment. Given the equipment, and therefore the labour embodied in it, there is no way for output per head to change if the interest rate at which the cost of this labour is capitalized, or the wage rate at which this cost is reckoned, changes in the first place. To put it differently: the amount of labour embodied in a particular piece of equipment is one thing, the cost of this labour reckoned at a particular wage and interest rate is another. Whereas the former corresponds to the 'amount' of investment, the latter adds up to its 'cost'; what makes output per man to increase is an increase in the *former*, not in the *latter* variable.

To highlight the difference between 'amount' and 'cost' of investment in the expression 'investment per head' and, therefore, the existence of two distinct concepts for JR's degree of mechanization, we shall call *pure degree of mechanization* the relation between 'amount of investment per head' and output per head, and we shall continue to use JR's 'degree of mechanization' for the relation between 'cost of investment per head' and output per head.

In the light of this distinction, the relationship between investment per head and output per head (which is the only way by which output per head can increase when the technical progress of the first classification is ruled out) should be looked at in two different ways depending on whether this relationship is considered from the point of view of an individual entrepreneur or from the point of view of the economy as a *fait accompli*. These different ways may be rendered, respectively, as follows:

(a) if an entrepreneur aims to increase output per head he must incur a higher 'cost' of investment per head;
(b) output per head increases if the 'amount' of investment per head rises.

While the second statement implies the Austrian principle of roundaboutness and shows the mechanism by which the productivity of labour, a technical phenomenon, can increase in a particular sector or economy (when technical progress assumes the capital-using form contemplated by the second classification), the first statement points to the mechanism by which the entrepreneur, a decision-making individual, is induced to choose a technique with a higher degree of mechanization. In this connection the relationship between investment per head and output per head presents itself

(a) as a 'technical' relation instrumental to the study of a 'change' of technique, if looked at in the spirit of the second statement; and
(b) as a 'social' relation instrumental to the solution of the problem of 'choice' of technique, if looked at in the spirit of the first.

The point of view of the individual entrepreneur is dropped, however, when JR moves to comparing different economies at different positions of the mechanization frontier. The new approach is developed, first, with regard to the determination of the mechanization frontier in a series of economies with different wage rates and with or without the same spectrum of techniques; and, secondly, with regard to shifts, in each economy, of the mechanization frontier itself under the assumption that capital is increasing either with a constant or with a changing population. In consistency with the new approach JR's arguments are therefore focused on the *effects*, rather than on the causes, of the behaviour of entrepreneurs 'contemplating investment' (i.e. facing the choice of the degree of mechanization). They are focused, accordingly, on *sectors* rather than on entrepreneurs.[9] Also in consistency with the new approach is JR's important conclusion that 'a low degree of mechanisation is a symptom of the underlying cause of low real wages, not a cause of low wages in itself'. This conclusion descends from the argument that one thing is (via the behaviour of entrepreneurs) the cause–effect relationship between the (increasing) wage rate and the (increasing) degree of mechanization, and that another is the determination of the wage rate itself. This determination belongs to the second part of the new approach in the sense that the pace of capital accumulation above or below the pace of population growth is shown to be the cause of, respectively, a scarcity or surplus of labour, and therefore (via the labour market) of increases or decreases in the wage rate, and therefore again (via the behaviour of entrepreneurs) of the corresponding changes in the degree of mechanization.

THE REAL-CAPITAL RATIO: A CRITIQUE

We have seen above that the degree of mechanization is related by JR sometimes to the *cost* of investment per head and sometimes to the *amount* of investment per head, and that the first meaning is as suitable for the analysis of the *choice* of technique as it is unsuitable for the analysis of its *changes*. It is in the context of the transition from the former to the latter type of analysis that JR correctly suggests replacing the notion of 'value of capital in terms of commodities' by the notion of 'capital in terms of labour time':

> This is in some ways the most significant way of measuring capital, for the essence of the productive process is the expenditure of labour time, and labour time expended at one date can be carried forward to a later

> date by using it to produce physical objects (or to store up knowledge) which will make future labour more productive, so that capital goods in existence today can be regarded as an embodiment of past labour time to be used up in the future.
>
> (Robinson 1965: 121)

This sentence is worth noticing because it is nothing but, incidentally, a rewording of the principle of roundaboutness, and, fundamentally, a statement on a technical relationship. There is no doubt, therefore, that the notion of 'capital in terms of labour time' is more appropriate than the notion of 'value of capital in terms of commodities' when it comes to this particular point of view. But the reason why this is more appropriate does not coincide with the reason provided by JR. For not only the element of wages (which is consistently included in the latter and excluded from the former notion) but also – it should be pointed out – the element of interest (which, on the contrary, is included in the latter as well as in the former notion) should be equally excluded from the concept of 'capital in terms of labour time' when the purpose is either to make comparisons between different economies or to deal with the productivity of productive capacity (pure degree of mechanization). The embodiment of a price (the rate of interest) in the magnitude (the labour accumulated up to the present) corresponding to this concept makes it impossible to regard it as JR (1965: 123) does, i.e. as implying the conception of capital as a *technical* factor of production and, therefore, as the core of a 'technical' relation.

This is not without consequences when JR comes to the construction of her new notion of the 'real-capital ratio'. On the one hand, this is defined as the ratio of capital reckoned in terms of labour time to the amount of labour currently employed, while, on the other, the two terms of the ratio are said not to be *in pari materia* for 'one consists of past labour time, compounded at interest, embodied in a stock of capital goods, the other is a flow per unit of time of current labour'. Since, however, the real-capital ratio is designed to deal with the stock of capital goods existing in an economy *after* the techniques in use have already been chosen (and, indeed, chosen in different moments of the past so that different techniques may be in use at the same moment), this ratio eventually incorporates the same ambiguities as the notion of 'capital in terms of labour time' and is equally unsuitable for dealing with the changes in technical relations that lie behind changes in, or differences between, different economies.

It should be admitted, however, that if only the rate of interest is squeezed out of the nominator the resulting ratio becomes most suitable for dealing with economies as a *fait accompli*. In this different version this ratio might be called, to stress the elimination of the distributive variable, *real-real-capital ratio* or, more briefly, *indirect labour per man*, depending on whether JR's or Böhm-Bawerk's early terminology is preferred. The similarity between the 'real-real-capital ratio' and the 'pure degree of mechanization' as defined above can be easily seen at this point. Although the pure degree of mechanization relates to a particular technique (or to a technique in relation to another, though not from the point of view of an entrepreneur) and the real-real-capital ratio to the whole of a particular sector or economy, the two notions may be used for the same purpose: this consists in providing an *index of capital deepening* in the context of the economy as a *fait accompli*. This is, after all, the very role assigned by JR herself to her real-capital ratio, except that the intrusion of the rate of interest makes this notion unsuitable for use in the context of the theory of reproduction (as distinct from distribution) of national wealth.

THE TWO POINTS OF VIEW: A SUMMING UP

The different implications of a transition to a higher degree of mechanization from the point of view of a decision-making entrepreneur (as highlighted by JR herself) and in the economy as a *fait accompli* (as highlighted above) can be collapsed at this point in the following statements (the colloquial form and the Marshallian terms have been used in order to highlight the first point of view and to reveal Marshall's shadow behind JR's construction):

The transition to a higher degree of mechanization from the point of view of an individual entrepreneur

If, as an entrepreneur, you want to cut the labour cost per unit of output when the spectrum of techniques, the wage rate and the rate of interest are given you will have to face an increase in the cost of capital per unit of output.

You will actually want to change your cost structure if the cut in the labour cost per unit of output exceeds the increase in the capital cost per unit of output.

You will definitely want to change your cost structure when the wage rate rises beyond a certain point.

Leaving aside the difference between changes in the total fixed cost of a firm and in the cost of total fixed capital but including the similarity between the investment required to save labour and the investment required to save any current input, you will have to face an increase in the supplementary costs of a given level of output if you want to cut its prime costs.

You will actually want to change your cost structure if the reduction in prime costs exceeds the increase in supplementary costs, or, to put it differently, if the quasi-rent relating to a given level of output rises, or at least does not fall, after the change.

You will definitely want to change your cost structure when the price for any current input rises beyond a certain point.

The transition to a higher degree of mechanization from the point of view of the economy as a *fait accompli*

In the absence of the forms of technical progress that do not require an act of ad hoc accumulation, output per head can increase only if the amount of investment per head rises.

The cause–effect relationship between the amount of investment per head and output per head is a technical relationship independent of the levels of – and changes in – the wage rate and the interest rate.

The relationship between the amount of investment per head and output per head is nothing but the relationship between indirect labour per unit of direct labour, on the one hand, and output per unit of direct labour, on the other. This relationship may be called the pure degree of mechanization.

The indirect labour per unit of direct labour may in turn be called indirect labour per man or, squeezing interest out of the nominator of JR's real-capital ratio, real-real-capital ratio. It would be better, however, to call it with its traditional name of capital–labour ratio once it is clear that this ratio underlines a technical relation and that the capital of the nominator stands for a given amount of indirect labour – and for nothing else.

When the capital–labour ratio in this sense rises, the economy is experiencing a process of capital deepening.

CONCLUDING REMARKS

Starting from the distinction between choice and change of technique, and from the broader (and older) distinction between the point of view of an individual entrepreneur and the point of view of the economy as a *fait accompli*, we have shown above that JR's treatment of the transition to a higher degree of mechanization is affected by a number of ambiguities. Some of these concern her inability to distinguish between changes in technical knowledge, on the one hand, and technical progress and technical change, on the other. The difference, in particular, between technical progress (as a reduction in coefficients) and technical change (as a change in coefficients) was argued to be at the root of the need to split JR's classification of technical progress into two different classifications depending on whether technical progress is or is not considered in conjunction with the accumulation of capital (or, to put it in a different perspective, depending on whether the accumulation of capital is considered in its deepening or widening form). In addition, it was argued that the neglect of the distinction between choice and change of technique is also at the root of the question as to whether the transition to a higher degree of mechanization should be considered as an increase in the cost (and therefore as a 'social' relation) or as an increase in the volume (and therefore as a 'technical' relation) of investment per head in relation to output per head. This ambiguity was in turn shown to be at the root of the further question as to whether JR's notion of the real-capital ratio is really able to reflect the older notion of capital per head in the sense of the volume, rather than of the cost, of past investment (in the sense, that is, of the amount of indirect labour embodied in the existing capital goods). The terms 'pure degree of mechanization' and 'real-real-capital ratio' were eventually suggested *in lieu* of JR's corresponding expressions in order (a) to stress the elimination of the distributive variable (the rate of interest or the rate of interest plus the rate of wages) from JR's corresponding concepts; and (b) to provide, through the simple notion of indirect labour per head, an index of capital deepening from the point of view of the economy as a *fait accompli*.

NOTES

1 The very structure of, and relations between, the three sections of Book II of TAC may be regarded as a signal of the ambiguities embodied in some of their arguments. The contents of these sections may be distinguished and summarized as follows.

Section I: Change-of-technique outlook (without choice of technique). It is here assumed that at any moment the only technique known is also the technique in use (the accumulation of capital is accordingly studied either in connection with a constant technique and the resulting stationary state, or in connection with changing techniques, with new techniques being superior to older techniques at every level of wages).

Section II: Choice-of-technique outlook (with and without change of technique). This section can be divided into two ideal parts. The first part is focused on the choice of technique (at any moment entrepreneurs face a 'spectrum' of techniques arranged according to a 'hierarchy' of output/labour ratios in which a 'technical frontier' between the most profitable technique and the others is determined by the level of the wage rate), while the second part is mostly focused on changes of technique (throughout this part comparisons are made not between alternative techniques from the standpoint of decision-making entrepreneurs but between different economies or different states of the same economy). Here the analysis is focused (a) on different economies with different technical frontiers and either different wage rates or different spectra of techniques; and (b) on the transition from one frontier to another, either with capital accumulation and population constant (scarcity of labour and rising wage rate), or with increasing population and constant capital (surplus of labour and falling wage rate). The aim of this part is to show that the wage rate, which plays a crucial role in the solution of the problem tackled in the first part, is determined by the interaction between the accumulation of capital and the growth of population.

Section III: Change-of-knowledge outlook (with changes of technique). Here the process of accumulation is studied in the context of a two-sector economy in which changes in technical knowledge continuously alter the spectrum of techniques while technical progress (neutral, capital using and capital saving) modifies the techniques in use.

2 See JR (1975b: 159n): 'This paper has not previously been published. I wrote it to clear my own mind on some fundamental points of theory. I hope it will not have the opposite effect on others.'

3 See JR (1965: ch. 9, 132–3; ch. 17, 418–20). See also JR (1962a).

4 It is this type of progress that is dealt with (along with an independent, albeit stronger or weaker, process of accumulation) in the part of chapter 9 ambiguously titled 'Accumulation and technical progress' and in the similarly titled Section III, Book II, of TAC.

5 The two classifications above are derived from JR's own classification as put forward in (1962a). The difference between the two classifications is implied, however, by JR herself when she comes to the discussion of the 'superiority of one spectrum of techniques over another' (1965: ch. 13). After distinguishing between a movement along a given spectrum (rising degree of mechanization) and a shift of this spectrum, JR defines the (neutral or biased) superiority of one spectrum over another in terms of the (equiproportional or non-equiproportional) reduction from spectrum to spectrum of coefficients in the two sectors (i.e. in terms of technical progress without accumulation). The difference between two economies is then said to be due either to a 'higher degree of mechanisation' or to 'technical superiority' (1965: 135).

6 But they are used elsewhere; see, for instance, JR (1960) and (1962b).

7 Whereas in case (a) the end of the process of widening – and of the accumulation of capital itself – is brought about by capital growing faster than population (labour force) until wages absorb the whole product and the rate of profit falls to zero, in case (b) technical coefficients are brought down in both sectors (with different intensity) by technical progress as an independent force. When technical progress is neutral, and the balance between capital and population is unaltered (which entails the case of widening if these two forces grow at the same pace, and of the stationary state if they do not grow at all), productivity increases at the same rate as productive capacity, the division of the labour force between the two sectors remains unchanged, and real wages rise while the rate of profit is constant. Of the forces that bring about the collapse of this situation (with or without accumulation in its widening form and, respectively, without or with neutral technical progress) one is that neutral technical progress sooner or later becomes biased, and another is that capital accumulation sooner or later fails to keep pace with technical progress. In the latter case JR argues that, with accumulation 'strong' (i.e. faster than technical progress), productive capacity increases faster than productivity, and that, with accumulation 'weak' (i.e. slower than technical progress), productivity increases faster than productive capacity.

8 See JR herself (1960: v) and the third of her 'methodological rules'.

9 Hence JR's statement that, with a higher degree of mechanization, 'a smaller number of workers are required to produce the given output of commodities' while 'a unit of productive capacity requires a larger investment of labour time' (investment, that is, in a quantitative sense) (1965: 125). Hence her new view of an increase in the degree of mechanization as a transition taking place in time (an anticipation of Hicks' 'traverse'; see Hicks 1973) rather than as a switch occurring in the mind of the forward-looking entrepreneur.

REFERENCES

Hicks, J. R. (1973) *Capital and Time*. Oxford: Clarendon Press.

Pasinetti, L. (1981) *Structural Change and Economic Growth*. Cambridge: Cambridge University Press.

Robinson, J. (1965) *The Accumulation of Capital*, 2nd edn. London: Macmillan.

——— (1960) *Exercises in Economic Analysis*. London: Macmillan.

——— (1962a) A Model of Technical Progress. In *Essays in the Theory of Economic Growth*. London: Macmillan, 88–136.

——— (1962b) A Neoclassical Theorem. In *Essays in the Theory of Economic Growth*. London: Macmillan, 120–36.

——— (1975a) Introduction. *Collected Economic Papers*, vol. II, 2nd edn. Oxford: Blackwell.

——— (1975b) Capital, Technique and Relative Shares. In *Collected Economic Papers*, vol. II, 2nd edn. Oxford: Blackwell.

23

TECHNICAL PROGRESS IN JOAN ROBINSON'S ANALYSIS[1]

Bruno Jossa

Joan Robinson was one of the very first economists to concern herself thoroughly and keenly with the economic theory of technical progress. As she addressed this topic time and again and her contributions in this field are found in a great many writings, a thorough analysis of all the conclusions she arrived at would obviously run to an exceeding length and consequently lies outside the scope of this study. What I am setting out to do here is to draw attention merely to a few basic propositions contained in Robinson's analyses. In particular, I intend to address only the case of fixed coefficients, with which Joan Robinson concerned herself most often, and not the case of variable coefficients, which she likewise analysed in a number of celebrated studies.[2] Accordingly I am going to refer to the model Robinson used in what is perhaps her major work, *The Accumulation of Capital* (1956).

JOAN ROBINSON'S GROWTH MODEL

In the first part of *The Accumulation of Capital*, Joan Robinson uses at first a simplified model based on the following assumptions:[3] (a) the system produces only two commodities, a consumer good X and a capital good Y (a 'machine'); (b) the manufacturing processes of both these commodities have fixed production coefficients; (c) there is a 'reserve' of unemployed workers; (d) there are only two 'factors' of production and, therefore, two classes of income-earners, workers and capitalists; (e) workers do not save and capitalists do not consume; (f) the quality of the consumer good is not affected by technical progress.

On the basis of these assumptions, it is possible to write the following equations:

$$a_{ky}Y + a_{kx}X = K \qquad (1)$$

$$a_{ly}Y + a_{lx}X = L \qquad (2)$$

where L is employment, K the capital available, and each a stands for the number of factor units required to manufacture one unit of the relevant commodity. It is likewise assumed that all the capital available is employed and equation (1) reflects the way it is distributed in the two sectors; equation (2) consequently indicates the employment made possible by the existing quantity of capital and the state of the art then available.

$$R = VPK + WL \tag{3}$$

$$R = PY + X \tag{4}$$

where V is profit per single machine, P is the price of one machine in terms of consumer goods, and W is the wage earned by one worker. Equations (3) and (4) are two definitions of income, R.

$$Wa_{\mathrm{ly}}Y = (1 - Wa_{\mathrm{lx}})X \tag{5}$$

$$\frac{(1 - Wa_{\mathrm{lx}})}{a_{\mathrm{kx}}XP} = \frac{X(P - Wa_{\mathrm{ly}})Y}{a_{\mathrm{ky}}YP} \tag{6}$$

$$V = \frac{Y}{K} = k \tag{7}$$

Equation (5) reflects the well-known condition at which, given the above assumptions, the wages earned in the sector that produces the machinery must equal the profits earned in the sector producing the relevant consumer goods. Equation (6) requires that the rate of profit earned in the consumer goods sector is equal to the rate of profit earned in the investment goods sector. On the basis of equation (7) the rate of profit must be equal to the rate of accumulation; as is well known, this is explained by observing that, if only capitalists save and provided they put aside all their income, the value of their profits will equal the value of their investments.

The system is described by seven equations with seven unknowns: X, Y, L, P, R, V and W.[4]

In the model, the rate of accumulation, k, is given; this is a key assumption, and it is also the distinctly Keynesian aspect of the model.[5] Consequently, if the system is solved for X, the result is:

$$X = \frac{(1 - a_{\mathrm{ky}}k)K}{a_{\mathrm{kx}}}. \tag{8}$$

This equation shows that, with a given quantity of capital available, the resources used to manufacture consumer goods increase according as the value of k decreases and the productivity of the capital used in the two sectors increases. It is worth mentioning that the value of X is in no way influenced by labour productivity. If, consequently, the technique is given, the distribution of capital in the two sectors is affected merely by the rate of accumulation.

Solving equation (2) for L/K and substituting from equation (8), the result is:

$$\frac{L}{K} = a_{ly}k + \frac{a_{lx}}{a_{kx}}(1 - a_{ky}k). \tag{9}$$

This equation calculates the equilibrium combination of labour and capital as a function of k and of the productivity of the two factors. It shows that, when k increases, the labour–capital ratio increases or decreases according as:

$$\frac{a_{ly}}{a_{ky}} \gtrless \frac{a_{lx}}{a_{kx}},$$

namely, according as the manufacturing process of the capital goods is more or less capital intensive than that of the consumer goods.

If equation (5) is solved for W, substituting from equation (8) the result is:

$$W = \frac{1 - a_{ky}k}{(a_{kx}a_{ly} - a_{ky}a_{lx})k + a_{lx}}. \tag{10}$$

Equation (10) yields wages as a function of the capital accumulation rate and of labour and capital productivity in the two sectors. From equation (7) we infer that the wage rate must decrease according as k increases because, with the income produced remaining unvaried, a rise in the rate of accumulation must result in boosting the rate of profit. The derivative of equation (10) for k is, in fact:

$$\frac{dW}{dk} = \frac{-a_{ky}a_{lx}}{[(a_{kx}a_{ly} - a_{ky}a_{lx})k + a_{lx}]^2},$$

an expression with a negative value.

Lastly, the value of P is calculated from equation (6) as follows:

$$P = \frac{a_{ky}}{a_{kx}} - \left(\frac{a_{ky}a_{lx}}{a_{kx}} - a_{ly}\right)\left(\frac{1 - a_{ky}k}{a_{kx}a_{ly} - a_{ky}a_{lx})k + a_{lx}}\right). \tag{11}$$

This equation shows that, as k increases, the price of the machines will tend to increase or decrease according as the capital goods are more or less capital intensive than the consumer goods.

Equations (7), (8), (9), (10) and (11) yield the values of V, X, L/K, W and

P as functions of k. The values of the other two unknowns, R and Y, can easily be calculated from (3) and (4).

The autonomous variable, let us repeat, is investment, and, provided the production coefficients are given, it determines all the remaining variables.

Employment – Robinson contends – is strictly determined by the existing capital stock.[6] As we can see, however, employment too, notwithstanding the absolute rigidity of production coefficients, is determined by investment. In fact it is the rate of accumulation that determines how the existing capital will be distributed in the two sectors: if the rate of accumulation is high, a substantial proportion of the capital available is employed in the sector of capital goods, and vice versa; as shown by equation (9), when the existing capital stock is given, employment will be higher or lower according as the capital is employed in the sector where the labour coefficient (a_1) is higher or lower.

The relationship between profit and accumulation, Robinson argues, is twofold. If any profit is to be generated, the labour productivity of the consumer goods sector must exceed the subsistence wage. But even if conditions are such as to make profit possible, this does not mean that it will come about in actual fact. Profit can be generated only if entrepreneurs make investments: if the total wages paid equal the consumer goods produced, it is only by allocating more resources to produce investment goods that wages can be compressed. Because equation (7) demonstrates that the rate of profit equals the rate of accumulation, it throws light on this twofold relation.[7]

A system with unemployment can experience growth at any rate. However, if labour supply is steady or increases at a slow pace, sooner or later full employment is achieved. When full employment is achieved, the wage rate will tend to rise and this will in turn result in raising the price level. Two results are possible in such a case. If capitalists keep viewing investment in real terms and abstain from reducing investment as prices rise, the system will experience a steady inflationary trend: if k is constant and greater than the growth rate of the working population (in the absence of technical progress), wages will tend to grow throughout, and so will prices, but monetary demand for goods will rise in the same proportion and will constantly exceed the level of supply. If, on the contrary, capitalists view investment in monetary terms and do not change their investment spending as prices rise, sooner or later the system will achieve the equilibrium state: as prices rise, k diminishes, tending to equal the working population growth rate. The question as to which of these two borderline cases is more likely to be attained in actual fact, only experience can tell.[8]

TECHNICAL PROGRESS IN JOAN ROBINSON'S ANALYSIS: INTRODUCTORY REFLECTIONS

Let us consider three kinds of technical progress, respectively termed type A, B and C. In the model here under review, type A progress results in reducing a_{ly} or a_{lx} (or both), depending on the sector in which it is adopted, and type B progress reduces a_{ky} or a_{kx} (or both), depending on the sector in which it is adopted. π_{lx}, for instance, is the rate to which a_{lx} declines with the passing of time. Type C, instead, is the kind of technical progress that reduces a_l and a_k at the same rate, so that $\pi_{ly} = \pi_{ky}$ and/or $\pi_{lx} = \pi_{kx}$.[9]

Let us mention that Robinson mainly analysed technical progress of type A: indeed, in her earliest fundamental analyses of the economics of technical progress she strictly confined herself to type A progress only. It may even be said that for years her neglect of technical progress of types B and C was a peculiar aspect and a shortcoming of her models (the misjudgements to which this gave rise will be addressed later on).[10] This circumstance is worth emphasizing because neither Joan Robinson nor any others have ever thrown light on the fact that in *The Accumulation of Capital* technical progress is constantly type A.[11]

At this point, as we turn to the effects of three different kinds of technical progress, a first observation to be made is that the primary effect of innovations, whatever their type, is to raise the capital accumulation rate. In this regard, however, it is all but easy to add anything else, because the model illustrated above is unsuited to bear out the extent to which technical progress raises the rate of accumulation.[12] This is why, having specified this, I am going to assume *k* as constant throughout the rest of this study.[13]

On the basis of the assumptions made above, however, the cost of the two commodities considered, the machine and the consumer good, results merely from two very simple elements: a 'labour cost', which is equal to the number of working hours required to produce one unit of the commodity using the capital available, and a 'capital cost' equal to the interest (or return) on the value of the machinery that is used to produce a single product unit. Following Robinson's suggestion, we can measure capital in terms of working hours; namely, we may think of the value or cost of a machine as being equal to the ratio of the value or cost of the machine in terms of consumer goods to the wage per man hour (in terms of consumer goods). In so doing, the value of one machine is equal to the number of working hours whose cost equals the cost of one machine to the manufacturer. If capital is measured in terms of working hours (in units of real wages), an innovation that, the rate of profit remaining unchanged, does not affect the capital per man hour (or capital per head, since working hours are assumed to be constant) employed in the relevant production process, this is a neutral invention in line with Harrod's definition. Indeed, an innovation that does not affect the capital per man hour employed to produce a given commodity is an innovation that reduces the capital cost of the relevant commodity in the same proportion as the labour cost and that consequently reduces the cost of the commodity in proportion to the capital cost. Hence an innovation that, the rate of profit remaining unchanged, increases (reduces) the capital per man hour employed in production is an innovation that increases (reduces) the capital cost of the production process as compared with the cost of labour and, at the same time, also the capital–output ratio in terms of value. This is why it is a capital-using (or capital-saving) innovation according to Harrod's definition.[14] If this holds true, the problem we are setting out to examine can also be posed in the following terms: with the rate of profit unchanged, which innovations leave capital per man hour unaltered and which increase or reduce capital per man hour in the model here under review?[15]

THE EFFECTS OF TYPE A INNOVATIONS

First of all let us consider type A technical progress arising in the consumer goods sector: as k is constant by hypothesis, this type of technical progress leaves the distribution of capital between the two sectors unchanged; and as capital productivity in the two sectors is constant, its only effect is to lessen employment and increase wages in the sector, without affecting the quantity of consumer goods produced.

However, with the rate of profit, the capital available and the outputs of the two commodities remaining unchanged, the distribution of income will change as a result of the change in the price of capital goods.

Let us add that, if type A innovations are introduced only in the consumer goods sector, the 'capital cost' remains constant in both sectors, while the 'labour cost' diminishes in the consumer goods sector. Consequently, with the rate of profit unchanged, the cost of machinery will also remain constant, while the cost of consumer goods will diminish. The capital–output ratio (in terms of value) will accordingly be constant in the capital goods sector, whereas in the consumer goods sector it will rise at a rate lower than the increase in labour productivity. With the rate of profit unchanged, therefore, the introduction of type A technical progress only in the sector of consumer goods shifts distribution to the benefit of the class of capitalists.[16]

Let us now consider the case in which type A innovations are introduced merely in the capital goods sector, namely the case in which only the machinery used to manufacture other machinery is perfected in such a way as to result in saving resources. If this type of innovation proceeds at a rate equal to π_{ly}, it reduces employment in the capital goods sector at the rate π_{ly}. Hence, the output of consumer goods remaining unaltered, the wage rate will increase. But what will be the relevant impact on distribution?

If type A innovations are adopted only in the capital goods sector, capital costs decrease in both sectors because machinery is manufactured with less labour, while the labour cost diminishes in the capital goods sector and remains unaltered in the consumer goods sector. As the physical productivity of machinery is constant, the capital–output ratio expressed in terms of value, being by definition equal to the reverse of average physical machinery productivity, must also remain constant in the capital goods sector. But if the capital–output ratio (in terms of value) remains constant in the capital goods sector, the capital cost of the machinery must decrease in the same proportion as the labour cost. Consequently the unit cost of the machine diminishes proportionally to the increase of the man–output ratio obtained in the sector. On the contrary, the cost of a consumer good will decrease less than the unit cost of a machine because labour cost is constant. Consequently the capital–output ratio must diminish in the sector considered.

From what has been said so far it follows that type A innovations introduced only in the capital goods sector do not affect the capital–output ratio in the sector of capital goods, while in the consumer goods sector they reduce the capital–output ratio in a lesser proportion than the increase in labour productivity in the capital goods sector (with the rate of profit unchanged). And this holds true regardless of the capital intensity of the consumer goods manufacturing process. This is why, the rate of profit remaining unchanged, the share of labour in income distribution rises.

Lastly let us consider the case in which type A technical progress is introduced in both industries at the same rate, namely the case in which the new machinery that is produced yields the same output as before, although it is manned by a number of workers π_1 times smaller in both industries. This case is a combination of the two examined before.

It is worth mentioning that type A innovations adopted in the capital goods sector leave the capital–output ratio of the capital goods sector unaltered and lessen the capital cost of the consumer goods sector proportionally to the increase in the man–output ratio in the capital goods sector. By definition, then, type A innovations lessen the labour cost of the consumer goods proportionally to the increase in the man–output ratio in the consumer goods sector. Consequently, if the man–output ratio diminishes at the same rate in both of the sectors considered, both the labour cost and the capital cost of consumer goods diminish in the same proportion. Therefore type A innovations adopted in both sectors leave the capital–output ratio unchanged both in the capital goods sector and in the consumer goods sector (always assuming that the rate of profit remains unchanged) and, hence, have no impact on distribution.[17] These are the peculiar conditions of the 'golden age'.[18]

All of the foregoing can be confirmed by a more formal analysis, but I shall confine myself to examining only the impact of technical progress on the wage rate, the most difficult problem to analyse verbally.

Assuming k to be constant, the derivatives of equation (10) for a_{lx} and a_{ly} are, respectively:

$$\frac{\mathrm{d}W}{\mathrm{d}a_{\mathrm{lx}}} = \frac{(1 - a_{\mathrm{ky}}k)\ (a_{\mathrm{ky}}k - 1)}{[(a_{\mathrm{kx}}a_{\mathrm{ly}} - a_{\mathrm{ky}}a_{\mathrm{lx}})k + a_{\mathrm{lx}}]^2}$$

$$= - \frac{(1 - a_{\mathrm{ky}}k)^2}{[(a_{\mathrm{kx}}a_{\mathrm{ly}} - a_{\mathrm{ky}}a_{\mathrm{lx}})k + a_{\mathrm{lx}}]^2} \quad (12)$$

$$\frac{\mathrm{d}W}{\mathrm{d}a_{\mathrm{ly}}} = - \frac{(1 - a_{\mathrm{ky}}k)\ a_{\mathrm{kx}}k}{[(a_{\mathrm{kx}}a_{\mathrm{ly}} - a_{\mathrm{ky}}a_{\mathrm{lx}})k + a_{\mathrm{lx}}]^2}. \quad (13)$$

We expect these expressions to be negative, because type A technical progress, being labour saving, must raise the wage rate. Expression (12) is negative at first sight. But does the same hold true of (13)? To answer this question, we must consider that a_{ky} is the reverse of the average capital–output ratio in the two sectors and that consequently $1/a_{\mathrm{ky}}$ must be greater than V (because wages cannot be reduced to zero); as $k = V$, $1 - a_{\mathrm{ky}}k$ is positive; hence (13) is negative.

THE IMPACT OF TYPE B AND C INNOVATIONS

I proceed to analysing type B technical progress.

When type B technical progress is adopted in the consumer goods sector, it too leaves the distribution of capital unaltered in both sectors (as k is assumed to be constant); because labour productivity does not change in either sector, its impact will be to increase total output and employment within the consumer goods sector in equal proportions: if the rate of technical progress is π_{kx}, the rate of change that technical progress will bring about in the consumer goods output of the sector and in its employment level will be π_{kx}. If k were zero, total employment would grow in the same proportion as the consumer goods output level and the wage rate would remain constant; if, conversely, k is greater than zero, total employment grows at a lesser rate than consumer goods output, so that wages increase as well. In the consumer goods sector, type B technical progress will consequently result in boosting the wage rate. Because employment in the capital goods sector is constant whereas the workers employed in the consumer goods sector have grown in number, each worker in the consumer goods sector, though yielding the same output as before, must contribute a lesser share of the total consumption of the workers operating in the capital goods sector.

As for the capital–output ratio in the case here under examination, it obviously remains constant in the capital goods sector and diminishes in the consumer goods sector. With the rate of profit unchanged, therefore, type B technical progress adopted only in the consumer goods sector shifts distribution to the advantage of workers.

If, conversely, type B technical progress is adopted in the capital goods sector, it changes the distribution of capital in the two sectors even if these use identical 'machinery'. Because the extent of the existing capital stock is given, the smaller a_{ky} is, the smaller is also the portion of the existing capital that will be required by a given amount of investment. Type B technical progress adopted in the capital goods sector will consequently result in increasing both total consumer goods output and employment. Even in the case of an increase in employment, technical progress will raise the wage rate both because output in terms of consumer goods will grow and because the relevant increase in output will be proportionally greater than the increase in employment.

As for distribution, when type B innovations are adopted only in capital goods sector, they lessen the capital–output ratio in both the capital goods and consumer goods sectors; if the rate of profit is constant, consequently, they will lessen the share of capital in distribution.

It is worth mentioning that, when type B innovations are adopted in both sectors, they cut the capital costs of both commodities for two reasons: by reducing both the machinery–output ratio and the machinery unit cost. More generally, wherever type B innovations are adopted, they cut the capital cost of at least one of the commodities for at least one of the two above-mentioned reasons, while they always leave labour cost unaffected. Therefore type B innovations always lessen the per-man capital in terms of wage units that is employed in manufacturing and, with a constant rate of profit, always shift distribution to the benefit of labour.

From all that goes before it follows, in particular, that if type B innovations are adopted in both sectors while the rate of profit remains stable, they lessen the capital–output ratio by the same rate, and this rate will change in a greater or lesser proportion than the machine–output ratio, depending on the capital intensity of the consumer goods manufacturing process. If they are adopted only in the machinery sector and the rate of profit remains stable, the capital–output ratio of the economy overall will diminish in a greater proportion than the machine–output ratio. If they are adopted only in the consumer goods sector and the rate of profit is likewise left unaltered, the capital–output ratio diminishes by a lesser rate than the machine–output ratio.

The foregoing propositions can be confirmed by mathematical analysis, but in this case too I am going to confine myself merely to examining the changes in the wage rate arising, depending on the kind of technical progress.

If we find the derivatives of equation (10) for a_{kx} and a_{ky} (and always assume k to be constant), the results obtained are, respectively:

$$\frac{dW}{da_{kx}} = \frac{-(1 - a_{ky}k)\, a_{ly}k}{[(a_{kx}a_{ly} - a_{ky}a_{lx})k + a_{lx})]^2} \qquad (14)$$

$$\frac{dW}{da_{ky}} = \frac{-\ a_{kx}\ a_{ly}k^2}{[(a_{kx}a_{ly}\ -\ a_{ky}\ a_{lx})k\ +\ a_{lx}]^2} \tag{15}$$

These two expressions are also evidently negative.

As mentioned before, it follows also that type B progress increases the wage rate, although it does not increase labour productivity in either sector. And these equations enable us to appraise the impact the single factors have on the wage rate as a result of the introduction of type B technical progress.[19]

At this point I shall proceed to analysing the introduction of type C innovations, namely innovations that increase output with the same combination of machinery and workers. Here too I shall start from the case in which innovations are adopted only in the consumer goods sector.

The introduction of type C innovations only in the consumer goods sector obviously causes no changes in the capital goods sector, so that the capital–output ratio of this sector remains constant. Conversely, in the consumer goods sector an equal number of machines operated by an equal number of workers afford greater output. Capital costs and labour costs consequently diminish at a rate equal to the increase in the man–output ratio, so that the cost of the consumer goods diminishes in the same proportion; the capital–output ratio in terms of value consequently also remains unchanged in the consumer goods sector.[20]

By their nature, accordingly, type C innovations do not alter the capital–output ratio of the economy overall when they are adopted only in the consumer goods sector and the rate of profit remains unchanged.[21]

Let us now examine the case in which type C innovations are adopted only in the capital goods sector.

With the rate of profit unchanged, in the case here under review the capital cost of the machinery diminishes necessarily in a greater proportion than the cost of labour; the machine–output ratio of the capital goods sector diminishes proportionally to the labour–output ratio, namely in the same proportion as labour cost, and thus the cost of machines diminishes. The manufacturing cost of the machines thus diminishes by a rate greater than the increase in labour productivity in the capital goods sector.

Furthermore, the capital cost of the consumer goods diminishes more than proportionally to the labour productivity increase of the capital goods sector, whereas the labour cost of the consumer goods remains steady. Accordingly the cost of the machinery diminishes to a greater extent than the consumer goods cost as a result of the fall in the capital–output ratio in terms of value observed in the consumer goods sector.

The conclusion is that, when type C innovations are adopted only in the capital goods sector, they lessen the capital–output ratio in both sectors.

Lastly let us address the case in which type C innovations are adopted in both sectors of the economy at the same rate.

Consistently with the foregoing, in this case – and always provided that the rate of profit remains unchanged – the capital costs of both commodities must necessarily diminish to a greater extent than the cost of labour, and the production costs of both commodities must diminish by a greater proportion than the increase in labour productivity. It follows, therefore, that when type C innovations are adopted in both industries they cannot but lessen the capital–man ratio (in real wage units) of the relevant production process.

Always assuming the rate of profit remains unchanged, in the case under review consumer goods costs may diminish more or less than proportionally to the machinery cost even if the technical progress rate is the same in both sectors. Indeed, whatever the fall in the machinery unit cost of the consumer goods sector, the capital cost of the consumer goods diminishes in a greater proportion and the labour cost in a lesser one. Accordingly the capital–output ratio in terms of value may diminish more or less than proportionally to the machine–output ratio. If the machinery–workers ratio is the same in both sectors, instead, the cost of the consumer goods and the cost of the machinery must diminish in the same proportion.[22] Hence it follows that, provided always that the rate of profit undergoes no change, the capital–output ratio of the consumer goods sector diminishes more or less than proportionally to the machine–output ratio according as the capital goods manufacturing process is more or less capital intensive than the consumer goods manufacturing process.

PRELIMINARY FINDINGS

The analysis conducted in the previous paragraphs suggests the following preliminary findings:

With the rate of profit remaining constant,

(a) type A innovations, namely innovations increasing only labour productivity, leave the capital–output ratio unchanged in the economy as a whole if they are introduced in both sectors, they raise the capital–output ratio if they are introduced only in the consumer goods sector, and they lessen the capital–output ratio if they are introduced only in the capital goods sector;
(b) type B innovations, namely innovations raising machine productivity only, always lessen the capital–output ratio, whatever the sector in which they are introduced;
(c) type C innovations, namely innovations raising both labour and capital productivity in the same proportion, leave the capital–output ratio unchanged only if they are introduced exclusively in the consumer goods sector; otherwise they result in lessening the capital–output ratio;
(d) if type A innovations are introduced in both sectors, they reduce the cost of consumer goods and that of machinery in the same proportion even

though the production cycles of these two sectors are characterized by a different capital intensity;

(e) if type B or C innovations are introduced in both sectors, they lessen the capital–output ratio in a proportion that is greater or less than or equal to the increase in machine productivity according as the capital intensity of the machinery production process is greater or less than or equal to the capital intensity of the consumer goods manufacturing process;

(f) if innovations are introduced only in the machinery sector, they lessen the capital–output ratio of the machinery in proportion to the increase in the machinery productivity level in the capital goods sector;[23]

(g) if innovations are introduced only in the consumer goods sector, the capital–output ratio of the consumer goods sector declines or remains unchanged according as labour productivity grows more or less than or at the same rate as machinery productivity;

(h) the capital intensity of the manufacturing processes of the two commodities is always uninfluential in terms of the increase, decline or constancy of the capital–output ratio following upon the introduction of technical progress.

NEUTRAL INNOVATIONS: A CRITICAL ASSESSMENT OF ONE OF ROBINSON'S STATEMENTS

Joan Robinson repeatedly stated that innovations are neutral in Harrod's definition if labour productivity increases in the same proportion in both the capital goods sector and that of consumer goods; she also emphasized that they are capital using or capital saving according to Harrod's definition according as labour productivity increases in a greater proportion in the sector of consumer goods or in that of capital goods.

> An increase in output per head at an even pace in all lines of production is equivalent, from the point of view of potential output, to an increase in the labour force at the corresponding rate.... Now, when the system is working in such a way that productive capacity increases at the same pace as output per head, there is steady employment of the given labour force over the long run. The division of the labour force (and of the productive capacity of capital goods) between the investment sector and the consumption sector then remains unchanged as time goes by. A given number of workers in the investment sector produce plant (for both sectors) of an ever increasing productive capacity, and a given number of workers in the consumption sector operate it to produce an ever increasing output. Real wages rise with output per man, and the rate of profit remains constant.
>
> (Robinson 1956: 87–8)

This proposition is responsible for the widespread assumption that innovations are neutral and *capital using* or *capital saving* according to Harrod's definition if they are introduced at the same rate in both sectors, at a greater rate in the consumer goods sector or, conversely, at a greater rate in the capital goods sector.[24]

In contrast, the analysis conducted so far has shown that innovations are not neutral when labour productivity grows in the same proportion in both the consumer goods sector and the investment goods sector.

The above proposition will hold true only if capital productivity too does not grow in either sector; and this is observed only in the case in which innovations increasing labour productivity fit into type A, and not also when they fit into type C.

In other words, Robinson's proposition holds up only in a special case, namely when innovations are *only* type A. Conversely, it does not hold up when innovations fit into types B or C, i.e. when they are also capital saving.

The analysis conducted so far also disproves the belief of all those who contend that, in the absence of specific reasons to the contrary, technical progress can be assumed to be neutral in the long run.

This opinion is widely shared. As mentioned before, in *The Rate of Interest and Other Essays*, for instance, Joan Robinson herself wrote: 'In general there is no reason to assume that innovations save less capital than labour' (1954: 43); and, in *The Accumulation of Capital*, she re-emphasized: 'There is no reason to expect technical progress to be exactly neutral in any one economy, but equally there is no reason to expect a systematic bias in one way or the other' (i.e. a greater diffusion of *capital-using* or *capital-saving* technical progress as defined by Harrod) (1956: 170).

The assumption we are dealing with here is grounded in the conviction that technical progress is neutral when it is introduced in both sectors and that in such a case there is no reason to assume that technical progress proceeds systematically at a greater rate in one of the two sectors. If this assumption holds up, then to deny the assumption from which this line of reasoning sets out would involve denying also the corresponding conclusions.

The foregoing analysis has shown that, *within the limits of the assumptions made*, in the long run technical progress ought to be *capital saving*. In actual fact, of the three types of technical progress that have been considered, only type A technical progress is neutral when it is introduced in both sectors of the economy, while type B and type C technical progress are *capital saving* regardless of the sector in which they are introduced and can never be *capital using*.

Special attention ought to be given to type C technical progress, namely the kind of technical progress that results in increased output when the quantity of capital and working hours employed remains unchanged. If any type of technical progress is to be held out as the prototype of all varieties of technical progress, it must be type C technical progress, which does not alter production coefficients. As shown above, type C technical progress is neutral only if it is introduced exclusively in the consumer goods sector; otherwise it is capital saving.

The fact that this model constantly produces technical progress of the capital-saving type is obviously due to the very assumptions underlying the model itself, in particular the assumption that changes in the prices of factors do not result in any substitution between production techniques. In actual fact the capital-saving nature of technical progress, with the consequential reduction in the price of capital goods, will lead to the introduction of more capital-intensive techniques. And this may explain why our conclusions are in contrast with what is being observed.

THE 'SILVER AGE'

If we now assume that workers do not save, but that capitalists consume part of their income, the rate of profit is:

$$V = \frac{k}{S_c}, \tag{16}$$

where k is the rate of capital accumulation, S_c is the capitalists' propensity to save, and the share of capital in the income produced is:

$$Q_k = \frac{VK}{R},$$

where R is the total output produced.

Let us assume that technical progress is both type A and type B and that entrepreneurs wish to accumulate capital at a constant rate. As is known, type B technical progress causes the physical productivity of the capital good to increase at the rate π_k in both sectors in successive periods of time. Let us also assume that the price of capital goods expressed in consumer goods is constant. In point of fact the latter assumption greatly restricts the validity of the model, because in essence it involves assuming a one-sector model; nevertheless it is justified because, by its very nature, type B technical progress increases the productivity of investments *of a given cost*.

If capital must be fully utilized, the following must apply:

$$r = k + \pi_k \tag{17}$$

where r is the growth rate of output.

As the propensity to save of society as a whole is equal to:

$$S = \frac{S_c VK}{R}, \tag{18}$$

when capital is fully utilized, the capitalists' propensity to save is constant and, hence, V is constant too, the following applies:

$$s = s_c + v + k - r = -\pi_k, \tag{19}$$

where the small letters indicate the growth rates of the corresponding capital letters. Equation (19) is compatible with the assumption of a constant rate of capital accumulation; indeed, if *ex ante* savings and *ex ante* investment are equal, i.e.

$$k = \frac{SR}{K},$$

then in the case under review the rate of capital accumulation is constant when:

$$\frac{\dot{k}}{k} = s + r - k = 0, \tag{20}$$

where $\dot{k}/k$ is the rate of change of k.

Thus a situation of long-term equilibrium exists, in which:

$$r = k + \pi_k = \text{cost}$$

$$V = \text{cost}$$

$$l = r - \pi_l = \text{cost}$$

$$q_k = v + k - r = -\pi_k$$

$$s = k - r = -\pi_k$$

where l is the growth rate of employment, π_l is the growth rate of labour productivity brought about by technical progress of type A, and q_k is the rate of change of the share of capital in the income produced.

This equilibrium state with constant growth is similar to that of the 'golden age', but differs from it because the capital–output ratio and, hence, the proportion of capital in income diminish at constant rates. This equilibrium state can be termed 'the silver age'.

At first sight, the 'silver age' is somewhat paradoxical: the capital accumulation rate and the income growth rate are constant although society's propensity to save and the investment–income ratio decline continuously. The paradox is explained if one observes that in an equilibrium state the rate of capital accumulation (SR/K) reflects the savings put aside by society (which diminish at a rate equal to π_k) and capital productivity (which advances at a rate equal to π_k).

The foregoing implies that the age of silver is associated with a kind of technical progress that raises the productivity of capital goods, namely exactly the kinds of technical progress, type B and/or C, that have so often been ignored in Keynesian growth models. And this is where the novelty of the result lies.

NOTES

1 This essay further develops and elaborates upon the reflections contained in Jossa (1965; 1966: chs X and XI).

2 In this connection it is worth spending a few words on the so-called 'Robinson theorem', according to which, with constant returns to scale and under a number of additional restrictive assumptions concerning the function of production, technical progress is neutral in Harrod's sense if, and only if, it is 'labour-augmenting' (see Robinson 1937–8, and, for a more formal demonstration, Uzawa 1960–1 and Ramanathan 1982: 78–83).

3 For the model examined here below, see, from among Robinson's many writings, Robinson (1952a, 1956, 1957, 1960, 1962b).

4 For this formalization of Robinson's model and the relevant solution, see Worswick (1959), Lancaster (1960) and Findlay (1963). A formalization of Robinson's model is also found in Asimakopulos and Weldon (1963).

5 This aspect of Robinson's model was already pointed out in the earliest comments (see, *inter alia*, Barna 1957: 491, Lerner 1957: 694ff). At times, however, it has given rise to misinterpretations (see Findlay 1963, and Robinson's comment in Robinson 1963: 408–9).

6 See Robinson (1956: 73).

7 See Robinson (1956: 76).

8 See Robinson (1956: 78–83); also see Robinson (1962b: vi), Findlay (1963), Konijn (1965), Asimakopulos (1965).

9 For the classification of the inventions concerned into types, see Jossa (1966: chs II and III). For the convenience of a classification of innovations at the microeconomic instead of the macroeconomic level, see Pasinetti (1981: 212–14).

10 Joan Robinson examined type C innovation in a model with fixed coefficients in Robinson (1962b).

11 In two-sector models there are labour- or capital-saving innovations in the consumer goods sector and labour- or capital-saving innovations in the capital goods sector. Consequently Asimakopulos and Weldon's analysis of the effects of technical progress in a two-sector model with fixed coefficients seems to result in a certain degree of confusion because, according to these two authors, labour-saving innovations are those reducing the labour–output ratio in the consumer goods sector (see Asimakopulos and Weldon 1963: 374, 383ff).

12 Robinson's comment on this point is: 'To understand the motives for investment, we have to understand human nature and the manner in which it reacts to various kinds of social and economic systems in which it has to operate. We have not got far enough yet to put it into algebra' (Robinson 1964: 101).

13 In her analyses, Robinson mostly uses the so-called naive approach to the theory of technical progress, an approach based on the assumption that innovation is

obtained at no cost and is independent both of relative prices and of the accumulation rate (see Chaudhuri 1989: 105–6). For a number of exceptions, however, see, for instance, Robinson (1956: 96, 1962b: 51–2).

14 See Harrod (1937: 329, 1948: 22–3, 1961: 300–1, Robinson (1937–8, 1952b: 40ff, 1956: 132–3), Pasinetti (1981: 208–9).

15 Robinson showed that Hicks' and Harrod's definitions of neutrality coincide when capital is measured in terms of real wage units (see Robinson 1956a: 132–3, 1962b: 113; Jossa 1963, 1966: 269–71).

16 For the earliest demonstrations of this proposition, see Robinson (1952b: 40ff, and 1956: 87–9, 132–3 and 159–60).

17 Joan Robinson analysed this case in Robinson (1952b: 40ff, and 1956: 99–100 and 159ff). In this connection Fellner writes: 'It is tempting, but quite wrong, to argue that when, say, "automation" gains ground at the expense of other types of innovations, then the labour-saving (capital-using) character of this change will express itself in higher capital–output ratios' (Fellner 1961: 59). My analysis confirms this finding.

18 In its present use, the notion of the 'golden age' goes back to Robinson herself (Robinson 1952b: 90ff, 1956: 99ff). Robinson wrote that in using the phrase 'golden age' she wanted to represent a mythical state of affairs not likely to be obtained in any actual economy (see Robinson 1956: 99, and 1962a: 52).

19 Type B innovations, i.e. innovations leaving the labour–output ratio unchanged, have been termed 'neutral in the sense of Solow' (see Solow 1963: 59, and Hahn and Matthews 1964: 1830). But whereas Solow's definition of neutrality involves that the respective income shares of capital and labour remain constant, this assumption is never met in our model. As observed by Pasinetti, therefore, the analogy between type B technical progress and neutrality in the sense of Solow should be posited only when the output–labour ratio is taken as a benchmark for neutrality (see Pasinetti 1981: 211–12).

20 For the earliest formulations of this proposition, see Solow (1961: 260ff, for a model with variable coefficients); Findlay (1963: 8), Asimakopulos and Weldon (1963: 384–5). Robinson did not analyse this case. In a study of Joan Robinson's model the authors remarked that the use of two sectors merely resulted in making the model unnecessarily complex (see Asimakopulos and Weldon 1963: 312). The fact that a one-sector model would be sufficient to reach the main results of Robinson's model is an interesting conclusion. But from the foregoing it is possible to infer that the contention is correct merely because Robinson failed to draw from her model exactly those results that only two-sector models can afford.

21 Type C innovations have been equated with neutral innovations in the sense defined by Hicks (1932: 121–2). Hicks' definition, however, requires that, with the capital–labour ratio remaining constant, the marginal productivity of both factors should increase in the same proportion; in a model where marginal productivity has no place, therefore, it can be used only by analogy. Moreover, Hicks' neutrality involves the income shares of capital and labour remaining constant, whereas in our model this has been shown to be the case only when type C technical progress is introduced only into the sector of consumer goods. As suggested by Pasinetti, therefore, the analogy between type C technical progress and Hicks' definition of neutrality should be posited only when the constancy of the capital–labour ratio is taken as the benchmark for neutrality (see Pasinetti 1981: 210).

22 In this case, in fact, the model behaves in the same way as a one-sector model.

23 The fact that innovations introduced only in the capital goods sector are always

capital saving in Harrod's definition has been explicitly emphasized by Pasinetti (1959: 272ff). However, Pasinetti failed to make it clear that this proposition holds only if fixed coefficients are assumed (see Jossa 1966: 361ff).

24 From among the numerous passages where one or the other of these two propositions is reported, see Robinson (1937–8: 177–8, 1949: 70–1, 1951: 22, 1956: 97ff and 133), Harrod (1948: 23), Lowe (1955: 622–3), Andreatta (1958: 76–7), Kahn (1959: 146), Davidson (1959: 78–9), Kaldor and Mirrlees (1962: 177), Arcelli (1962: 76) and Capolupo (1990: 95).

REFERENCES

Andreatta, N. (1958) *Distribuzione del reddito e accumulazione di capitale*. Milan: Giuffrè.

Arcelli, M. (1962) *La Cobb–Douglas strumento per la programmazione*. Rome: ISCO.

Asimakopulos, A. (1965) Findlay's Robinsonian Model of Accumulation: A Note, *Economica*, 32.

Asimakopulos, A. and Weldon, J. C. (1963) The Classification of Technical Progress in Models of Economic Growth, *Economica*, 30.

Barna, T. (1957) The Accumulation of Capital, *Economic Journal*, 67.

Capolupo, R. (1990) *Progresso tecnico e disoccupazione*. Bari: Cacucci.

Chaudhuri, P. (1989) *The Economic Theory of Growth*. New York: Harvester.

Davidson, P. (1959) *Theories of Aggregate Income Distribution*. New Brunswick, NJ: Rutgers University Press.

Fellner, W. (1961) Appraisal of the Labour-saving and Capital-saving Character of Innovations. In F. A. Lutz and D. C. Hague, eds, *The Theory of Capital*. London: Macmillan.

Findlay, R. (1963) The Robinsonian Model of Accumulation, *Economica*, 30.

Hahn, F. H. and Matthews, R. C. O. (1964) The Theory of Economic Growth: A Survey, *Economic Journal*, 74.

Harrod, R. F. (1937) Review of *Essays in the Theory of Employment*, *Economic Journal*, 47.

——— (1948) *Towards a Dynamic Economics*. London: Macmillan.

——— (1961) The Neutrality of Improvements, *Economic Journal*, 71.

Hicks, J. R. (1932) *The Theory of Wages*. 2nd edn, London: Macmillan, 1963.

Jossa, B. (1963) Hicks ed Harrod sulla neutralità delle invenzioni: una conciliazione, *Studi economici*, 18(5–6).

——— (1965) Sviluppo a tasso costante e riduzione del rapporto investimento reddito, *Studi economici*, 20(1–2).

——— (1966) *Analisi economica del progresso tecnico*. Milan: Giuffrè.

Kahn, R. F. (1959) Exercises in the Analysis of Growth, *Oxford Economic Papers*, 11.

Kaldor, N. and Mirrlees, J. A. (1962) A New Model of Economic Growth, *Review of Economic Studies*, 30.

Konijn, H. S. (1965) Findlay's Robinsonian Model of Accumulation: A Note, *Economica*, 32.

Lancaster, K. (1960) Mrs Robinson's Dynamics, *Economica*, 27.

Lerner, A. P. (1957) The Accumulation of Capital, *American Economic Review*, 47.

Lowe, A. (1955) Structural Analysis of Real Capital Formation. In *Capital Formation and Economic Growth*, National Bureau of Economic Research. Princeton, NJ: Princeton University Press.

Pasinetti, L. L. (1959) On Concepts and Measures of Changes in Productivity, *Review of Economics and Statistics*, 41.
——— (1981) *Structural Change and Economic Growth.* Berlin: Springer Verlag.
Ramanathan, R. (1982) *Introduction to the Theory of Economic Growth.* Berlin: Springer Verlag.
Robinson, J. (1937–8) The Classification of Inventions, *Review of Economic Studies*; reprinted in AEA, *Readings in the Theory of Income Distribution*, London: Allen & Unwin, 1950.
——— (1949) Mr Harrod's Dynamics, *Economic Journal*, 59.
——— (1951) Introduction to Rose Luxemburg, *The Accumulation of Capital.* London: Macmillan.
——— (1952a) Notes in the Economics of Technical Progress. In *The Rate of Interest and Other Essays.* London: Macmillan.
——— (1952b) *The Rate of Interest and Other Essays.* London: Macmillan.
——— (1956) *The Accumulation of Capital.* London: Macmillan.
——— (1957) La théorie de la répartition, *Economie appliquée*, 10(4).
——— (1960) Capital, Technique and Relative Shares. In *Collected Economic Papers*, vol. II. Oxford: Basil Blackwell.
——— (1962a) A Model of Accumulation. In *Essays in the Theory of Economic Growth.* New York: St Martin's Press.
——— (1962b) A Model of Technical Progress. In *Essays in the Theory of Economic Growth.* New York: St. Martin's Press.
——— (1963) Findlay's Robinsonian Model of Accumulation, *Economics*, 30.
——— (1964) *Economic Philosophy.* Harmondsworth, Middx: Pelican.
Solow, R. M. (1961) A Wicksellian Model of Distributive Shares. In F. A. Lutz and D. C. Hague, eds, *The Theory of Capital.* London: Macmillan.
——— (1963) *Capital Theory and Rate of Return.* Amsterdam: North Holland.
Uzawa, H. (1960–1) Neutral Inventions and the Stability of Growth Equilibrium, *Review of Economic Studies*, 28 (76).
Worswick, G. D. N. (1959) Mrs Robinson on Simple Accumulation: A Comment with Algebra, *Oxford Economic Papers*, 11.

Part VI

METHOD

24

JOAN ROBINSON'S CHANGING VIEWS ON METHOD

A tentative appraisal[1]

Andrea Salanti

> [The economist] must have a capacity for abstract thinking combined with its least usual bed-fellow – simple commonsense. But the temperament of the economist is even more strange. He must have a strong interest in human welfare . . . but he must have the capacity for a detachment of mind which makes it possible for him to accept the assertion that the subject matter of economics is neither more nor less than its own technique.
>
> (Robinson 1932: 4)

> My saying 'A serious subject is neither more nor less than its own technique' was a half truth, but it is the important half. In the natural sciences experiments can be repeated and observations checked so that a false hypothesis is quickly knocked out.
>
> (Robinson 1979a: 116)

Joan Robinson addressed herself to explicit methodological reflections on at least three occasions: in the juvenile pamphlet *Economics Is a Serious Subject*, in the more mature essays of *Economics and Philosophy*, and finally in 'Thinking about Thinking' (a rather pessimistic view of the state of economics in the late 1970s).[2] Furthermore, as her readers know very well, most of her writings are punctuated by metatheoretical (if not strictly methodological) remarks, notably on the limited explanatory power of 'pure' economic theory and on the pervasive and subtle influence of ideology within economics.

However, in spite of such an abundance of source material,[3] it is far from easy to bring together her various ideas on a single subject in order to obtain a coherent picture of the whole. This is surely due to a number of concurrent reasons (some of which will be pointed out in the course of this paper), but primarily, I believe, to Joan Robinson's peculiar attitude towards methodological enquiry. Indeed, she never engages herself in a comprehensive and dispassionate discussion of 'the scope and method' of economics with explicit reference to some well-established epistemological perspective. On the contrary, she frequently uses methodological arguments either in support of the particular piece of economic research she is pursuing, or against that particular facet of 'mainstream' economics she is challenging at that moment. Take for instance the following passages, excerpted from the 1974 introduction to the second edition of volume III of her collected papers:

> My critical pieces are understood only by those who agree with me and do not need to read them. Evidently, we are in a clash of paradigms. In *Structures of Scientific Revolutions* [Kuhn 1962] the examples are drawn from physics, chemistry and biology. . . . We cannot command the methods that have led to their success – precise observation of exact recurrences or controlled experiments. . . . But as an academic profession . . . we have much in common with the scientific community which Kuhn describes. When I read his accounts of a 'crisis' in the development of a scientific discipline, I recognised exactly what I had lived through in the Keynesian revolution.
>
> (1975: iii–iv)

Two observations spring immediately to mind. First, had she read Kuhn for his own sake, she would surely have abstained from the commonsensical asides on the 'superiority' of natural science (just one of the traditional beliefs within the philosophy of science that Kuhn, and the subsequent literature on the 'growth of knowledge', so vigorously disputes). Secondly, such a crude and sketchy allusion to the 'Keynesian revolution' and to the capital controversy makes apparent that Joan Robinson's beliefs were antecedent to (and independent of) her reading of Kuhn. The reference to the Kuhnian notion of 'paradigm' is purely instrumental, so that the methodological point appears as nothing but another rhetorical device parenthetically added to her usual bunch of critical arguments, neither completely pursued nor particularly appreciated in all its implications.

One of the aims of this paper is to show that the very same approach is easily observable in all her various methodological pronouncements, and consequently, because at different times in the course of her long career she focuses on different issues, that it is by no means surprising that she makes use of a variety of not mutually compatible methodological judgements. This is not, however, the sole common feature we can trace in the different periods of Joan Robinson's scholarly activity. In the following sections it is also argued that we may detect, behind her changing views on method, different answers to the same unchanging question(s) and different attempts to overcome the same really methodological problem.

A BRIEF SKETCH OF CHANGING VIEWS

As pointed out by a number of sympathetic commentators (Gram and Walsh 1983, Turner 1989, Harcourt 1990, Rima 1991) and openly acknowledged by Joan Robinson herself in her 1979 essay 'Thinking about Thinking', there can be no doubt that her view on economic methodology passed through different (and, in some cases, apparently contradictory) phases. Behind such transformations, however, it is easy to identify some elements of continuity. The first, as previously stated, is that her differing methodological perspectives were always instrumental to the particular field of research she was interested in at the time. This may be easily shown with reference to her three major works on method.

In Robinson (1932) the main message is that 'a serious subject, in the academic sense, is neither more nor less than its own technique' (ibid.: 3). Admittedly, this elliptic and somewhat enigmatic sentence may be interpreted in a number of different ways. However, if it is taken to mean that we should define 'the subject matter of economics as anything on which that technique can be made to work' (ibid.: 10) and therefore that 'economists must get all the results which are just as complicated, but no more complicated, than their technique can produce, hoping gradually to build up a more and more complicated technique as time goes by' (ibid.: 9–10), we have a proper account of what Joan Robinson herself is trying to accomplish in *The Economics of Imperfect Competition*, published the year after *Economics Is a Serious Subject*. It may well be that she 'soon ceased to believe in its main argument – that if the economists could avoid certain bad habits and arrive at a consistent set of assumptions, however abstract, they could approach reality step by step merely by making more complicated models', as she herself tells us in Robinson (1979a: 110), but this does not lessen the striking affinity between the methodological thesis put forth in 1932 and her famous 1933 piece of analysis on the theory of the firm along Pigouvian lines. Later on, indeed, she dismisses her own work on the theory of imperfect competition as a 'wrong turning' erroneously based 'on static assumptions'.[4] What she never dismissed, however, is the other main argument in her 1932 pamphlet on method. As Harcourt rightly puts it:

> [The] problem is related to the age-old problem of the gap between the world 'out there' that the techniques and theory of the discipline are meant to illuminate and the techniques themselves – the method and the resulting theory itself. The theory has in effect to pass two tests. The first is its own logical consistency and coherence; the second (which is probably even more important) is its ultimate applicability.
>
> (Harcourt 1990: 414)

Those readers acquainted with Robinson's subsequent work will here surely recognize two of her favourite themes, namely the necessity of distinguishing clearly between these two different types of criticism in order to avoid unnecessary misunderstandings, and, when discussing the adequacy of assumptions, the intellectual duty to isolate the implicit ideological premises.

In the same vein it is by no means surprising to find in the first essay ('Metaphysics, Moral and Science') in Robinson (1962), written in a period when she was becoming more and more conscious of the hidden ideological bias behind the different attempts to rebuild a new orthodoxy after the 'Keynesian revolution' (see, for example, Robinson 1962: 73–98), the following recognition of Popper's demarcation criterion:

> The hallmark of a metaphysical proposition is that it is not capable of being tested.... It can never be proved wrong...; it claims to be true by definition of its own terms.... Adopting Professor Popper's [1959] criterion for propositions that belong to the empirical sciences, that they are capable of being falsified by evidence, it is not a scientific proposition.
>
> (ibid.: 3)

When the main purpose is to separate 'science' from 'ideology', Popper's solution is surely quite appealing. What has to be noted in this respect, however, is that Joan Robinson's advocacy of the Popperian demarcation criterion does not involve a complete acceptance of Popper's falsificationist methodology, nor is it indifferent to possible dangers. Unlike Terence Hutchison, a former student of hers at the time of *Economics Is a Serious Subject*, she never advocated the adoption of a falsificationist methodology in order to improve the 'seriousness' of economics. On the contrary, in the same essay previously quoted it is clearly said that:

> The process of science, as Professor Popper maintains, consists in trying to *disprove* theories.... [L]acking the experimental method, economists are not strictly enough compelled to reduce metaphysical concepts to falsifiable terms and cannot compel each other to agree as to what has been falsified. So economics limps along with one foot in untested hypotheses and the other in untestable slogans. We shall find no neat answers to the questions that it raises.
>
> The leading characteristic of the ideology that dominates our society today is its extreme confusion. To understand it means only to reveal its contradictions.
>
> (Robinson 1962: 22–4; italics in the original)

By the end of her life, as noted by Harcourt (1990: 411),

> she was almost nihilistic about economic theory, method, and their potential development. She rejected the idea of providing a rival 'complete theory' to replace the orthodox neoclassical one (as she saw

> it) . . . She said that 'any other complete theory would be only another box of tricks. What we need is a different habit of mind – to eschew fudging, to respect facts and to admit ignorance of what we do not know' [Robinson 1979a: 119].

Although it is undoubtedly true that her progressive disillusionment with method paralleled her increasing dissatisfaction with the state of economic theory, it is important to note that the premises to her gloomy 1979 conclusions on economic method were already present in her previous observations on the inapplicability of falsificationism in economics.

Indeed, in the passages previously quoted from Robinson (1962) we find the crucial point of her argument about the difficulty of unveiling the more or less hidden ideological substratum of mainstream economics. If in economics we could consistently apply Popperian falsificationism, then the problem would be solved, because we should need only to identify those cases where the demarcation criterion of falsifiability is not fulfilled. But unfortunately in economics (and in all the other social sciences, for that matter) the experimental method is not available, so that it becomes difficult, not to say impossible, to reach a general agreement on precise criteria of falsifiability (or falsification).[5]

The problem here is that we cannot use Popper's criterion of demarcation in order to ascertain the possible presence of metaphysical assumptions if at the same time we reject his falsificationism methodology. This would be possible if, and only if, all the assumptions were independently falsifiable, but for a number of reasons it may well happen that we test – that is, in a Popperian perspective, attempt to falsify – only some of the conclusions (or, if you prefer, 'predictions') of the theory.

IDEOLOGY AND SCIENCE

Joan Robinson was not interested in Popper's methodology (and epistemology, for that matter) for its own sake. Not only her main contributions on the subject, but also a large number of passing remarks on methodological questions in other writings clearly show that she was mainly interested in the problem of the widespread influence of ideology on economics, as if her main concern were about the possibility of separating, within the different traditions of economic thought, what can be rationally argued from what should be more properly considered as ideological padding.[6] Coherently, Joan Robinson never ceased to state her own ethical values and ideological convictions openly (coming to depict herself explicitly as 'the archetypical left-wing Keynesian') and to draw our attention, of course for critical purposes, to the (often deliberately disguised) ideological message embedded in the various strands of neoclassical theory.

Although the former practice does not call for any particular methodological argument (if anything, we may only applaud it as an expression of an unusual intellectual integrity), the latter raises more than one problem of methodological appraisal.

Indeed, in order to claim to be able to separate what is 'science' (and therefore susceptible of rational discussion) from what is mere ideology (perhaps indispensable as a source of relevant questions in the social sciences, but to be eliminated as much as possible from the answers), we should have at our disposal a sound criterion of demarcation. I am not sure if Joan Robinson fully realized that her blunt rejection of falsificationism, justified as it might be, rendered more difficult the solution to the problem (of greater concern to her) of uncovering ideological biases within economic theory. It is worth noting in the passage quoted on page 288 her implicit grounds for criticizing the ideological component of the dominant economic theory. Although there is no explicit reference to the criterion of non-contradiction as substitutive of that of falsifiability (or of other criteria set forth in the empiricist tradition before Popper) in order to justify the distinction between 'science' and 'ideology', such a criterion seems to be the only basis of the seemingly fortuitous circumstance of the self-contradictory nature of the 'dominant' ideology (characterized by 'confusion' and 'contradictions'). Because there are no *a priori* reasons for assuming that any ideological position must perforce prove to be self-contradictory, one may well wonder how it could be possible (in less fortunate circumstances) to identify the ideological ingredients of science independently from their (possible) formal correctness.

The same ambivalence can be recognized in other well-known remarks made by Joan Robinson on the same topic. On the one hand, indeed, in the second volume of her collected papers we are told that it is 'foolish to refuse to learn from the ideas of an economist whose ideology we dislike' and 'equally unwise to rely upon the theories of one whose ideology we approve'. An economic theory 'cannot be accepted as correct until it has been tested by an appeal to the facts. The business of the disciples of a great economist is not to propagate his doctrines but to test his hypotheses' (Robinson 1960: 12).

On the other hand, in the fourth volume she openly acknowledges that '[w]hen two economic theories differ in their ideology the most important distinction between them lies in the sphere of political action, but the best sport that they offer is to trace the difference in the logical structure of the systems' (Robinson 1973: 249). Apart from a spontaneous feeling of solidarity towards those ill-fated disciples to whom is assigned such a thankless task (so difficult that the great economists themselves, normally busily occupied in the practice of a more rewarding sport, are unable to do it satisfactorily), we may well wonder whether critical analyses of the 'logical consistency' of theoretical frameworks could ever be as effective as is here presumed.

Before attempting to answer this point, it must be pointed out that, in order to isolate the 'logical structure' of any theoretical system, we must not only dispose of its ideological components but also have to hand a clear-cut distinction between what is simply a matter of logic and what is a matter of empirical judgement. After all, as will be argued below, the real methodological difficulty that Joan Robinson repeatedly encounters in her methodological detours is nothing but one of the most important unsolved (and probably simply irresolvable) epistemological problems (at least before the recent post-modernist assault), that is, the explanation of how objective and progressive scientific knowledge can ever emerge from the subjective and fallible endeavour of the scientists.

THE REAL METHODOLOGICAL DIFFICULTIES

In the end, as we have already seen, Joan Robinson solves that dilemma by denying the progressiveness of economics, depicted by her as a discipline in a permanent state of crisis. There is one instance, however, in which she comes close to making explicit a more optimistic view on the working of economic theory. In the concluding chapter of *Economic Heresies*, we find that

> It is easy enough to make models on stated assumptions. The difficulty is to find the assumptions that are relevant to reality. The art is to set up a scheme that simplifies the problem so as to make it manageable without eliminating the essential character of the actual situation on which it is intended to throw light.
>
> (Robinson 1971: 141)

Behind these observations, with which nobody would disagree because apparently in compliance with the simplest common sense, it is not difficult to see the presence of two important methodological problems: how to justify (in an intersubjective sense) the relevance of the chosen assumptions and how to prove the adequacy of the explanans with respect to the explanandum. As is well known, the repeated attempts to solve precisely these problems constitute the core of both empiricism and rationalism, that is, the two main epistemological traditions in the history of western philosophy. Within the former the ultimate criterion of validation is always given by the correspondence of the 'theory' to the 'facts' (either simply observed or experimentally replicated) that it is meant to explain; while in the latter the main attention is always placed on the logical consistency of the theory (in the sense of the correctness of the deductive inference from the basic postulates to their implications) accompanied by the most disparate justifications of the initial assumptions.

In the economics of the 1960s and 1970s (and nowadays too, for that matter) these two traditions are represented, respectively, by Friedman's instrumentalism together with Hutchison's or Lipsey's strands of Popperian falsificationism on one side,[7] and by von Mises' rationalistic apriorism and Debreu's mathematical formalism on the other. Each of these perspectives, however, is open to question and none of them, indeed, has been able to attain a general consensus within the discipline.[8] What instead can be said to represent the (frequently hidden) methodological beliefs of the representative economist is that strange mixture of rationalism and empiricism that could be labelled as 'empirical apriorism', in other words nothing but the old methodological tradition of Senior–Cairnes–Mill subsequently revived by John Neville Keynes and Lionel Robbins (and recently reinstated by Hausman 1992). According to Klant (1994), such a perspective is characterized by two main 'plausibility strategies', which are meant to fill the gap that derives from the difficulty of testing in economics. One of these strategies is concerned with the realisticness[9] of assumptions and the other with the method of 'diminishing abstractions' or, as is more often said, successive approximations. Both these strategies, of course, are taken to work for logically coherent theories.

As we have already seen, shortly after *Economics Is a Serious Subject*, Joan Robinson ceased to believe in the plausibility of 'approaching reality step by step merely by making more complicated models', but she did not completely escape from the whole tradition of empirical apriorism, continuing to maintain (for lack of better alternatives?) the other building blocks of that methodological perspective: that is, the realisticness of assumptions and the internal consistency of the models. Indeed, we find all that once again in her 1977 essay ('What Are the Questions?'), where she explicitly says that '*Before a model can be confronted with empirical tests, it has to be examined for internal consistency and for the a priori plausibility of its assumptions*'; indeed we may easily detect 'a whole branch of the subject – that which carries the highest prestige – which is concerned simply with criticizing and defending hypotheses' (Robinson 1979b: 4).

Some readers will surely be surprised to realize that these sentences (and especially the italicized one) are firmly grounded in the general tradition of empirical apriorism, and furthermore, if we credit de Marchi (1988b),[10] that they match Robbins' particular version of it startlingly well. Of course, Joan Robinson's judgement on the '*a priori* plausibility' of hypotheses such as the rationality principle or the assumption of maximizing behaviour was completely opposite to that of Robbins. Nevertheless she seems to share the same methodological position; no wonder, therefore, that she had the distasteful experience of seeing her own objections to the assumptions of neoclassical theory more or less ignored and her attacks on its logical consistency continually parried.

Although, alas, there is little or nothing to add on the problem of how we could establish the realisticness of each single assumption, the question of what is implied by a critique directed at the logical consistency of a theoretical structure may be worthy of further scrutiny.

THE PROBLEM OF 'INTERNAL' CRITICISMS

An important implication of 'empirical apriorism' is that, when debating contentious subjects, economists are supposed to make a clear distinction between 'internal' (or 'logical') and 'external' (or 'empirical') critiques. The former would be uniquely concerned with the logical consistency of the analytical structure of the theory (a matter that should lend itself to compelling arguments), whereas the latter would deal with (*pace* Friedman 1953 and Machlup 1955) the more disputable issue of the realisticness of its assumptions.[11]

The distinction between the two types of criticism may well appear as self-evident because we are accustomed to the distinction between 'logical truth' and 'material (or factual) truth' that can be found in every textbook on formal logic (see, for instance, Quine 1982: 53). However, as I argued at some length in Salanti (1989), what is commonly considered as a purely logical criticism usually implies, in addition, some confidence in a number of 'correspondence rules' (to use the terminology of logical empiricists).[12] But such correspondence rules, as we will see below with reference to the controversy on capital theory, involve arguments that do not pertain to the realm of pure logic alone.

Let us consider, for example, the debate on 'reswitching' in capital theory. In the concluding section of the 1967 essay 'The Badly Behaved Production Function' by Robinson and Naqvi, the authors point out that:

> [T]here is no point in discussing which is most 'likely to be found in reality'. First, the argument concerns comparisons of equilibrium positions with different rates of profit and the same 'state of technical knowledge'. These are not found in nature and cannot be observed. Second, *the argument is concerned with a point of logic, to which the number of instances has no relevance one way or the other*. The benefit of the discussion is only to dispel illusions.
>
> (Robinson 1973: 86, italics added)[13]

Although it is beyond question that to appeal to empirical evidence in such a context would be decidedly out of place, it might be doubted that we are facing an argument uniquely concerning the pure logic of a piece of theory.

How could it be possible, indeed, to make a 'point of logic' about the aggregate production function as used in neoclassical one-sector models of growth (and distribution) by showing that conclusions drawn from them no longer hold in a multi-sectoral linear model of production? Such an argument makes sense if, and only if, we agree (as all participants to that debate on capital theory were in fact prepared to do) with the idea that one of the obvious features of capital goods is their heterogeneity and, at least to a certain degree, their complementarity rather than their substitutability. Indeed, it was just the general approval of this 'correspondence rule' about the meaning of the term 'capital' as we understand it that made such a critique quite effective. The strength of that criticism, therefore, depends not on its being concerned with a point of pure logic in the usual sense of the term (otherwise the target of the criticism should have been Euler's theorem on homogeneous functions, but we know that this was by no means the case), but on its being based on a 'correspondence rule' that is virtually impossible to disallow: it would hardly be possible, indeed, to disagree with the plain observation that, for instance, personal computers, trucks and drilling-machines are heterogeneous capital goods and serve quite different purposes.

A favourable situation like that, however, is more the exception than the rule in the evolution of economic thought. More often it happens that the advocated correspondence rules leave (ample) room for disagreement, partly because such rules may be not completely spelled out or may be easily replaced without having to modify the analytical structure of the theory. This is precisely what happened to the great majority of critiques that have been raised over time against the concept(s) of equilibrium as dealt with in neoclassical theories. In this case, indeed, the implied correspondence rules are much less self-evident than in the case of reswitching (because we may, on request, easily exhibit the most disparate kinds of capital goods, whereas in no way can we observe an economy in equilibrium), so that it is not surprising to see that the same kind of criticism, in a different context, ends by proving to be scarcely effective. The methodological lesson is thus that 'internal' criticisms are much less conclusive than they are usually maintained to be, simply because the soundness of a correspondence rule is not a matter of logic alone and greatly changes according to the particular issues at stake.

SOME CONCLUDING REMARKS

As noted at the outset of this paper, the peculiar way in which Joan Robinson (more or less) incidentally ventured into the field of economic methodology undoubtedly makes it difficult to reconstruct a coherent outline of her thought on the matter. Nevertheless, it seems to me that at least the following three points can be safely maintained: (a) she rightly dismisses the applicability of Popperian falsificationism to economics, but for the incorrect reason of the supposed differences between economics and natural (or experimental) sciences; (b) in spite of the 'half recantation' of her early view on method, she remained basically within the British tradition of empirical apriorism; and, consequently, (c) she places too much hope in the supposed effectiveness of 'logical' criticism.

The decidedly pessimistic tone of her later views on economic method (and theory, for that matter) might have been somewhat mitigated if she had acknowledged that the relevant difference between social and natural sciences lies not so much in the different possibility of having access to laboratory experiments, as in the way the problems to be tackled are chosen within each group of disciplines. The point was raised as early as in Kuhn (1962), one of the very few texts on the history or philosophy of science that Joan Robinson explicitly quotes in her writings. Kuhn notes that natural scientists may often choose their research subjects according to their own judgement on the feasibility of the involved research activity, whereas social scientists are often obliged to deal with problems (whether or not they are sufficiently equipped to do so) whose importance depends on practical reasons at the individual or social level.

Given this situation, it would be surprising if the results achieved in the social sciences were as impressive as those achieved by the natural sciences (whose achievements, in spite of the possibility of taking advantage of the laboratory, are much less impressive than usual just when natural scientists are required to solve problems because of their practical or social urgency), and the task for the social sciences becomes even more difficult when faced with the formidable questions that Joan Robinson was not afraid of forcefully raising. When the issues at stake relate to the subtle nature of capitalism, it would be really surprising if we could attain easy and generally agreed solutions. In any case, a more optimistic attitude would be required: apart from methodological puzzles (which may not ever be solved), there must be a way of reasonably arguing about these kinds of problem. They are too important and pressing to allow us to wait, before tackling them, until we know exactly how 'scientific' the advanced solutions might be.

All this does not mean, however, that Joan Robinson's late pessimism was fully unjustified. If I had to suggest a possible explanation, I should say that it can be justified by the Cartesianism that has been deeply embedded in economics since its early stages. This association is to some extent unavoidable because of the peculiar characteristics of the subject matter of economics and is not devoid of some merits, for, as Klant acutely points out:

> The [economic] theory consists of two parts. The evident theory is produced by contemplating the world and determines the construction of the whole. The contingent theory, which is interwoven with it and fills the space structured by clear ideas, requires empirical research.... Those philosophers who saw society as a machine but fell short of the mark in systematic observation and experimentation in comparison to physicists, could easily, despite their Newtonian intentions, go in the direction of Descartes. The more clearly the predictive power of their theories fell short, the greater their need for evident theory.
>
> (Klant 1984: 52)

Our discipline has followed a very similar route since then. But all this has not been without costs for a social science such as economics, for within Cartesian epistemology there is no room for history – history to which Joan Robinson attributed more and more importance in the last period of her intellectual itinerary. Indeed, if we look for generally valid principles, we cannot pay much attention to a history that, alas, does not suitably replicate itself, and we must abstract from differences in time and space.[14] The only time for which there is place in such a context, as Joan Robinson acutely perceived, is logical time, not the historical time in which we actually live.

Let me conclude by saying that Joan Robinson's struggle with methodological difficulties may be depicted as common sense in the service of (ethically) good reason(s). Perhaps common sense is not compelling enough to convince the majority in the economics profession: what is left to those who are willing to take up her intellectual heritage is to try to go beyond her brave but incomplete suggestions.

NOTES

1 Without bearing any responsibility, Cristina Marcuzzo deserves my warmest thanks for her comments and suggestions on an earlier draft of this paper. A grateful acknowledgement is also due to the Italian Ministry of University and Scientific Research (MURST) for financial support.

2 The exact references are, respectively, Robinson (1932, 1962 and 1979a: 110–19).

3 For an impressive list of quotations from Joan Robinson's writings on her own value judgements, see Jensen (1991).

4 Compare the preface to the second edition of Robinson (1933) and Robinson (1978: ix–xi). See also the perceptive reconstruction of that 'wrong turning' made by Loasby (1991).

5 On this point see also Robinson (1965: 156, 1979b: 2–3 and 1979a: 116).

6 Note, for example, that in the *General Index* of her *Collected Economic Papers* (Robinson 1980) there is no entry on 'method' whereas we may find careful references under 'Ideology (and logic)' (1980: 22), 'Religion (and science distinguished)' (1980: 47), and 'Theology' (1980: 55).

7 One might expect to find here at least a mention of the tradition of logical empiricism. However, for a number of reasons that we cannot discuss here (see Salanti 1987), in economics such a tradition has never achieved a complete manifestation.

8 Popperian falsificationism (even in its Lakatosian version) has been found to be unsuitable for economics, and perhaps for any scientific discipline as is actually practised (see, for instance, the various essays in de Marchi 1988a and in de Marchi and Blaug 1991), while Friedman's instrumentalism has never convinced either empiricists of other traditions or the Austrians of any persuasion (see Hirsch and de Marchi 1990). To approve von Mises' radical apriorism one should accept the Kantian notion of synthetic *a priori* judgements (i.e. propositions about reality that are necessarily true but cannot be proved by empirical experience), a category of thought nowadays quite out of fashion. Finally, Debreu's formalism cannot avoid the unpalatable conclusion, already known at the beginning of this century – see the first chapter ('Definition of Pure Mathematics') in Russell (1903) – that from pure mathematics nothing can be deduced about what actually exists. In the past fifteen years the literature on these issues has reached a very impressive size: for an idea of the present state of the debate see the various essays in Backhouse (1994).

9 The usual phrase is 'realism of assumptions'. However, as pointed out by Maki (1989), there are good reasons for abandoning the bad habit of confusing an ontological perspective (realism) with a property of representations (realisticness).

10 'Robbins was Professor of Economics, Analytical and Descriptive, and his seminar was the focus of theoretical endeavour within the School [LSE]. The style of the seminar was the then common one of analytical dissection. Theory was regarded as "a method of classifying the universe of possible cases" (H. G. Johnson 1951: 826; cf. Lange 1944). Models were examined for the realism of their assumptions and for internal consistency. Results might be tested for robustness (to assumption change) but were rarely subjected to quantification using actual numbers.' To the second-last sentence the following footnote is appended: 'Cf. Harry Johnson's remark about Cambridge in the 1950s: "the examination of the realism or unrealism of analytical assumptions as a test of the validity of a theory . . . provided a basic technique of British theoretical discourse in the 1930s and on well into the 1950s (1978: 158)"' (de Marchi 1988b: 143).

11 Note that the real bone of contention among all the different methodological perspectives mentioned in the previous section is about the right way of testing the factual truth of theories, while the stipulation that logical consistency must hold is virtually commonplace. It follows that the problem of specifying the proper domain of internal criticism is common to all of them.

12 To give a rigorous definition of 'correspondence rule' after the rebuttal of the theoretical/observational dichotomy (see Quine 1953 and Putnam 1962), and consequently of the traditional notion of 'partial interpretation' of theoretical terms (Suppe 1971), is far from easy: for an introductory discussion let me refer to Salanti (1989). Anyway, we may informally define correspondence rules as the set of propositions whose function is to establish a link between the bare logical or mathematical structure of a theoretical model and testable (or, at least, understandable with reference to a possible world) propositions derived from it. Note that, as Nooteboon (1986: 204) aptly remarks, correspondence rules 'are not specified as an integral part of a theory, and their role is to some extent taken over by the standard applications, which indicate the rules implicitly, by illustrating their use. Often, the specification of the rules is sparse or even nonexistent'.

13 I have chosen this passage both because of its clarity and because it has been repeatedly quoted in the subsequent literature: compare, for instance, Harris (1978: 136), Cohen (1984: 623) and Kurz (1985: 20). The same point, however, is repeated eight years after in 'The Unimportance of Reswitching', in the following (even more straightforward) way: 'How is it possible to have a controversy over a purely logical point? When various theorists each set up their assumptions clearly, after eliminating errors, they can agree about what conclusions follow from what assumptions' (Robinson 1979c: 76).

14 For a comprehensive analysis of the Cartesian legacy in the method of economics, see Mini (1974). Apart from some idiosyncratic judgements on the various 'schools' in the history of economic thought, this (somewhat unduly neglected) book has the merit of having lucidly pointed out, well before the recent upsurge of interest in economic methodology, one of the main issues at stake.

REFERENCES

Backhouse, R. E., ed. (1994) *New Directions in Economic Methodology.* London: Routledge.

Cohen, A. J. (1984) The Methodological Resolution of the Cambridge Controversies, *Journal of Post Keynesian Economics*, 5: 614–29.

Friedman, M. (1953) The Methodology of Positive Economics. In *Essays in Positive Economics*. Chicago: University of Chicago Press, 3–43.

Gram, H. and Walsh, V. (1983) Joan Robinson's Economics in Retrospect, *Journal of Economic Literature*, 21: 518–50.

Harcourt, G. C. (1990) Joan Robinson's Early View on Method, *History of Political Economy*, 22: 411–27.

Harris, D. J. (1978) *Capital Accumulation and Income Distribution*. London: Routledge & Kegan Paul.

Hausman, D. (1992) *The Inexact and Separate Science of Economics*. Cambridge: Cambridge University Press.

Hirsch, A. and de Marchi, N. (1990) *Milton Friedman. Economics in Theory and Practice*. Ann Arbor: University of Michigan Press.

Jensen, H. E. (1991) The Role of Values in the Economics of Joan Robinson. In I. H. Rima, ed., *The Joan Robinson Legacy*. Armont, NY: M. E. Sharpe, 20–33.

Johnson, E. S. and H. G. Johnson (1978) *The Shadow of Keynes*. Oxford: Blackwell.

Johnson, H. G. (1951) The Taxonomy Approach to Economic Policy, *Economic Journal*, 61: 812–32.

Klant, J. J. (1984) *The Rules of the Game. The Logical Structure of Economic Theories*. Cambridge: Cambridge University Press.

——— (1994) The Core of Economic Methodology. In *The Nature of Economic Thought. Essays in Economic Methodology*. Aldershot: Elgar; 63–72.

Kuhn, T. S. (1962) *The Structure of Scientific Revolutions*. Chicago: University of Chicago Press.

Kurz, H. (1985) Sraffa's Contribution to the Debate on Capital Theory, *Contributions to Political Economy*, 4: 3–24.

Lange, O. (1944) *Price Flexibility and Employment, Cowles Commission*, Monograph no. 8. Bloomington, Ill.: Principia Press.

Loasby, B. J. (1991) Joan Robinson's 'Wrong Turning'. In I. H. Rima, ed., *The Joan Robinson Legacy*. Armont, NY: M. E. Sharpe, 34–48.

Machlup, F. (1955) The Problem of Verification in Economics, *Southern Economic Journal*, 22: 1–21.

Maki, U. (1989) On the Problem of Realism in Economics, *Ricerche Economiche*, 43: 176–98.

de Marchi, N., ed. (1988a) *The Popperian Legacy in Economics*. Cambridge: Cambridge University Press.

——— (1988b) Popper and the LSE Economists. In N. de Marchi, ed., *The Popperian Legacy in Economics*. Cambridge: Cambridge University Press: 139–66.

de Marchi, N. and Blaug, M., eds (1991) *Appraising Economic Theories. Studies in the Methodology of Research Programs*. Aldershot: Edward Elgar.

Mini, P. V. (1974) *Philosophy and Economics. The Origins and Development of Economic Theory*. Gainesville, Fla.: The University Press of Florida.

Nooteboon, B. (1986) Plausibility in Economics, *Economics and Philosophy*, 2: 197–224.

Popper, K. R. (1959) *The Logic of Scientific Discovery*. London: Hutchison Education; originally published in German in 1934.

Putnam, H. (1962) What Theories Are Not. In E. Nagel, P. Suppes and A. Tarsky, eds, *Logic, Methodology and Philosophy of Science*. Stanford, Cal.: Stanford University Press, 240–51.

Quine, W. V. O. (1953) Two Dogmas of Empiricism. In *From a Logical Point of View. Logico-Philosophical Essays*. Cambridge, Mass.: Harvard University Press, 20–46.

——— (1982) *Methods of Logic*, 4th edn. Cambridge, Mass.: Harvard University Press.

Rima, I. H., ed. (1991) *The Joan Robinson Legacy*. Armonk, NY: M. E. Sharpe.

Robinson, J. (1932) *Economics Is a Serious Subject. The Apologia of an Economist to the Mathematician, the Scientist, and the Plain Man*. Cambridge: Heffer.

——— (1933) *The Economics of Imperfect Competition*. London: Macmillan; 2nd edn, 1969.

——— (1960) *Collected Economic Papers*, vol. II. Oxford: Blackwell.

——— (1962) *Economic Philosophy*. London: Watts & Co.

——— (1965) *Collected Economic Papers*, vol. III. Oxford: Blackwell.

——— (1971) *Economic Heresies*. London: Basic Books.

——— (1973) *Collected Economic Papers*, vol. IV. Oxford: Blackwell.

——— (1975) *Collected Economic Papers*, vol. III, 2nd edn. Oxford: Blackwell.

——— (1978) *Contributions to Modern Economics*. Oxford: Blackwell.

——— (1979a) Thinking about Thinking. In *Collected Economic Papers*, vol. V. Oxford: Blackwell.

——— (1979b) What Are the Questions? In *Collected Economic Papers*, vol. V. Oxford: Blackwell.

——— (1979c) The Unimportance of Reswitching. In *Collected Economic Papers*, vol. V. Oxford: Blackwell.

——— (1980) *Collected Economic Papers. General Index*, edited by M. Milgate and P. Kerr. Oxford: Blackwell.

Russell, B. (1903) *The Principles of Mathematics*. London: Allen & Unwin.

Salanti, A. (1987) Falsificationism and Fallibilism as Epistemic Foundations of Economics: A Critical View, *Kyklos*, 40: 368–92.

——— (1989) 'Internal' Criticisms in Economic Theory: Are They Really Conclusive? *Economic Notes*, 19: 1–15; reprinted in B. Caldwell, ed., *The Philosophy and Methodology of Economics*. Aldershot: Elgar, 1993, vol. III, 445–59.

Suppe, F. (1971) On Partial Interpretation, *Journal of Philosophy*, 68: 57–76.

Turner, M. S. (1989) *Joan Robinson and the Americans*. Armonk, NY: M. E. Sharpe.

25

ARE ECONOMIC THEORIES HISTORICALLY SPECIFIC?

Bertram Schefold

It may seem strange to present a paper on the historical relativity of economic theories in a volume dedicated to the memory of Joan Robinson, since she was known to the world primarily as a progenitor and critic of the theory of contemporary capitalism, not of the economic systems of the past. But, at times, she revealed a different aspect of her intellectual personality:

> For the serious students, I would take the bull by the horns and start from the beginning to discuss various types of economic systems. Every society (except Robinson Crusoe) has to have some rules of the game for organizing production and the distribution of the product. Laissez-faire capitalism is only one of the possible sets of rules, and one in fact which is unplayable in a pure form. It always has to be mixed with some measures of collective control. The Indian scene provides examples of pre-capitalist, capitalist and socialist games being played side by side.
>
> (Robinson 1975b: 4)

As a matter of fact, I can testify that she was glad to get involved in discussions about the different character of the forms of economic life in different historical epochs, even if she never pretended to be an economic historian, and she displayed a keen interest in economic differences connected with different contemporary cultures – she even said, comparing economic developments in Latin American and East Asian countries, 'there is something after all in national character' (Robinson 1975b: 213) – a reluctant admission, given her socialist views.

In what follows, I shall defend the historicist thesis according to which different economic models have to be used to capture the characteristics of different economic formations – if the expression is permitted: different economic theories apply to different economic systems. I shall adduce some evidence that Joan Robinson was inclined to take such a view and I shall use one of her favourite examples but, in accordance with the fact that she did not wish her students to argue from authority, I shall primarily summarize results based on my own research[1] rather than attempting to reconstruct an interpretation of her approach.

HISTORY AND ECONOMIC MODEL-BUILDING

Stages: The character of technology

Polanyi regarded 'the term *economic*' as a

> compound of two meanings.... The first..., the formal, springs from the logical character of the means–ends relationship.... The second, the substantive meaning, points to the elemental fact that human beings... cannot exist for any length of time without a physical environment that sustains them.
>
> (Polanyi 1977: 23)

Polanyi traces the distinction to the second, posthumous edition of Carl Menger's *Grundsätze*. Neoclassical economists, starting from the formal definition alone, have often claimed that economic theory, defined as a science of human action, should be applicable to all forms of economic behaviour encountered in history. For a long time, it was regarded as a problematic consequence of this formalist interpretation of the task of economic science that almost anything could then be interpreted in terms of economic considerations, even a rational use of the means of destruction in war. Today, the opinion prevails that most social activities and interactions are better understood and explained in terms of constrained maximization or rational choice.

The substantivist interpretation of economics also had its difficulties. If economics is concerned with the understanding of material reproduction, the definition is too narrow because it seems to exclude services and too large because no clear separation from other disciplines such as engineering is provided (Godelier 1968). Meanwhile, the Chicago School has largely put aside earlier scruples about the invasion of neighbouring fields. Family life, law and morals are now subjected to formalized economic analysis. The new institutional economics is also concerned with the description of historically specific forms of economic life. Bazaars, the marriage market in different set-ups, even the allocation of time between different activities in societies of hunters and gatherers are analysed in terms of the calculation of rational action. Savings of transaction costs are introduced to explain the emergence of non-market institutions in history as well as in the modern firm (North 1981, Posner 1988: 149–206).

Although economists such as Posner use different variants of their theory to capture peculiar features of different societies, they pride themselves on the claim that they apply essentially the same theory to different circumstances. Not much seems to have remained of the older view according to which economic theories appropriate for different economic stages were thought to be quite different. The subdivisions of history into stages inherited from antiquity (Aristotle 1972: 1256 b 1; Dikaiarch) represent an instance of the substantivist interpretation to the extent that the stages were distinguished according to the means of producing the means of subsistence (hunters, nomads, farmers, etc.). Adam Smith (1961) later added commerce.

The members of the historical school, often writing in a more theoretical vein than is commonly thought, tried to improve on this by distinguishing stages according to some unifying criterion. Hildebrand (1922: 325–57), to take a prominent example, distinguished a barter economy, a money economy and a credit economy, on the basis of the technique of transaction. He knew that stages could not be neatly separated from each other. When he treated barter, using both ancient sources (Homer) and contemporaneous examples of barter in less developed economies, he was aware that credit relationships of a primitive kind are characteristic of commercial exchanges without money. For if there is no immediate coincidence of wants in an act of barter, the obvious solution is to exchange a good against the promise of the delivery of another good. Another mixture of stages occurs in a money economy, when advance payment is made at the beginning of the agricultural year against a promise to deliver part of the harvest at its end. But these early credit relationships that permeate both barter and money economies are not based on the extensive use of the instruments of credit creation such as bills and banking that allow the extension of the sphere of transactions in space and in time, at the expense of requiring controls. Hildebrand was at pains to demonstrate the primitive character of banking in antiquity, especially in Rome, in order to emphasize the key role of credit and finance in modern times by contrast.

Thus, there is a striking parallelism between the functions of different forms of exchange as seen by Hildebrand and North's distinction between 'Personal Exchange' and 'Impersonal Exchange with Third-Party Enforcement' (North 1990: 33–5, 120–5), both at the theoretical level (the simpler forms entail higher transaction costs for each individual transaction, the more complex forms presuppose the creation of costly institutions) and at the level of the historical applications. Hildebrand's theory was not formalized but intuitive, in that he tried to explain what he meant by his three stages as he went along, discussing historical illustrations. Hence the misunderstanding that arises if one takes terms such as a stage of barter too literally – the stage theory then is obviously theoretically pure but trite and historically false – and the other misunderstanding that such enquiries of the historical school were concerned only with facts and devoid of theoretical content.

The historical character of classical models

It seems to be a universal feature of stage theories that they describe an evolution from simple to more complex forms, which then also require more developed theoretical tools for their analysis. Marx and Engels were prominent defenders of the thesis that, by and large, less complex economic categories also apply to earlier stages. The Marxian theory of the forms of value reflects this idea – less so in the first volume of *Das Kapital* than in earlier formulations (Backhaus 1978: 19). A more famous and more striking example is provided by the labour theory of value, which, following Smith, was ascribed by Engels to earlier and simpler forms of social development in his Postscript to the third volume of *Das Kapital*. The ascription is based on a quote from Marx: 'The entire difficulty comes about because commodities are exchanged not simply as *commodities* but as *products of capitals* which participate in relation to their magnitude . . . in the total mass of surplus value' (Marx 1969: 905; my translation) and further: 'The exchange of commodities at their values or approximately at their values requires a *much lower stage* than exchange at prices of production, for which a definite level of capitalist development is required' (Marx 1969: 905; my translation). Marx goes on to defend the idea that it is appropriate to regard the values of commodities not only theoretically but also historically as the antecedent of prices of production. The idea is said to apply to states in which the means of production are owned by the workers, and such states are said to be found both in the old and in the modern world, among both landowning farmers and artisans. Even guilds are included in the consideration because they represent instances of a division of labour where it is difficult to shift the means of production from one line of industry to the other. Engels then generalized these hints and reached the assertion that the labour theory of value was valid – 'to the extent that economic laws are valid at all' (Marx 1969: 909; my translation) – for an entire period of 'simple commodity production', that is, from the beginning of exchange prior to written history down to the fifteenth century.

As is well known, Joan Robinson did not think much of this argument.

> There is no reason to suppose that there was ever a moment when prices were all proportional to values, still less a time when capitalism had been generally established without any change in prices having occurred. This piece of history is even less plausible than Adam Smith's anthropology.
>
> (Robinson 1979: 101)

Why should there be a division of labour among hunters, giving rise to commodity exchange? Are the means of production of artisans not to be advanced? Do guilds not exert monopoly rights that may lead to very significant differences in the remuneration of labour time? Is labour time the relevant measure of effort in traditional societies?

It is easy to knock down and even to ridicule the notion that there has ever been a society of simple commodity production. But this is not the point. One can be convinced of the importance of prices of production, based on the uniform rate of profit in the face of a world with imperfect competition, if a way is found to explain differentials in profit rates as systematic deviations from the tendency towards a uniform rate of profit that would obtain in the absence of these imperfections. Engels, who had still seen the guilds in systematic operation, must have known that there was imperfect competition between them, so that there was something to the idea of using labour values as benchmarks against which the power of guilds to influence usages and to raise prices in specific branches could be measured.

Nevertheless, I tend to agree that the labour theory of value – whatever its importance in the history of economic thought – is not all that helpful. We do not have to dwell on the reasons why it is inadequate as a basis for the explanation of prices of production. As an explanation of pre-capitalist forms of production, it is misleading – among other things – because it suggests that the quantitative measure of labour time has always been the essential determinant of price (a problem to which we shall return). The classical theory of value has been given a new form in the work of Sraffa, and this may also be used to characterize different economic systems.

Cartelier (1976), apparently taking up an idea first expressed by Gilibert (1976), has proposed a modern interpretation of physiocratic theory in order to visualize the physiocratic account of the distribution of the surplus with its associated definition of manufacturing as 'sterile'.[2] In the following formulae,

$$\begin{aligned} (1+R)(a_{11}p_1 + a_{12}p_2) &= p_1 \\ a_{21}p_1 + a_{22}p_2 &= p_2, \end{aligned} \tag{1}$$

the first line describes the production of corn in agriculture, the second manufacturing in the city. The amounts of corn needed for production in the countryside and in the city are a_{11} and a_{21}; a_{12} and a_{22} are the necessary quantities of the manufactured commodities as a mean of production. The corresponding prices are p_1 and p_2. A surplus is produced of both commodities, i.e. we have both $a_{11} + a_{21} < 1$ and $a_{12} + a_{22} < 1$.

The point is the 'rule of distribution': the surplus in monetary form is levied in agriculture and accrues to the owners of the land (the monarch, the church, the feudal lords) so that there is a rate of a surplus product R only in the first process. R is the larger, the smaller the needs of reproduction. These may be reduced by means of technical progress. But it should be noted that the input coefficients do not only contain the means of production that are necessary for technical reasons. They also contain the necessaries of the workers, who on the land are largely dependent peasants while in the city they are free labourers, artisans, unskilled workers, etc. Wages may remain at a subsistence level while the surplus product increases with productivity.

The rule of distribution therefore expresses the curious physiocratic doctrine of the sterility of manufacturing and of the genesis of the surplus product in the countryside. The rule may be justified by invoking the monopoly power of landowners and the competitive character of manufacturing. The formal representation allows land to appear as solely productive without denying that manufacturing also contributes to the existence of a surplus. The labour theory of value does not allow us to capture this structural characteristic of the pre-revolutionary French economy because the model implies that there are obstacles to the mobility of labour while there is trade in commodities. The free labourers in the city have no free access to land while the labourers on the land can produce only under the constraint that they must hand over the surplus to the owner of the land. Oppenheimer called this the 'land barrier' ('*Bodensperre*').

Sraffa's book clarifies the reasons why prices of production cannot be explained in terms of labour values for logical reasons. His approach may also be used to criticize the 'historical' transformation of values into prices. As I have argued earlier (Schefold 1989a: 344–6), the simplest form of capitalist competition is represented by

$$(1 + R)\mathbf{Ap} = \mathbf{p}. \tag{2}$$

where $\mathbf{p}$ is the vector of prices and R the rate of profits.

The coefficients of the input matrix $\mathbf{A}$ again contain the necessaries of the workers; the entire surplus is appropriated by the owners of capital. Nothing is said as yet about the status of labourers – whether they are free, or whether they are serfs or slaves.

This general image of capitalist production is different from that proposed by Marx. He spoke of capitalist production only when production was undertaken by means of free labourers, the proletariat. He was aware that capitalist commerce was much older than this. But his scheme did not allow capitalist production by means of slaves, of which examples are found in antiquity, especially in late antiquity and in Byzantium.

Of course, capital has never flowed freely between all productive activities. In classical Athens, maritime trade was thought to be more profitable than agriculture, partly on account of risk – at any rate, more interest was charged on maritime loans. Formula (1) is a simple formalization of a specific monopoly of landowners. Formula (2) expresses the idea that capitalist competition precedes the formation of a free and mobile workforce, which was in fact only the historical product of the later mercantilist period, as a result of a long process of transition, at the beginning of which there is the commutation of the forced labour of serfs into rents and the migration of landless peasants to the cities. Such formulae are not of much use in a concrete analysis of past economic systems but they help to establish the logical possibility that wage labour may be regarded as the product of capitalism rather than as a presupposition of what one obtains eventually:

$$(1 + r)\mathbf{Ap} + w\mathbf{l} = \mathbf{p}, \tag{3}$$

l is now the labour vector and *w* the wage rate. The description of how wage labour developed its characteristic forms is not susceptible of formal analysis.

Joan Robinson's position

We have thus seen that there is a historical dimension even to the modern formulation of the classical theory. But it would be rash to take the variations of models that we have considered as different theories of different stages. We have only begun to address the problem of classification of different economic systems, of the theory to be formulated for each and of the transitions between them – this last aspect being the most difficult. In the eyes of Joan Robinson, 'the most important point in which the Marxist system of ideas has failed to stand the test of experience is the concept of stages of history which every society must pass through' (Robinson 1975b: 158). Joan Robinson's doubts are mainly concerned with the sequence capitalism–socialism, but many authors – Max Weber perhaps being the most prominent among them – have pondered over the problem of 'capitalism in antiquity' – what does evolution mean if there was such a thing? And it turns out that Marx himself had doubts in this regard.

Let us first continue with the relatively modest task of considering variations of a given theory that help us to understand changing historical constitutions, without as yet attempting to separate systems from each other by means of general criteria. There are several respects in which the 'core' of classical theory (Garegnani 1981) is open to historical, social and institutional consideration. Instead of simply repeating this triad, I want to provide one other example for the historical element by concentrating on one aspect, distribution, in relation to one author, Joan Robinson.

At times, Robinson seemed to affirm the Anglo-Italian theory of distribution as a general truth, but then she would look in different directions.

> It used to be said that income from property is an inducement to accumulation. The rich are useful to society because they save. But nowadays industry does not depend upon saving from individual households. The whole of investment – sometimes even more than the whole – is covered by retentions. This does not mean, of course, that no firm ever goes to the market for funds, but it does mean that by and large, taking them together, the saving provided out of profit margins is sufficient to finance the total outlay on investment. Legally, the firm is saving on behalf of its shareholders but this is legal fiction. The shareholders can realise the capital gains that arise from ploughing profits back into real assets, and when they do so, the same money is being spent twice over. This is the extraordinary economic system that we are living in. It has been evolved by a historical process; no one

thought it out or designed it, and no one has yet been able to give a rational account of it.

(Robinson 1973: 65–6)

This is the Anglo-Italian theory, interpreted explicitly – which is rare in Robinson's writings – as a peculiar characteristic of a peculiar economic system. In a socialist system, the turnover tax has one of the functions ascribed by her to profit margins in the capitalist system:

> Prices of consumption goods exceed the wages bill for producing them in such a way as to provide for all the other expenses of the economy, including investment. The gap between wages and prices is arranged partly by profit within each enterprise, but mainly by means of turnover tax. This turnover tax (given wage rates) has to be higher the smaller the proportion of consumption to total output. Thus the turnover tax fulfils the same function as profit margins in the capitalist economy. The function both of the turnover tax and the profit margins is to prevent the consumption-sector workers from buying the whole of their own product, so that the rest of the workers also can consume.
>
> (Robinson 1975a: 94)

At the time when she wrote this essay (1957), she seemed to believe that socialism was 'going to beat capitalism at its own game, and the reason that it will do so is that it is a far more powerful instrument than capitalism for extracting the investible surplus from an economy' (Robinson 1975a: 98).

She was expecting a long period of coexistence. I believe that economists need some knowledge about systems that are not capitalist in order to understand capitalism. For Joan Robinson this meant mainly studying socialism and conditions in underdeveloped countries. She knew, of course, about the importance of a given real wage for the understanding of capitalism before the middle of the nineteenth century, and sometimes she speculated about conditions when the rate of exploitation is the primary determinant. She proposed a kind of historical model:

> Capitalism insinuates itself into an artisan economy by means of some innovation in organization or technique which enables an employer to raise output per head of workers over that of artisans. While the artisan sector is still predominant, the wage rate that an employer must offer cannot be less than the earnings of an artisan (there is 'a moral and historical element' in the level of wages depending on the 'habits and degree of comfort in which the class of free labourers has been formed'), while the level of prices at which he sells is set by artisan products. The share of gross profits in the value of output is fixed by the ratio of the value of output per man employed to the wage. The rate of profit then depends upon the value of capital per man, which depends upon the technical characteristics of the method of production that is

> being introduced. With this share of profit, the capitalist can now expand his business as fast as he likes, taking the market from the artisans by underselling them and employing their children as workers. His wife's habits of consumption are formed by the amount of profit that he allows her to spend. In this situation, clearly, the rate of exploitation governs the rate of profit, not *vice versa*.
>
> (Robinson 1975b: 178–9)

To me, it is a pity that Joan Robinson was not prepared to admit that there are conditions, to be formulated in abstract form but applying at certain times to actual conditions, such that the rate of interest is a relevant direct determinant of the rate of profit (Pivetti 1991, Schefold 1993c). But even without adding this last ingredient to Robinson's menu of variations of her theory of distribution, it is clear that her approach to economics was not an attempt to formulate one general theory, thought to be capable *a priori* of accommodating different historical circumstances as special cases. Rather, she sought to adapt her theory to different historical situations as she encountered them in real life or in intellectual debates.

DIFFERENT FORMS OF RATIONALITY

The models that we have been considering so far have in common that they describe functional relationships among economic variables that are conditioned by institutions, without explaining the emergence of those institutions, and they represent early economic forms as simpler and less developed than later ones; one might almost say that they portray them as incomplete forms of capitalism. It must be stressed that this is true also of many more sociologically oriented interpretations of economic history, which speak of a rationality that has not yet fully developed as long as the motives of profit and utility maximization are not clearly perceptible. Joan Robinson did not usually venture into the difficult territory of a description of earlier forms of economic organization in positive terms. Her book *Freedom and Necessity* (1970) speaks of 'The Origin of Society', invoking the evolutionary theory of biological behaviour, and interesting use is made of anthropological material in her second chapter on 'Isolated Economies', where she touches on the opposition between gift exchange and commodity exchange, status as a basis for distribution, and other such matters. Only in the chapter 'Land and Labour' does she deal with a model of feudal society, which also reappears in the textbook by Robinson and Eatwell (1973). This is essentially a critique of Domar's contention that feudalism could be explained in neoclassical terms. It insists on the existence of a more specific rationality.

Domar had observed that a ruling class that disposes of much land but little labour will attempt to restrict the freedom of workers in order to prevent them from becoming free farmers. The form of the bondage may be thought to be conditioned by historical traditions as well as by technical considerations, serfdom being associated with agriculture and slavery with plantations. Domar's leading example was the so-called second feudalism of Eastern Europe, which had traits of its own and contrasted with medieval conditions because of its export orientation.

Domar thought that the land left to the peasants for their own cultivation and the land of their lord, to be cultivated by forced labour, would be worked upon with equal intensity. He adduced empirical evidence of pre-revolutionary Russia and, as a theoretical argument, the forces of competition to argue that marginal products would tend to get equalized on the land of the lord and on the land of the peasant. By contrast, Joan Robinson sided with those who believe that there is an inner logic to domination such that lords will tend to try to keep most of the land to themselves and give away as little as possible to the peasants, especially when they grow in number, so that the intensity of labour will be higher on the land of the serfs than on manorial land. The labour–land relation is lower on the land of the lord because it is difficult to enforce discipline where the effort cannot be controlled through wages; there is also the extra-economic argument that lords like to keep land to themselves as forests and hunting grounds. Eighteenth-century Cameralists in Germany deplored the inefficiency of working according to feudal obligations and favoured land-lease and rent-payments (Schefold 1993c). One might also object to Domar that there was little economic competition among feudal lords in medieval times, not despite but because there was much rivalry between them as warriors.

The functioning of the economic system can thus not always be understood without taking into account a specific political logic. In his *The Economics of Feudalism*, Trout Rader (1971) made a grand attempt to model pre-capitalist systems in terms of general equilibrium economics. His model of feudalism is essentially driven by the goal-orientation of the lords, who wish to maximize their consumption of the products of the artisans of the cities, which they obtain in exchange for the agricultural surplus. The rural population grows while mortality is higher in the cities. If the lords leave a higher share to their peasants, they prevent them from migrating to the cities, so that production in the cities is reduced. If they extract a higher surplus, more peasants will migrate and the lords obtain more luxury products but they lose their labour force. There is therefore a share of the agricultural product that is optimal from the point of view of the landlords in that it allows them to maximize their utility from luxury consumption. Rader tries to show that this equilibrium can be approached in cycles even if the lords do not have perfect foresight.

The construction seems far-fetched and its central idea clearly refers to later stages of feudalism rather than to its classical form. But it is a brilliant illustration of how even the neoclassical apparatus of thought leads to different results if it is applied to take account of different constitutions (here, relationships of power), 'natural' characteristics (the distribution of population between town and countryside with a specific dynamic) and institutions (serfdom).

ECONOMIC STYLES

What are our theoretical concepts for subdividing economic history? The Marxian separation of a mode of production of antiquity, of feudalism and of capitalism corresponds to the most conventional historical distinction between antiquity, the Middle Ages and modernity. The parallelism did not stand up to more detailed investigations, e.g. regarding the economic transformations following upon the decline of Rome – not even in Marx's own writings, which do not generally sustain a generalization of a mode of production based on slavery to the entire development from classical Greece to the fall of the Western empire. The older and the younger historical school down to Schmoller hesitated to associate economic stages and cultural epochs. Schmoller actually polemicized against attempts to associate the characterizations of cultural periods with phases of economic development, such as that of the historian Lamprecht (Schefold 1989b).

But the theories of stages of the historical school, each based on a single criterion to distinguish one stage from another, are today regarded as crude. With his concept of ideal type, Weber abandoned the pretension of constructing a stage or a mode of production to which reality would correspond like any given rose to the definition of roses in the classification of the botanist. The ideal type is a mental construction with which reality is compared only in order to emphasize some significant aspect. 'Solche Begriffe sind Gebilde, in welchen wir Zusammenhänge unter Verwendung der Kategorie der objektiven Möglichkeit konstruieren, die unsere, an der Wirklichkeit orientierte und geschulte Phantasie als adäquat beurteilt' (Weber 1988: 194) – 'such concepts are formations in which we construct interdependencies using the category of objective possibility which our imagination regards as adequate, being educated and oriented by reality' (my translation; see also Eisermann 1993: 88). For cultural phenomena and their meaning, the ideal type seems to be somewhat similar to what models are for economic interdependencies and their functioning. And just as a number of more or less connected models may be used to shed light on the working of an economy in a given period, different related ideal types are used by Weber to describe a complex phenomenon with its specific rationality such as what he called the 'political capitalism' of imperial Rome.

Weber accepted evolution, but he was fully aware of the ambiguity of progress, in particular of the process of rationalization. Marx had believed that the development of the forces of production was responsible for the impossibility of containing growing contradictions within a given mode so that a transformation eventually had to take place, the leading example, of course, being that of the growth of capitalist production within the feudal mode, which rendered the old relations of production obsolete. Don Quixote was his illustration of the fate of those who attempted to preserve old forms in a new framework. Technological determinism is not confined to the Marxian tradition:

> Few inventions have been so simple as the stirrup, but few have had so catalytic an influence on history. . . . Inevitably this nobility [chivalry] developed cultural forms and patterns of thought and emotion in harmony with its style of mounted shock combat.
>
> (White 1981: 38)

Schmoller (1989) shared the belief, so typical of his time, in a parallel progress of man in regard to both the growth of his technical abilities and the improvement of his moral faculties. Nietzsche's scepticism in this regard began to be widely shared only after World War I (Nörr, Schefold and Tenbruck 1994). Weber's objectivity obliged him to clarify the causes of the emergence of capitalist rationality while recognizing other forms of rationality as valid in their own right. The challenge now was to associate levels of technological evolution, the economic and social constitution and forms of rationality without falling into the traps of a one-sided determinism or of the idea of a general and all-encompassing progress. As an example, let us consider Weber's analysis of the 'political capitalism' of imperial Rome.

As far as antiquity is concerned, Weber saw a kind of capitalism because there was a free disposition of the means of production in the market: slaves and land were bought and sold. On the other hand, he observed limits to the division of labour in the workshops, he saw cities as centres more of consumption than of production, and he emphasized the economic importance of tributes and rents rather than profits. Because slaves were capital, much capital was required per unit of labour time, there was little flexibility in its use, its cost was difficult to ascribe to the product, and slavery became an obstacle to the creation of material incentives. Moreover, Weber interpreted many forms of acquisition as comparatively irrational processes, including tax farming, usury and the selling of offices. Thus, he envisaged a special form of accumulation, which was fostered by the formation of empires, and a special interaction between the form of the state and the economy (Schefold 1992b). The legal forms of enterprises were particularly significant to him and, in the absence of any analogue to modern company law, he carefully analysed the relationships between masters and slaves who were employed to work in semi-independent shops, with capital entrusted to them, but also with their own capital and their own slaves. Here and with regard to clients, personal and political obligations modified the rationality of capitalist acquisition. These relationships, irrational as they may seem, allowed the integration of economy and society in the order of the Roman universe, despite much opposition from individuals and minorities.

The same institutions that appear deficient in comparison with their modern counterparts thus reveal their own political and cultural meaning if they are seen in their own context. Another example, mentioned by Weber but also by others, is provided by the liturgies, the semi-voluntary contributions of rich citizens to religious ceremonies and the war effort in classical Greece. The gifts to the state were not provided in a spirit of pure altruism; the giver could be assured of prestige. One possible analogue is the display of splendour analysed by Smith in his *Theory of Moral Sentiments*, which resulted in a distribution of riches, as if guided by an 'invisible hand' (1976: 184). Two modern analogues seem to be the payment of personal taxes and contracts. Both are misleading, however. Taxes are compulsory and the sanction imposed on the evader is not general contempt but a fine. The contract, once concluded, also represents a strictly binding obligation. Aristotle, by contrast, thought that the association of free citizens was characterized by their readiness to give liberally for the public good, i.e. without formal constraints always being imposed; otherwise, the city would be a forced community.

We thus come back to the question of how cultural factors are to be represented as features and possibly as determinants of economic formations. The theory of economic styles of Spiethoff (1932: 891–924) followed Weber and Sombart in postulating an 'economic spirit', a specific form of rationality that, together with the natural and technical preconditions, the constitution of the society, the constitution of the economy and the dynamic character, was thought to characterize an economic style. This conception broke with a purely materialist determination and also with the liberal hypothesis according to which the dynamics of the economy depend on the economic order alone: if markets are free, growth will follow. To illustrate the point in Keynesian terms: by regarding the dynamics of the economy as a separate characteristic, Spiethoff stressed that the forces of accumulation are not fully determined by legal conditions and technology; room was left for something like 'animal spirits', even if the heir of the historical school used different terms.

ECONOMIC SYSTEMS

In the discussions after World War II, economic styles became unfashionable. Eucken (1990) is the real founder of the theory of the comparison of different economic systems. His concept of system rests on the assumption that the elements of neoclassical theory are sufficient to represent the structure and the functioning of economic systems. One primary datum is the economic order, the legal framework, which defines property rights in particular. Another is the combination of units of decision taking and of institutions: the economy can be centrally administered or it can be coordinated through the market; there are various forms of imperfect competition and different monetary regimes. Just as a molecule is composed of a finite set of atoms, ordered according to the periodical system of elements, a given economic system was thought by Eucken to be composed of functional units (individuals, companies, etc.) that coordinated planned actions through market and command, according to a list of possible combinations.

In this view, the economy was 'embedded' in a cultural environment; the cultural characteristics were not endogenous. The methodology of the analysis of economic systems is inspired by mechanics, while that of the analysis of economic styles is phenomenological. The multitude of modern economic models has rendered impossible the task of representing all conceivable economic systems in terms of a combination of functional elements, taken from a reasonably small set of fundamental elements. But, otherwise, the theory of economic systems is still essentially that described by Eucken.

I believe that economic styles and economic systems are complementary, not mutually exclusive concepts, as I argue at greater length elsewhere (Schefold 1995). On the one hand, some of the more complex forms of motivation can now be modelled, such as gift exchange or the influence of risk aversion on investment, which helps to explain the quasi-stagnant character of many traditional societies. A formal analysis of economic systems is thus able to take cultural modifications of the rationality guiding economic behaviour into account. On the other hand, the somewhat naive concept of an economic spirit has given way to more differentiated accounts of changing mentalities. Style refers to the way in which problems are solved, which compromise is thought to reconcile conflicting goals such as that of efficiency and redistribution. A way of transforming economies is also to promote technological paradigms, such as 'Fordism'. Such paradigms are advocated by political and economic interest groups and may eventually crystallize in programmatic form as new ways or styles to solve economic problems (Dockès 1993).

It should be noted that the intentionality implied by the concept of style is not in contradiction with the basic insight gained by Smith, and emphasized by Hayek, according to which the economic process is in some sense a superior result of actions that are not coordinated *a priori*. A certain compromise between efficiency and redistribution may have been established by tradition in a modern country reinforced by institutions such as social security payments. The intention is to preserve an established social order. Whether the nation will succeed, surrounded by international competitors, or whether it will fall back because it redistributes too little and creates social tension, or because it redistributes too much, discouraging investment, remains to be seen. Intentionality and competition therefore interact. A Smithian example of unintended consequences is the transformation from feudalism to capitalism, with landlords losing prestige because they buy luxury goods instead of entertaining their followers, and with petty traders ('much less ridiculous' – Smith 1961, I: 440) opening up the market. But the unintended consequence is no reason not to represent the long and slow transition as a style in which the mentalities of an increasingly luxury-oriented nobility and of merchants (who are profit-oriented but who all too soon also aspire to the standards of the aristocracy) are complementary. Attitudes cannot diverge indefinitely from norms imposed by circumstances. If an early medieval lord had tried to alter his lifestyle and exchanged the maintenance of his warriors for splendid paintings and other precious amenities, he would not have enjoyed his comfort for long.

Mentalities and other determinants of an economic style are related. The history of economic thought helps us to understand these relationships, as we have seen here, using the examples of Aristotle, mercantilist authors and Adam Smith. The interpretation of one author such as Aristotle can have as much importance for our interpretation of his time as masses of archaeological material, and the same may be said of an author such as Petty: we understand mercantilism and the archives of trading companies because we have at our disposal texts that suggest the essential connections.

In what sense, then, can economic theories be historically specific? Primarily, I believe, by being theories of a specific style or system. Models and ideal types may have been invented to shed light on particular situations but their domain of application is *a priori* indeterminate. The same may be said of theories, but both gain in specificity insofar as one tries to improve one's comprehension of a given reality by combining models and ideal types – by adapting them to the task at hand, by understanding the cultural meaning of economic phenomena and by linking these approaches to form a specific theory.

Of course, it is easier and more common to reverse the proposition: the same theory does not fit all economic forms encountered in history, unless one uses the most abstract concepts. But the challenge considered here is to have theories not only of abstract concepts, such as theories of 'capitalism' in terms of supply and demand, the surplus approach, etc., but as directed to the understanding of a more concrete reality such as Western Europe in the mercantile period, or, more remote and more surprising, the planned economy of Ptolemaic Egypt (Rostovtzeff 1972: 255–422), which has been described as the superimposition of an Oriental theocracy, with much central administration, by Hellenistic rationality. It involved the use of an international language and of a new script. With the country being considered as the household of the king, agricultural labour was surveyed, textile production directed, domestic animals were counted. Alexandria became the port of communication with the Mediterranean 'world' market – a symbiosis resembling that of Red China and Hong Kong a few years ago. The theory then is not a set of deductions derived from a number of given axioms but an articulation of heterogeneous approaches, some using idealized descriptions, others referring to conceptions such as planning and market exchange that can be clarified by means of formal models. The former would be more typical for an understanding of the economy as an economic style, the latter for the analysis of a system.

One could go on to compare economies that have essential elements in common as systems, but differ in style, and others that share style characteristics but exhibit systematic differences. Examples could be discussed but it may suffice to point to the principle in order to indicate in what sense theories may be historically specific after all.

NOTES

1 I should like to thank my collaborators, notably H. Peukert and O. Volckart, in the research project 'Wirtschaftssysteme im historischen Vergleich' (Economic Systems in Historical Perspective), financed by the Fritz Thyssen-Stiftung. The usual caveat applies.

2 Some paragraphs that follow represent a revised version of the last section of my paper 'Value and Price in a Historical Context' (1993a).

REFERENCES

Aristotle (1972) *Politics*, with an English translation by H. Rackham. Cambridge, Mass.: Harvard University Press.

Backhaus, H.-G. (1978) Materialien zur Rekonstruktion der Marxschen Werttheorie 3, *Gesellschaft, Beiträge zur Marxschen Theorie 11*. Frankfurt a.M.: Suhrkamp, 16–117.

Cartelier, J. (1976) *Surproduit et reproduction*. Grenoble: Maspero.

Dockès, P. (1993) *Paradigme socio-technique et théorie de l'innovation*. Lyon: Centre Auguste et Léon Walras, Université de Lyon Lumière II.

Eisermann, G. (1993) *Max Weber und die Nationalökonomie*. Marburg: Metropolis.

Eucken, W. (1990) [1940] *Die Grundlagen der Nationalökonomie*. Düsseldorf: Verlag Wirtschaft und Finanzen.

Garegnani, P. (1981) *Marx e gli economisti classici*. Turin: Einaudi.

Gilibert, G. (1976) *Dispense di analisi economica*. Turin: Giappichelli.

Godelier, M. (1968) *Rationalité et irrationalité en économie*. Paris: Maspero.

Hildebrand, B. (1922) [1864] Natural-, Geld- und Kreditwirtschaft. In idem, *Die Nationalökonomie der Gegenwart und Zukunft und andere ges. Schriften*, edited by H. Gehrig, vol. I. Jena: G. Fischer.

Marx, K. (1969) [1894] *Das Kapital. Kritik der politischen Ökonomie*, vol. III. In *Marx-Engels-Werke*, vol. 25. Berlin: Dietz.

Nörr, K. W., Schefold, B. and Tenbruck, F., eds (1994) *Deutsche Geisteswissenschaften zwischen Kaiserreich und Republik. Zur Entwicklung von Nationalökonomie, Rechtswissenschaft und Sozialwissenschaft im 20. Jahrhundert*. Stuttgart: Steiner.

North, D. C. (1981) *Structure and Change in Economic History*. New York: Norton.

——— (1990) *Institutions, Institutional Change and Economic Performance*. Cambridge: Cambridge University Press.

Pivetti, M. (1991) *An Essay on Money and Distribution*. London: Macmillan.

Polanyi, K. (1977) *The Livelihood of Man*, edited by H. W. Pearson. New York: Academic Press.

Posner, A. (1988) A Theory of Primitive Society, with Special Reference to Law. In G. J. Stigler, ed., *Chicago Studies in Political Economy*. Chicago: University of Chicago Press.

Rader, T. (1971) *The Economics of Feudalism*. New York: Gordon & Breach.
Robinson, J. (1970) *Freedom and Necessity. An Introduction to the Study of Society*. London: Allen & Unwin.
——— (1973) *Collected Economic Papers*, vol. IV. Oxford: Blackwell.
——— (1975a) *Collected Economic Papers*, vol. II, 2nd edn. Oxford: Blackwell; 1st edn 1960.
——— (1975b) *Collected Economic Papers*, vol. III, 2nd edn. Oxford: Blackwell; 1st edn 1965.
——— (1979) *Collected Economic Papers*, vol. V. Oxford: Blackwell.
Robinson, J. and Eatwell, J. (1973) *An Introduction to Modern Economics*, Maidenhead: McGraw Hill.
Rostovtzeff, M. (1972) [1941] *The Social and Economic History of the Hellenistic World*, vol. I. Oxford: Clarendon.
Schefold, B. (1989a) *Mr. Sraffa on Joint Production and Other Essays*. London: Unwin Hyman.
——— (1989b) Normative Integration der Einzeldisziplinen in gesellschaftswissenschaftlichen Fragestellungen. In M. Bock, H. Homann and P. Schiera, eds, *Gustav Schmoller oggi/Gustav Schmoller heute*. Bologna: Il Mulino and Berlin: Duncker & Humblot, 251–69.
——— (1992b) Antiquity and Capitalism: Max Weber and the Sociological Foundations of Roman Civilization (J. R. Love), *Manchester School of Economic and Social Studies*, 60: 208–10.
——— (1993a) Value and Price in a Historical Context. Paper presented to the annual meeting of the Institute for Economic Research, Hanshin University, Seoul, Korea (to be published in Korea).
——— (1993c) Glückseligkeit und Wirtschaftspolitik: Zu Justis 'Grundsätzen der Policey-Wissenschaft'. Einleitung zur Neuausgabe von Justis Werk. Kommentarband ('Vademecum') zur Faksimileausgabe des Werkes in der Reihe *Klassiker der Nationalökonomie*. Düsseldorf: Verlag Wirtschaft und Finanzen, 5–27.
——— (1995) Theoretical Approaches to a Comparison of Economic Systems from a Historical Perspective. In P. Koslowski, ed., *The Theory of Ethical Economy in the Historical School*. Berlin: Springer.
Schmoller, G. (1989) [1900–4] Grundriß der Nationalökonomie. In *Klassiker der Nationalökonomie*. Düsseldorf: Verlag Wirtschaft und Finanzen.
Smith, A. (1961) [1776] *The Wealth of Nations*, vols I and II. London: Methuen.
——— (1976) [1759] *The Theory of Moral Sentiments*. Oxford: Clarendon.
Spiethoff, A. (1932) Die allgemeine Volkswirtschaftslehre als geschichtliche Theorie. Die Wirtschaftsstile. In *Schmollers Jahrbuch 1932* (= Festschrift für Werner Sombart).
Weber, M. (1988) Die 'Objektivität' sozialwissenschaftlicher und sozialpolitischer Erkenntnis. In J. Winckelmann, ed., *Gesammelte Aufsätze zur Wissenschaftslehre*. Tübingen: J. C. B. Mohr.
White, L. (1981) [1962] *Medieval Technology and Social Change*. Oxford: University Press.

26

SOME REFLECTIONS ON JOAN ROBINSON'S CHANGES OF MIND AND THEIR RELATIONSHIP TO POST-KEYNESIANISM AND THE ECONOMICS PROFESSION[1]

G. C. Harcourt

Until her very last years, I think it is true to say that Joan Robinson's bark was often worse than her bite (both measured high on their appropriate Richter scales), that her *analysis* was not *that* far removed from the mainstream mould. It is true that Keynes in the 1930s wondered why she always had to be so fierce in debate and she (sort of) apologized for being so (she passionately believed in seeking truth); and Hayek reproached her for assuming that, if people did not agree with her, they must be of extremely low intelligence, with their morals probably not the best either, so that argument back and forward with her was often difficult, to say the least. Indeed, I can remember when Joan 'debated' with Bob Solow before the undergraduates in Cambridge after Solow's 1963 Marshall Lectures (on a mythical creature called 'Joan' and another called 'Nicky') and they hardly ever joined in argument. She would tell him that he had been knocked over on this point (often before he had had time to reply) and that they would now move on to the next point. But when we look at the *substance* of her analysis as she moved towards her final stance, which put her well and truly within the post-Keynesian rubric – of course it does for, despite an unhealthy American post-Keynesian attempt at hegemony to the contrary, Joan *was* an original pioneer – we find her Marshallian, even Pigovian, background tending to break through.

In order to argue for this point of view – and I do not want to push it too far, for often she would be demonstrating to the 'enemy' how they should have done their own dirty work – I shall concentrate on some key watersheds in her life's work, so as to show the nature of and the reasons for the movements towards her final stance.

To do this, it might be helpful if I briefly refer to the strands of post-Keynesianism that Omar Hamouda and I identified in our 1988 survey article, 'Post Keynesianism: from criticism to coherence?'. As we said in the survey, the umbrella term, post-Keynesian[2] is useful for gathering in groups of economists who, historically, have interacted with one another's work (not always uncritically or positively), as well as being hostile to mainstream economics, both neoclassical microeconomics and bastard Keynesianism. In one sense, therefore, they are under this same umbrella for *historical* as much as for analytical, method of approach or purely logical reasons.

The attempted classification was based, first, on the 'vision' of the economies and societies they predominantly analysed and, secondly, on their principal method or methods of analysing them. As some of the people concerned changed their views over their lives (not least, Joan Robinson), their later views were taken as the evidence for their particular classification – a definite limitation when, as in Joan's case, they made radical changes over their lifetimes. In the survey article we identified the American post-Keynesians, the neo-Ricardians and the Kaleckians/Robinsonians as the three main strands. In addition, we argued that Nicholas Kaldor, Richard Goodwin and Luigi Pasinetti could not be fitted into any one category, because they had (at least some of) the characteristics of two or even all strands, and that Wynne Godley and his colleagues were unique rather than easily classifiable. We should also have included a role for institutionalists and institutions, especially as John Kenneth Galbraith is the patron saint of the *Journal of Post-Keynesian Economics* and Joan Robinson herself always put much emphasis on asking what were 'the rules of the game' of the economy being analysed, what were its institutions and how did they arise.

Let me say emphatically at this stage, because Bruce McFarlane has recently taken me to task for giving the, quite unintended, impression (in the Introduction to Baranzini and Harcourt 1993: 38, n2) that Michal Kalecki was a minor post-Robinsonian, that I am well aware that though there was mutual and long-sustained interaction between these two great friends, causation did, most of the time, run more *from* Kalecki *to* Joan Robinson than the other way around. Increasingly, I believe, her own mode of thought and analysis were moulded by her absorption of Kalecki's approach, to the propagation of which she lent her very considerable powers of exposition. I think this is as true of the main propositions of *The Accumulation of Capital* (1956) and the papers that run up to and follow it, as it is of her superb account of Kalecki on capitalism in the 1977 *Oxford Bulletin* Memorial Issue for Kalecki.

It is ironic that the economists most attacked by Joan Robinson – Hahn, Samuelson, Solow, Stiglitz, for example – were sympathetic to her points on methodology: witness the rise of path-dependent equilibrium models over the past ten years or so. (Joan Robinson – and Kaldor, of course – was inclined in the end to argue that there may not even be equilibria out there to be found.) But though their views on methodology may have overlapped – and Joan never accepted this, probably correctly, if Samuelson's way of putting of the case is at all representative[3] – their 'visions' did only in regard to Keynes, and even he – or his conjectures – were often wrongly included in a framework that was Walrasian/Fisherian, not classical *cum* Marxist. (Furthermore, we must be careful, even here, because Hahn, for example, regards general equilibrium not as *descriptive* theory but as a reference point for truth.) By contrast, though Joan Robinson and the neo-Ricardians have largely overlapping 'visions' – Kalecki is not as acceptable to the neo-Ricardians as Keynes is – they were at loggerheads on method. Joan thought that their methods were at one with her view of neoclassical methods, of which she strongly disapproved; while they argued that she had thrown in her lot with the enemy as far as method is concerned, abandoning the one method – long-period positions – that allows general theoretical propositions to be derived. Thus, to them, it is not surprising that she became nihilistic at the end of her life, arguing that she had been doing theory for fifty years and that it had come to pieces in her hands; for if you did not do long-period analysis, you were left with the ephemera of the short period about which no worthwhile generalizations could be made. The American post-Keynesians overlapped with Joan Robinson's views as far as emphasizing the need to theorize about what reasonable people do in uncertain environments, and what are the systemic consequences of this, but, with the exception of Jan Kregel and the partial exception of Hyman Minsky, the agents in their stories are far too close to those of the neoclassical 'enemy' (even though they come from the work of Marshall and Keynes in particular) and too far away from the class society of the classicals and the Marxists, in which conflict is ever present and profit-making and accumulation are a way of life for the principal decision-makers. *Analytically*, in the neoclassical schema, life-time utility-maximizing individuals drive the system along, and all the institutions of society – markets, stock exchanges, firms, for example – are but agencies, the better to allow the former to do their thing.

Looking back in retrospect, Joan Robinson herself saw her early work, e.g. *The Economics of Imperfect Competition* (1933) and the papers surrounding it, as criticizing from within the Marshallian/Pigovian theory of the firm and industry, using their static method. This she was to call 'a shameless fudge' – the idea that business people could find by trial and error the equilibrium profit-maximizing, cost-minimizing prices on their downward-sloping demand curves without affecting *endogenously* the position of the curves themselves in the process. Here is a very succinct statement by her, one of many, this one dating from 1953:

> In my opinion, the greatest weakness of the *Economics of Imperfect Competition* is one which it shares with the class of economic theory to

> which it belongs – the failure to deal with time. It is only in a metaphorical sense that price, rate of output, wage rate or what not can move in the plane depicted in a price-quantity diagram. Any movement must take place through time, and the position at any moment of time depends upon what it has been in the past. The point is not merely that any adjustment takes a certain time to complete and that (as has always been admitted) events may occur meanwhile which alter the position, so that the equilibrium towards which the system is said to be *tending* itself moves before it can be reached. The point is that the very process of moving has an effect upon the destination of the movement, so that there is no such thing as a position of long-run equilibrium which exists independently of the course which the economy is following at a particular date.
>
> (Robinson 1960a: 234)

This part of her early work concerned value and distribution. As she joined in the arguments of the 'Circus', 'spied' (with others) on Keynes' lectures, and wrote her progress reports on what was emerging in the discussions and lectures following the publication of Keynes' *A Treatise on Money* (1930), she wrote in 1933 that Keynes was developing, without realizing it, a 'long-period analysis of output' (1951: 56).

Putting it this way was a hangover from the *Treatise on Money* in which full stock-flow equilibrium occurs when profits are at their *long-period* normal level, as also are wages, and saving is equal to investment on the *Treatise on Money* definitions, but the real and money dichotomy inherited from Marshall was beginning to break down. There is a remnant of all this left in *Introduction to the Theory of Employment* (1937) where in the chapter on the rate of interest, especially in the section on the rate of interest as the regulator of the economic system, she argues that it 'contains an important element of truth … Within very broad limits the system does regulate itself. Very severe unemployment does, slowly and imperfectly, bring about its own cure' (1937: 83–4). There then follows a simple Keynesian argument of the impact of unemployment (and the reverse case, high employment), through the price level and activity, on the demand for money and the rate of interest, and of its feedback effects on aggregate demand. She concludes:

> For the discussion of problems involving broad changes over the course of generations, in population, the rate of technical progress or the general social forces influencing thriftiness, it is possible to regard fluctuations in employment as a secondary consideration, and to conduct the discussion in terms of a self-regulating system.
>
> (1937: 84)

But that Keynes' *General Theory* (1936) itself was, for the most part, set in a short-period context was acknowledged by Joan when she tried out his system in a long-period setting – very much economics for the economists but nevertheless she was able to show that some of his most important rcsults, e.g. the paradox of thrift, went through (see Robinson 1947). Though Joan Robinson had taken on board with enthusiasm the revolutionary theory of output and employment as a whole (and the general price level), she was still prepared to use a neoclassical theory of distribution, marginal products and all that. The elasticity of substitution was all the rage at that time with many of the contributors to the pages of the youthful *Review of Economic Studies*. (This, incidentally, throws doubt on her retrospective claim that one of the principal explicit aims of *The Economics of Imperfect Competition* was to knock over the marginal productivity theory of distribution, 'the doctrine that wages are determined by the marginal productivity of labour' – Robinson 1973a: x.)

She was also fending off, along with Keynes and Kahn, Piero Sraffa's criticisms of neoclassical capital theory – witness Piero Sraffa's letter of October 1936 to Joan, to which I have often referred (e.g. Harcourt 1990: 49), in which he suggests, in effect, that she ask her gardener what a quantity of capital is, and other evidence in Keynes' *Collected Writings*, that Keynes, Joan and Kahn were trying to keep at a distance Sraffa's 1925 and 1926 critique of the theory of the firm and industry, and of partial equilibrium analysis generally, and also Sraffa's emerging/emerged views on value and distribution theory, which he was discussing with, at least, Keynes. Keynes, Kahn and Joan regarded all these as side issues when considered alongside producing a clear and persuasive account of the theory of effective demand. (There is some evidence that Keynes did go deeply into capital theory in the early 1930s following Hayek's criticism that one of the weaknesses of his system in the *Treatise on Money* was its lack of a coherent understanding of capital-theoretic puzzles. It seems reasonable to suppose that Keynes would have talked to Sraffa about this, for Sraffa was clearly aware of these puzzles when he wrote, at Keynes' request, his critique of Hayek's *Prices and Production* 1931 – Sraffa 1932.)

Now a sea change occurs in Joan Robinson's thought as Karl Marx comes over the horizon, first (and at second hand), when she reviewed (1936) Strachey's *The Nature of Capitalist Crisis* (1935) and, then, with the beginning of her friendship with Michal Kalecki. This led to the making of her *Essay on Marxian Economics* (1966). This was subject to a critical review article by Gerald Shove (1944), not so much for either her understanding or exposition of Marx's views, as for her lack of understanding, in his opinion, of neoclassical economics – read, mostly, Marshall. There is also Keynes' evaluation of Marx, as a result of Keynes reading Joan's *Essay*, together with both Keynes and Joan reaffirming the short-period structure of the system in *The General Theory* and their sympathy with the classical political economists' practice of measuring key concepts in terms of labour time. (Keynes was more sympathetic to the latter procedure than was Joan Robinson, who always had a blind spot about what the labour theory of value [LTV] really entailed. This is as evident in her long preface to the second edition – see 1966: vi–xi – written in 1965, twenty-five years on, as it was in the first edition of the *Essay*. Basically, she insisted on seeing the LTV as a theory of relative prices rather than as a portmanteau term for Marx's explanation of the origin of profits in capitalism, an explanation that entailed, as a necessary corollary, an analysis of the deviations of the prices of production around their underlying labour values.)

The relevant passages from Keynes' letter of 29 August 1942 to 'Mrs Austin Robinson' (who was, as well, 'My Dear Joan') are:

> I found it most fascinating, – as well written as anything you have done. This is in spite of the fact that there is something intrinsically boring in an attempt to make sense of what is in fact not sense. However, you have got round it by making no undue attempt in this direction. I hope you will have done something to give the quietus to these discussions by doing Marx that justice he deserves. But I expect that the faithful will regard your attempt, such as it is, to make sense of him rather irreverent.
>
> I am left with the feeling, which I had before on less evidence, that he had a penetrating and original flair but was a very poor thinker indeed, – and his failure to publish the later volumes probably meant that he was not unaware of this himself.
>
> Your footnote about me on page 23 [I have not been able to find the footnote but the issue being discussed is clear – GCH]: – I do not plead guilty here. Certainly I never intended to suggest that the wage unit is a stable measure of real output for purposes of comparison between periods widely different in other respects. At the top of page 214, . . . I said expressly that I am thinking of the unit of labour as 'operating in a given environment of technique, natural resources, capital equipment and effective demand'. How could I have protected myself more completely and more wordily from your accusation? I never connect the wage unit with real output, and merely remark that, subject to the above assumption as to the given environment, it is 'the sole physical unit which we require in our economic system apart from units of money and time'.
>
> Yours ever,
> JMK

In the *Essay on Marxian Economics*, after discussing Marx's definitions and the LTV, Joan went systematically through the 'big' issues in economic doctrine – long-period employment, falling rate of profits, for example – trying to set out and then contrast Marx's answers with those of the orthodox ('academic') economists. This way of proceeding was increasingly to characterize her mode of writing for the rest of her life. It led, as I have often pointed out, to some grievous misunderstandings – that she was in fact a closet neoclassical in her analysis when what she was trying to do in fact was to give the orthodox answers to some of the questions that the orthodox had posed. This is true, for example, of many of the papers that cluster around the publication of *The Accumulation of Capital* (1956). Nevertheless, she did try in a number of places, including *The Accumulation of Capital*, to integrate the orthodox analysis of the choice of technique, emanating more from Wicksell than from Marshall, into her own positive analysis. She warned us that the difficulty of the analysis exceeded the importance of the issues in the whole scheme she had in mind – but it was there. Ultimately, of course, she was to reject it, even as a minor part of the analysis. She argued that the traditional distinction between the movement along a production function in a given state of knowledge and the movement of the function itself because of the influence of technical progress was to mis-specify the investment process both at the level of the individual firm and industry and for the economy as whole. In one of her many discussions of this point, she says: 'To discuss the choice of technique, we must look, not at total stock of capital as a point on a pseudo-production function, but at the investment plans which are being made at each moment' (1971: 104). Having analysed the accumulation process 'in an environment of near full employment' in which a large firm is not 'provided with a predigested "book of blue-prints" [but has to] find out what the possibilities are and assess them as best it may', she concludes:

> Since, as output per head rises, prices are likely to rise less than in proportion to wage rates, it is possible to see long spells of accumulation in which real wage rates are rising but the rate of profit is not falling. In this sense, 'substitution of capital for labour' is the essence of industrial development, but it has nothing whatever to do with the factor prices shown on a pseudo-production function.
>
> (1971: 106–7)

As I often pointed out to her, what she was saying here was, in essentials, much the same as what Salter had to say in his seminal work on productivity and technical change (Salter 1960, 1965). She did not disagree, for, despite all the evidence to the contrary, she never regarded his work as being in the neoclassical tradition!

As far as Joan Robinson's personal quest is concerned, a number of significant papers follow *An Essay On Marxian Economics*. In particular, there is her 1953 booklet *On Re-reading Marx*. The third lecture is called 'An Open Letter from a Keynesian to a Marxist' – read Ronald Meek – in which she claimed that she understood 'Marx far and away better than you do . . . [because she had] Marx in [her] bones and you have him in your mouth' (1973b: 265). From the point of view of our task in this paper, though, it is the 'Lecture Delivered at Oxford by a Cambridge Economist' (to one thoroughly scared Tutor and his/her pupil) that is significant. Joan Robinson sets out her views on the nature of equilibrium, of how in her opinion you cannot get into it, or even tend toward it. Here, I think, she may have had Hayek in her sights as well. I recently re-read his brilliant 1937 *Economica* article on economics and knowledge. It made me realize, first, how small and parochial the profession was then and, secondly, how fundamental were the concepts with which they grappled, only to have both their questions and their attempted answers lost to the modern generation of economists, especially those trained in the United States. In many ways Joan's discussion of the nature of time and equilibrium is more fresh and exciting (and insightful even) than it was to be in the 1953–4 *Review of Economic Studies* paper and *The Accumulation of Capital*. What *is* strange is that this aspect of her critique was rather neglected, even by herself, as people chased after the conundrum of measuring capital within the neoclassical framework, and the intricacies of golden age models and so on. Again, if she had published the preface to a subsequent edition of *The Accumulation of Capital* (see Harcourt 1990: 51), her purposes would have been better understood and the sea change in her views then emerging better realized, even by herself. For she certainly gave some fuel to the misconceived view of what she was doing, not least in her early response to Sraffa's Introduction to *The Works and Correspondence of David Ricardo* (Sraffa 1951) and her review of Sraffa's 1960 book, *Production of Commodities by Means of Commodities* (Robinson 1961a), and, later on, when the reswitching debate was in full swing, with her 1967 paper with K. A. Naqvi on it all in the *Quarterly Journal of Economics*. Not that her position was not covered by appropriate qualifications; it was, rather, that the significance of the latter was not understood by mainstream readers, or by the neo-Ricardians and the American post-Keynesians.

At the same time as Joan Robinson was writing about 'high theory' from a critical point of view and attempting to generalize *The General Theory* to the long period, she was also being both philosophical and practical about China. This was partly a reflection of her view that to understand an economy we must always start from its history, institutions and 'rules of the game', especially when the economist concerned is actually trying to influence the form that the latter two should take. There may be overlaps of analysis at certain points between one sort of economy and another – for example, her discussion of the choice of technique in *The Accumulation of Capital*, which is derived from Wicksell, has a part to play in her 1950s lectures in China (and her debate with Dobb and Sen over their rationalization of Stalinism) – but the changed setting has to be (and it is) made explicit. Again, many of her exercises in *Exercises in Economic Analysis* (1960b) reflect her thoughts on current issues in China.

Most of all, her difficult but profound essay, 'The Philosophy of Prices' (1960c), which was too much for the Russians and Poles to take, reflects her musings on the nature of the society being analysed. Basically, she grappled with the inescapable facts of life of *any* society in which commodities are exchanged, having been produced by labour and commodities, and a price mechanism rules: there is a two-way interchange between incomes and prices and that the appropriate price structure for the desired development of the economy may not throw up incomes for significant sections of the population that are consistent with society's perception of what is a decent, acceptable and humane standard of life. This problem is as acute for a planned economy as for a freely competitive capitalist one. The problem is made even more complicated by the fact that, in one form of (pure) price system, incomes arise from prices that are related to commodities produced by specific factors, whereas in the other form of pure price system that she identifies factors are not specific and can operate in *any* sector.

By the late 1960s Joan Robinson herself was putting all the emphasis on the methodological critique of neoclassical theory and arguing for a change to process analysis in historical time in a Kaleckian mode. This distanced her from the approach taken by the neo-Ricardians. She recognized this and had many a brawl with Garegnani and, to a lesser extent, with John Eatwell, Murray Milgate and Krishna Bharadwaj. She remained appreciative of Luigi Pasinetti's work. For example, she wrote a most favourable review of his 1974 collection of essays. She said that he had 'played a notable part in the development and exposition of… "Post-Keynesian" theory'. She quoted, with approval, Pasinetti's main theme: 'Keynes' theory of effective demand, which has remained so impervious to reconciliation with marginal economic theory, raises almost no problems when directly inserted into the earlier discussions of the Classical economists' (1975: ix), and, even more perhaps, the resemblance that Pasinetti discerned between Ricardo's method of analysis and the method that Keynes had revived: looking for fundamentals, direct stating of assumptions, singling out the variables believed to be most important, 'freezing out' the others – for the moment – by simple assumptions, to as to produce 'a system of equations of the "causal type" as opposed to a completely interdependent system of simultaneous equations' (Pasinetti 1974: 43–4). Joan Robinson goes on to show how thought experiments may be done with this approach and how the point of Pasinetti's 'golden age' analysis, for example, in his 1962 paper, belongs to 'the sphere of doctrine – it shows that there is no room for a theory of profits based on "marginal productivity of capital" or the "rate of return" on saving' (Robinson 1975: 398).

Her final assessment of Sraffa's purposes and contributions is contained in two papers, 'Spring Cleaning' (1985) and 'Accumulation and Exploitation' (Bhaduri and Robinson 1980), in which she and Bhaduri attempt to link up Sraffa and Kalecki's modes of analysis. The latter paper is more optimistic in tone than the former, urging coming generations to discuss 'the influence of changes in technology on demand for labour, on accumulation and on effective demand' (Bhaduri and Robinson 1980: 111) – a request that is even more pertinent today than when it was first published. In both papers, Joan

Robinson distinguished between, on the one hand, the first two parts of Sraffa's 1960 book, where change was explicitly ruled out, and, on the other, the third part, where the choice of technique is discussed and changes are allowed. She interpreted the first two parts as an attack on 'the amorphous moralising Marshallian theory of "factors of production" receiving "rewards" consonant with their respective productivities' (ibid.: 111), but I think that Krishna Bharadwaj, Garegnani and Pasinetti have shown that Sraffa's 'Prelude to a Critique' was intended to encompass the entire corpus of supply and demand theories of distribution. She was unable to accept that changes are allowed in Part III. Sraffa himself saw it as a critique of the concept of price as an index of scarcity in the theory of distribution – here the rate of profits (r) – by showing that there was no *necessary* inverse relation between r and the 'quantity' of capital.

Their viewpoints mesh, however, when, having argued that 'the given position in an economy is a purely logical structure', she adds that such a construction may be used to answer the question 'what would be different if... ?' (1985: 161). 'Keynesian' analysis, by contrast, is developed by making predictions about the consequences of change – 'what would follow if...?' (ibid.). It 'starts ever afresh from the short-period position that past history has brought into existence "today" and attempts to understand what consequences will follow from recent changes in it' (ibid.). Kalecki, using this method, allows us to operate in 'historical time' because '[we] know something about how the share of wages in the value of net output is affected by monopoly power and the pricing policy of corporations, by particular scarcities, by effective demand, by bargaining power and the social and political climate in which it operates; and about the "inflation barrier" which drives money wages irresistibly upward when real wages are pushed too low', (Bhaduri and Robinson 1980: 111). I have already noted above the underdeveloped set of questions that complement this and that Joan Robinson argues may be tackled by 'Sraffaesque' models that encompass 'distribution according to Marx and realisation according to Kalecki' (Bhaduri and Robinson 1980: 104).

In 1979 Joan Robinson contributed a Foreword (Robinson 1979a) to Alfred Eichner's edited collection of the papers on various aspects of post-Keynesianism that were originally published in *Challenge*. There, she identified Keynes' realization, set out most explicitly and succinctly in his 1937 answers to his critics, that 'the main distinction [between him and the school from which he was struggling to escape] was that he recognized . . . the obvious fact that expectations of the future are necessarily uncertain. It is from this point that Post-Keynesian theory takes off' (Robinson 1979a: xi). From this starting point she tells us that the authors of the papers in the volume are 'exploring, from various points of view, the problems of prices, employment, accumulation, distribution, growth, and stagnation in the actual, historical evolution of an ever changing world. In the nature of the case, definitive answers cannot be found quickly. There is plenty of work still to do' (Robinson 1979a: xxi).[4] This seems to me a good place to leave off – more optimistically than Joan herself was to be in her last year, or rather last months, in Cambridge. Her spell of teaching at Williams in the autumn of 1982 had cheered her up (see Turner 1989: 204–7); it was the return to Cambridge in late December 1982 that disorientated her. She told me that for the first time in her working life she had no new projects to get on with. I tried to reassure her by suggesting that she look through what she had accomplished and that I get the research students to come and meet her, individually or in small groups, so that they could be inspired to carry on the torch that she had so decisively lit. I was not, I'm afraid, successful. Nevertheless, I believe, passionately, that Joan Robinson has set out for us a vital post-Keynesian agenda – and an approach with which to implement it.

NOTES

1 I am most grateful to Philip Arestis, Jan Kregel and Cristina Marcuzzo for their comments and suggestions on the original conference paper, but, of course, take responsibility for the final product.

2 I was rather surprised to be reminded that Joan wrote in the Introduction to volume II of the *Collected Economic Papers* in December 1959 that: 'The bulk of the present volume was written within the last five years and all . . . within the last eight. It belongs to the field of what is sometimes called post-Keynesian economics' (1960d: v).

3 Samuelson writes:

> I do not think that the real stumbling block has been the failure of a literary writer to understand that when a mathematician says, '*y* rises as *x* falls', he is implying nothing about temporal sequences or anything different from 'when *x* is low, *y* is high'.
>
> (1979: 85)

Samuelson goes on to argue that, though it is possible in theory to design efficient transition paths between one long-period position and another, it is nevertheless legitimate to doubt whether either a planned economy or a competitive capitalist economy could have the skills 'to *approximate* in real life such warranted paths' (Samuelson 1979: 85).

Joan Robinson commented that Samuelson had reminded

> us that a plane diagram can show relations between only two variables . . . that a mathematician knows that a functional relationship is timeless . . . makes no reference to history or to the direction of change [so that] there cannot be a movement between points on a plane diagram . . . However, Professor Samuelson continues to use his construction to describe a *process* of accumulation that *varies* wages, *alters* technology and *changes* a stock of inputs made, say, of wood into one made of iron and then into copper.
>
> (Robinson 1979b: 88)

4 I hope that those who join the chase will read Joan and Richard Kahn's work on money and the rate of interest in the 1950s and early 1960s. There, as well as expositing and extending Keynes' insights, they show by example (i.e. by not

doing so) the incoherence of modelling systemic behaviour by the use of *one* representative agent. See Robinson (1961b) for a good example of what I have in mind.

REFERENCES

Baranzini, M. and Harcourt, G. C., eds (1993) *The Dynamics of the Wealth of Nations. Growth, Distribution and Structural Change. Essays in Honour of Luigi Pasinetti.* London: Macmillan.

Bhaduri, A. and Robinson, J. (1980) Accumulation and Exploitation: An Analysis in the Tradition of Marx, Sraffa and Kalecki, *Cambridge Journal of Economics*, 4: 103–15.

Hamouda, O. F. and Harcourt, G. C. (1988) 'Post Keynesianism: From Criticism to Coherence?' *Bulletin of Economic Research*, 40: 1–33; reprinted in C. Sardoni, ed., *On Political Economy and Modern Political Economists. Selected Essays of G. C. Harcourt.* London: Routledge, 1992.

Harcourt, G. C. (1990) On the Contributions of Joan Robinson and Piero Sraffa to Economic Theory, In M. Berg, ed., *Political Economy in the Twentieth Century*, New York and London: Philip Allan, 1990; 35–67; reprinted in C. Sardoni, ed., *On Political Economy and Modern Political Economists. Selected Essays of G. C. Harcourt.* London: Routledge, 1992.

Hayek, F.A. (1931) *Prices and Production.* London: Routledge & Kegan Paul.

——— (1937) Economics and Knowledge, *Economica*, 4: 33–54.

Keynes, J. M. (1930) *A Treatise on Money*, 2 vols. London: Macmillan. In *Collected Writings*, vols V and VI.

——— (1936) *The General Theory of Employment, Interest and Money.* London: Macmillan. In *Collected Writings*, vol. VII.

——— (1937) The General Theory of Employment, *Quarterly Journal of Economics*, 51: 209–23; reprinted in *Collected Writings*, vol. XIV.

Pasinetti, L. L. (1962) Rate of Profit and Income Distribution in Relation to the Rate of Economic Growth, *Review of Economic Studies*, 29: 267–79.

——— (1974) *Growth and Income Distribution. Essays in Economic Theory.* London: Cambridge University Press.

Robinson, J. (1933) *The Economics of Imperfect Competition.* London: Macmillan.

——— (1936) Review of J. Strachey, *The Nature of Capitalist Crisis, Economic Journal*, 46: 298–302; part of article reprinted as 'Some Reflections on Marxist Economics' in *Essays in the Theory of Employment.* London: Macmillan, 1937.

——— (1937) *Introduction to the Theory of Employment.* London: Macmillan.

——— (1947) [1937] *Essays in the Theory of Employment*, 2nd edn. Oxford: Blackwell.

——— (1951) [1933] The Theory of Money and the Analysis of Output. In *Collected Economic Papers*, vol. I. Oxford: Blackwell.

——— (1953–4) The Production Function and the Theory of Capital, *Review of Economic Studies*, 21: 81–106.

——— (1956) *The Accumulation of Capital.* London: Macmillan.

——— (1960a) *Imperfect Competition* Revisited. In *Collected Economic Papers*, vol. II. Oxford: Blackwell.

——— (1960b) *Exercises in Economic Analysis.* London: Macmillan.

——— (1960c) The Philosophy of Prices. In *Collected Economic Papers*, vol. II. Oxford: Blackwell.

——— (1960d) Introduction. In *Collected Economic Papers*, vol. II. Oxford: Blackwell.

——— (1961a) Prelude to a Critique of Economic Theory, *Oxford Economic Papers*, 13, 53–8.
——— (1961b) Own Rates of Interest, *Economic Journal*, 71: 596–600.
——— (1966) [1942] *An Essay on Marxian Economics*, 2nd edn. London: Macmillan.
——— (1971) *Economic Heresies. Some Old-fashioned Questions in Economic Theory*. London: Macmillan.
——— (1973a) Foreword to J. A. Kregel, *The Reconstruction of Political Economy. An Introduction to Post-Keynesian Economics*. New York: Wiley, Holsted Press.
——— (1973b) [1953] *On Re-Reading Marx*. Reprinted in *Collected Economic Papers*, vol. IV. Oxford: Blackwell.
——— (1975) Review of L. L. Pasinetti, *Growth and Income Distribution*, *Economic Journal*, 85: 397–9.
——— (1977) Michal Kalecki on the Economics of Capitalism, *Oxford Bulletin of Economic Studies*, 39: 7–17.
——— (1979a) Foreword to A. S. Eichner, ed., *A Guide to Post-Keynesian Economics*. New York: M. E. Sharpe.
——— (1979b) The Unimportance of Reswitching. In *Collected Economic Papers*, vol. V. Oxford: Blackwell.
——— (1985) [1980] Spring Cleaning, mimeo, Cambridge; published as The Theory of Normal Prices and the Reconstruction of Economic Theory, in G. R. Feiwell, ed., *Issues in Contemporary Macroeconomics and Distribution*. London: Macmillan, 1985.
Robinson, J. and Naqvi, K. A. (1967) The Badly Behaved Production Function, *Quarterly Journal of Economics*, 81: 579–91.
Salter, W. E. G. (1960) *Productivity and Technical Change*. London: Cambridge University Press; 2nd edn 1966.
——— (1965) Productivity Growth and Accumulation as Historical Processes. In E. A. G. Robinson, ed., *Problems in Economic Development*. London: Macmillan.
Samuelson, P. A. (1979) [1975] Steady-State and Transient Relations: A Reply on Reswitching. In J. Robinson, *Collected Economic Papers*, vol. V. Oxford: Blackwell, 83–7.
Shove, G. F. (1944) Mrs Robinson on Marxian Economics, *Economic Journal*, 54: 47–61.
Sraffa, P. (1925) Sulla relazione fra costo e quantità prodotta, *Annali di Economia*, 3: 277–328.
——— (1926) The Laws of Returns under Competitive Conditions, *Economic Journal*, 36: 535–50.
——— (1932) Dr Hayek on Money and Capital, *Economic Journal*, 42: 42–53.
——— (1960) *Production of Commodities by Means of Commodities. Prelude to a Critique of Economic Theory*. London: Cambridge University Press.
——— (1951) Introduction to vol. I of *The Works and Correspondence of David Ricardo*. Edited by P. Sraffa with M. Dobb. Cambridge: Cambridge University Press.
Strachey, J. (1935) *The Nature of Capitalist Crisis*. London: Victor Gollancz.
Turner, M. S. (1989) *Joan Robinson and the Americans*. Armonk, NY: M. E. Sharpe.

THE WRITINGS OF JOAN ROBINSON

Maria Cristina Marcuzzo

This is the fifth version of the bibliography of the writings of Joan Robinson that I have produced so far.

The first was published in *Studi Economici* (no. 16, 1982), as the result of work I had started a few years before, following correspondence I had with Joan Robinson in 1974 requesting her to provide me with information about the list of her published writings.

The second was prepared when the Joan Robinson papers were brought to King's College, after her death, and I had a chance to look at them before they were catalogued. It appeared as 'Materiali di Discussione' (no. 1, Dipartimento di Economia Politica, Modena, 1985).

The third is contained in I. Rima (ed.), *The Joan Robinson Legacy* (New York: M. E. Sharpe, 1991) and benefited from the inspection of the catalogue of Joan Robinson papers prepared by the then King's College Modern Archivist, Mr M. Hall.

The fourth is published as an Appendix to Joan Robinson, *Occupazione, distribuzione e crescita*, ed. M. C. Marcuzzo (Bologna: Il Mulino, 1991) and benefited from the inspection of the R. F. Kahn papers, with the help of the present King's College Modern Archivist, Ms J. Cox.

Besides correcting inaccuracies and filling minor gaps in the references, this version includes 65 items more than the third version and 13 items more than the fourth version, which, however, is not available in English.

NOTATION

Each publication listed in this bibliography has been assigned a number in brackets at the beginning of each entry that corresponds to the chronological order of publication. Where there is more than one edition of the same text, subsequent editions are noted in parentheses at the end of the listing for the first edition. Modifications that appear in later editions are noted separately under the year in which such changes were introduced. Essays that appear in different collections are listed by the number assigned to them for their first appearance in this bibliography. Account has not been taken of all the anthologies, essay collections and the like in which a particular article may have been republished, except for any edited by Joan Robinson herself. This suits the purpose of the present work, which is to date Joan Robinson's works and establish their order and sequence, rather than to provide a complete inventory of where her various writings may be found. If an article or essay appears in one or more of Robinson's own collections, the corresponding abbreviation appears in brackets and the year of the article's first publication appears in parentheses. Variations in titles among different sources, indications regarding modifications and other explanatory details are given in the notes.

ABBREVIATIONS

Journals

Ac: *Accountancy*
ACE: *Annals of Collective Economy*
AEP: *Australian Economic Papers*
AER: *American Economic Review*
AJS: *American Journal of Sociology*
ApEP: *Applied Economic Papers*

Ba: *Banker*
BAS: *Bulletin of the Atomic Scientists*
Bs: *China Policy Study Group Broadsheet*
BSEA: *Bulletin de l'Institut du Science Economique Appliquée*

Ca: *Capital* (Calcutta)
CD: *Canadian Dimension*
CdJE:: *Canadian Journal of Economics*
CdJE(ns): *Canadian Journal of Economics, New Series*
CE: *Critica Economica*
CF: *Canadian Forum*
Ch: *Challenge*
CI: *Cahiers internationaux*
CmJE: *Cambridge Journal of Economics*
CN: *China Now* (formerly SACU)
CPE: *Contributions to Political Economy*
CQ: *Cambridge Quarterly*
CR: *Cambridge Review*
Cs: *Co-existence*

DC: *Development and Change*

EA: *Economie appliquée*

Ec:	*Economica*
Ec (ns):	*Economica, New Series*
EH:	*Eastern Horizon*
EI:	*Economia Internazionale*
EJ:	*Economic Journal*
Em:	*Econometrica*
En:	*Encounter*
EPW:	*Economic and Political Weekly*
ER:	*Economic Record*
ERw:	*Economic Review* (Tokyo)
EW:	*Economic Weekly*
FR:	*Frontier*
FQ:	*Fabian Quarterly*
GER:	*Greek Economic Review*
GR:	*Girton Review*
His:	*History*
IA:	*International Affairs*
IE:	*Investigation Economica* (Mexico)
IEJ:	*Indian Economic Journal*
IER:	*Indian Economic Review*
JCA:	*Journal of Contemporary Asia*
JDA:	*Journal of Developing Asia*
JEL:	*Journal of Economic Literature*
JES:	*Journal of Economic Studies*
JMCB:	*Journal of Money, Credit and Banking*
JPE:	*Journal of Political Economy*
JPKE:	*Journal of Post-Keynesian Economics*
JRAS:	*Journal of the Royal Asiatic Society*
JRSA:	*Journal of the Royal Society of Arts*
JRSS:	*Journal of the Royal Statistical Society*
Ky:	*Kyklos*
LR:	*Left Review*
Ls:	*Listener*
Me:	*Mercurio*
MR:	*Monthly Review*
MS:	*Manchester School of Economics and Social Studies*

Na: *The Nation*
NC: *New China*
NLR: *New Left Review*
N Sc: *New Scientist*
Ns: *New Statesman and Nation*
NT: *Nationaløkonomisk Tidsskrift*
NYRB: *New York Review of Books*
NYT: *New York Times*

OBES: *Oxford Bulletin of Economics and Statistics*
OEP: *Oxford Economic Papers*
OIS: *Oxford Institute of Statistics*

PEJ: *Pakistan Economic Journal*
PQ: *Political Quarterly*
PSQ: *Political Science Quarterly*

QJE: *Quarterly Journal of Economics*
QREB: *Quarterly Review of Economics and Business*

REP: *Revue d'économie politique*
RES: *Review of Economic Studies*
RPE: *Rivista di Politica Economica*

SACU: *Bulletin of the Society for Anglo-Chinese Understanding* (later *China Now*)
SaS: *Science and Society*
SC: *Socialist Commentary*
ScSc: *Social Scientist*
Se: *Seminar*
Sp: *Spectator*
SS: *Soviet Studies*
SSI: *Soviet Studies Information*
StG: *Studium Generale*

TJ: *Trade Journal*
Tm: *The Times*
TT: *Time and Tide*

URL: *Universities and Left Review*

ZN: *Zeitschrift für Nationalökonomie*

Collections of essays

CEP I:	*Collected Economic Papers*, vol. I (1951)
CEP II:	*Collected Economic Papers*, vol. II (1960)
CEP III:	*Collected Economic Papers*, vol. III (1965)
CEP IV:	*Collected Economic Papers*, vol. IV (1973)
CEP V:	*Collected Economic Papers*, vol. V (1979)
CME:	*Contributions to Modern Economics* (1978)
ETE:	*Essays in the Theory of Employment* (1937)
ETG:	*Essays in the Theory of Economic Growth* (1962)
FCM:	*Further Contributions to Modern Economics* (1980)
GGT:	*Generalisation of the General Theory* (1979)
NFC:	*Notes from China* (1964)
RFC:	*Reports from China* (1977)
RIE:	*The Rate of Interest and Other Essays* (1952)
RRM:	*On Re-reading Marx* (1953)

BIBLIOGRAPHY

1930

[1] Review of H. Clay, *The Problem of Industrial Relations*
PQ 1: 293–6, April

1932

[2] *Economics is a Serious Subject. The Apologia of an Economist to the Mathematician, the Scientist and the Plain Man* Cambridge: Heffer
[3] Review of L. S. S. O'Malley, *Indian Caste Customs*
CR 54: 138, 25 November
[4] Imperfect Competition and Falling Supply Price
EJ 42: 544–54, December

1933

[5] *The Economics of Imperfect Competition*
London: Macmillan (2nd edn 1969)
[6] A Parable on Saving and Investment
Ec 13: 75–84, February
[7] The Imperfection of the Market: Comments on G. F. Shove's Note
EJ 43: 124–5, March
[8] Shakespeare and Mr. Looney
CR 54: 389–90, 12 May
[9] Review of A. Da Empoli, *Theory of Economic Equilibrium.* A study of Marginal and Ultramarginal Phenomena
EJ 43: 666–9, June
[10]Review of P. H. Wickstead, *The Coordination of the Laws of Distribution*
EJ 43: 301–4, June

[11] Decreasing Costs: A Reply to Mr Harrod
EJ 43: 531–2, September
[12] The Theory of Money and the Analysis of Output
RES 1: 22–6, October [CEP I] [CME]
[13] Comments on R. G. Hawtrey, *Public Expenditure and Trade Depression*
JRSS 96: 464–5, Part III

1934

[14] Mr. Fraser on Taxation and Returns
RES 1: 137–40, February
[15] Review of J. E. Meade, *The Rate of Interest in a Progressive State*
EJ 44: 282–5, June
[16] Euler's Theorem and the Problem of Distribution
EJ 44: 398–414, September [CEP I]
[17] Review of G. T. Jones, *Increasing Returns*
JPE 42: 694–6, October
[18] What Is Perfect Competition?
QJE 49: 104–20, November [CEP I]

1935

[19] Review of A. D. Gayer, *Monetary Policy and Economic Stabilization*
CR 56: 351, 3 May
[20] A Fundamental Objection to *Laissez-Faire*[1]
EJ 45: 580–2, September [CEP I]
[21] Review of H. S. Ellis, *German Monetary Theory*
EJ 45: 729–31, December

1936

[22] Dr. Machlup's Commonsense of the Elasticity of Substitution
RES 3: 148–50, February
[23] The Long Period Theory of Employment[2]
ZN 7: 74–93, March [ETE]
[24] Review of P. Einzig, *Bankers, Statesmen and Economists*
EJ 46: 122–3, March
[25] Banking Policies and the Exchanges
RES 3: 226–9, June
[26] Disguised Unemployment
EJ 46: 225–37, June [ETE] [CEP IV]
[27] Review of J. Strachey, *The Nature of Capitalist Crisis*[3]
EJ 46: 298–302, June
[28] Review of N. Angell, *The Money Mystery*
IA 15: 598–9, July
[29] Review of R. F. Harrod, *The Trade Cycle*
EJ 46: 691–3, December [CEP I]
[30] Review of *Britain without Capitalists* by a Group of Economists, Scientists and Technicians
EJ 46: 704–6, December
[31] Review of A. Redford, *Patterns of Economic Activity*

EJ 46: 706–7, December
[32] Disguised Unemployment: A Rejoinder
EJ 46: 759–60, December
[33] Mr. Keynes and Socialism. Review of A. L. Rowse, *Mr. Keynes and the Labour Movement*
LR 2: 853, December

1937

[ETE] *Essays in the Theory of Employment*
London: Macmillan (2nd edn 1947)
[34] Foreword
[35] Full employment [CEP IV]
[36] Mobility of Labour
[37] Certain Proposed Remedies for Unemployment
[26] Disguised Unemployment (1936) [CEP IV]
[23] The Long Period Theory of Employment[4] (1936)
[38] The Concept of Zero Saving
[39] Disinvestment
[40] Diagrammatic Illustrations
[41] The Foreign Exchanges [CEP IV]
[42] Beggar-my-Neighbour Remedies for Unemployment [CEP IV] [CME]
[43] Indeterminacy
[44] An Economist's Sermon [CEP IV]
[45] Some Reflections on Marxist Economics[5]
[46] *Introduction to the Theory of Employment*
London: Macmillan (2nd edn 1969)
[47] Review of R. L. Hall, *The Economic System in a Socialist State*
CR 58: 289–90, 26 February
[48] Review of A. W. Knight, *Abolish Slumps*
EJ 47: 339–40, June
[49] Review of S. E. Harris, *Exchange Depreciation*
EJ 47: 669–701, December

1938

[50] The Classification of Inventions
RES 5: 139–42, February
[51] The Concept of Hoarding
EJ 48: 231–6, June [CEP I] [CME]
[52] Review of C. Bresciani Turroni, *The Economics of Inflation*[6]
EJ 48: 507–13, September [CEP I]

1939

[53] Review of G. Myrdal, *Monetary Equilibrium*
EJ 49: 493–5. September [CEP I]

1940

[54] Review of J. Strachey, *A Programme for Progress*
PQ 11: 280–3, April–June
[55] Review of R. A. Lester, *Monetary Experiments*
EJ 50: 280–2, June
[56] Review of G. Crowther, *Ways and Means of War*, and of J. K. Horsefield, *The Real Cost of the War*
EJ 50: 505–7, December
[57] Consumption and Prices
Tm: 5, 3 December

1941

[58] The Financial Problem of 1941
Ba 57: 8–13, January
[59] Rising Supply Price
Ec (ns) 8: 1–8, February [CEP I]
[60] Review of R. F. Bretherton, *Public Investment and the Trade Cycle in Great Britain*
EJ 51: 127–9, April
[61] Marx on Unemployment[7]
EJ 51: 234–48, June
[62] Review of M. Dobb, *Soviet Economy and the War*
EJ 51: 489, December

1942

[63] *An Essay on Marxian Economics*
London: Macmillan (2nd edn 1966)
[64] *Private Enterprise or Public Control*
Handbooks for Discussion Groups, no. 11, London: Association for Education in Citizenship
[65] Review of S. E. Harris, *Economics of Social Security*
EJ 52: 241–3, June
[66] Review of G. H. J. Pierson, *Full Employment*
EJ 52: 240–1, June
[67] Review of N. H. Borden, *The Economic Effects of Advertising*
Ec (ns) 9: 294–6, August [CEP I]
[68] Industry and the State
PQ 13: 400–6, October
[69] Review of T. Wilson, *Fluctuations in Income and Employment*
EJ 52: 352–4, December
[70] Review of L. E. Hubbard, *Soviet Labour and Industry*
CR 63: 348–9, 30 May

1943

[71] *The Future of Industry*
London: Commonwealth Publication
[72] *The Problem of Full Employment: An Outline for Study Circles*

Workers' Educational Association Study Outlines, London (2nd edn 1949; 3rd edn 1953)

[73] Creating Money
Ac 54: 64–5, January

[74] Planning
FQ 36: 4–8, January

[75a] Planning Full Employment I: The need for a constructive approach
Tm: 5, 22 January [CEP I]

[75b] Planning Full Employment II: Alternative solutions of a dilemma
Tm: 5, 23 January [CEP I]

[76] Review of A. L. Bowley (ed.), *Studies in National Income*
PQ 14: 112–3, January–March

[77] Review of R. T. Norris, *The Theory of Consumer's Demand*
EJ 53: 115–17, April [CEP I]

[78] The International Currency Proposals
EJ 53: 161–75, June

[79] Do We Need World Markets?
Ls 30: 490–1, 501, 28 October

[80] Review of J. A. Schumpeter, *Capitalism, Socialism and Democracy*
EJ 53: 381–3, December [CEP I] [FCM]

[81] Review of G. D. H. Cole, *The Means to Full Employment*
Ns 26: 372–3, 4 December

1944

[82] Abolishing Unnecessary Poverty
In N. Kaldor *et al.* (eds), *Planning for Abundance*, Peace Aims Pamphlets, no. 21, London: National Peace Council

[83] Can Planning Be Democratic
In H. Morrison, T. W. Agar, B. Wootton, C. E. M. Joand, J. Robinson and G. H. Cole, *Budgeting in the Post-War World,* London: Routledge

[84] The Currency Plan
SC 9: 246–50, June

[85] Review of H. B. Larry (ed.), *The United States in the World Economy*[8]
EJ 54: 430–7, December [CEP I]

1945

[86] Review of W. B. Bennett, *The American Patent System*
Ec 12: 38–9, February

[87] Review of Oxford Institute of Statistics, *The Economics of Full Employment*
EJ 55: 77–82, April [CEP I]

[88] Review of B. Wootton, *Freedom under Planning*
GR 129: 20, Michaelmas term

[89] Review of League of Nations, *International Currency Experience*
EJ 55: 405–7, December

1946

[90] Obstacles to Full Employment
NT 84(5): 169–78, [CEP I] [CME]

[91] Budget et Inflation
BSEA: 4–11, September

1947

[ETE bis] *Essays in the Theory of Employment*, 2nd edn
London: Macmillan (1st edn 1937)
[92] Foreword to the second edition of *Essays in the Theory of Employment*
[93] Note to the reissue of *Introduction to the Theory of Employment*
[94] The Pure Theory of International Trade
RES 14(2): 98–112
[95] Professor from War Returning. Review of L. Robbins, *Economic Problem in Peace and War*
Ns 34: 375, 8 November

1948

[96] Case for a Double Price Level
Ls 39: 363–4, 4 March
[97] Marx e Keynes[9]
CE 2: 33–45, May [CEP I]
[98] Review of E. V. Morgan, *The Conquest of Unemployment*
Ns 35: 359, May
[99] Review of A. P. Lerner and F. D. Graham, *Planning and Paying for Full Employment*, and of T. Morgan, *Income and Employment*
EJ 58: 248–50, June
[100] La théorie générale de l'employ
EA 1: 185–96, April–September
[101] Review of H. Montgomery-Hyde, *The Amazing Story of John Law*
Ns 31: 59–60, 17 July

1949

[72 bis] *The Problem of Full Employment: An Outline for Study Circles*, Workers' Educational Association Study Outlines, London (1st edn 1943; 3rd edn 1953)
[102] Mr. Harrod's Dynamics
EJ 59: 68–85, March [CEP I]
[103] Review of M. Dobb, *Soviet Economic Development since 1917*[10]
SS 1: 60–4, June [CEP I]
[104] Review of D. Lynch, *The Concentration of Economic Power*
EJ 59: 580–1, December

1950

[105] Review of R. Schlesinger, *Changing Attitudes in Soviet Russia: The Family*
SS 1: 235–7, January
[106] Exchange Equilibrium
EI 3: 396–406, May [CEP I]
[107] Review of E. Böhm-Bawerk, *Karl Marx and the Close of His System*; R. Hilferding, *Böhm-Bawerk's Criticism of Marx*; L. Bortkiewicz, *On the*

Correction of Marx's Fundamental Theoretical Construction in the Third Volume of Capital (ed.) by P. M. Sweezy)[11]
EJ 60: 358–63, June [CEP I]

1951

[CEP I] *Collected Economic Papers*, vol. I
Oxford: Blackwell
[108] Introduction
[16] Euler's Theorem and the Problem of Distribution (1934)
[18] What Is Perfect Competition? (1934)
[59] Rising Supply Price (1941)
[77] *The Theory of Consumer's Demand* by R. T. Norris (1943)
[67] *The Economic Effects of Advertising* by N. H. Borden (1942)
[20] An Inherent Defect in *Laissez-Faire*[12] (1935)
[12] The Theory of Money and the Analysis of Output (1933) [CME]
[29] *The Trade Cycle* by R. F. Harrod (1936)
[51] The Concept of Hoarding (1938) [CME]
[52] The Economics of Hyper-Inflation[13] (1938)
[53] *Monetary Equilibrium* by G. Myrdal (1939)
[75] Planning Full Employment (1943)
[109] War Time Inflation
[87] *The Economics of Full Employment* by Members of the Oxford Institute of Statistics (1945)
[90] Obstacles to Full Employment (1946) [CME]
[110] Economic Consequences of a Decline in the Population of Great Britain
[97] Marx and Keynes[14] (1948)
[107] The Labour Theory of Value[15] (1950)
[80] *Capitalism, Socialism and Democracy* by J. Schumpeter (1943) [FCM]
[102] Mr Harrod's Dynamics (1949)
[103] The Theory of Planning[16] (1949)
[92] The Pure Theory of International Trade (1947)
[85] The United States in the World Economy[17] (1944)
[106] Exchange Equilibrium (1950)
[111] Beauty and the Beast [CME]
[112] Introduction to Rosa Luxemburg, *The Accumulation of Capital*
London: Routledge & Kegan Paul, 1951 [CEP II]
[113] Review of J. A. Schumpeter, *Capitalism, Socialism and Democracy*, 3rd edn
EJ 61: 141–2, March
[114] The Rate of Interest[18]
Em 19: 92–111, April [RIE] [CEP II] [CME] [GGT]
[115] Preparation for War[19]
MR 3: 194–5, October

1952

[RIE] *The Rate of Interest and Other Essays*[20]
London: Macmillan
[116] Introduction [GGT]
[114] The Rate of Interest[21] (1951) [CEP II] [CME] [GGT]
[117] Notes on the Economics of Technical Progress [GGT]

[118] The Generalisation of the General Theory
[119] Acknowledgements and Disclaimers[22] [CEP II] [GGT]
[120] *Conference Sketch Book: Moscow, April 1952*
Cambridge: Heffer & Sons
[120] Moscow 1952
MR 4: 157–72, September
[121] The Model of an Expanding Economy
EJ 62: 42–53, March [CEP II]
[122] 'Full Cost' and Monopolistic Competition: A Comment
EJ 62: 325, March
[123] Review of C. Bettelheim, *Les problèmes théoriques et pratiques de la planification*
SS 4: 53–58, July
[124] Monetary Policy Again. Comments[23]
OBES 14: 281–4, August [CEP II]
[125] Review of J. K. Galbraith, *American Capitalism: The Concept of Contervailing Power*
EJ 62: 925–8, December

1953

[72 ter] *The Problem of Full Employment: An Outline for Study Circles*, Workers' Educational Association Study Outlines, London (1st edn 1943; 2nd edn 1949)
[RRM] *On Re-reading Marx*
Cambridge: Student's Bookshop
[126] Would You Believe It? [CEP IV]
[127] A Lecture Delivered at Oxford by a Cambridge Economist [CEP IV] [CME]
[128] An Open Letter from a Keynesian to a Marxist [CEP IV] [FCM]
[129] *Imperfect Competition* Revisited
EJ 63: 579–93, September [CEP II] [CME]
[130] The Production Function and the Theory of Capital[24]
RES 21(2): 81–106, No. 55 [CME] [CEP II]
[131a] Letters from a Visitor to China, July 1953
MR 5: 302–10, November, Part I [RFC]
[131b] Letters from a Visitor to China, July 1953
MR 5: 397–410, December, Part II [RFC]

1954

[131c] Letters from a Visitor to China, July 1953
MR 5: 477–80, January, Part III [RFC]
[131d] Letters from a Visitor to China, July 1953
MR 5: 536–43, February, Part IV [RFC]
[131] Letters from a Visitor to China
Cambridge: Students' Bookshop [RFC]
[132] The Labour Theory of Value: A Discussion
SaS 18(2): 141–51 [CEP II]
[133] The Impossibility of Competition
In E. H. Chamberlin (ed.) *Monopoly and Competition and their Regulation*, Papers and Proceedings of the International Economic Association Conference, London: Macmillan

[134] Britain and China
Na 179: 125–8, 14 August

1955

[135] Marx, Marshall and Keynes
Delhi School of Economics, Occasional Paper no. 9, University of Delhi [CEP II] [CME]
[136] The Production Function
EJ 64: 67–71, March
[137] A Theory of Long Run Development
ERw 6: 382–5, October
[138] The Production Function and the Theory of Capital: A Reply
RES 23(3): 247

1956

[139] *The Accumulation of Capital*
London: Macmillan (2nd edn 1965; 3rd. edn 1969)
[140] Mr Wiles' Rationality. A Comment
SS 7: 269–73, January
[141] Employment and the Plan
EW 8: 355–6, 24 March
[142] The Industry and the Market
EJ 66: 360–1, June
[143] Review of K. Marx, *The Poverty of Philosophy*
EJ 66: 334–5, June
[144] The Choice of Technique
EW 8: 715–8, 23 June
[145] British–Soviet Trade Prospects
British–Soviet Friendship: 2–3, 5, October
[146] Time and the Choice of Technique. Letter
EW 8: 1333, 17 November
[147] Review of J. Strachey, *Contemporary Capitalism*
EJ 66: 697–8, December
[148] Unemployment and Planning: India 1955
Ca 7–9, Annual Supplement, December [CEP III]

1957

[149] What Remains of Marxism?
In 'A Contribution to a Symposium'[25] [CEP III]
[150] Notes on the Theory of Economic Development
Annales de la Faculté de Droit de Liège [CEP II]
[151] Une lettre sur le capitalisme contemporain
CI 82: 27–8, January
[152] The Control of Monopoly in British Industry
Ls 48: 459–60, 475, 21 March
[153] Full Employment and After
URL 1: 66–8, Spring
[154] Economic Growth and Capital Accumulation: A Comment

ER 33: 103–8, April
[155] Choice of Technique Letter
EW 9: 537, 27 April
[156] The Indian Mixture. Review of M. Zinkin, *Development for Free Asia*
Ns 53: 844–5, 29 June
[157] The Policy of Backward Nations. Review of P. Baran, *The Political Economy of Growth*
Na 184: 485–6, 1 June
[158] Review of E. E. Nemmers, *Hobson and Underconsumption*
EJ 67: 511–2, September
[159] La Théorie de la Répartition[26]
EA 10: 523–38, October–December [CEP II]

1958

[160] *China: An Economic Perspective* (with S. Adler)
Fabian Tract no. 314, London: Davenport Press
[161] Birth Control in China
Ns 55: 66–7, 18 January
[162] Plein emploi et inflation[27]
Bulletin de Conjoncture Regionale, Rennes, 3: 26–30, March [CEP II]
[163] Review of L. Robbins, *Robert Torrens and the Evolution of Classical Economics*
CR 80: 489–91, 26 April
[164] Some Reflections on the Philosophy of Prices[28]
MS 26: 116–35, May [CEP II] [CME]
[165] The Real Wicksell Effect
EJ 68: 600–5, September [CEP II]
[166] Il mito della concorrenza[29]
Me 9: 15–20, December [CEP II]
[167] Poblacion y desarollo[30]
IE 18: 275–81

1959

[168] Economic Possibilities of Ceylon
In 'Papers by Visiting Economists', Planning Secretariat, Colombo
[169] The Falling Rate of Profit: A Comment
SaS 23(2): 104–6
[170] A Comment on G. D. N. Worswick, Mrs Robinson's Simple Accumulation
OEP 11: 141–2, January
[171] Some Problems of Definition and Measurement of Capital
OEP 11: 157–66, June [CEP II]
[172] Review of K. Kurihara, *The Keynesian Theory of Economic Development*
EJ 69: 352–3, June
[173] Letter to the Editor on Capital Theory
Em 27: 490, July
[174] Accumulation and the Production Function
EJ 69: 433–42, September [CEP II]
[175] Depreciation
RPE 49: 1703–17, November [CEP II]

1960

[CEP II] *Collected Economic Papers*, vol. II
Oxford: Blackwell (2nd edn 1975)
[176] Introduction
[135] Marx, Marshall and Keynes (1955) [CME]
[119] Notes on Marx and Marshall[31] (1952) [RIE] [GGT]
[164] The Philosophy of Prices[32] (1958) [CME]
[135] The Labour Theory of Value (1954)
[112] Rosa Luxemburg's Accumulation of Capital (1951)
[121] The Model of an Expanding Economy (1952)
[150] Notes on the Theory of Economic Development (1957)
[167] Population and Development[33] (1960)
[130] The Production Function and the Theory of Capital[34] [CME]
[174] Accumulation and the Production Function (1959)
[159] The Theory of Distribution[35] (1957)
[177] Capital, Technique and Relative Shares
[165] The Real Wicksell Effect (1958)
[178] Saving Without Investment
[171] Some Problems of Definition and Measurement of Capital (1959)
[175] Depreciation (1959)
[129] *Imperfect Competition* Revisited (1953) [CME]
[166] *Imperfect Competition* To-day[36] (1958)
[114] The Rate of Interest[37] (1951) [RIE] [CME] [GGT]
[124] A Note on the Bank Rate[38] (1952)
[162] Full Employment and Inflation[39] (1958)

[167] Population and Development[40]
PEJ 10: 1–7, March [CEP II]

[179] Exercises in Economic Analysis
London: Macmillan

[180] Teaching Economics
EW 12: 173–5, January [CEP III]

[181] Review of T. J. Hughes and D. E. Luard, *The Economic Development of Communist China 1949–58*
EJ 70: 409–10, June

[182] Review of B. S. Keirstead, *Capital, Interest and Profits*
CdJE 26: 488–90, August

[183] Mirth Killer. Review of J. K. Galbraith, *The Liberal Hour*
TT 41: 1342, 5 November

[184] 'General Liquidity'
Ba 110: 790–5, December [CEP III]

[185] The Present Position of Econometrics. The Choice of Models: A Discussion
JRSS 123(3): 274–8

1961

[186] Prelude to a Critique of Economic Theory
OEP 13: 53–8, February [CEP III] [FCM]

[187] Equilibrium Growth Models
AER 51: 360–9, June [CEP III]

[188] Beyond Full Employment
ACE 32: 159–67, April–June [CEP III]

[189] From the United States to Cuba
Ls 52: 265–7, 280, 24 August
[190] Own Rates of Interest
EJ 71: 596–600, September [CEP III]
[191] Review of S. Tsuru, *Has Capitalism Changed?*
MR 13: 265–71, October [CEP III] [CME]
[192] Review of S. Tsuru, *Has Capitalism Changed?*
JPE 69: 504–5, October
[193] Review of S. Kuznets, *Lectures on Economic Growth*
JPE 69(1): 74
[194] Thinking about China: The Economic Impact of Communism (with R. Berger)
Ls 65: 220–2, 2 February

1962

[195] *Economic Philosophy*
London: Watts and Co. (reprinted in Pelican Books, 1964)
[ETG] *Essays in the Theory of Economic Growth*
London: Macmillan (2nd edn 1963)
[197] Normal Prices[41] (1962)
[198] A Model of Accumulation
[199] A Model of Technical Progress (1962)
[200] A Neo-classical Theorem[42] (1962)
[197] The Basic Theory of Normal Prices[43]
QJE 76: 1–19, February [ETG]
[199] A Model of Technical Progress
RPE 52: 147–75, February [ETG]
[200] A Neoclassical Theorem
RES 29: 219–26, June [ETG]
[201] Draft of a Multilateral Trade Clearing Agency (with R. Frisch)
Memorandum from the Institute of Economics University of Oslo
[202] Cuba and the USA
EW 14: 473–6, 17 March
[203] Latter Day Capitalism
NLR 2: 37–46, August [CEP III] [CME]
[204] Review of H. G. Johnson, *Money, Trade and Economic Growth*[44]
EJ 72: 690–2, September [CEP III]
[205] Review of E. S. Kirby (ed.), *Contemporary China. Economic and Social Studies*
EJ 72: 734, September
[206] Marxism: Religion and Science
MR 14: 423–35, December [CEP III] [FCM]
[207] Comment on the Production Function Symposium
RES 29: 258–66, June
[208] Review of R. Frisch, *Planning for India. Selected Explorations in Methodology*
JRSS 125(3): 504–6

1963

[ETE bis] *Essays in the Theory of Economic Growth*, 2nd edn
London: Macmillan (1st edn 1962)
[209] Foreword to the second edition of *Essays in the Theory of Economic Growth*
[210] Review of A. K. Cairncross, *Factors in Economic Development*
IA 39: 97, January
[211] Review of P. Moussa, *The Underprivileged Nations*
IA 39: 93–4, January
[212] Public or Private Enterprise
ApEP 3: 1–12, March
[213] Review of J. M. Montais, *Central Planning in Poland*
EJ 73: 124–6, March
[214] Meaning of Alignment
Se 45: 27–9, May
[215] Review of J. Maynard, *Economic Development and the Price Level*
EJ 73: 299–300, June
[216] The Chinese View
Se 50: 44–6, October
[217] Learning by Doing. A Further Note
RES 30: 167–8, October
[218] Findlay's Robinsonian Model of Accumulation[45]
Ec (ns) 30: 408–11, November [CEP III]
[219] Are We Exerting Ourselves Enough? An Interview
Yojana 7(1): 7–8

1964

[NFC] *Notes from China*
Oxford: Blackwell
[220] Foreword
[224] The Chinese Point of View(1964)
[225] The People's Communes (1964)
[221] Communes in China
Ls 55: 177–9, 30 January
[222] Notes from China[46]
EW 16: 195–203, February [RFC]
[223] Review of L. Zeitlin, *Life's Value in Cash*
EJ 74: 219–20, March
[224] The Chinese Point of View
IA 40: 232–44, April [RFC] [NFC]
[225] A British Economist on a Chinese Commune[47]
EH 3: 6–11, May [RFC] [NFC]
[226] Chinese Agricultural Communes
Cs 1: 1–6, May
[227] Factor Prices not Equalized
QJE 78: 202–7, May [CEP III]
[228] Statement Submitted to Committee on Resale Price Maintenance (with R. Cohen, R. Kahn and W. B. Reddaway)
OIS 26: 113–21, May
[229] Solow on the Rate of Return

EJ 74: 410–17, June [CEP III]
[230] Review of H. G. Shaffery (ed.), *The Soviet Economy. A Collection of Western and Soviet Views*
CR 85: 491–3, 6 June
[231] China 1963: The Communes
PQ 35: 285–97, July [CEP III]
[232] The Final End of *Laissez-Faire*
NLR 4: 3–9, August [CEP III]
[233] Review of S. Chou, *The Chinese Inflation, 1937–1949*
EJ 74: 680–1, September
[234] Pre-Keynesian Theory after Keynes
AEP 3: 25–35, December [CEP III] [CME]
[235] Prospects for China
N Sc 22: 756, 18 June
[236] India Wake-up
EW 16: 1917–20, 5 December
[237] Review of C. Cheng, *Communist China Economy 1949–1962. Structural Changes and Crisis*
IA 40: 560, July
[238] Planning for Economic Development
TJ: 5–7, June–July

1965

[139 bis] *The Accumulation of Capital*
London: Macmillan (1st edn 1956; 3rd edn 1969)
[CEP III] *Collected Economic Papers*, vol. III
Oxford: Blackwell (2nd edn 1975)
[239] Introduction
[180] Teaching Economics
[186] Prelude to a Critique of Economic Theory[48] (1961) [FCM]
[187] Equilibrium Growth Models (1961)
[227] Factor Prices Not Equalized (1964)
[229] Solow on the Rate of Return (1964)
[218] Robinson on Findlay on Robinson[49] (1963)
[240] Harrod's Knife-Edge
[234] Pre-Keynesian Theory after Keynes (1964) [CME]
[241] Consumer's Sovereignty in a Planned Economy (1965)
[242] Wiles on the Political Economy of Communism[50]
[243] Kalecki and Keynes[51] [CME]
[204] The General Theory after Twenty Five Years[52] (1962)
[188] Beyond Full Employment (1961)
[203] Latter Day Capitalism (1962) [CME]
[184] General Liquidity (1960)
[190] Own Rates of Interest (1961)
[233] The Final End of *Laissez-Faire* (1964)
[206] Marxism: Religion and Science (1962) [FCM]
[149] What Remains of Marxism? (1957)
[191] Has Capitalism Changed? (1961) [CME]
[244] A Reconsideration of the Theory of Value[53] (1965)
[148] India, 1955: unemployment and planning (1956)
[231] China, 1963: the communes (1964)

[245] Korea, 1964: economic miracle (1965)
[241] Consumer's Sovereignty in a Planned Economy
In *On Political Economy and Econometrics*, Oxford: Pergamon Press [CEP III]
[244] Piero Sraffa and the Rate of Exploitation[54]
NLR 5: 28–34, January [CEP III]
[245] Korean Miracle[55]
MR 16: 541–9, January [CEP III]
[246] What's New in China
EH 4: 11–15, January [RFC]
[247] Cuba 1965
EW 17: 1341–5, 28 August
[248] Review of T. C. Liu and K. Yeh, *The Economy of the Chinese Mainland, National Income and Economic Development 1933–59*
EJ 75: 604, September
[249] Review of C. Bettelheim, J. Charrier, H. Marchisio, *La construction du socialisme en Chine*
Bs 2: 1–3, October

1966

[63 bis] *An Essay on Marxian Economics*, 2nd edn.
London: Macmillan (1st edn 1942)
[242] Review of P. J. D. Wiles, *Political Economy of Communism*[56]
IER 1: 145–52, April [CEP III]
[243] Kalecki and Keynes[57]
In *Problems of Economic Dynamics and Planning. Essays in honor of M. Kalecki*, Oxford: Pergamon Press [CEP III] [CME]
[247] Cuba 1965
MR 17: 10–18, February
[249] Review of C. Bettelheim, J. Charrier, H. Marchisio, *La construction du socialisme en Chine*
Cs 3(1): 105–7
[250] *Economics: An Awkward Corner*
London: Allen & Unwin (2nd edn 1968)
[251] Introduction[58]
In M. Kalecki, *Studies in the Theory of Business Cycles 1933–39*
Oxford: Blackwell
[252] *The New Mercantilism*
Cambridge: Cambridge University Press [CEP IV] [CME]
[253] Review of K. R. Walker, *Planning in Chinese Agriculture: Socialization and the Private Sector 1956–1962*
IA 42: 159–60, January
[254] The Communes and the Great Leap Forward. Reviews of I. and D. Crook, *The First Years of Yangyi Commune* and R. Dummond, *La Chine Surpeuplé, tiers monde affamé*
NLR 6: 69–72, May–June
[255] Comment on D. M. Bensusan-Butt, *Pre-Keynesian Theory: A Modest Defence*
AEP 5: 45–6, June
[256] Review of A. K. DasGupta, *Planning and Economic Growth*
EJ 76: 397–8, June
[257] China Today: The Organization of Agriculture
BAS 22: 28–32, June

[258] Review of C. Chi-Yi, *La Réforme agraire en Chine populaire*, and of Y. L. Wu, *The Steel Industry in Communist China*
IA 42: 546–8, July

[259] Comment on Samuelson and Modigliani
RES 33: 307–8, October

[260] Organisation of Agriculture
In R. Adams (ed.), *Contemporary China*, London: Peter Owen and New York: Pantheon Books

1967

[261] Socialist Affluence
In C. H. Feinstein (ed.), *Socialism, Capitalism and Economic Growth*, Cambridge: Cambridge University Press [CEP IV] [CME]

[262] Opening Remarks
In K. Martin and J. Knapp (eds), *The Teaching of Development Economics*, London: Frank Cass

[263] Review of R. Lekachman, *The Age of Keynes*[59]
NYRB 8: 20–2, 26 January [CEP V]

[264] Review of Yuan-Li Wu, *Economy of Communist China: An Introduction*; D. H. Perkins, *Market Control and Planning in Communist China*; J. L. Buck, O. L. Dawson and Yuan-Li Wu, *Food and Agriculture in Communist China*
IA 43: 192–3, January

[265] Contribution to Sanity
EPW 2: 111, 28 February

[266] Growth and the Theory of Distribution
ACE 38: 3–7, March [CEP V]

[267] The Soviet Collective Farm as a Producer Cooperative: A Comment
AER 57: 222–3, March

[268] Review of A. N. Young, *China's Wartime Finance and Inflation, 1937–45* and Chi-Ming-Hou, *Foreign Investment and Economic Development in China 1840–1937*
IA 43: 404–6, April

[269] Marginal Productivity
IER 2: 78–84, April [CEP IV]

[270] Review of H. Portisch, *Eyewitness in China*
IA 43: 611–12, July

[271] Review of R. Pellisier, *The Awakening of China, 1793–1949*
IA 43: 797, October

[272] The Badly Behaved Production Function (with K. A. Naqvi)
QJE 81: 579–91, November [CEP IV]

[273] The Economic Reforms
MR 19: 45–50, November

[274] Review of G. Grossmann, *Economic Systems*
EJ 67: 871–3, December

[275] Review of M. Wolfson, *Reappraisal of Marxian Economics*
PSQ 82: 627–8

[276] China and China Specialists
SaS 31: 338–41, Summer

[277] The Chinese Cultural Revolution
Now, 22 December

1968

[250 bis] *Economics: An Awkward Corner*, London: Allen & Unwin (1st edn 1966)
[278] Review of G. Myrdal, *Report from a Chinese Village*
IA 44: 152–3, January
[279] Intensive Look at China
SACU 3: 1–5, February
[280] Review of W. Leontief, *Essays in Economics: Theories and Theorising*
Em 36: 431–2, April
[281] The Poverty of Nations
Ls 80: 509–10, 17 October
[282] The Cultural Revolution in China
IA 44: 214–27, April
[283] Review of F. M. Gottheil, *Marx's Economic Predictions* and of W. Leontief, *Input–Output Economics*[60]
IER 3: 57–64, April [CEP IV]
[284] Reply to Sussex Internationalists Attack
SACU 3: 5, June-July
[285] Reply to D. Willet, *A Defence of Adam Smith's Deer and Beaver Model*
JES 3: 33, July
[286] China Today: Economic Organisation
JRSA 116: 683–93, July
[287] Review of G. Myrdal, *Asian Drama. An Enquiry into the Poverty of Nations*[61]
CQ 3: 381–9, Autumn [CEP IV]
[288] One Quarter of Mankind
CF 48: 150, October
[289] Value and Price
SSI 7: 632–72, December [CEP IV]
[290] Review of A. Donnithorne, *China's Economic System*
SACU 3: 5, December

1969

[46 bis] *Introduction to the Theory of Employment*,[62] 2nd edn
London: Macmillan (1st edn 1937)
[139 ter] *The Accumulation of Capital*, 3rd edn
London: Macmillan (1st edn 1956; 2nd edn 1965)
[281] Poverty of Nations. Review of G. Myrdal, *Asian Drama*
CD 5: 27–30, February
[291] Postcript to the third edition of *The Accumulation of Capital*
[292] *The Cultural Revolution in China*[63]
Harmondsworth: Penguin (2nd edn 1970)
[293] Preface to N. Brunner, *China Economy*, London: Anglo-Chinese Educational Institute
[294] Preface to the second edition of *Introduction to the Theory of Employment*
[295] Too Much for the 'Times' (with J. Needham)
SACU 4: 1–2, January
[296] Ten Years of the Communes
Bs 6: 3, January
[297] A Further Note on Kaldor–Mirrlees's Growth Model Concerning the Degree of Monopoly
RES 36: 260–2, April

[298] A Model for Accumulation Proposed by J. E. Stiglitz
EJ 79: 412–3, June
[299] The Theory of Value Reconsidered
AEP 8: 13–19, June [CEP IV] [CME]
[300] Macroeconomics of Unbalanced Growth: A Belated Comment
AER 59: 632, September
[301] Review of A. Leijonhufvud, *On Keynesian Economics and the Economics of Keynes*
EJ 79: 581–3, September
[302] India and China: A Comparison
Ls 82: 816–18, 11 December

1970

[303] *Freedom and Necessity*
London: Allen & Unwin
[304] Society and Economics in China Today
In R. Jungk et al., *China and the West: Mankind Evolving*, London: Granstone Press.
[305] Chinese Economic Policy
StG 23(12): 1267–74
[306] Economics Today
Basler Wirtschaftswissenschaftliche Vortrage 2, Zurich: Polygraphischer Verlag [CEP IV]
[307] Foreword
In E. L. Wheelwright and B. McFarlane, *The Chinese Road to Socialism*, New York: Monthly Review Press
[308] Capital Theory up-to-date
CdJE(ns) 3: 309–17, May [CEP IV] [CME]
[309] Reply to A. J. Watson, *The Cultural Revolution: Two Views*
CN 4: 4, June
[310] Review of R. C. Ferguson, *The Neoclassical Theory of Production and Distribution*
EJ 80: 336–9, June
[311] Reviews of K. Buchanan, *The Transformation of the Chinese Earth* and of T. R. Tregear, *Economic Geography of China*
Bs 7: 4, July
[312] Chinese Economic Policy. Prescription for Development
CN 4: 5–8, August
[313] Harrod after Twenty-one Years
EJ 80: 731–7, September [CEP IV]
[314] Harrod after Twenty-one Years: A Reply
EJ 80: 741, September
[315] Quantity Theories Old and New
JMCB 2: 504–13, November
[316] Review of C. B. Turner, *Analysis of Soviet Views of John Maynard Keynes*
SS 22: 134–5, July

1971

[317] *Economic Heresies*
London: Basic Books

[318] Chinese Economic Policy
In J. Needham et al., *Hand and Brain in China and Other Essays*, London: Anglo-Chinese Educational Institute
[319] The Relevance of Economic Theory
MR 23: 29–37, January [CEP IV]
[320] Continuity and the 'Rate of Return'
EJ 81: 120–2, March [CEP IV]
[321] The Existence of Aggregate Production Functions: Comment
Em 39: 405, March
[322] Capital Theory up-to-date: Reply to Ferguson[64]
CdJE(ns) 4: 254–6, May [CEP IV]
[323] Comment on Going to Europe Again. A Symposium
En 36: 5–6, June
[324] The Measure of Capital: The End of Controversy
EJ 81: 597–602, September [CEP IV]
[325] Michal Kalecki[65]
CR 93: 1–4, 22 October [CEP IV]
[326] Something to Live for. Review of G. Myrdal and G. Kessle, *The Revolution Continued*
Ns 81: 631–3, 7 May
[327] Review of R. Solow, *Growth Theory: An Exposition*[66]
Ky 24: 189–92 [CEP IV]

1972

[328] For Use Not for Profit. A Report on a Recent Visit to China
EH 11(4): 6–15
[329] Review of T. K. Rymes, *On Concepts of Capital and Technical Change*
Ky 25: 427–9
[330] The Second Crisis of Economic Theory
AER 62: 1–9, May [CEP IV] [CME]
[331] Through Western Spectacles. Reviews of K. Mehnert, *China Today* and of K. Ling, *Red Guards*
Sp 229: 321, 19 August

1973

[CEP IV] *Collected Economic Papers*, vol. IV
Oxford: Blackwell
[332] Foreword
[252] The New Mercantilism (1966) [CME]
[333] The Need for a Reconsideration of the Theory of International Trade (1973) [CME]
[283] Economics versus Political Economy[67] (1968)
[261] Socialist Affluence (1967) [CME]
[289] Value and Price (1968)
[299] The Theory of Value Reconsidered (1969) [CME]
[313] Harrod after Twenty-one Years (1970)
[272] (with K. A. Naqvi) The Badly Behaved Production Function (1967)
[325] Michal Kalecki[68] (1971)
[330] The Second Crisis of Economic Theory (1972) [CME]

[287] The Poverty of Nations[69] (1968)
[319] The Relevance of Economic Theory (1971)
[306] Economics Today (1970)
[269] Marginal Productivity (1967)
[327] Solow Once More[70] (1971)
[308] Capital Theory up-to-date (1970) [CME]
Capital Theory up-to-date: A Comment (by C. E. Ferguson)
[322] A Reply[71] (1971)
[320] Continuity and 'The Rate of Return' (1971)
[324] The Measure of Capital: The End of the Controversy (1971)
[334] Essays 1935: Introduction
[35] Full Employment (1937) [ETE]
[26] Disguised Unemployment (1936) [ETE]
[41] Foreign Exchanges (1937) [ETE]
[42] Beggar-My-Neighbour Remedies for Unemployment (1937) [ETE] [CME]
[44] An Economist's Sermon (1937)
[335] Essays 1953: Introduction
[126] Would You Believe It? (1953) [RRM]
[127] A Lecture Delivered at Oxford by a Cambridge Economist (1953) [RRM] [CME]
[128] An Open Letter from a Keynesian to a Marxist (1953) [RRM] [FCM]

[333] The Need for a Reconsideration of the Theory of International Trade
In M. B. Connolly and A. K. Swoboda (eds), *International Trade and Money*, London: Allen & Unwin [CME] [CEP IV]

[336] *Introduction to Modern Economics* (with J. Eatwell)
Maidenhead: McGraw-Hill (2nd edn 1974)

[337] *Economic Management in China 1972*
London: Anglo-Chinese Educational Institute (2nd edn 1975)

[337a] Planning and Management in China Today[72]
CR 94: 106–20, 2 March

[337b] Structure of Management[73]
CN 7: 10–11, February

[338] What Has Become of the Keynesian Revolution?
In J. Robinson (ed.), *After Keynes*, Oxford: Blackwell [CEP V]

[339] Foreword in J. Kregel, *An Introduction to Post-Keynesian Economics*, London: Macmillan

[340] Ideology and Analysis. A Contribution to the Festschrift for Eduard Marz, Europa Verlags, A. G. Wien [CEP V]

[341] Chinese Agricultural Communes
In C. K. Wilber (ed.), *The Political Economy of Development*, Random House: New York

[342] Review of T. Brus, *The Market in a Socialist Economy*
EJ 83: 558–60, March

[343] Formalistic Marxism and Ecology Without Classes. Review of A. Emmanuel, *Unequal Exchange*. A Study of the Imperialism of Trade, and of R. G. Wilkinson, *Poverty and Progress*
JCA 3(4): 457–61 [CEP V]

[344] Review of G. Myrdal, *Against the Stream*[74]
NYT: 31, 23 September [CEP V] [FCM]

[345] Samuelson, Marx and Their Latest Critics
JEL 11: 1367, December

[346] Review of L. S. Reynolds, *World Economics*
PSQ 88: 114–15

1974

[338] What Has Become of the Keynesian Revolution?
Ch 16: 6–11, January [CEP V]
[347] History versus Equilibrium
London: Thames Polytechnic [CEP V] [CME]
[347] History versus Equilibrium
IEJ 21: 202–13, March [CEP V] [CME]
[348] Reflections on the Theory of International Trade
Manchester: Manchester University Press [CEP V]
[349] The Abdication of Neoclassical Economics
In A. Mitra (ed.), *Economic Theory and Planning: Essays in honor of A. K. Das Gupta*, New Delhi: Oxford University Press [CEP V]
[350] On the Pollyanna of Economic Growth. Review of W. Beckerman, *In Defence of Economic Growth*
Sp 233: 19–20, 6 July
[351] Two Revolutions
Bs 11: 4, October
[352] Inflation West and East
Fr: 19 October [CEP V]
[353] Achievements of a Generation
CN, no. 45: 2–3
[354] False Development. Review of J. White, *The Politics of Foreign Aid*
Sp 233: 401–2, 28 September
[355] Inflation and Stabilisation: A Neo-Keynesian View
Sp 233: 488–9, 19 October

1975

[337 bis] *Economic Management in China, 1972*
London: Anglo-Chinese Educational Institute (1st edn 1973)
[356] Postcript to the second edition of *Economic Management in China, 1972*
[357] Value before Capitalism
Ky 28(1): 143–8 [CEP V]
[358] The Unimportance of Reswitching
QJE 89: 32–9, February [CEP V]
[359] The Unimportance of Reswitching: A Reply
QJE 89: 53–5, February [CEP V]
[360] Review of L. L. Pasinetti, *Growth and Income Distribution. Essays in Economic Theory*
EJ 85: 397–99, June
[361] National Minorities in Yunnan
EH 14(4): 32–43 [RFC]
[362] Review of L. R. Marchant, *The Phoenix Seat: An Introductory Study of Maoism and the Chinese Quest for a Paradise on Earth*
His 60: 272–3, June
[363] Introduction 1974: Reflections and Reminiscences[75]
In *Collected Economic Papers*, vol. II, 2nd edn, Oxford: Blackwell (1st edn 1960) [FCM]
[364] Introduction 1974: Comments and Explanations[76]
In *Collected Economic Papers*, vol. III, 2nd edn, Oxford: Blackwell (1st edn 1965) [FCM]

[365] Foreword to P Manger et al., *Education in China*, London: Anglo-Chinese Education Institute
[366] In the Deep Southwest. The Thai People of Yunnan before and after Liberation
NC 1: 21–3, Fall
[367] The Fall of Lin Piao. Review of P. Worsley, *Inside China*, and of K. S. Carol, *The Second Chinese Revolution*
Sp 235: 217, 16 August
[368] Hsishuang Panna
CN, no. 55: 10–11

1976

[369] Introduction
In M. Kalecki, *Essays on Developing Economies*, Atlantic Highland, NJ: Harvester Press
[370] Introduzione[77]
In R. F. Kahn, *L'occupazione e la crescita*, Torino: Einaudi, 1976
[371] Planning Models: Two Views. Review of A. Rudra, *Indian Plan Models*
EPW 11: 361–3, 28 February
[372] Michal Kalecki: A Neglected Prophet
NYRB 23: 28–30, 4 March
[373] The Age of Growth
Ch 19: 4–9, May–June [CEP V] [FCM]
[374] Review of J. Collier and E. Collier, *China's Socialist Revolution*
MR 28: 50–1, October
[375] Review of I. G. Shivji, *Class Struggle in Tanzania*
JCA 6(3): 344–5
[376] Review of J. K. Fairbank, E. O. Reischauer and A. M. Craig, *East Asia: Tradition and Transformation*
JRAS 102(1): 91–2
[377] Review of E. S. Kirby, *Russian Studies in China*
Sp 236: 17, 17 January

1977

[RFC] *Reports from China: 1953–1976*
London: Anglo-Chinese Educational Institute
[378] Foreword (1976)
[131] Letters from a Visitor to China (1953)
[379] Reminiscences[78]
[380] Economic Recovery[79]
[224] The Chinese Point of View (1965)
[246] What's New in China (1965)
[292] The Cultural Revolution[80] (1969)
[381] Reports and Conversations (1967)
[382] Retrospect (1972)
[383] Postscript
[361] National Minorities in Yunnan (1975)
[384] Employment and the Choice of Technique
In K. S. Krishnaswamy, A. Mitra, I. G. Patel and K. N. Srinivas (eds), *Society and Change*, Oxford: Oxford University Press [CEP V]

[385] The Labour Theory of Value as an Analytical System
A Contribution to the Conference of the Economic Section of the Academy of Science of Montenegro [CEP V]
[386] Guidelines of Orthodox Economics
JCA 7(1): 1–22 [CEP V]
[387] Michal Kalecki on the Economics of Capitalism[81]
OBES 39: 7–17, February [CEP V]
[388] What Has Become of Employment Policy? (with F. Wilkinson)
CmJE 1: 5–14, March [CEP V] [CME]
[389] Qu'est ce que le capital?[82]
REP 87: 165–79, March [CEP V] [CME]
[390] Education
ScSc 5: 131–7, June
[391] Economics in Disarray
NYT: 21, 12 August
[392] Review of E. Brun and J. Hersch, *Socialist Korea. A Case Study in the Strategy of Economic Development*
MR 29: 60–2, October
[393] Review of R. L. Meek, *Studies in the Labour Theory of Value* (2nd edn)[83]
MR 29: 50–9, December [CEP V] [FCM]
[394] What Are the Questions?
JEL 15: 1318–39, December [CEP V] [FCM]
[395] M. Kalecki
Ch 20: 67–9, November–December

1978

[CME] *Contributions to Modern Economics*[84]
Oxford: Blackwell
- [396] Preface
- [397] Reminiscences
- [330] The Second Crisis of Economic Theory (1972) [CEP IV]
- [12] The Theory of Money and the Analysis of Output (1933) [CEP I]
- [90] Obstacles to Full Employment (1946) [CEP I]
- [51] The Concept of Hoarding (1938) [CEP I]
- [114] The Rate of Interest[85] (1951) [RIE] [CEP II] [GGT]
- [243] Kalecki and Keynes[86] (1966) [CEP III]
- [135] Marx, Marshall and Keynes (1955) [CEP II]
- [130] The Production Function and the Theory of Capital[87] (1953) [CEP II]
- [234] Pre-Keynesian Theory after Keynes (1964) [CEP III]
- [308] Capital Theory up-to-date (1970) [CEP IV]
- [389] The Meaning of Capital[88] (1977) [CEP V]
- [347] History versus Equilibrium (1974) [CEP V]
- [127] A Lecture Delivered at Oxford by a Cambridge Economist (1953) [RRM] [CEP IV]
- [164] The Philosophy of Prices[89] (1960) [CEP II]
- [129] *Imperfect Competition* Revisited (1953) [CEP II]
- [299] The Theory of Value Reconsidered (1969) [CEP IV]
- [42] Beggar-My-Neighbour Remedies for Unemployment [ETE] [CEP IV]
- [252] The New Mercantilism (1966) [CEP IV]
- [333] The Need for a Reconsideration of the Theory of International Trade (1973) [CEP IV]

[191] Has Capitalism Changed? (1961) [CEP III]
[203] Latter-day Capitalism? (1962) [CEP III]
[261] Socialist Affluence (1967) [CEP IV]
[388] What Has Become of Employment Policy? (1977) [CEP V]
[111] Beauty and the Beast (1951) [CEP I]

[398] The Organic Composition of Capital
Ky 31(1): 5–20 [CEP V] [FCM]

[399] Morality and Economics
Ch 22: 62–4, March–April [CEP V]

[400] Keynes and Ricardo
JPKE 1: 12–8, Fall [CEP V] [FCM]

[401] Review of J. Steedman, *Marx after Sraffa*[90]
JCA 8(3): 381–4 [CEP V]

[402] Understanding the Economic Crises. Review of R. L. Heilbronner, *Beyond Boom and Crash*
NYRB 25: 33–4, 21 December

[403] The Organic Composition of Capital. A Reply
Ky 31(4): 692

[404] China 1978: Comments on Bettelheim
CN, no. 80: 4–7

[405] Review of Mao Tse-Tung, *A Critique of Soviet Economics*
CN, no. 80: 26–7

1979

[404] Comment on China since Mao
MR 31: 48–56, May

[404] Ambitious Plans and Careful Steps
NC 5: 27–9, Spring

[405] Review of Mao Tse Tung, *A Critique of Soviet Economics*
MR 30: 52–3, January

[CEP V] *Collected Economic Papers*
Oxford: Blackwell

[406] Preface
[394] What Are the Questions? (1977) [FCM]
[349] The Abdication of Neoclassical Economics (1974)
[399] Morality and Economics (1978)
[347] History versus Equilibrium (1974) [CME]
[389] The Meaning of Capital[91] (1977) [CME]
[266] Growth and the Theory of Distribution (1967)
[358] The Unimportance of Reswitching (1975)
[359] The Unimportance of Reswitching. A Reply (1975)
[407] The Disintegration of Economics [FCM]
[357] Value before Capitalism (1975)
[344] Gunnar Myrdal[92] (1973)
[408] Thinking about Thinking [FCM]
[373] The Age of Growth (1976) [FCM]
[348] Reflections on the Theory of International Trade (1974)
[409] Markets[93] (1979)
[338] What Has Become of the Keynesian Revolution? (1973)
[263] Smoothing out Keynes[94] (1967)
[387] Michal Kalecki[95] (1977)

[388] What Has Become of Employment Policy? (1977) [CME]
[400] Keynes and Ricardo (1978) [FCM]
[352] Inflation West and East (1974)
[386] The Guidelines of Orthodox Economics (1977)
[384] Employment and the Choice of Technique (1977)
[343] Formalistic Marxism and Ecology without Classes[96] (1973)
[410] Who Is A Marxist?
[340] Ideology and Analysis (1973)
[398] The Organic Composition of Capital (1978) [FCM]
[401] Formalism versus Dogma[97] (1978)
[393] The Labour Theory of Value[98] (1977) [FCM]
[385] The Labour Theory of Value as an Analytical System (1977)

[409] Markets[99]
In *Encyclopedia Britannica*, 15th edn, vol. 11: 511–15, Chicago: Benton Publisher [CEP V]

[411] *Aspects of Development and Underdevelopment*
Cambridge: Cambridge University Press

[GGT] *The Generalization of the General Theory and Other Essays*[100]
London: Macmillan
[412] Introduction
[118] The Generalisation of the General Theory [RIE]
[117] Notes on the Economics of Technical Progress [RIE]
[119] Acknowledgements and Disclaimers[101] [RIE] [CEP II]
[114] The Rate of Interest[102] [RIE] [CEP II] [CME]

[413] Foreword
In K. Kuhne, *Economics and Marxism*, 2 vols, London: Macmillan

[414] Résumé des débats
In J. Robinson and P. K. M. Tharaka (eds), *The International Division of Labour and Multinational Companies*, Farnborough, England: European Centre for Study and Information on Multinational Corporations

[415] Foreword
In A. S. Eichner (ed.), *Guide to Post-Keynesian Economics*, London: Macmillan

[416] Commento all'articolo di Garegnani[103]
In P. A. Garegnani, *Valore e domanda effettiva*, Torino: Einaudi (Appendix A)

[417] Un ulteriore commento[104]
In P. A. Garegnani, *Valore e domanda effettiva*, Torino: Einaudi, (Appendix C)

[418] Has Keynes Failed?
ACE 50: 27–9, January–March

[419] Review of D. Patinkin and J. C. Leith, *Keynes, Cambridge and the General Theory*
CdJE(ns) 12: 118–20, February

[420] Garegnani on Effective Demand
CmJE 3: 179–80, June

[421] Misunderstandings in the Theory of Production
GER 1: 1–7, August [FCM]

[421] Misunderstandings in the Theory of Production
In R. F. Feiwel (ed.), *Samuelson and Neoclassical Economics*, Boston: Kluwer-Nijhoff

[422] Keynes Today (with F. Cripps)
JPKE 2: 139–44, Fall

[423] Surplus Value and Profits
DC 10: 693–5, October
[424] Employment and Inflation[105]
QREB 19: 7–16, Autumn [FCM]
[424] Solving the Stagflation Puzzle[106]
Ch 22: 40–6, November–December [FCM]
[425] Modernization: Which Road Will China Take (with F. M. Kaplan and N. P. Peritore)
NC 5: 21–9, Spring
[426] Pros and Cons
CN, no. 86: 25–6

1980

[FCM] *Further Contributions to Modern Economics*
Oxford: Blackwell
[427] Introduction
[394] What Are the Questions? (1977) [CEP V]
[373] The Age of Growth (1976) [CEP V]
[424] Stagflation[107] (1979)
[408] Thinking about Thinking (1979)
[428] Accumulation and Exploitation: An Analysis in the Tradition of Marx, Sraffa and Kalecki (with Amit Bhaduri)[108] (1980)
[400] Keynes and Ricardo (1978) [CEP V]
[429] Time in Economic Theory (1980)
[407] The Disintegration of Economics (1979) [CEP V]
[363] Survey: 1950s[109] (1975) [CEP II bis]
[364] Survey: 1960s[110] (1975) [CEP III bis]
[430] Debate: 1970s
[431] Retrospect: 1980
[421] Misunderstandings in the Theory of Production (1979)
[80] Joseph Schumpeter: *Capitalism, Socialism and Democracy* (1943) [CEP I]
[186] Piero Sraffa: *Production of Commodities by Means of Commodities*[111] (1961) [CEP III]
[344] Gunnar Myrdal: Against the Stream[112] [CEP V]
[206] Marxism: Religion and Science (1962) [CEP III]
[128] An Open Letter from a Keynesian to a Marxist (1953) [RRM] [CEP IV]
[398] The Organic Composition of Capital (1978) [CEP V]
[393] The Labour Theory of Value[113] (1977) [CEP V]
[430] Marxism and Modern Economics
[428] Accumulation and Exploitation: An Analysis in the Tradition of Marx, Sraffa and Kalecki (with A. Bhaduri)[114]
CmJe 4: 103–15, June [FCM]
[429] Time in Economic Theory
Ky 33(2): 219–29 [FCM]
[432] Introduction
In W. Walsh and H. Gram, *Classical and Neoclassical Theories of General Equilibrium. Historical Origins and Mathematical Structure*, New York and Oxford: Oxford University Press
[433] Review of N. Maxwell, *China Road to Development*
Bs 17: 4, March

[434] Review of *The Collected Writings of J. M. Keynes*, Vol. XXIX, *The General Theory and After*
EJ 90: 391–3, June
[435] Review of H. Chenery et al., *Structural Change and Development Policy*
JDA 15: 131–2, October
[436] Review of J. F. Becker, *Marxian Political Economy. An Outline*
AJS 85: 1474–6, May

1982

[437] The Arms Race
In S. M. McMurrin (ed.), *The Tanner Lectures on Human Values*, Salt Lake City: University of Utah Press
[438] One Hundred Issues
CN no. 100: 3
[439] The Current State of Economics
CPE 1: 47–9, March
[440] Shedding Darkness: A Note. Review of A. Leijonhufvud, *Information and Coordination*
CmJE 6: 295–6, September

1983

[441] Economics of Destruction
MR 35: 15–17, October

1984

[442] Logica e ideologia (with Frank Wilkinson)[115]
In F. Vicarelli (ed.), *Rilevanza di Keynes*, Bari: Laterza

1985

[442] Ideology and Logic (with Frank Wilkinson)[116]
In F. Vicarelli (ed.), *Keynes's Relevance Today*, Philadelphia: University of Pennsylvania Press and London: Macmillan
[443] The Theory of Normal Prices and Reconstruction of Economic Theory[117]
In G. R. Feiwel, *Issues in Contemporary Macroeconomics and Distribution*, London: Macmillan

ACKNOWLEDGEMENTS

For the fourth version I benefited from the work done by Pervez Tahir in his PhD thesis, 'Some Aspects of Development and Underdevelopment. Critical Perspective on Joan Robinson', University of Cambridge, 1990. For the present version I benefited from the work done by Claudia Heller in the preparation of her PhD thesis, 'Oligopoly and Technical Progress in Joan Robinson's View', Universitade Estadual de Campinas, São Paulo, Brazil.

NOTES

1 Reprinted in CEP I as An Inherent Defect in *Laissez-Faire*.
2 In ETE, section 5 is omitted.
3 Part of this article is in Some Reflections on Marxist Economics in ETE (1937).
4 See note 2.
5 Part 1 in Review of J. Strachey, *The Nature of Capitalist Crisis* (1936).
6 Reprinted in CEP I as The Economics of Hyper-Inflation.
7 Parts 1 and 2 also in Marx e Keynes (1948) [CEP I].
8 Reprinted in CEP I as The United States in the World Economy.
9 Parts 1 and 2 also in Marx on Unemployment (1941).
10 Reprinted in CEP I as The Theory of Planning.
11 Reprinted in CEP I as The Labour Theory of Value.
12 Previously published as A Fundamental Objection to *Laissez-Faire*.
13 Previously published as Review of C. Bresciani Turroni, *The Economics of Inflation*.
14 See note 9.
15 Previously published as Review of E. Böhm-Bawerk, *Karl Marx and the Close of his System*; R. Hilferding, *Böhm-Bawerk's Criticism of Marx*; L. Bortkiewicz, *On the Correction of Marx's Fundamental Theoretical Construction in the Third Volume of Capital* (ed. by P. M. Sweezy).
16 Previously published as Review of M. Dobb, *Soviet Economic Development Since 1917*.
17 Previously published as Review of D. Lynch (ed.), *The United States in the World Economy*.
18 Last section omitted in CEP II and CME.
19 Originally published in *Cambridge Today*, an undergraduate magazine.
20 Reprinted with a new Introduction and the order of essays reversed as [GGT] (1979).
21 See note 18.
22 Parts 1 and 2 only are reprinted in CEP II as Notes on Marx and Marshall.
23 Reprinted in CEP II as A Note on the Bank Rate.
24 Reduced version in CEP II and CME.
25 The original version could not be traced.
26 English version appears in CEP II as The Theory of Distribution.
27 English version appears in CEP II as Full Employment and Inflation.
28 An amended version of this article is published as The Philosophy of Prices in CEP II and CME.
29 Italian version of Imperfect Competition Today.
30 Spanish version of Population and Development (CEP II and in PEJ, 1960).
31 Previously published as Acknowledgments and Disclaimers. Only Parts 1 and 2 are reprinted in CEP II.
32 An amended version of Some Reflections on the Philosophy of Prices.
33 English version of Poblacion y Desarollo (1958).
34 Reduced version of the article published in RES (1953).
35 English version of La Théorie de la répartition.
36 English version of Il mito della concorrenza.
37 The last section of the 1951 article is omitted in CEP II and CME.
38 Previously published as Monetary Policy Again. Comments.
39 English version of Plein emploi et inflation.
40 English version of Poblacion y desarollo (1958).
41 Shortened version of The Basic Theory of Normal Prices.
42 Shortened version of the RES article (1962).

43 Shortened version reprinted in ETG as Normal Prices.
44 Reprinted in CEP III as The General Theory after Twenty Five Years.
45 Reprinted in CEP III as Robinson on Findlay on Robinson.
46 Reprinted partly in RFC as Economic Recovery.
47 Reprinted partly in RFC as Economic Recovery.
48 Reprinted in FCM as Piero Sraffa: *Production of Commodities by Means of Commodities*.
49 Previously published as Findlay's Robinsonian Model of Accumulation.
50 In CEP III the reference to the original article is given as IER 1965 instead of IER 1966.
51 In CEP III and CME the reference to the original text is given as 1964 instead of 1966. There are two editions of the volume *Problems of Economic Dynamics and Planning. Essays in Honor of M. Kalecki*. In the first edition (Warsaw: Polish Scientific Publisher, 1964) Joan Robinson's contribution is not included.
52 Previously published as Review of H. G. Johnson, *Money, Trade and Economic Growth*.
53 Previously published as Piero Sraffa and the Rate of Exploitation.
54 Reprinted in CEP III as A Reconsideration of the Theory of Value.
55 Reprinted in CEP III as Korea, 1964: Economic Miracle.
56 See note 50.
57 See note 51.
58 First two pages are the same as the first two pages of Kalecki and Keynes (1966).
59 Reprinted in CEP V as Smoothing out Keynes.
60 Reprinted in CEP IV as Economics versus Political Economy.
61 Reprinted in CEP IV as The Poverty of Nations.
62 The Note to the re-issue of 1947 is omitted.
63 Excerpts reprinted in RFC.
64 Reprinted in CEP IV as A Reply.
65 Review of M. Kalecki, *Selected Essays in the Dynamics of a Capitalist Economy*.
66 Reprinted in CEP IV as Solow Once More.
67 Previously published as Review of F. M. Gottheil, *Marx's Economic Predictions*, and of W. Leontief, *Input–Output Economics*.
68 See note 58.
69 Previously published as Review of G. Myrdal, *Asian Drama. An Enquiry into the Poverty of Nations*.
70 Previously published as Review of R. Solow, *Growth Theory. An Exposition*.
71 Previously published as Capital Theory up-to-date: Reply to Ferguson.
72 Extracted from *Economic Management in China, 1972*.
73 Extracted from *Economic Management in China, 1972*.
74 Reprinted in CEP V as Gunnar Myrdal.
75 An amended version is reprinted in FCM as Survey: 1950s.
76 An amended version is reprinted in FCM as Survey: 1960s.
77 Written for the Italian edition; never published in English.
78 New version of a report written in 1957, which Joan Robinson was unable to trace.
79 Article taken partly from *Notes from China* (1964) and partly from A British Economist on a Chinese Commune (1964).
80 Excerpts from *The Cultural Revolution in China*.
81 Reprinted in CEP V as Michal Kalecki.
82 French version of The Meaning of Capital in CEP V and CME.
83 Reprinted in CEP V and FCM as The Labour Theory of Value.

84 There are three reprints of this volume: *Contributions to Modern Economics*, New York: Academic Press 1978; *What Are the Questions and Other Essays*, New York: M. E. Sharpe, 1981; *Contributions to Modern Economics*, New Delhi: Heritage, 1985.
85 The last section of the 1951 article is omitted in CEP II and CME.
86 First two pages are the same as the first two pages of [251].
87 Reduced version of the article published in RES (1953).
88 English version of Qu'est ce que le capital?
89 An amended version of Some Reflections on the Philosophy of Prices.
90 Reprinted in CEP V as Formalism versus Dogma.
91 See note 88.
92 Previously published as Review of G. Myrdal, *Against the Stream* and reprinted in FCM with the original title.
93 An expanded version of the article published in *Encyclopedia Britannica*. In CEP V the reference to the original text is erroneously given as 1974 instead of 1979.
94 Previously published as Review of R. Lekachman, *The Age of Keynes*.
95 Previously published as Michal Kalecki on the Economics of Capitalism.
96 Previously published as Review of A. Emmanuel, Unequal Exchange. *A Study of the Imperalism of Trade*, and of R. G. Wilkinson, *Poverty and Progress*.
97 Previously published as Review of J. Steedman, *Marx after Sraffa*.
98 Previously published as Review of R. L. Meek, *Studies in the Labour Theory of Value*.
99 The version in CEP V is an expanded version of this article.
100 A reprint of RIE (1952) with the order of essays reversed and a new Introduction.
101 Parts 1 and 2 only are reprinted in CEP II as Notes on Marx and Marshall.
102 The last section of the 1951 article is omitted in CEP II and CME.
103 Published in English in P. Garegnani, 'Some Notes on Capital, Expectations and the Analysis of Change', in G. R. Feiwel (ed.), *Joan Robinson and Modern Economic Theory*. London: Macmillan, 1989: 360–1.
104 See note 103.
105 Reprinted in FCM as Stagflation.
106 Reprinted in FCM as Stagflation.
107 Previously published as Employment and Inflation and Solving the Stagflation Puzzle.
108 Reprinted without the mathematical appendix.
109 Previously published as Introduction 1974: Reflections and Reminiscences.
110 Previously published as Introduction 1974: Comments and Explanations.
111 Reprinted in CEP III as Prelude to a Critique of Economic Theory.
112 Reprinted in CEP V as Gunnar Myrdal.
113 See note 98.
114 Reprinted in FCM without the mathematical appendix.
115 Italian version of Ideology and Logic. Published posthumously.
116 Published posthumously.
117 Published posthumously. Original title: Spring Cleaning.

INDEX